INFORMATIVE
WRITING

INFORMATIVE WRITING

EUGENE R. HAMMOND
University of Maryland

McGRAW-HILL BOOK COMPANY

New York   St. Louis   San Francisco   Auckland   Bogotá
Hamburg   Johannesburg   London   Madrid   Mexico
Montreal   New Delhi   Panama   Paris   São Paulo
Singapore   Sydney   Tokyo   Toronto

INFORMATIVE WRITING

1 2 3 4 5 6 7 8 9 0 DOC DOC 8 9 8 7 6 5 4

ISBN 0-07-025891-0

This book was set in Bembo by Better Graphics. The editors were
Emily G. Barrosse and James R. Belser; the production supervisor
was Marietta Breitwieser; the designer was Elliot Epstein.
R. R. Donnelley & Sons Company was printer and binder.

See Acknowledgments on pages 341–342. Copyrights included on this page by reference.

Library of Congress Cataloging in Publication Data

Hammond, Eugene.
   Informative writing.

   Includes index.
   1. English language—Rhetoric. I. Title.
PE1408.H323 1985   808'.042   84-14406
ISBN 0-07-025891-0

*To my partners
in crime:
Ann Allen, Lucy Schultz,
Carolyn Hill, Betsy Cohn,
Sally Glover, Rosalie Gancie,
and the writing staff
at College Park*

Contents
in Brief

◆
Contents

Preface

Structure of course

Informative Writing tries to approach the writing course from the students' point of view. It tries to recognize areas where students are willing to work hard and also areas that they are tired of repeating. Its most distinguishing feature is that it emphasizes writing activities rather than explanations. Recent research and my experience suggest that students learn and remember more from "workshop" classes, where they are busy writing and helping each other with writing, than they do in either "lecture" or "discussion" classes, in which they read and discuss model essays or chapters from a textbook. The most unusual chapter in the book is the chapter on grammar, "Sentence Sense," which teaches students grammar and punctuation through their construction of their own sentences.

The chapters are broken down as follows:

Chapter 1: "Where Do We Start?" This chapter consists of various exercises that help students determine what they value in "good" writing and then compare what they value with the standards of their teacher and their classmates. It also tries to get students to think about why they're taking this course.

Chapter 2: "Telling Details." This chapter will send students out searching for details which can tell the reader something. Such a search is essential early in the semester if we expect our students to write specifically. The chapter is based largely on Ken Macrorie's ideas about telling facts (in *Telling Writing*), but it applies the principle of telling facts to all forms of writing—not just narration and description.

Chapter 3: "Facts, Inferences, and Theses." This chapter includes several exercises in the most crucial skills for a writer distinguishing facts from inferences, and then drawing inferences from facts. Students will learn through this chapter how to use fact-inference pairs as a prewriting technique and how to use inferences as tools for organizing a paper.

Chapter 4: "Writing for a Reader." This chapter tries to get students to picture a reader as they write. It includes several examples of writing, mostly in some inflated, vague, or "official" style. Students are asked to choose which writers they'd like to hear more from. Then they are shown several ways (including timed writing) that they can use to develop a confident voice.

Chapter 5: "Organization I: Writing Systematically." This chapter focuses on a week-long exercise of practice in the so-called *rhetorical modes* (definition, cause-effect, problem-solution, comparison-contrast, etc.). It emphasizes the use of these strategies as tools for making your thinking clear to your reader. It concludes with a brief explanation of how useful these organizational strategies can be when writing essay exams.

Chapter 6: "Organization II: Paragraphing, Introductions, and Conclusions." This chapter consists almost entirely of exercises designed to help students develop both a conscious and an intuitive sense of how best to handle these three important writers' problems.

Chapter 7: "Thinking." This chapter, which is not related to any specific assignment and could have been placed anywhere in the book, is meant to remind students of the crucial importance to a writer of curiosity, reflection, and creativity. Several exercises are included which encourage students to make connections, and distinctions, judgments, and to qualify assertions.

Chapter 8: "Sentence Sense." This chapter tries to teach students practical punctuation and the use of different grammatical forms for varying emphasis. It includes sentence-imitation and sentence-building exercises which teachers can easily modify or supplement depending on their students' individual needs. This chapter can be used as appropriate throughout the semester. It is placed in the middle of the book to make reference to it easier and to remind students that grammar, though not the end-all of writing, is more than merely matter for an appendix.

Chapter 9: "Persuasion." This chapter tries to explain induction and deduction in practical ways so that students can make use of them. It also introduces the terms *ethos, logos*, and *pathos* as critical standards that students can apply to writing. All writing, I believe, is persuasive, but specifically persuasive techniques are more necessary when one's readers are not inclined to agree. The chapter contains several questions and exercises that get students to think about what the best strategies are for persuading others. I remind students that many of the best arguments are not overtly arguments, and I explain Carl Rogers' theory that care for one's reader makes successful persuasion possible.

Chapter 10: "The Writing Process." This chapter begins by asking students to describe their writing processes in different circumstances—when they are writing an assignment, when they are writing for fun, when they are proud of what they write, and when they hate writing. It then includes descriptions of the writing process and portions of descriptions—from a filmmaker, a sculptor, and both student and professional writers.

Chapter 11: "Revision." This chapter contains several flawed student essays for students to practice revision on. It also tries to teach rethinking, reorganization, and further research, as well as tightening and making word choice more precise, as typical revision strategies.

Chapter 12: "Reading." This chapter includes practice in reading comprehension, but not simply comprehension of "the main points." It encourages students to be alert to matters of *ethos, logos,* and *pathos,* or what we might call voice, substance, and attitude toward the reader. It repeats some of the lessons of finding facts and drawing inferences that were practiced in Chapter 3. It will help students learn how to write papers about works of literature.

Chapter 13: "Research." This chapter includes exercises to be undertaken in any library to show students the often odd and lively sources of information that they usually neglect when they head dutifully for the card catalog. It also includes advice about the use of the new MLA guidelines for parenthetical references and lists of "Works Cited."

Chapter 14: "Interviewing." The exercises in this chapter get the students used to collecting information from other people. Once they master this skill, they will have a much greater fund of information from which to draw when they write.

Chapter 15: "Suggested Assignments." This chapter includes ten assignments, explained in a way that helps students proceed systematically, from which a teacher may choose or adapt as many as he or she finds use and time for. All assignments require research—of people, of places, or of books and artifacts. No assignment can be done in a student's room the night before it's due. The assignments can easily be adapted to the interests of various programs, personal interests, and student abilities.

Chapter 16: "What Next?" This chapter tries to get students to take stock of what they've learned and to think about how they will go about improving their own writing after they leave this course.

The advantages of this text over others are as follows:

1. The students practice everything, so they internalize more of what they learn.

2. The papers encourage observation, selection, and judgment: skills which will be necessary in any writing situation students later find themselves in.

3. Students finish the course knowing enough grammar to be literate representatives of our universities and community colleges, but they learn through practice and not through analysis.

4. Students read more flawed work than they do models, so they are encouraged to develop their critical abilities.

5. Students most often write about subjects that they know more about than their teachers; consequently, they produce work that they're proud of, and they come to like writing.

6. Teachers using this book, after first becoming acquainted with it, need to do far less preparation, since so many useful exercises are provided, and much emphasis is placed on students taking responsibility for their work into their own hands. This leaves teachers free to devote their energy to reading and responding to finished student papers, which is itself challenging and time-consuming work.

7. The text tries to understand and acknowledge the attitudes that both teachers and students have toward required writing courses. It doesn't pretend that we all love this work, but it does show how we can learn more about it and at the same time enjoy it much more than we ordinarily do.

As Instructor's Manual, available from McGraw-Hill, provides guidelines for the use of all the exercises in this book.

Acknowledgments

I'd like to thank the many teachers and editors (in addition to those I've cited in the text) who have helped to improve this work with their examples, their suggestions, and their goodwill. Just because each name is buried in this long list doesn't mean that I don't feel particularly grateful in each case: Phil Butcher, Laura Berkshire, Jim Belser, George Dillon, Jeanne Fahnestock, Michael Marcuse, Betty Day, Carleton Jackson, Sara Edinger, Donna Coyle, Nancy Smith, Sheryl Witkin, Betsy Cohn, Joyce Middleton, Greta Coen, Tom Berninghausen, Trudi Walsh, John Hyman, Theresa DePaolo, Dody Parris, Kristy Beattie, Gail Rossman, Tom Cole, Aimee Doyle, Lucy Schultz, Carolyn Hill, Jane O'Brien, Kathy Riley, Nancy Runion, Kathleen Burke, Tom Moore, Tom Holbrook, Jade Gorman, Patti Rosenberg, Cristina Cheplik, Michael Forschler, Joe Miller, Bobbie Daniels, Margo Hammond, Rebecca Butler, Dan Keranen, Rae Rosenthal, Rowena Cross, Vic Caroscio, Jane McGettrick, Gerry Higgins, Jeanne Marie Etkins, Dragana Perovic, Chenliang Sheng, Pat Noone, Alice Tracy, Kofi Aidoo, Judy Kreger, Douglas Meyers, Ed James, Mary Kay Jordan, Sara Mate, Matthew Wong, Mack Siddoris, Jud Sage, Craig Stoltz, Monika Bilby, Marsha Markman, Anasuya Basu, Margaret Della Torre, Nikhilesh Banerjee, Alba Ben-Barka, Harry Crosby, Richard Marius, Virginia Beauchamp, Leigh Ryan, Betsey Blakeslee, Robert Coogan, Beth Lambert, Brian McLaren, Susan Rosen, Joyce Joyce, Leonard King, Emily Barrosse, Susan Kleimann, Mary Jane Hurst, Bobby Fong, Ernest Fontana, Blair Halsey, Geneva Parker, Nancy McCracken, Jack Folsom, Albert Labriola, Ronald Maxwell, Gratia Murphy, David Rankin, Jim Dodd, and R. Baird Shuman.

Eugene R. Hammond

1

♦

Where Do We Start?

Rhetoric . . . should be the study of misunderstanding and its remedies.

I. A. Richards

Writing is an art that requires more soul and sweat than I'm willing to give.

student

Welcome to a course in the practice of writing. If you don't have them already, pick up, in the next day or two, a pen you like to write with and plenty of paper you like to write on. (In this book, I'll call whatever paper you use your "notebook.") These, along with a typewriter or perhaps a word processor, are the tools of our trade. With these tools in the next several weeks, you can expect to improve your writing in at least sixteen ways:

1. You'll become more observant.

2. You'll become an avid collector and user of telling details.

3. You'll learn how to find what you need or want in a library.

4. You'll learn how to organize any chaotic pile of information.

5. You'll become confident (if you aren't already) about your grammar.

6. You'll master the use of commas, semicolons, dashes, and periods.

7. You'll learn to make every sentence in your writing count.

8. You'll learn to write so that your readers can learn easily from you.

9. You'll learn to paragraph in a way that makes reading easier for your readers.

10. You'll learn to link your sentences smoothly.

11. You'll learn how to rethink and revise your first drafts.

12. You'll learn how to write effective introductions and conclusions.

13. You'll learn to write effectively to unsympathetic readers.

14. You'll learn to write with a voice that readers can recognize as yours.

15. You'll learn to write clear essays in class under pressure.

16. You'll learn to compare writing with other forms of communication such as talking, photography, and filmmaking.

You can accomplish all this even if, like most of us, you don't especially like to write. But there is one condition: that you *want* to improve your writing. If you don't want to learn, you might as well drop the course now, sell this book back, get into another course, and come back another semester when you're ready. You can succeed in this course if you're shaky about your grammar or if you think your writing is awkward. You can succeed if you think your aptitude is not for English but for engineering or computers. But if you're not curious, if you're not patient, if you're not willing to work hard, or if you're only taking this course because it is a requirement, you may have real trouble with it. The work load in this course is going to fall not on your teacher but on you. Neither your teacher nor this book can tell you how to write better. You must decide for yourself that *you* want to improve. If you write badly now, it's not because you are not intelligent but because you haven't been *attentive* about improving your writing. That attention is where we want to start.

You can't learn to write if you don't want to learn. You also can't learn to write by studying about writing. You learn to write by writing (and by *thinking* while you write—if you don't learn something in the process of writing a paper, your reader isn't likely to learn anything in reading it). In this class you will try to produce writing that you and your teacher and your classmates can genuinely admire. Much of your progress as a writer will come from practice—repeated papers in this class and others, repeated essay exams in this class and others, (and later, perhaps) repeated application letters that fail to get you a job, repeated memos that are sent back once you do get a job. You can practice writing—and gain some understanding of yourself—any time you like by writing letters or by keeping a journal of your dreams, your conflicts, your decisions. But you can also practice, in this class, by writing assigned papers for your teacher and for your class-mates and by doing the exercises suggested in this book.

Exercises enable you to practice and develop skills one or two at a time until all the skills become part of your intuitive resources, thus improving your writing performance and giving you greater confidence as a writer. All the assignments, discussions, readings, and writing you do in this course will go into building your writing intuitions—intuitions for how to begin, how to organize, how to please your readers, and so on. Writing is a complex task which requires everything from getting your spelling right to making your voice distinctive enough to be heard. Writing any new assign-ment requires a combination of thought, hard work, and intuition; the more you can rely on intuition for, the more energy you have left for thinking about matters that are really new.

One of the most profitable ways to build up your intuitions is to read—or at least show—your writing to others. When you do so, listen to what people suggest. See how many options you have. As the semester pro-gresses, you'll learn new options from your teacher, from your classmates, from me, and from your increasingly good judgment. Your progress in developing both writing ability and confidence will be gradual but sub-stantial.

In this course you will not simply be delivering enough gradable noise on paper for your teacher to correct. Every paper will require you not just to arrange materials but to think. No paper will be able to be written the night before it's due. You'll be thinking and taking notes about your subject from the day each paper is assigned. Also, you'll be trying to learn much more about writing than simply how to develop a good "style." You'll find that collecting information, sorting it out, and drawing conclusions from it are the most crucial writing skills. If you learn to present pertinent information clearly, you'll find that you have developed, without even trying to, your own style. From the start, <u>information</u> will be your best friend. The more information you have, the better a paper you can write. But once you have selected the information you most want to pass on, you may find yourself becoming concerned about your writing as a craft. You'll find yourself wanting to present the information you've selected as well as you possibly can. You'll develop your own standards of what way is best with your teacher's help, with the help of your classmates, and with the help of the advice in this book.

This book contains very few rules. If you think you'll do well in college or in life (or in writing) by following rules, you're mistaken. There are guidelines for most situations, writing or otherwise, but success lies in making the most of the options you have within these guidelines. Some so-called *rules* of writing were merely fashions which are now as dead as men's wigs: "Never begin a sentence with *and* or *but*"; "Never end a sentence with a preposition"; "Never split an infinitive." Other "rules" of writing ("Grab the attention of your readers"; "Outline everything you write") are merely rules of thumb: they are useful in many cases, but certainly not in all. The key to good writing is not learning to follow rules but learning what your choices are—choices in tone, in words, in paragraphing, in punctuation. Throughout this course you'll practice making choices. Your teacher and your classmates may make other choices than you make. Pay attention to the choices of the others. And examine at the same time your own choices. Yours may be better in some cases. Theirs may be better in others. But by the end of the semester, you ought to have an excellent sense of how varied your choices are.

Throughout this book, I'll stop talking to you as often as possible to give you time to try exercises that will help develop your thinking about writing. You may interpret the heads that introduce these exercises as invitations to skip over to my next comments. If you do, though, you'll be squandering the money and effort you've invested in this course. My thoughts about writing may stay with you for six months (an optimistic estimate); but your thoughts about writing, as you discover them in these exercises, will stay with you for life.

Exercise 1-1

All of you are starting this course with different writing strengths and different writing weaknesses. So before we can begin sensibly to work on improvement, we have to find out what your current writing abilities are. Perhaps you feel confident about your writing; more likely you do not. To let your teacher know your strengths and your weaknesses, *write*—as well as you can within the limitations of twenty-five minutes and beginning-of-a-course nerves—*a page or two in your notebook about your training in English to this point and about what kind of writer you now are as a result of that training.*

• Be as specific as possible.

- You may write about just a single English class if you prefer.

- Cross out and revise as much as you wish. Don't worry about neatness.

- You might want to stop for a few minutes and take a few notes before you begin.

Exercise 1-2 — *evaluations*

For much of your life, you've handed in samples of your writing to be evaluated. Do you know what your teachers have thought about as they read that writing? Perhaps you should try on the role of evaluator yourself. On a new page in your notebook, write at least four or five sentences in which you express your opinion about each of the following three pieces of writing. What do you like? What do you dislike? As you read, underline and make marginal notes so it will be easier to write your comments. When you've finished noting your opinions, you may want, in preparation for discussion, to give each of the pieces a quality rating between 1 (poor) and 10 (excellent).

A. A FEATURE ARTICLE IN A SMALL-TOWN NEWSPAPER — *to entertain*

"BUT I NEVER SAID I COULD TAKE A PICTURE . . ."
RUTH HAMMOND
***Waseca's* [Minnesota] *Daily Journal*, February 24, 1976**

w.c. — to attribute or impute or assign as assign to and work should be subscribe to contribute

1 Next to the American automobile, the machine I like least in this world is the Japanese camera. I ascribe to the old school of thought which still holds that if man had meant to be photographed, he would have been born as a two-dimensional still engraving.

2 No one ever warned me that taking pictures would be part of my job before I came here. But the day I started, Tony went over the camera for me part by part, explaining aperture, light meter, strobe, and other foreign terms. I listened and pretended to understand. We took a few practice shots with no film in the camera. If I'd stayed at that level, I'd be doing fine.

3 But no. I was soon supposed to be taking pictures of people. My first shot was of half an FDA lady. I don't know what happened; I'm sure she was whole before I took her picture. Roger said I was too close to the end of the film roll.

4 By this time both halves of the FDA expert had left town and there was no chance of retrieving what I'd missed. I conjured up cutlines such as: "Mrs. Smith's better half bravely smiles for the camera as her face gets eaten away from the left by a cloud of molten black."

5 Better yet, I decided to go over to Ron's Jack and Jill and take a picture of some of the fruit juice the woman had been talking about. I rushed in, snapped shots of V-8 Juice and Gatorade from every angle, returned to the JOURNAL then meekly went back to Ron's and asked the clerks if I could take some more pictures, this time using a flash.

6 My tool has always been the pen, and even in France, if I saw something I liked, I wrote it down. That's my way of freezing impressions. Put a Minolta in my hands and my lack of self-confidence jumps two hundred per

cent. "You're too timid with the camera," a friend who was visiting from Madison this weekend complained. Why shouldn't I be, after all that cameras have done to me? I'm shy on either side of the lens.

7 One of the many things I can't do is to get people to smile as I take their pictures. I feel it's not my place to demand that anyone fabricate happiness and besides, any human being who's had a camera trained on him for ten minutes while I fiddle around with readings, light meters and apertures, is likely to look irate and contemptuous more than anything else. I get a shot of the winterized Minnehaha Falls flashing me an icy glare and that's okay to run; but the frozen countenances of all my other subjects aren't exactly front page material.

8 A few weeks ago, when temperatures skyrocketed, I was told to go out and get some pictures of kids coming out of school into the warm air. I don't know how to capture warmth in pictures. I toyed with and quickly disposed of the idea of getting someone to climb up and stand in front of the neon temperature reading at First National Bank.

9 Instead I tracked down four kids and asked if I could take their picture for the JOURNAL: "We're going to have our picture in the paper," one of them squealed.

10 "Don't count on it," I ventured as I fumbled with the focusing lens. I can never figure out if it's the muck on my contact lenses or my inept fingers that makes everything blurry.

11 I had the kids stand behind one deep puddle and I stood in another on the other side of the street and released the shutter a few times, trying to radiate some warmth into my shots. "Why don't you take off your mittens and unzip your jackets?" I asked. The kids readily complied. I fearfully imagined myself having all the mothers in town on my back the next day for running pictures that advocate unzipped jackets in 46-degree weather.

12 That picture turned out only slightly hazy. Others haven't fared as well. If I ran all the pictures I've attempted, I'd have to be writing cutlines like: "Looking at the snapshot above, please squint and try to discern . . ." or "Carefully concealed behind the thumb blobbed across the trick photo at left, kindly imagine . . ."

13 I had somewhat better luck just recently when the camera was frozen to my frigid fingers nearly all weekend. The first event I had to cover was the Sleigh and Cutter Parade. I stood just outside the fairgrounds and started snapping away. The trouble was, by the time I got into focus on each shot, the vehicle had passed out of my view. In my head I was beginning to contrive cutlines like "Above please notice the finely-focused thin air through which a decorative, single-horse buggy has just passed." It was either that or turning around and getting rear shots of all the horses.

14 A few of the photos turned out, though, which is more than I can say for the roll I took at the Penny Carnival. "What would you advise me to get pictures of?" I asked a 4H leader at Hartley School.

15 "Oh, get some shots of the kids playing. Jo always takes such good pictures. She even climbs on tables and takes them."

16 Not to be outdone in enthusiasm, only in talent, I climbed onto a bench and got a picture of some cute little girls playing a ring toss game. I got a picture of 4H leaders flipping tiger-striped pancakes, a picture of kids

playing basketball, toddlers gazing at Bingo boards and boys shooting rubber balls. I got a whole roll of blank film.

17 "What happened?" I asked Dan in the developing room on Monday.

18 "It could be any one of a number of things."

19 Next time I'll have to learn to avoid any-one-of-a-number-of-things. The most important thing to avoid, I'm convinced, is the camera.

20 I've never thought of myself as a photographer, only as someone who inadvertently has a camera in her hands. So I was rather nonplussed at the Blue and Gold Banquet Sunday when the cubmaster asked if the JOURNAL photographer was there yet. I raised my hand to indicate I was and then 29 Cub Scouts, five Webelos, 68 parents and 53 brothers and sisters all turned to look at me as if I really were a photographer. I smiled, nudged my camera, and tried to look as if I knew what I was doing. A few minutes later when my flash refused to go off, it became apparent that I didn't. A man with an instamatic saved the day.

21 When all the tricks Tony taught me fail, I resort to gentle coaxing: "—–?*/." (Read: Dash hyphen, you question-mark asterisked son-of-a-slash camera.)

22 Lately I've decided that the language barrier has made my coaxing ineffective. You can't cuss English horizontal to a Japanese camera which only listens in vertical. So from now on it's going to be

–

+

&

!

or nothing at all. Preferably nothing at all.

23 Whatever misguided soul said, "A picture is worth a thousand words" certainly didn't have one of my photos in mind. Even at my ineloquent worst, the value of my writing always surpasses that of my photography.

24 Writing this column isn't going to make my subjects any more comfortable next time I show up with my Minolta, but if I had my choice between writing about how I hate cars and how I hate cameras, my aversion to cameras would win out every time—just for the sake of the town's stability. If I wrote an article on my finesse behind the wheel, frightened Toyotas would be hopping into trees to get out of my way every time I turned on my engine. We can't have that happen. The roadside trees in Waseca are having a hard enough time staying up as it is.

B.   A LETTER TRYING TO RAISE MONEY

Dear Friend:

1 On top of the Capitol dome is a woman statue facing east. The rest of Washington faces west—the Mall, federal buildings, art galleries, the reflecting pool. The woman statue's name is Freedom, but in yet another Washington irony, she was forged in a slave foundry. The statue has stood there for decades—watching, listening. What does she see today? Whose voices does she hear?

2 I believe she sees, in the buildings below her, systematic changes

taking place through choices made in the federal budget—transfers of money from the poor to the Pentagon. Those who lose out are hidden. Do legislators see the elderly poor losing more from an already minimal Social Security payment? Do they see the Chicana woman's loss of legal services? Do they see the hungry who lose food stamps?

3 And as the woman statue gazes far to her right, what does she see? In Nicaragua, a country struggles for reconstruction and self-determination; while in Guatemala, the Indian population find themselves caught in a government program of political murder. Salvadorans engage in a struggle for basic human needs, as their government denies them access to land and the means of production. The resolute mothers of the missing persons in Argentina risk their lives to demand information about their children.

4 As she looks across the Atlantic, she sees unrest and tension in Northern Ireland and Poland and the starving refugees in Somalia. When she turns toward the Cape of Good Hope, she sees the black majority in South Africa struggling for independence, for legal justice, for the right to participate fully. Across the South China Sea, she sees the people of the Philippines crying out for political independence and for freedom from US military and corporate dominance.

5 And scattered throughout the globe, she sees weapons of unspeakable destruction bristling in silos, poised on submarines, encased in bombers, causing worldwide anxiety and dread. In too many places additional weapons are being prepared, arms traded, persons anticipating war, if not actually fighting one another. And she watches the world's limited resources being diverted to swords rather than plowshares.

6 Then she listens to the response of US policymakers. What does she hear from the Administration and Congress? What do you hear? Does current US policy adequately reflect your values, your vision of a just world?

7 NETWORK, a Catholic social justice lobby founded in 1971, attempts to apply the Old Testament's principles of justice, Jesus's challenge to meet people's basic human needs and the Catholic Church's social teaching to public policy. In so doing, we believe that current policy does not reflect social justice principles and call upon equally concerned people to join us in resisting these trends while offering alternative possibilities. As a NETWORK member you are encouraged to respond actively to legislative initiatives and to take responsibility for policy decisions made in your name.

In Hope and Struggle,

Carol Coston

C. THE PREFACE TO A BOOK ABOUT PLUMBING FOR HOMEOWNERS

"PREFACE"
CARE AND REPAIR OF THE PLUMBING AND HEATING SYSTEM IN YOUR HOME
CHARLES GEISER

1 The purpose of this book is not to make a Plumber out of the Home Owner or Tenant, but to give the necessary information on the Care and

Repair of the Plumbing and Heating System, etc. WHETHER YOU EVER DO ANY OF YOUR OWN REPAIRING OR NOT. THIS BOOK SHOULD BE READ by the Home Owner, Tenant, Housewife, Maid, etc., in fact anyone left to care of the Home during the Summer as well as the Winter seasons. If the instructions are carefully followed, you will, no doubt, find it a WONDERFUL HELP IN CASE OF SUDDEN OR UNEXPECTED REPAIRS, in eliminating accidents, damaging property, unnecessary expense, etc.

not necessary

2 DO NOT THINK THAT PARTS IN THIS BOOK ARE OLD-FASHIONED, or behind the times, DO YOU KNOW this book is being sold all over the Country. About one third of the population live in Small Towns, Farms, Villages, etc., and have no City Sewer, Gas, City Water, etc., U.S. Official Census 1960, Urban 125,268,759, Rural 54,054,425, Total Population 179,323,175. Where the majority have Gas or Oil for fuel, others have to use Coal or Wood.

3 The contents give the necessary information on Care, Repair, etc., especially of the Plumbing System, but not on new installations. The author does not approve of any installation of drainage, venting material, or the installing of plumbing fixtures where direct connections to the sewer are to be made by anyone but a mechanic who thoroughly understands this particular line of installation.

4 PLUMBING NOT INSTALLED PROPERLY IS A MENACE TO THE PUBLIC HEALTH, see p. 162.

5 A deep or thorough knowledge on the subject of Plumbing, Heating, Ventilation, Gas, etc., is not essential to anyone except a licensed mechanic in that particular line. On the other hand, the public (home owner, tenant, apprentice, etc.) SHOULD BE THOROUGHLY INFORMED AS TO CERTAIN PARTS OF THE SYSTEM. The author has endeavored to place in the foregoing pages the knowledge that the PUBLIC SHOULD ACQUIRE or have for ready reference on Plumbing, Heating, etc.

6 The author in a total of many years of experience, has come across some very sad accidents, and the remark that is usually made with a regretting sigh, "IF I HAD ONLY KNOWN." There are many serious accidents that occur every year, especially DURING THE WINTER MONTHS, simply because of the ignorance of the fact that the proper precautions should have been taken, or because of the carelessness commonly called "TAKING A CHANCE." Do not wait until the auto is missing before locking the garage door. Be prepared when it comes to looking after your Plumbing, Heating, Ventilation, etc.

7 The information on Care of the Plumbing, Heating, Systems, etc. is not only on the first few pages, but throughout the entire book, as the CARE instructions are part of the REPAIR instructions. The reader may think that the information contained in this book is somewhat scattered, but the contents are not intended to a continued story, simply REFERENCE AND INSTRUCTIONS on some particular subject, which you will find after reading over a few pages. The instructions along with the illustrations are very USEFUL when used in a practical way. Some of the illustrations in this book are not drawn exactly according to scale and some are in odd positions or angles but the reason for this is, that the necessary details may be more clear.

8 This book is written from practical experience (not technical or trade

school experience) having been in the Plumbing and Heating business for many years in Chicago, Chicago Suburbs, Colorado, Kansas, Wyoming, and Canada, so became acquainted with the many different State Laws, License, Examination Tests, Codes, Sanitary Engineering, etc.

9 You will find this book placed in many Libraries in the U.S., in the world's largest, in Washington, D.C.

10 MEMORIAL: The net proceeds from this book is being given to Orphan Homes, Blind, Mental Institutions, Missionary Work. If you only followed one of the many items in this book, what you save on, for instance, on fuel alone during the Winter season (25–50 dollars) not saying anything about the healthful results received, what you save, remember just a little for some charitable work.

11 This book is written in the hope of helping and assisting the reader along the lines for which it is intended.

Chicago, Illinois   Charles J. Geiser
January 2, 1963

Once you've taken all your notes, discuss with your classmates, in small groups or as a class, your opinions of these writings. You may all agree that one piece is terrible or that another is very good. But at the same time you should be giving your reasons for saying that one piece is good or that another is not so good. Your reasons undoubtedly will differ from those of your classmates. Perhaps some of you will even disagree strongly about whether a piece is good or bad. We have the same disagreements about movies, about politics, and about religion, so it shouldn't be surprising that we have these differences about writing.

Exercise 1-3

The differences we have in evaluating writing are most often due to differing standards of what is important. So before we go too far in a writing course, we should try to find out what our standards are. The best way to start, perhaps, is to stop and write down what you look for when you read. List in your notebook the three things you think are most important in a piece of writing.

Once you have three items, extend the list to five. These last two will be more difficult to come up with.

Now set aside these criteria and take the following survey.

PRIORITIES: A SURVEY OF OPINION

1. Mark with an *H* the three items below that you think should have highest priority in this writing class.

2. Mark with an *L* the three items that you think should have lowest priority.

When you've finished marking your highest and lowest priorities, your teacher will survey the results and tell you his or her current opinion. Note down the totals, and compare your teacher's and the group's opinions with your own. My own H's the last time I took the survey went to "using supporting details," "developing a distinct tone of voice," and "becoming aware of one's readers." My L's went to

2

♦

Telling Details

Fred got up from the table, put on his pants, and said he was going to cook me a pork chop, because I looked hungry and ought to eat something. It was about noon, and I was even hungrier than I may have looked, so I gratefully accepted his offer, which was a considerable one. There are two or three small general stores in the pines, but for anything as fragile as a fresh pork chop it is necessary to make a round trip from Fred's place of about fifty miles. Fred went into the kitchen and dropped a chop into a frying pan that was crackling with hot grease. He has a fairly new four-burner stove that uses bottled gas. He keeps water in a large bowl on a table in the kitchen and ladles some when he wants it. While he cooked the meat, he looked out a window through a stand of pitch pines and into the cranberry bog. "I saw a big buck out there last night with velvet on his horns," he said. "Them horns is soft when they're in velvet." On a nail high on one wall of the room that Bill and I were sitting in was a large meat cleaver. Next to it was a billy club. The wall itself was papered in a flower pattern, and the wallpaper continued out across the ceiling and down the three other walls, lending the room something of the appearance of the inside of a gift box. In some parts of the ceiling, the paper had come loose. "I didn't paper this year," Fred said. "For the last couple months, I've had sinus." The floor was covered with old rugs. They had been put down in random pieces, and in some places as many as six layers were stacked up. In winter when the temperature approaches zero, the worst cold comes through the floor. The only source of heat in the house is a wood-burning stove in the main room. There were seven calendars on the walls, all current and none with pictures of nudes.

John McPhee, *The Pine Barrens*

On March 14, 1983, Ruben Zamara, a negotiator for Farabundo Marti National Liberation Front, a coalition of five El Salvador guerilla groups, complained about the progress of talks between the guerillas and the Salvadoran government: "Let's use fewer adjectives and more facts" (Hall, 2.1.1). If adjectives like "communist" and "imperialist" and "terrorist" were preventing communication from taking place in the 1983 El Salvador peace talks, so also do adjectives like "weird" or "interesting" or "terrible" hinder genuine communication when we write. Which of the two statements below, each taken from a student's paper, tells you more?

1. On the very day that Goebbels spoke (June 28, 1936), the statue of Athena, goddess of wisdom, was torn from the gateway of the University of Heidelberg's main building, and was replaced by a golden swastika. The inscription, "to the eternal spirit," that accompanied Athena, was exchanged to pay tribute "to the German spirit."

2. So far I haven't had as much of a problem adjusting to college as I thought I would have. I have met some interesting people, and some not so interesting people.

Photographers and filmmakers don't have adjectives at their disposal, so they've become quite skilled at finding facts that make their points. The photograph opposite, using a "telling" fact, could replace many an editorial page. Movies use "telling" facts almost constantly. Since most movies try to tell, in two hours, stories which would take thirty or forty hours to read, they focus on crucial incidents. In *Coal Miner's Daughter,* for example, about the country singer Loretta Lynn and her husband "Doo," Doo's bachelor character is presented to us in a thirty-second sequence in which he tries to race his new jeep up an impossibly steep incline. The task seems pointless, but Doo is stubborn—and he is finally successful. In thirty seconds, the director has "told" us how stubborn (and yet finally successful) Doo will be as a husband. Later in the same movie, when Doo has for a long time been ignored by Loretta, we see him flirting with a circus worker, and we "know" he's feeling sexually frustrated. Still later, we see him surprising Loretta with a staked-out area for a new house, and we "know" that he is again feeling domestic and willing to please.

Readers, no less than filmgoers, learn most from facts that carry a clear message. Ken Macrorie calls these "telling facts" (32); others call them "telling" or "revealing" or "significant" details. If you become able—after this chapter, or by the end of this course—to find telling facts and use them in your writing, you will have mastered one of the most difficult skills (and the most crucial) in the art of writing. Decide now that you're willing to spend the time necessary to understand, collect, and use these telling facts. Here's a start.

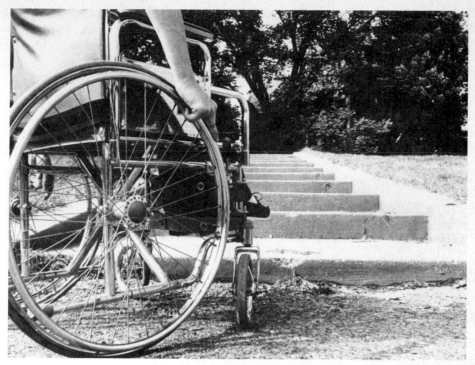

© *Pamela S. Hinden, 1981*

stopped 401/501

Exercise 2-1

Think back to the home you grew up in. Write down some detail from your kitchen or attic or basement that would, by itself, give your teacher and class some idea of the character of either your father or your mother. (Your response might be a single sentence, or two or three.) Now compare your results with those of other people in the class (either by being called on in class or, in your next class, by checking a list selected by your teacher).

Have some of you succeeded in using a fact or detail to give us an idea of a parent's character? Be strict in your standards—you have nothing to lose if you don't succeed now, but you have everything to lose if you don't learn through your mistakes. Here are a few successful examples from a fall 1982 class:

1. One corner of our basement is a large paneled room with 3 fluores-cent lights hanging from the ceiling and plenty of 3-pronged out-lets.

2. As you walk through the living room into the kitchen, immediately you see the table set with 4 places, just as a top restaurant might look. It's only 3:30 in the afternoon.

3. Opening the refrigerator door is always an adventure. The top shelf is usually empty. On the next, there are containers of food which haven't been opened in weeks. Hamburger expected to be cooked for dinner nights ago sits on the shelf slowly turning brown. The freezer looks like a perfect place for cross-country skiing.

This kind of success is rare. Three or four students from a class of twenty tend to succeed on their first try. You'll undoubtedly find as you read each other's samples that details haven't come easily. There are three ways to describe a person or a place: by stating a *quality*, by giving a *detail*, or by suggesting a *comparison.* Stating a quality (through an adjective) comes most easily to us, but it is least helpful to those we're trying to tell something to:

1. The kitchen in my present house has a tendency to be a bit *sloppy* by the end of the day.

2. I have always been overwhelmed by the *strong* and *dictative* atmosphere that the basement of my house possesses.

3. He's *weird*.

Comparisons can be more helpful. The cross-country skiing comparison in the last sentence of the third successful telling fact gives us a vivid picture of a freezer, but comparisons are not always so successful:

1. As I entered the basement I felt as if I were entering a dentist's office.

2. Our kitchen looks like it came out of a catalogue.

The value of almost any piece of writing depends not on its comparisons or on its assertions of qualities but on its details. A good letter of recommendation, written for you, for example, will make a much better impression with details about your performance than with adjectives like "brilliant," "helpful," or "studious." Every fact included in such a recommendation reflects the writer's interpretation (since it is selected), but readers enjoy drawing their own meanings from the facts, while they resent being given those meanings through opinionated adjectives. The facts are therefore more persuasive. Comparisons (if carefully selected) help, and qualities are sometimes a useful shortcut when we're in a hurry, but by far the most effective description is achieved through details.

Exercise 2-2

Look at the following notes toward a description of a neighborhood where one of my students grew up. Which notes are statements of quality, which are comparisons, and which are details (or telling facts)? Which do you find most effective?

Every kid should be raised in a ghetto. Predominantly white, Irish-Catholic neighborhood with a sprinkling of a few black-haired, tanned-skinned,

Italians. Something out of an Irish Soap commercial. A Black, Oriental, or Jew nowhere to be found and Protestants treated like illegal aliens. One-way street so narrow one could spit across it (popular game). Stick ball, wise ball, half ball (called hemisphere), step ball—city games—make do. 23 row houses attached one to another on both sides of 1-way street. Unread pages of the *Philadelphia Bulletin* blowing up and down the street making the ordinary trash somewhat more intellectual. Not unlike the floor of the N.Y. stockmarket during a bull market. 45 good Catholic families who have littered the street with over 150 children. Chalk designs on the street, crying babies, fighting children while parents do some city socializing on front steps. Ice Cream and Water Ice Trucks make their respective ritualistic appearances at 9:07 and 9:35. The sound of horns blowing accompanies the youth's shouts for the money from parents. The only universal sound emanating from households is the sound of the radio's baseball broadcast.

The evening ends with the last out of the ninth inning. The final roundup of camaraderie and community of purpose or maybe plight. Young and old. Sporadic crying, yelling, laughing, and coughing. No air conditioning. The heat which for 12 hours bakes the city's concrete carpeting. A night with little promise of relief.

Has the writer found enough details to begin a description?

One more point. Not all details are telling. If I were to describe the room I usually teach in by saying "The room is painted light green," I wouldn't have told you much. You'd have a much better picture if I noted that "The paint on the back wall is peeling, the ceiling is covered with water stains, and the exposed pipes rattle every time a toilet is flushed upstairs." Telling facts are facts which *tell a reader something*; they imply more than they say.

Exercise 2-3

Take five or ten minutes to try to write some telling facts. After five minutes, offer your attempts to the class to see what they think. If, after hearing from others a few successful telling facts, you decide that one of yours is clearly unsuccessful, offer it to the class as an unsuccessful attempt and see if you can explain why. You can often learn more, at this point, from failures than from successes.

Here are a few good telling facts that my students have come up with during the above exercise:

- My professor had a copy of *Winning by Intimidation* on the corner of his desk. (*Implication: The professor likes the power of his position.*)
- Karen's grammar book was used to prop up the broken leg of her stereo set. (*Implication: Karen is more concerned about music than about English.*)
- When the grease that coats the top of the stove is splattered, it hits all

four walls of the kitchen. *(Implication: The room is small, and its cooks are sloppy.)*

- He begrudgingly agreed to lend her $2 but then found that the smallest bill he had was a twenty. *(Implication: The richer a person is, the less likely he'll be generous.)*
- When he was introduced, his handshake was firm, but his palms were damp with sweat. *(Implication: He was nervous, though pretending not to be.)*

Of course, our efforts are not always so successful. Here are a few attempts that the class decided were inadequate:

- As he walked down the street, the beer and ale called out to him from the passing restaurants and bars. *(Not a fact.)*
- Giant "Eiffel Tower" steel electric generators stand on a sweep of smooth bright grass. *(Not focused. What implication is intended?)*
- After two drinks, she could dance a fair polka; after three drinks, she was Polish. *(The second half is not a fact.)*
- The Professor's desk was piled high with dusty books and papers. *(Perhaps a telling fact, but one used so often that it has become a cliché.)*

A common type of attempt at writing a telling fact follows:

1. In the attic of the house I grew up in was a box placed so high I could not examine its contents until I was 8 or 9; then I discovered it contained dozens of letters, yearbooks, corsages—all sorts of artifacts from my parents' lives. They must have kept everything!

2. My mother uses her own set of kitchen knives and keeps her knives in a special drawer so that no one else can use them. To her, the art of cooking lies in the right way of cutting.

In both cases above, a strong telling fact in the first sentence is weakened by a lame explanation or comment in the second sentence. Try, for now, to resist the urge to explain. In your writing later, you will, of course, do some explaining, but explaining is easy, while finding the facts that convince is much more difficult. If you want to learn to be a good writer, you have to learn to *earn* the right to make a comment by starting with well-chosen details.

Exercise 2-4

Coming up with a telling fact is difficult—thinking specifically is difficult—it means clearing out the cobwebs. But it's also difficult because so far you've been trying to recall telling facts rather than write them from observation. Telling facts are easier to collect than to recollect. So for homework for the next class, stop somewhere to observe for a while—allow yourself at least an hour—and write out five telling facts to bring to class. (It should be clear by now that the word *fact* is not limited to statistics; a fact is anything that can be observed.)

You can check your ability to find these telling facts by comparing yours, in your next class, with those of your classmates. One effective way to compare notes is to divide into groups of three or four in which you decide on the group's best five and worst five telling facts. Once a group has come to a decision, it can rejoin the class and read the facts chosen randomly. The class may then vote whether each example is or is not a telling fact. The class should vote the facts "telling" (when they have clear implications) or "boring" (when they call forth only a "so what" response). Finally, you might hand your facts in to your teacher to get a more experienced opinion.

Deciding whether a fact is telling or boring will always be somewhat subjective; our judgments will often depend upon our degree of familiarity with the subject. And many facts that a writer uses do their work (like supplying context) without calling attention to themselves as telling facts. But telling facts are always worth striving for. The quest for them will keep any writer—a professional writer, a student A-writer, or a student D-writer—challenged while working on any writing assignment. Every paper needs strong details to support and explain its purpose. *No amount of correct or clever writing can substitute for a mass of telling facts in helping a writer achieve his or her ends.* If you didn't come up with five good facts the first time, try the same exercise again until you're more comfortable with selecting and writing them. Force yourself to sit quietly in a busy place and observe. Once you get the knack for finding telling facts, all your writing this semester will be easier and more effective.

In most writing situations, you will first gather facts from observation (of places, people, books, or films), and then you'll come to interpretations of the facts you've gathered. Sometimes, though, you'll write because you already have an interpretation, or opinion, that you want to get across. That opinion will look a little naked until you find some facts to support it. You may find some facts in the library, or by asking other people, but other facts you'll have to get by checking your memory. And you can't let your memory be satisfied with vague recollections, as in one of the sentences that introduced this chapter:

- I have met some interesting people, and some not so interesting people.

You can't let sentences like that quit. They remain opaque to the reader, and three or four in succession, or six out of eight, will put the reader to sleep.

Exercise 2-5

Search the following passage for genuine details. Note where the writer has allowed herself to be satisfied with vague recollections.

Some girls join sororities to increase their social interests, but a smart girl joins for a chance to better herself. She comes to the sorority to escape the anonymity of a large university. She works to become a person, an identity with feelings, instead of number 000-11-7777. Living with a large group of girls, she becomes more aware of others' wants and needs. By working with others, she learns to express her ideas and interests and become a leader. The sorority gives her the opportunity to work with the underprivileged and the disabled, helping her to grow mentally. As she works to become a part of the sorority, she grows stronger as an individual. With the support of the other members, she is fulfilled by the increase in her self image.

There's a lot of feeling in this passage, but the message that gets through to the reader is muddy. Don't let yourself be satisfied with such careless, undetailed writing.

To see how you can build an essay out of specific details, you might try, at this point, to write a description of a place you'd like to study (see Assignment 1 in Chapter 15). When I say "description," I don't want your mind to leap immediately to "beauty." There's no point in writing fantasy like the following:

> My first glimpse of the beach was from a distance. I was standing on a hill gaping at what seemed to me the perfect beach. The scenic view looked like it belonged in a travel agency poster. There was a thick grove of coconut palms and a strip of virgin white sand that separated the trees from the deep blue Caribbean Sea.

You'll miss the whole point of a description assignment if you aim for beauty. When you write description, you should be aiming *not for beauty but for honesty*.

DESCRIPTION ≠ BEAUTY

DESCRIPTION = HONESTY

What is your place really like? What makes it distinctive? How do people use it? (Places are only distinctive—and thus worth writing about—because people have made them so. People have conceived them, built them, and perhaps neglected them. Now other people frequent them, or pass by them as quickly as possible. How? Why?)

Your raw material for any description paper will be telling facts that you collect by observing, patiently observing. Here is part of what one of my students, Geneva Parker, saw when she took a pencil and notebook to a seat in the lounge of the athletes' dorm at the University of Maryland:

> During the course of the evening, an uncountable number of Snoopy caps, Pumas, warm-up suits, and red vinyl jackets passed by, giving

me curious looks or an occasional "Hello" or "How ya doin'?" There were arms in slings, legs in casts, and muscles . . . lots and lots of muscles. Girls in dancing dresses and high heels slid through side doors, their whispers and giggles mingling with the creaks of the door. At 8:30, a troop of knees and elbows emerged from the "vator" (elevator). They were all dressed in suits, and were it not for their lanky bodies and a cue from the guy sitting next to me, I would not have known that they were basketball players. The elbows soon found themselves making way for three warm-up suits walking in time to the syncopated bounce of the basketball. "Thwump! Thwump! Thwump!" While the bouncer hailed the vator, the other two went over to harass the Macke machine. He stood at the vator doors, bouncing patiently, until the other two joined him and together they bounced aboard.

One great virtue of telling facts like these is that they allow us to recognize meaning in the most ordinary details of our lives.

This habit of observing patiently, of respecting what facts can tell us, and of seeking out the facts that resonate most will make all your paper writing more successful. Observation, after all, is not only useful in describing objects. When we read a book well, we underline various words, sentences, and paragraphs. By doing so, we implicitly acknowledge that these are "telling" words, "telling" sentences, "telling" paragraphs. They express, in miniature, much more than they actually say. If you were writing a paper on, say, Henry Kissinger's *White House Years* (Boston: Little, Brown, 1979), you'd want to look back at your carefully observed underlinings to find "telling quotations" to use in your review. If you were to interview a woman in a nursing home, you would observe carefully how she acts and what she says. Some of how she looks would be "telling"; you'd be sure to include those details. Some of what she says would also be "telling"; you'd of course include that too. By seeking out "telling" facts and then drawing responsible inferences (conclusions) from them, you would be likely to write a fresh, honest, thoughtful paper.

Research of all kinds, then, is simply a form of observation. The same keen observation, the same research methods, apply in a description, in an interview, in using the library, in film watching, in book reading, in newspaper or magazine reading. It takes practice in each to look through the raw material and find what's significant, what's thought-provoking, what's of human interest. It takes practice in each to find the telling facts, to determine the meanings that those telling facts reveal. Collecting information through research, like collecting facts for a description of a place or collecting statements for an interview, requires patience. You don't always find what you want right away. But the patient exploration the writer goes through each time follows the same pattern. And once you're confident that you can find evidence, you'll never again have to sit at your desk for hours staring at a blank page and worrying about how you're going to fill it.

Work at noticing telling facts until you can select them almost instinctively. Our ability to write "telling" facts is a reflection of our ability to discriminate, to select, to distinguish meaning from the lack of it. A couple of years ago, I was talking in the hall with a student who was trying to decide whether to take my section of English 101 or someone else's. Another student in the hall saw us talking and interrupted, "Are you taking his class? If you do, you should know—he likes details." That's a rumor I'd be happy to help spread. Telling details are the foremost tools of photographers, filmmakers, fiction writers, informative writers—anyone who wants to get a point across economically and vividly.

3

♦

Facts, Inferences, and Theses

George Bernard Shaw once said that as he grew older, he became less and less interested in theory, more and more interested in information. The temptation in writing is just the reverse. Nothing is so hard to come by as a new and interesting fact. Nothing is so easy on the feet as a generalization.

John Kenneth Galbraith

Exercise 3-1

Before we start, I'd like you to answer some questions in your notebooks. You'll remember better the principles of this chapter if at the end of the chapter you come back and check what you've learned against your original opinion.

1. What's an inference?

2. What's an implication?

3. What's a thesis statement?

4. What makes newspapers sell?

As much as I have emphasized facts so far, I don't mean to suggest that facts are to be used by a writer without analysis, without commentary, without conclusions or judgments that the writer draws from those facts (it is an insecure lawyer or manager who stuffs a chaotic pile of facts into a brief or a report in the hope that some of the facts might convince). We build a paper out of facts, but the glue that holds a paper together is the *inferences* that we can draw from the facts we put on paper. *Inferences,* I know, is a word that you either haven't heard before or are a little fuzzy about. You don't hear it much in everyday conversation—we take inferences for granted. But drawing careful inferences is crucial to becoming a good writer.

An *inference* is a judgment based on at least one fact. You drew inferences in Chapter 2 whenever you decided what you thought a telling fact "meant." *Inference* is very closely related to a much more commonly used term, *implication.* When a writer uses a telling fact—"Most of the people who fill the university's trash baskets are white, but most of those who empty them are black"—she is *implying* that there is some injustice here. When you or I read the same telling fact, we are likely to *infer* that there is some injustice. We're both going in the same direction—*from* the fact *toward* injustice—but the word used to describe the writer's action is *imply,* and the word used to describe the reader's action is *infer.* This chart may help:

S. I. Hayakawa, in *Language in Thought and Action,* has explained inferences so clearly that I'll call on him here to help me (41):

> An inference . . . is a *statement about the unknown made on the basis of the known.* We may *infer* from the material and cut of a woman's clothes her wealth or social position; we may *infer* from the character of the ruins the origin of the fire that destroyed the building; we may *infer* from a man's calloused hands the nature of his occupation; we may *infer* from a senator's vote on an armaments bill his attitude toward

Russia; we may *infer* from the structure of the land the path of a prehistoric glacier; we may *infer* from a halo on an unexposed photographic plate that it has been in the vicinity of radioactive materials; we may *infer* from the sound of an engine the condition of its connecting rods. Inferences may be carelessly or carefully made. They may be made on the basis of a broad background of previous experience with the subject matter, or no experience at all. For example, the inferences a good mechanic can make about the internal condition of a motor by listening to it are often startlingly accurate, while the inferences made by an amateur (if he tries to make any) may be entirely wrong. But the common characteristic of inferences is that they are statements about matters which are not directly known, statements made on the basis of what has been observed.

Drawing inferences responsibly is a very important thinking skill. In this chapter, you'll practice "drawing" several kinds of inferences from several different kinds of facts.

Geologists and archaeologists are masters at drawing inferences. Most of the Western world in the eighteenth century believed that Noah, about 3000 B.C., had built an ark and survived a forty-day flood. Then James Hutton in the 1780s discovered clam fossils embedded in Scotland's granite. Thinking about the fact of the embedded fossils, Hutton inferred that much of Scotland was at one time under water—not 5000 years earlier, as the biblical story of Noah suggested, but perhaps 6 million years earlier. Hutton's inference was a bold one in 1785, but much evidence since then has tended not only to confirm it but also to suggest an even older earth (McPhee, *Basin and Range,* 91–108). Geologists look at surviving artifacts from millions of years ago and try to interpret them, or draw reasonable inferences from them.

Archaeologists work the same way. They sift through the remains of more recent times, the times since the human race made its appearance. Their method of working is well described in a forthcoming book by Craig Stoltz:

> Professor Joe Dent arrives to the first meeting of "Archaeology 451" with a plastic trash bag slung over his shoulder. He grabs the bag by the corners and shakes its contents onto the floor: several institutional memos, a Bach Festival brochure, a Coke can. A small paper envelope imprinted with the name of an English industrial archaeology museum, a "Dear Friend" direct mail piece from an historical society, a black plastic cannister the size of a thread spool. A cellophane pipe tobacco packet, a twisted pipe cleaner, flecks of charred tobacco, and a scattering of papers, some handwritten, others typed, a few dittoed. Some are balled up.
>
> "This," says Dent, spreading the mess around with his foot, "is what archaeologists deal with—garbage." He's dumped onto the teacher's platform what has accumulated in his trash can since 7:30

that morning. The students of Archaeology 451 don't say much, but just look at the trash, their pens poised at their notebooks. They had planned on merely taking notes. "So what does this garbage tell us?" Dent asks. "Anything?"

We begin to speculate, carefully at first. That Dent is a nonlover of classical music. No, of Bach. Maybe. He doesn't read memos. Well, maybe he *reads* them but doesn't *keep* them. He's literate. We guess. That he has a mild addiction to caffeine. No, practically everybody drinks Coke. At least he's not a health nut—he smokes. But a pipe. A clean pipe. *Was* dirty, though. Probably a tourist type, with a decent camera. Those balled up papers—he has a temper. Or was bored. Maybe shoots baskets. Maybe shares an office. Or someone else put that trash in his can.

We continue for twenty minutes or so, leaping from fact to rickety inference, back to solid fact, on to other facts. Valid inferences, we find, are hard to draw: each must be checked in relation to other facts and inferences. After twenty minutes of pawing and grabbing, we know little about the man behind the garbage. Even this morning's trash, it turns out, doesn't yield many answers.

Archaeologist that he is, Dent has also brought in some "real" artifacts—the kind we'd planned on taking notes about. One is what we call an "arrowhead" of brown stone (later, we'll learn to call such things "projectile points"); another is an axe head the size of an open hand, a smooth finger-wide groove dividing it in two. Dent claims these are garbage too—cultural discards—but harder than fresh trash to draw inferences from: there are no other items with which to associate them. There is also a rectangular stone slab a-foot-and-a-half long and three-inches thick, half of its top face chipped an inch deep. This artifact has proved very difficult indeed to make assumptions about, Dent reports—to date, nobody has been able to figure out what it might have been used for. Such an item is known in archaeologist parlance as a "FRGOK": Funny Rock—God Only Knows.

"The archaeologist's real problem," Dent says, nodding back at the fresh trash scattered on the floor, is that "over time, almost everything disappears." If this trash were dumped outside, the paper and tobacco would decompose in a month; the plastic and metal would get kicked around, eventually buried, and biodegraded within a few hundred years. Even the gray plastic trash bags, always a target of angry environmentalists who complain that plastic lasts forever, would disintegrate within a millennium or two. So when archaeologists apply what may seem absurd scrutiny to chunks of stone, says Dent, holding the Funny Rock in his arms, it is not because they think these are the most telling cultural remains. They are not. It's because, most of the time, that's all a prehistoric culture has left behind. The rest has rotted away.

Exercise 3-2

Your teacher may not be so accommodating as to bring in the garbage, but you should be able to practice drawing inferences from the contents of your teacher's pockets, purse, briefcase, or bookbags: keys, inspector's tags, a bottle of Head and Shoulders or Allergy Relief Medicine, credit cards, aspirin—whatever. Every item (e.g., an American Express card) is a fact from which you may draw a timid inference ("she doesn't like to carry lots of money with her") or a bold inference ("she's rich") or even—we hope—a responsible inference somewhere between those two.

It will help you sort things out in your mind when doing this exercise with your own teacher if you make a list down the left-hand side of a piece of paper of the items in your teacher's purse (or pockets):

a "J. C. Penney" tag

five pens

a pocket dictionary

wire-rim glasses

Then, as you draw inferences, list those inferences opposite the facts with arrows between them:

a "J. C. Penney" tag ————→Doesn't spend much money on clothes

five pens ————→Writes a lot

a pocket dictionary ————→Not sure about how to spell

wire-rim glasses ————→Went to school during the 1960s

When you draw these inferences, do you have full confidence in them? What other facts would help you feel more sure?

At this point you should have some sense that inferences drawn from single facts are suspect, but more important, you should feel in your bones that you can distinguish a fact from an inference. If you're ever confused in the future, all you have to remember is—all those things from the purse or pockets? They're facts. All the things you said about your teacher? They're inferences. When you've exhausted your teacher's patience with your "bold" inferences, pair off with another student in the class and see how well you can infer things about each other using the objects each of you carries around.

Exercise 3-3

Now try the same exercise with a more revealing (or is it a less revealing?) kind of fact—statistics. The following is a breakdown of types of ads in two different magazines. Use these charts (one at a time) to draw as many inferences as you can about the audience—in terms of age, sex, marriage status, interests, and occupations—at which the magazine is aimed. Compare your results with those of the rest of the class, and note whether your inferences tend to be bolder or more timid than those of your classmates. You might want to guess what each magazine was; your teacher will tell you at the end of your discussion.

age - 18-21
sex - F
marriage status - S
interests - themselves
occupations - McDonalds

MAGAZINE 1   AUGUST 1980
Breakdown of Ads 1/4 Page and Larger

Product type	Total number of ads
Hair care	13
Jewelry	5
Makeup	16
Clothing	19
Shoes/boots	14
Fragrance	6
Health care/toiletries	33
Cigarettes	8
Education/employment	8
Lingerie	5
Travel	5
Food/drink	9

Other

1 Cross pen	1 Christian Children's Fund
1 Woolite	1 C&P Telephone
1 *People* magazine	2 china
2 wallet	

looking for jobs
Glamour

MAGAZINE 2   JUNE 30, 1980
Breakdown of Ads

The New Yorker

age 25-30
sex - m
m.S married
interest}
travel -
drinking
occupation -
banker

Product type	1/2 page and larger	Less than 1/2 page	Total
Automobile	4		4
Women's clothes	1	5	6
Liquor	8	2	10
Travel	5	11	16
Makeup	3		3
Women's shoes	1	2	3
Accessories for home	2	10	12
Stockbroker	1		1
Corporate PR	1		1
Charity	1		1
C&P Telephone	1		1
Camera	1		1
Bank		1	1
Men's clothes		2	2
Jewelry		1	1
Entertainment/dining		3	3
Books		9	9
Psychiatric hospital		1	1

Exercise 3-4

For more practice in drawing inferences, take a look at the photograph on the opposite page. Imagine that you are an archaeologist living in the year 2500 who has found this photograph (framed) buried in a pile of rubble along the shores of

© *Joan Clark Netherwood, 1979*

the Gulf of Mexico. As a class, examine the photo in detail, and begin to list details—not judgments—about the picture along the left side of a sheet of paper. Once the class has noted ten or fifteen details, put on the right side of your paper, opposite each detail, any conclusions that you feel the detail might justify. Again, you're drawing inferences from the facts (details) you've noted. Once the right side of your paper is pretty full, describe at the bottom of your sheet the overall impression that you think the photographer of this picture was trying to get across. What do you think the purpose of the picture was?

You'll find, I think, that your purpose will be some kind of summation, or summation with qualification, of the inferences that you've listed on the right side of your paper. Now write a quick paragraph about the picture explaining its purpose.

Your paragraph would most naturally begin with a sentence stating the purpose of the picture, and that sentence would be substantiated by a listing (perhaps with some explanation) of some of the details you first put down on the left side of your page. Compare your paragraph with those of several other students in the class.

You should now begin to see how most papers take shape. Your research begins with an examination of details, and yet your written paragraphs begin at the opposite end—with a summary of your inferences (a thesis). Rarely is a paper quite so straightforward as this exercise suggests, but any study of a body of material will take this basic form. You are practicing inductive, scientific reasoning.

Exercise 3-5

This kind of fact-inference-thesis exercise becomes more complex when we use our fact-selecting and inference-drawing powers to investigate a more complex piece of raw material, a newspaper. Have someone in the class pick up twenty to twenty-five copies (one for each member of the class) of some newspaper that you're not familiar with. Pay for your copy, and then read your paper through, thinking of yourself again as an archaeologist. Collect twenty telling facts about the paper—not the telling facts chosen by reporters to tell their stories, but facts *about* the paper itself that tell us something about the editors, or the owner, or the paper's intended audience. Look for evidence in the placement and length of articles, the types of articles favored, the pictures, the editorials, the advertisements, or anything else that strikes you about the newspaper. If, at first, nothing "strikes" you, compare the paper with one with which you are more familiar, and you'll more easily see distinctive features. Again, place distinctive facts about the newspaper along the left side of a sheet of paper, and put your inferences about the editors, owner, or intended audience opposite on the right. Here are some examples:

Facts	Inferences
The *Seattle Post-Intelligencer* prints a story of an explosion that injured three workers in an Ilwaco factory on page A-11 and reports the story matter-of-factly.	Readers probably are more proud of industrial productivity than they are alarmed about industrial accidents.
A *Sun* headline reading "Politicians' Egos on the Line" is set in special type.	The *Sun's* readers are interested in politics, but only superficially—in things like the psyches of politicians.
The *Village Voice* contains no reference to children or schools except a full-page ad for the Macy's parade and a small ad for a dance class.	The *Voice* is not a family newspaper. The Macy's parade must be an "in" event. If readers have children, they are precocious.
All the *Village Voice* ads for beer and wine are for foreign brands.	The readers have expensive tastes and are snobbish about what they drink.
The *Village Voice* contains very few furniture ads, but four full pages of J&R ads for stereos and a full page of Crazy Eddie's stereos.	Readers all have stereos, but not much furniture.
The *Rutland Herald* publishes elaborate, detailed obituaries of people from all social classes.	Many readers probably know each other. It's a close-knit community.

The first list that anyone makes is likely to have some strong elements and some weak ones, so to get help in setting standards of quality for yourself, bring your first list to class, get in a group of three or four students, and decide what are the ten best fact-inference pairs you've come up with among you. The "best" ones will include facts not everyone would have noticed and inferences not everyone would have thought of. Now that you see more clearly what constitutes "quality" in fact-inference pairs, go home and upgrade your list, keeping your best pairs and adding new ones until your list reaches twenty-five. When you come to class again, look over your list, and write out a thesis statement (a summary of the points you'd like to make) for a paper you could write if you were asked to characterize the newspaper or its audience. Here are some samples:

- The Friday, September 24, issue of the *New York Post* seems to indicate that it hopes to attract a wide variety of working-class people who are delighted with controversy, who are not politically knowledgeable, and who probably commute to work.

- The *Rutland Herald* addresses a group of rural, middle-aged, middle-class readers interested not only in local news but in international conditions. The majority of the readers are probably white and Protestant, and American by birth.

- The readers of the *Village Voice* see themselves as an exclusive, "in-the-know" group. They also see themselves as the champions of minorities and as politically "hip." They are most likely not your average New Yorkers, nor would they want to be considered so.

How did these writers come up with their theses? How did you come up with yours? They noticed the kinds of inferences that come up over and over again, and their theses were summaries of those inferences.

Compare your thesis with the theses of the other students in the class. You'll be curious to see not only how your judgments differ but how complex the theses are, how specific, how clearly thoughtful.

Next, ask your classmates how they would support their theses. Tell them how you would support yours. Now you should be able to see more clearly (1) how a thesis statement should be arrived at, after consideration of the evidence, and also (2) how to use evidence to support a thesis.

Fact-inference pairs can be used not only to arrive at a thesis that you can substantiate but also to help you paragraph your paper. Any inference that you've made three or four times could serve as the topic sentence, or main point, of a paragraph. Look at your list of fact-inference pairs, and collect a group with the same inference, or similar inferences. See whether, by listing all the facts together, you can make your inference more complex or thoughtful, as did a writer who was studying a copy of *The National Enquirer:*

Facts	Inferences (in sum)
Eleven articles about general health issues (arthritis, asthma, cancer, stress, high blood pressure, weight loss, "beating the blues," digestion, hypnotism to treat health problems)	Readers very concerned about health problems. Apparently more given to worry than to action. Especially concerned with weight loss and energy. Very sedentary. Not willing to make

Cover article is "Top Experts Reveal Easy Way to Lose Weight While You Sleep"

Eleven ads for diet and pep pills

No articles about exercise or nutrition (or ads for health spas or exercise programs)

Three ads for vitamins

Ad with the heading "Lose Pounds Fast, Lose Bulges, Bumps and Inches Instantly"

Ad with the heading "Instant Relief for Tired Aching Feet"

Five cigarette ads, all for light cigarettes (Virginia Slims, Golden Lights, Barclay, Marlboro Lights, Raleigh Lights)

major changes in their habits, although perhaps willing to make minor modifications. More oriented toward cures, especially miracle cures, than prevention. Not very skeptical of inflated promises for instant relief.

This writer now has a point to make (the inference) and facts to substantiate that point that will make up a solid paragraph or two.

Inferences that we draw are never wholly reliable. You'll note that even when the members of the class are all investigating the same newspaper, each member arrives at a slightly different (in some cases even a wildly different) thesis. Using the same newspaper and the same facts, some students will label the paper conservative, and others will label it liberal. Facts, even "telling" facts, can't yield 100 percent certain inferences. All inferences are personal—valuable, and yet vulnerable. Nevertheless, all inferences can be made more persuasive with the help of company. An inference substantiated by five facts is more reliable than one drawn from two. That's more reason for us to develop our ability to seek out the most pertinent, most telling facts.

As we learn to draw inferences, we must learn to draw responsible inferences. We cannot complacently assume that a single fact we've presented justifies the inference we'd like to draw. Occasionally, people will come up confidently proud with a "telling" fact that is implicitly racist:

- The clerk wearing a yarmulke put a dollar of his customer's change into his own pocket.

- Three white farm laborers were busy pulling weeds while three Mexicans snoozed under their sombreros.

One fact does not, of course, justify a conclusion. A single fact is always at least slightly unstable: from any fact several (more or less probable) inferences can be drawn. Since several inferences can be drawn, we see the need for additional facts to limit the number of possible inferences. If the

paint on my classroom wall is peeling, for example, it could be the maintenance crew's fault, or it could be the state legislature's fault. The added
detail that state funds for the university have been cut back 10 percent per
year for the past seven years might help to fix the inference and the blame.
The quality of an inference depends, too, on the expertise of the person
making it. A crack in a basement floor means more to a groundwater
geologist than it does to a new homeowner.

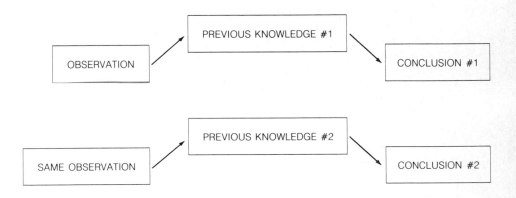

Since expertise is for the most part a matter of mastering more facts in a
given area, we should be making a lifelong effort to become more expert in
as many areas as possible so that we will be better able to interpret the new
facts we face every day.

Exercise 3-6

To test your sense of the vulnerability of inferences, try this exercise. Study the
following list of facts:

1. The university grounds crew has laid new sod in front of Skinner, Francis
   Scott Key, Jimenez, and Taliaferro Halls in the past four months.

2. Last summer new acoustical tile ceilings were installed in fourteen class-
   rooms in Taliaferro.

3. A new parking lot has been paved over the area left decimated when the
   World War II temporary buildings were torn down in October.

4. Twenty-five azalea shrubs have been planted next to the footpath crossing the library mall.

What inferences, what interpretation, can we draw from these facts? Would we be
willing to write a paper using just these facts as evidence? What other facts would
we look for to support our interpretation? Where would we look? One final question
before moving on. Might there be evidence to contradict our interpretation too?
What should we do about that evidence? When you write, your own fact-inference

pairs will be vulnerable, and you'll often find, when you'd like to begin writing, and even after your first draft, that you don't yet have enough facts.

You've begun to see now how complex the relationship between facts and their inferences is. If you want to write something that will gain attention, you'll have to be as specific as you can be with your facts, and then you'll have to be slightly daring in your inferences. Safe inferences are easy to make but not very interesting to readers. For example:

Fact	Inference
The Tuesday *Kenosha News* contains 12 pages of food ads.	People in Kenosha buy a lot of food.

Any reader can come up with that simple inference without any help. But once you try to make your inference more daring (e.g., people in Kenosha spend more on food than on housing), you'll see that you'll need more facts to back up that daring inference. Making the daring inference thus encourages you to improve your research.

You should see easily now that every assertion that we make imposes upon us a responsibility to substantiate it. When we make any assertion— *Tanya is a liar*, or *nuclear reactors are dangerous*, or *Salvador Allende was a communist*—we usually make it because we've heard someone in our family, or on the news, make the same assertion. Too easily, we accept these assertions, these inferences, as facts. But any written assertion is incomplete (and in most cases ineffective) until it is substantiated by facts. Substantiating our assertions is an acknowledgment that justice is more important than our desires.

Exercise 3-7

Look, one at a time, at the following list of reckless assertions. As a class, try with a few to find specific examples, specific details, that would substantiate these assertions so they would look less reckless. Then, for homework, give at least two details (or examples) to back up five of the assertions in the list.

1. _____ is a racist campus.
2. There's no racism any more at _____ .
3. The automobile is wrecking American life.
4. The automobile has finally made life worth living.
5. Men don't do their share of work in this society.
6. Men have far more responsibility than women in this society.
7. Young people are more ethical than old people.
8. Young people should learn from their elders.
9. *Smokey and the Bandit* (or a movie of your choice) was a great movie.
10. *Smokey and the Bandit* (or a movie of your choice) was a terrible movie.

11. Living in the suburbs is like not living at all.

12. The best American life is to be found in the suburbs.

13. Criminals commit crimes not because they are bad but because they've been injured by their families or society.

14. Criminals should be shot.

You'll now see that a reckless assertion is an insufficiently substantiated inference. Through this exercise you'll be learning to reveal yourself less recklessly in your own writing.

Facts and inferences are the building blocks of our writing skills. Any set of facts will yield at least slightly different inferences to every different writer. We can thus *guarantee* that any writer is a writer with originality. Even if the facts you present are the same as those of another writer, your inferences will be different. In addition, our understanding of facts changes with time, and from country to country, so different people in different places will draw different inferences from the same facts. From the same facts, our children will draw different inferences than we do. So you never have to worry about being original. At the same time, it will be pretty clear to others—to your teacher, and to your classmates—if you steal the inferences of someone else (whether a friend, an expert you know, or an author). They won't carry your voice. They won't *sound like* your inferences. You'll of course borrow your facts from other people. Facts are in the public domain. None of us can be expected to verify every fact we learn from others. But the inferences we make must remain our own. What we call intelligence in a person is very much a matter of the facts at that person's command combined with the thoughtfulness of the inferences that he or she consistently derives from those facts.

We are often advised to write by starting with a subject (say, the automobile), trying to decide on an idea about the subject (say, "the automobile is harming American life"), then "factoring" that idea into at least three parts (say, "the automobile is harming American life by polluting our cities, by distracting our 16-year-olds from their studies, and by distracting all of us from walking through our neighborhoods and talking to people"), and finally trying to substantiate each of those ideas with facts and examples. This method of finding a thesis and then a factored thesis is a good place to start if we are writing an essay exam, the purpose of which is to show someone what we already know about a subject. But if we're examining any subject seriously, we're on very shaky ground when we start to write with "ideas." Most often, our ideas on abortion, dorm life, gun control, automobiles, and other such issues are half-baked (more often quarter-baked) and based on the reflected opinions of parents and newscasters. The "ideas" we write down are surprisingly seldom our own, and surprisingly often contrary to our own feelings. Thesis statements constructed before a writer begins research and writing are dangerous invitations to muted or biased observation. And so we shouldn't allow ourselves to write "ideas," or theses, until they are earned with sufficient evidence. The first step in any assignment should be a search for the facts, the pertinent facts, the telling facts. Every fact you write down triggers an inference, which in turn may remind you that you have other facts at your disposal. And then the implications of those facts, in sum, will lead to an idea, a thesis, a proposition, that will always be more responsible than one arrived at through a deskbound search for an appropriate "topic" for a paper.

I'll be giving you a great deal of advice in this book about what you should take *out* of your prose. Now you know what you should put in— carefully selected facts and sound, thoughtful inferences.

4

◆

Writing for a Reader

A reader doesn't read from an insatiable need to applaud.

source unknown

I now think more about the people reading my paper and try to make it so that it would sound clear to them. Before I used to write unspecific things because I expected people to know already what I was talking about.

student

The most important thing I learned in this course was not to be a "selfish" writer.

student

Exercise 4-1

Try to answer these very different questions:

    1. What <u>tone</u> of voice of either of your parents gets on your nerves?

    2. Who reads what you write?

               reader

How often have you dipped into a book and found something like the following:

> Right-wing disbelief and hostility or unreadiness to think or listen one can comprehend. It is part and parcel of a more or less coherent lengthy process of ideological socialization (Worsley, 15).

How often have you opened a report and found something like:

> To maintain the day-to-day operations of the program, while expending other energies toward the fulfillment of department objectives, requires the careful and responsible commitment of resources (PLANNING, POLICYMAKING). The responsible commitment of human resources requires the substantiative involvements of staff in decision-making to (1) maximize use of a pool of differing skills and interests, to (2) further develop individuals' sets of skills, and to (3) deepen individuals' commitments to department growth (COMMUNICATIONS, MOTIVATION).

How often have you yourself written something like:

> It is hard to realize just how much you miss someone until you are away from this person. It seems that the time spent away from this person is wasted. You seem to wait and wait till you can see this person again. Then when the time comes it passes too quickly (Macrorie, 2).

Or when you have been asked to write a paper, how often have you delivered something like:

> The general notion of gymnastics brings to mind flips and swings on various apparatus. There exist various imposed requirements within men's and women's gymnastics which reflect the differences of these two sports. It is these requirements which make up the very essence which separates men's gymnastics from women's gymnastics. The difficulty of a woman's routine is set by a minimum requirement of one superior and two medium skills. Other skills are required for a routine, but they hold no difficulty value. The context of men's gymnastics is emphasized by the philosophy that a man will be strong, forceful and fluid. The framework of men's gymnastics is built on these concepts and dictates a design such that the aspects of strength and swing can be stressed. These differences go beyond the superficial

individuality of each event, and we can see that each sport seems to stress different points. It is this concept which indeed accounts for the wide differences between men's and women's gymnastics.

As Faulconbridge, in Shakespeare's *King John,* says after being lectured to by a citizen of Angiers, "Zounds, I was never so bethumped with words" (2.1.466). These passages fail, I'm afraid, to meet the standard for good writing established by the British Admiralty Pilots during World War II: "that it should be intelligible to a tired man reading in a bad light."

Ken Macrorie has called the type of writing in the above examples "Engfish"; one of my students who misheard the term calls it "Inkfish." Either is a good name for murky, bloated, pretentious language that results when a writer hasn't remembered that the job of a writer is to communicate. Swamped by writing like this, no wonder professors and students alike despair over the future of the written word. Writing like this keeps authors busy and paper companies solvent, but it communicates very little, and it enhances our lives not at all. When a television show doesn't tell us anything, we often sit and watch anyway because the flicker of light is calming. But when a writer doesn't tell us anything, we drop the book and fall asleep, because a printed page, as a printed page, is tiring. Many of us have self-destructively given up on books, not because books are incapable, even in this computer-and-television age, of entertaining us, informing us, and making us more human, but because we're not careful enough to be selective—to read only the best, and not to read books published because an issue is hot or because (in school) a certain body of materials needs to be "covered." Writers who provide these "demand" books don't write their best because they don't have enough time to think through their subject carefully. And when, as readers, we look into three or four dull books (often textbooks) in a row, we sometimes too easily give up on books in general.

In this writing course, and after it, try to avoid adding to our pile of unreadable writing. Take your time when you write; give the reader something for her money, something for her time, something for her effort. That something is information, news, something she didn't know before, something that will help her live the rest of her life in a better way than she has to this point. That something is not just information but also your interpretation of the information. The reader may disagree, but she can only disagree if she knows what you think and if she knows the facts that have led you to think as you do.

Writing that stands out from the morass of words like those on the first page or two of this chapter is writing that sounds like it is being spoken by someone. Nevertheless, most of us hold back our personalities as we write. Some of our teachers have told us to keep our selves out of our writing. But even without that advice, we often write in voiceless language out of fear of revealing too much. We don't want people to recognize what we perceive as our ignorance or our lack of confidence about what we're writing. Our reservations are not unfounded. When we write (or talk), we do give away a great deal about our personalities.

Exercise 4-2   *evidence to back up opinions*

Look at the following passages, for example, and note in your notebook what you learn about the character of each writer.

evidence and cockiness

1. C-130 rollin' down the strip.
   Airborne Rangers on a one-way trip.
   Mission unspoken, destination unknown,
   Don't give a damn if they ever come home.
   Locked and loaded, ready to kill,
   Always have and always will.
   Squeeze the trigger and let it fly,
   Hit the bastards between the eyes.
   Before he died, I heard him yell,
   "Airborne Rangers are bad as hell."
   [U.S. Army Ranger chant (Harris, 4.1–4.2)]

trying to be one of the guys

2. The ultimate revenge in this life, I think, is to come back to your high school as its commencement speaker. Imagine. Me. Not the president of my class, not the former chairman of the Latin Scrabble Club, not the head of the Keyettes (I think it was Nancy Immler, who would never go out with me). Not Goldie Hawn, with whom I once rode to the Hot Shoppe after the Bethesda–Chevy Chase game in the back seat of Pete Oldheiser's chopped-and-lowered Buick. Not Bob Windsor, the football player. But me, from the very bottom of my class. [Carl Bernstein, coauthor of *All the President's Men,* speaking at a high school graduation (5)]

careful, cautious, intellectual

3. I have never been in a strike before. It is like looking at something that is happening for the first time and there are no thoughts and no words yet accrued to it. If you come from the middle class, words are likely to mean more than an event. You are likely to think about a thing, and the happening will be the size of a pin point and the words around the happening very large, distorting it queerly. It's a case of "Remembrance of things past." When you are in the event, you are likely to have a distinctly individualistic attitude, to be only partly there, and to care more for the happening afterward than when it is happening. That is why it is hard for a person like myself and others to be in a strike. [Meridel Le Sueur, "I Was Marching" (229)]

bit officious but sense of responsibility within a tradition

4. On January 1, 1967, the Supreme Court of Arkansas will for the first time in a century seat four new judges, all at once. A majority of the seven. This impending influx of the uninitiated led me, some months ago, to turn from the question I so often put to myself, "What can my country do for me?", to a different question: What can I do for these novitiates who are about to outnumber me? That reverie led to this primer. I have decided, not without diffidence, to try to say to you four the sort of thing that I wish

my late colleague, Judge Frank Smith, then in his thirty-seventh year on the court, had said to me when as an infant of only thirty-seven years all told I became his devoted associate on the bench. [George Rose Smith, introducing "A Primer of Opinion Writing"]

Writing reveals our charm, our goodwill, our intelligence, but it also reveals our anger, our snobbery, our sexism, our racism. Still, you can't write well if you're afraid of what your writing will say about you. You want to write more than just gradable noise on paper. You want to get used to your voice. You want to see what your voice reveals and then—during revision—make whatever modifications you feel are necessary. Only by practice, that is, by trial, and error, and criticism of our errors, can we develop confidence and get away from the voiceless writing that plagues both student and professional writers. But the payoff is generous. Checking on and working on our voices is one of many ways in which learning to write better helps us to become more generally mature.

It is remarkably easy to slip into voiceless language. The patterns of voicelessness surround us. You'll find a ready-made guide below (*Newsweek,* 104):

0. integrated	0. management	0. options
1. total	1. organization	1. flexibility
2. systematized	2. monitored	2. capability
3. parallel	3. reciprocal	3. mobility
4. functional	4. digital	4. programming
5. responsive	5. modular	(program)
6. optimal	6. transitional	5. concept(s)
7. synchronized	7. incremental	6. time-frame
8. compatible	8. third generation	7. projection
9. balanced	9. state-of-the-art	8. hardware (software)
		9. contingency

The table above is a guaranteed Inkfish generator. Pick any three-digit number, and you have a ready-made, impressive-sounding addition to your prose:

> 357: parallel modular projection
>
> 502: responsive management capability
>
> 793: synchronized state-of-the-art mobility

This writing may seem ridiculous, but if you're not careful, you may find yourself writing it in six or seven years.

Exercise 4-3

There are no "functional incremental time-frames" in the following letter I found in the files when I took over my current job. Nevertheless, the writer has resorted to "Inkfish" rather than communication. See whether you can repair the damage.

Dear Dr. Washington:
Receipt of your letter of August 2, 1974, with reference to the offering of English 103 and/or 171 to Susan R. Trowbridge is hereby acknowledged. In view of the fact that she is currently out of the country and is not expected to return until after August the 20th, pursuant to my telephone conversation with your secretary, Ann Allen, I am requesting that the deadline for my daughter be postponed until after her return to enable her to exercise her option of taking either of the courses being offered.

Thank you for the courtesies extended and for your propitious consideration of this request!

Sincerely,

George Trowbridge, Consulting Psychologist (A concerned father)

What do you think of the writer of this letter? Rewrite the letter. Show Dr. Washington that you are indeed a "concerned father" and not just a consulting psychologist trying to show off your importance.

Of course, there's another extreme to the stilted voice, and that is the breezy, self-advertising voice. If you were browsing through a bookstore and you ran across the following preface (Bolles, 1–3), would you want to read the rest of the book? Has the writer won you over? Or distracted you from his message?

THE BACKGROUND TO THIS BOOK
COMMONLY CALLED
THE PREFACE

Hello, dear reader. You're browsing here in order to try to find out what kind of a book this is, right? You've flipped through the pages, back to front, the way we all do, and you've seen that it has lots of interesting cartoons, charts, and flair. You've perused the table of contents. And now you're checking out the preface.

Welcome. You want to know what this book is about? Well, it's essentially a book of ideas. Ideas about School, Work, and Retirement—what's wrong with them, what could be right with them, and how you might do something about that in your own life . . . now. There are separate books on the market already that deal just with School, or just with Work, or just with Retirement, but this book is unusual because it deals with all three at once. The reason for that is that this book is an introduction to LIFE/work Planning. And L/w P, by definition, means looking at all the parts of your life, together.

I volunteered, very reluctantly I might add, to write this book. I am the head of a project of United Ministries in Higher Education, which is called the National Career Development Project. We put out a Newsletter, run workshops, and create needed materials (more about this, at the very end of this book). People also ask us a lot of questions. And one of the most persistent has been, Where can I lay my hands on a good book that explains what LIFE/work Planning is all about? Well, there really isn't any (that we *know* about, anyway). So we decided that with all the experience the Project has had, in this field, we probably ought to fill the void.

I cannot *possibly* tell you the sacrifices that have had to be made, the mountains that have had to be climbed, the deserts that have had to be crossed, the rivers that have had to be swum, in order for this book to be completed. God knows. (Also my dear office-person, Erica Chambre-Hubartt, who has regularly beat off callers from the entrance to my cave, while I typed away inside.)

Anyway, here it is. A book of ideas, some of them really dazzling; I know, because they aren't mine. If you are enamored of a particular idea, you will of course want to know where it came from. Wherever possible, I tell you. I feel exceedingly protective toward idea people. They are creatures who are often given little recognition or reward— in this life at least. I mean, if you invent a product, *everybody remembers*. Every time there is a car accident, people automatically think of Old Whatsisname. But an idea? Ah that is a different kettle of fish. . . .

By now you're probably very nervous about what voice is your natural voice. You probably won't achieve that natural voice consciously, so let's get at it another way.

Exercise 4-4

Take out your notebook, begin on a new page, and write for ten minutes without stopping. You can write on any subject at all, but don't let your pen stop.

— only writer functions

Exercise 4-5

Consider that attempt a warm-up. Now write again for ten minutes without stopping, again writing on any topic at all. For homework this evening, write three more of these timed ten minute writings and see what you come up with. After the writing, note down anything that surprised you about what you wrote. Your teacher may want to look over and comment on one of the five timed writings that you've done.

You probably feel pretty awkward writing these timed writings. But as you practice them more and more often, you will find that they do several things for you. First, they show you that you are never without words. Second, they help you realize what your natural voice is. Third, they help you realize that writing can be used as a thinking technique: when you force yourself to keep your pencil moving, you'll find thoughts coming to your mind that you had forgotten were on your mind. (When you stop to take time to write, you have stopped to take time to think.) Finally, timed writings remind you that the first words off your pen are often not the best you can do and therefore that revision is a step in writing that should never be ignored.

Exercise 4-6

As the semester proceeds, you may find that you want to do timed writing regularly to keep up your skills. If you do, here are some topics that you may use to start yourself off:

1. Look ten, twenty, thirty, or forty years into the future and imagine yourself having just died. Write an obituary for yourself.

2. Give us your thoughts about the paper you just handed in.

   - I feel there is a good writer hidden away inside.
   - The paper I handed in today was one of the strangest essays I have ever written.
   - Writing my first composition in English 101 was kind of hectic, but I am sure glad that it is over.
   - Once I got rolling, I knew it would be okay.
   - My paper was a long time in the thinking stage.
   - I felt good about my first paper. I was pleased with myself.
   - I spent a good deal of time rereading my paper to see how it sounded and flowed.

3. Explain, in 500 words or less, how to write an F paper.

4. Explain in detail, based upon your experience, one important principle every child should be taught.

5. What problems are you having putting together the paper you're currently working on?

6. Writing is a game. True or false? Explain your answer.

7. Respond in writing to the comments you just received from your teacher on your paper.

8. What place do you have in your family? What effect has that place had on you?

9. You're now well past the legal age for leaving school. Why are you starting another school year?

10. Describe either the best or the most bizarre scientific experience you have had in a laboratory of your high school or college.

11. Describe a way of life that you admire but cannot take up yourself.

12. What kind of writing does your mother or father do?

13. Write a letter to the author of one of your books for this course. Assume that you are on friendly terms with him or her and that you are every bit

as intelligent, and ask at least two questions about the author's advice on writing. Try to include a part of the book, even a small part, in your questions.

This timed writing doesn't often result in a final version that you'd be proud to hand to a teacher, or to anyone. But it can form the *basis* of a final version that can be handed in. Once you have something written down, you can begin to choose what you want to include in a paper. The choices you make, much more than the words you put down the first time, will determine your success as a writer.

Of course, your voice will not sound the same every time you write. Sometimes you're trying to soothe the feelings of the person you're writing to; other times you're trying to move people to act or think more like you do. A variety of (honest) voices is at your disposal. You'll quickly see that variety if you imagine that you've had a motorcycle accident and then consider how you'd explain that accident (1) to a parent, (2) to the friend from whom you've borrowed the motorcycle, and (3) to the director of public safety, who is (indirectly) responsible for the malfunctioning traffic light that caused the accident (Gebhardt, "Imagination and Discipline," 31).

Many beginning writers, afraid of their own voices, feel that they could add some pep to their writing if they could just add some kind of "style," although they don't know quite how "style" is achieved. But you can't rush the steady climb toward a style you're proud of. Your style develops as your voice develops. And your voice can only be as sophisticated as you are. The more you learn, the more experience you get, the more you will have to offer in your voice. In a sense, your voice is dependent on your entire education, in and out of school. The more you learn, the more confidence, authority, and life your voice will carry.

In the meantime, we can achieve the best voice we're so far capable of not by adding some sort of "style" but by subtracting elements in our writing that we share with everybody else. This is why we've been told so often to avoid clichés like "hit the nail on the head" or "avoid it like the plague." Our use of a cliché tells readers that we understand life as well as most people do, but it doesn't tell readers our particular point of view on life. Conventions in writing are another form of clichés:

This paper will discuss . . .

The question of mercy killing is beyond the scope of this paper . . .

In conclusion . . .

Many of the words and phrases which come most easily off the pen are the words that we all share, the ones that are not distinctive. Pruning these clichés from our drafts leaves us with the word combinations, and the fact-inference combinations, that are our own. Such pruning is, of course, more than verbal: it includes cutting out the comfortable, conventional repetition of ideas that often passes for "thinking." The conventions are comfortable, but though we have come to expect conventional prose, we are quietly disappointed every time we read it.

Using conventions is the easiest way to get through life. If we get married too young, for example, we are likely to *imitate* fatherhood or motherhood instead of being good fathers or mothers. When we imitate, we tend to imitate only the surface features of fatherhood or motherhood. There is much to be learned, to be sure, from the way others have been fathers or mothers. But if we want to be our own best parents, we have to do what we think is best, adjusting our behavior occasionally after checking with the established patterns. The same strategy results in effective writing. We should start writing by noting what we see and by writing what we think ought to be said. Later we can fit what we have found into some conventional form so that readers can make use of it. But if we start with a model in our minds and not with what we want to say, we are condemned to repeating old truths and to writing voiceless papers.

You're beginning to see, I hope, that writing either wins or loses the prize, not because of its elegance but because of the way it affects a reader. When you write, you are not showing off, you are not expounding; you are performing a service for a reader. When you think of yourself as trying to talk to someone as you write, then you will be likely to sound like someone when you do write.

One way to begin to think more seriously about your readers is to do some analyzing of audiences. Assignment 3 in Chapter 15 asks you to do an audience analysis of the readers of some old magazine. There you try to infer, from the way the magazine is written and from the kinds of ads that the magazine uses, what kind of audience the magazine is aiming at. You can make some reasonable guesses about the audience. But, of course, in many cases you will be wrong. (You know yourself from your reading experience that the audience assumed by some of the writers you've read did not include yourself.) To get a sense of your own audience when you begin to write, you might ask yourself a couple of questions:

- Is there an audience that needs this information?
- Is there an audience that would like this information?

But writing for audiences has its pitfalls. When we write for an audience, we too easily assume that we have to write *down* to that audience.

Although we claim in this country to believe in democracy, we secretly distrust our fellows. "We forever hold back, on the theory that our neighbors are not so wise or remarkable as we are" (Mitchell, 3.1). It's easy, once you've defined an audience as "college freshmen," for example, or "university professors," to develop contempt for the group as a whole. But if you remember that every individual in that group will be very different and that any individual in that group might be you, you will be much more likely to write well. You will write *to* people, not *down to* them. To write well we must learn to picture a reader—not an audience, but one reader (at a time) in that audience. In this class that reader will often be your teacher but also, frequently, one of your fellow students. To give you some idea of how your teachers and students read, I've collected some samples:

STUDENT 1: When I read another student's paper, if the grammar (word choice & punctuation) is poor, I have to spend too much time trying to figure out what the writer is trying to say. Therefore, the majority of my time is spent reading the writer's mind and I have less time to enjoy the paper.

STUDENT 2: When reading someone's paper I can usually tell if it's going to be good by the confidence of the writer. Whether the content is interesting or boring, I can enjoy a paper whose writer has the ability to include his own style and opens with an interesting introduction. A paper that is stifled by poor grammar or is boring by an attempt to make everything grammatically correct or for an audience such as teachers (using large words that are vague) is not what I consider a good paper.

STUDENT 3: When I'm reading another student's paper I know it will be a good paper if it arouses some sort of feeling or response in me (such as sympathy or anger). If a paper can get me to think about that particular subject—it's a good paper. If I have absolutely no desire to go on reading, I know something is lacking in that paper. When I get the feeling that I can't wait to find out what's going to happen but at the same time want to savor every word and never finish reading—I know that's a good paper.

TEACHER 1: I always read a paper the first time for the content only, not marking anything. I always hope to read something I didn't know, or something old said or seen in a different way. It's so disappointing when the student sticks to the obvious details, the usual arguments. It means that she only tries to be acceptable instead of challenging herself to write something alive, worth reading by someone other than the teacher.

TEACHER 2: There are papers I read with frustration and self-flagellation and say "Oh no, not this again—I've talked about this *19* times!!" But then, others make up for it—I *do* remember what the preceding paper was like (in spite of students who call my office to say "This is Jane. Jane Doe. I'm in your 8:00 English 101 class . . .") and thoroughly enjoy seeing Jane working on the details or cleaning up a particular grammar problem. And then I feel an *immense* satisfaction, a simple pleasure that at least something is working somewhere. . . .

TEACHER 3: I usually read through the first paragraph quickly and if it is interesting, I continue reading. If it is not interesting, I throw it aside and tell myself I'll read it later. After reading through all the essays once (for content only), I then read through critically. Even though I try to be impartial, I cannot help responding more favorably to the ones that I enjoy.

In your one-on-one conferences with your teacher this semester, you'll see how your own teacher reads. And in draft workshops, you'll learn how your own classmates read. Think about what you learn as you write.

A genuine feeling for one's reader works surprising transformations in a writer's prose. Most poor writers are bound inside their own heads as they write. They make no imaginative leap to their reader's point of view. They see easily that their speech is a way of communicating, because they've known that most people listen when they talk. But if they haven't written many letters, most of their writing has been for teachers, and few students have taken the trouble to try to imagine what their teachers think as they read their papers. You know that readers come to an article looking for information, for surprises, for clean, clear expressions of ideas. Well, your teacher will come to your papers looking for the same things, and she'll also make some comments to help you achieve them. One of the first things that you'll have to learn if you want to improve your writing in this course is to overcome your contempt for your teacher as a reader. None of us would admit that we have contempt for our teachers, but if we would stop to consider how little effort we often put into our papers and how much effort the teacher must put into reading them, we would realize that we really are showing contempt when we write. Keep in mind that your teacher wants to read some good material this semester. She takes no satisfaction in being a gradable-noise grader. Teachers, like any other readers, like to be informed, and they like to learn without going to too much trouble trying to figure out what you mean. See whether you can get your teacher to enjoy reading. It may be that you can if you provide some of the things that readers and teachers look for, such as:

1. Density of details
2. Challenging interpretations of details
3. Paragraphs in which every sentence is purposeful
4. Thorough research
5. Careful distinctions
6. Thoughtful introductions and conclusions

As a teacher reads, though, it's a rare paper that will delight him throughout. So at the same time that he is looking for items to praise, he'll be noting every obstacle to his comprehension of the paper. Every time he comes up against an obstacle, he'll explain to you why he found what you did an obstacle. You'll then begin to see that your punctuation, for example, and your paragraphing, and your organization are worth improving.

Writing class priorities	High-rated		Low-rated	
	Self	Group	Self	Group
1. Writing thesis statements	✓			
2. Using supporting details *mE*	✓	✓		
3. Avoiding sentence fragments	✓		✓	
4. Knowing precise verb forms and subject-verb agreement			✓	
5. Spelling correctly			✓	
6. Punctuating correctly			✓	
7. Drawing inferences				
8. Writing introductions	✓			
9. Writing conclusions	✓		✓	
10. Developing a distinct tone of voice	✓			
11. Observing one's subject carefully				
12. Writing logically	✓	✓		
13. Connecting sentences coherently	✓			
14. Paragraphing clearly				
15. Learning to fear writing less				
16. Planning before writing			✓	
17. Revising a first draft				
18. Using words precisely	✓		✓	
19. Becoming aware of one's readers				
20. Getting practice in reading			✓	
21. Knowing correct manuscript form			✓	
22. Being concise	✓			
23. Learning to judge one's own work				
24. Other (specify) _____				

"knowing precise verb forms," "spelling correctly," and "knowing correct manuscript form." Looking at my L's reminds me that I consider even these items important, though not as important as the others. In this course we'll be working on everything. You may, though, want to focus on weak areas while building up your strengths in all.

What we'll be learning in this course has long been called *expository* writing. I prefer to call it *informative* writing. I don't much like the term *expository*. No one outside of school seems to know what it means. And expository writing is usually considered the opposite of so-called *creative* writing. In fact, though, all writing—not just fiction and poetry—is creative: our writing requires, even at its simplest, creative decisions about the selection of material, the interpretation of material, the arrangement of material, and the best way to persuade our readers.

Everyone in this class will be writing—creatively—in his or her chosen profession. You may not realize, though, how much of your time is going to be taken up with writing, because writing is private work, so we rarely watch people do it. Lawyers in television series spend their time in court; police officers in television series spend their time making arrests. But Chicago lawyers and Detroit police officers and Los Angeles sales managers spend much of their time writing. Job announcements even for routine work often ask for written communication skills. And promotions beyond college-exit jobs are almost always dependent on your communication skills. Schools and majors which test you exclusively through multiple-choice tests are (unintentionally) misleading you about your future. There are no multiple-choice tests after college. Whether you plan to be a teacher, an engineer, a marketing analyst, or a computer programmer, surveys show that you're likely to spend at least 25 percent of your working hours writing or planning writing—letters, reports on research, budget reports, grant proposals, business forecasts, press releases, speeches, management briefings, equipment justifications, technical bulletins (Faigley and Miller, 560–61). Much of the time you are not writing, you will be trying to be informative in other ways. What you learn in this course about writing will often help you conduct business in person or over the phone. It will also help you talk more clearly and specifically with friends. Even if you never write for the rest of your life (an unlikely possibility), you'll find the thinking, research, and organizational skills in this course useful.

This book is shorter than some writing course texts because in this course *you* are going to have to do most of the work. Newspapers, your city council, your local courtroom, a person whom you choose to interview, and your library's books, magazines, and videotapes will all expand this textbook. At the end of this course you won't carry away a fund of propositions or rules. You'll leave with a willingness to work hard and a good set of writer's intuitions that will make you confident in attacking college and professional writing assignments.

Of course, your teacher will not only read your essay but also grade it. Our society pays teachers (experts) to judge how well our students (candidates for jobs) have learned the necessary skills for these jobs. The teacher must step into that role of judge for five minutes each time he gives a paper a grade. But every other minute of the semester, including the time he spends writing comments on your papers, your teacher is an ally, a skilled reader trying to help you improve, trying to help you become a skilled reader of your own work. Many students seem to forget that this all-but-forty-five-minutes-of-the-course teacher exists.

It helps to know how your potential readers read, but to become a skilled writer, you must also gradually acquire the knack of becoming two distinct people yourself when you write. One self is a writer who scribbles out a draft, does some revising, and then types up that draft. The second self is a reader who reads that draft as if he hadn't written it. Reading your draft aloud (advice I'm sure you'll resist) may seem simplistic, but it makes you acutely aware of previously unconsidered needs of your readers. When you try to influence a reader through writing, you won't be there to smile, to demonstrate with your hands, to say "what I really mean is. . . ." Your separation from the reader is reflected in the following diagram (Linton, 27):

These gears show graphically that the written message is crucial. Only the message, never the writer, gets to touch the reader. The writer must therefore depend on what she has transferred to the message to do any communicating she wants to do. The first time you read a paper aloud in class, you'll want to change half your words, sentences, and paragraphs. It's not just a matter of hearing how your writing sounds but of becoming really conscious of your listeners. Once you're aware of your readers, you'll have much higher standards for your writing. You'll want to reveal something significant at least in every paragraph. You'll develop enough respect for your readers to believe that they will be convinced not by bullying but by a complete review of the information. You will remember that a reader wants to read rapidly, but wants to be mentally challenged.

All this effort to help your readers by becoming a reader yourself is much easier to undertake if you are working with a typed draft (or a draft on a word-processor screen). You're required to type your papers in a writing course much less to make reading easier for your teachers than to enable you to *see* your work, to become a reader of your own writing, to develop your second self. Your second self will also grow if you write self-critiques of the papers you write in this course ("I am satisfied with this paper because . . ." or "I am not yet satisfied because . . ."). That second self will also grow as you read the drafts of papers by other students in your class. It will grow steadily in sophistication as the course proceeds.

As you develop your second self, your internal reader, you should see that you don't please an outside reader by trying to find out exactly what the reader wants. The reader often doesn't know what she wants. Editors don't know what they want until they see what a writer has delivered to them. Similarly, a teacher doesn't have a fixed form of exactly what he wants. He's looking to be surprised. He's looking for some work from you that is genuinely different, genuinely worth reading. When you think about your readers, therefore, that doesn't mean you should be pandering to their presumed tastes; it means that you should be crafting the work so well that they will have no trouble comprehending it. Our job as writers is to eliminate obstacles for readers.

What are the implications, then, of learning to write for a reader? With the reader foremost in mind, we will come to share the values William Zinsser has identified as the four crucial values for writers: vitality, clarity, simplicity, and humanity (Zinsser, 131). Vitality engages the reader's interest; simplicity and clarity help the reader learn easily. But why humanity? Because we're human. Any understanding of our world is limited if we can't see the human dimensions of that understanding. Writing, like any other profession, requires both technical and human skills. Second, and very important, writing for a reader highlights the importance of revision. No one can write prose a reader would best understand on a first draft. Our minds work too fast; they are too concerned with getting matters from brain to paper in the first draft. The transition from first to final draft is best named, I think, the transition from "writer-based" to "reader-based" prose (Flower and Hayes, 449–61). The first stage—writer-based prose—is not a sign of weakness. It is essential. The stage is playful; it allows us to take risks, to try things out. It is also the best opportunity for us to think for ourselves. But a writer's patterns of thought should seldom be presented in the order that they occurred to him. A lab notebook, for example, is writer-based; it reflects the sequence of research. A published scientific paper, however, must be reader-based: the research material must be reworked to fit into the experiences of the readers of the paper. Readers need time and space coordinates at the beginning of an essay. Readers need good transitions between paragraphs. Readers need contrasts signaled and quotations introduced. Readers are distracted by irrelevant details, unnecessary repetition, and faulty punctuation. Readers, in short, expect the fruits of, not a record of, our research and thought.

You've just finished a crucial chapter. Now that you're aware of a reader, that reader will keep you on your toes. Worrying about that reader will incline you to read your work aloud before you hand it in. As you read, you'll often be embarrassed, but that embarrassment is useful because it will teach you how to revise what you've already written and what to avoid the next time you write. Reading aloud will often make you wish you knew more about your subject; that's not a bad thing either. Reading aloud will also help you with your punctuation, since punctuation was once a system of breathing directions and still reflects the way we breathe as we speak. But the main value of reading aloud is in helping you see the voice that you project. To be a better writer you'll have to develop that writer's voice; as you do, you will develop a sense of who you are, a sense of what tone you need for each writing assignment you're given, a sense of what words are appropriate for each writing assignment, and a sense of what effect your voice will have on your readers.

5

♦

Organization I:
WRITING SYSTEMATICALLY

I have many problems about writing essays but the biggest of which is organization.

student

Where there is no obscurity it will not be difficult to discover method.

Samuel Johnson

Exercise 5-1

To prepare yourself to get the most from this chapter, jot down some answers to the following questions:

1. How do you organize your weekend?
2. How do you organize your writing?
3. What does it mean to "define" a term? When is such a definition necessary?

Some of the professional writing you'll be doing will be expected to follow a predetermined order. If you plan to be a television screenwriter, you'll be asked, I hear, to include in each episode some "hooks" (situations that viewers can identify with), some "laid pipe" (background information on the characters), some "heat" (tension), some "topspin" (questions raised in the viewers' minds just before each commercial), and some "buttons" (clever remarks made by characters leaving the scene). If you're a personnel director, on the other hand, and you have to write a job description, you may be asked to include the following sections: "supervisor," "scope of responsibility," "specific duties," and "personal requirements." Some of your school papers must also follow a preestablished order: perhaps an introductory paragraph which ends with a thesis statement, a series of "body" paragraphs that all begin with topic sentences, and a conclusion in which you sum up your principal arguments. If your paper is of a particular kind, say a paper proposing a change in policy, you may be asked to use the following structure:

I. Introduction
  A. Opening words to win attention and goodwill by introducing your case in a favorable light
  B. History of the case
  C. Direct statement of your proposal
II. Body of argument
  A. Presentation of evidence in favor of your proposal
  B. Consideration of opposing views
  C. Concession and reply
III. Conclusion
  A. Recapitulation and summary of argument
  B. Final, heightened appeal for support

Most often when you write, though, you'll have to decide for yourself how to organize your material. It is you who decides how long you'll make your introduction, how many sections you'll divide your paper into, whether you'll use a formal thesis statement.

Organization is not a simple record of your thoughts. Neither is it a prearranged package, a method of "filling in the blanks." Organization is making order out of chaos. It results from decisions you make from the time you first start your research to the time, just before the final typing, when you may still be tinkering with scissors and Scotch tape. Form will seldom be your first consideration when you write. The principal elements which a writer considers are:

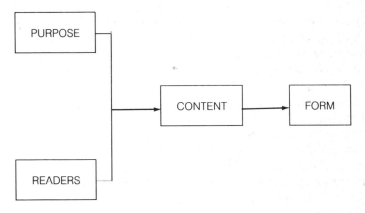

The decision to write starts in most cases in one of the two left-hand boxes. The writer starts with a desire to convey some information, or to explore a problem, or to persuade a reader, or simply to show off. She then searches for facts (content) which serve her purpose. Perhaps the facts she finds alter her purpose. But it is only after purpose, readers, and content are in mind that the writer faces the task of choosing an appropriate form for her given purpose.

Although form, or organization, is one of our later considerations as we prepare to write, it is a consideration that rarely works itself out easily. Whenever you find yourself saying "as I mentioned earlier," you know yourself that you haven't been systematic in explaining yourself. When other people complain about your structure, as they have complained about mine, they'll usually say that the piece isn't organized "logically." Although they use the word *logical,* they are only rarely talking about *induction* or *deduction,* the two forms of logic that will be examined in Chapter 9. What they mean, usually, is that the material hasn't been organized "systematically." Readers unconsciously expect systems when they read, and if we can adapt our writing to their systems, we can be much more easily understood. If writers don't order their material the way their readers unconsciously expect them to, they may bore their readers or make the readers laugh at them.

Exercise 5-2

To see how unsystematic ordering can destroy a message, read the following sentences and then try to rearrange them in such a way that they will not make you laugh.

1. Our spaceship brought back from the strange planet a large animal, two small green people, and a soil sample.

2. Cities are faced with countless problems, such as crime in the streets, littering, pollution, and traffic jams.

3. Although the controversial speaker tried to proceed, stones thrown at the platform, annoying catcalls, and a barrage of rotten fruit brought an end to the meeting.

My guess is that you've rearranged these sentences so that the most important item was saved for last. This order is often called *climactic* order. It is not always the best kind of order; you also need something solid at the beginning of your message to catch the reader's attention. And there are many kinds of order that are not climactic but yet are systematic. The following, for example, are all common and systematic *thought patterns*—ways of organizing material no matter what purpose we have in writing.

1. Problem-solution
2. Arrangement in space (description)
3. Narration (or explanation of a process)
4. Assertion with examples
5. Assertion with reasons
6. Definition
7. Cause and effect
8. Comparison-contrast
9. Classification
10. Building to a climax

These useful thought patterns are methods of putting subjects in context. They represent common ways of thinking. We find them, with equal frequency, in anthropologists' field notes, in grocery lists, in segments of the evening news. They are useful in writing because they are such common ways of thinking; no one really needs to be taught them. A reader is as likely to find a cause–effect sequence "logical" (that is, to find that he understands it) as the writer is, so it's a useful way to communicate. Since these thought patterns are common ways of thinking, they therefore become for us common *ways of*—or *strategies for*—*organizing our writing.*

Exercise 5-3

To get some idea of the systematic thought patterns available to you and to help yourself realize that those patterns are not infinite in number or complexity, try the following. Choose one subject from among the first three below, and write a one-page sketch organized according to any one of the ten thought patterns above.

First class	Second class	Third class
Procrastination	Money	Guilt
The Extended Family	Inferiority	The Best Movie I've Seen Lately
High School Education	Marriage	Working Mothers

When you've finished, write *a second sketch on the same subject,* using a second chosen pattern. During a class session, then, read, in turn, your papers aloud. After each reading by another student in the class, jot down (1) the method of organization you think the writer used and (2) a sentence or two explaining your decision. As soon as you've written down your estimates, compare them with those of other members of the class, and finally, ask the author what his or her intention was. You'll begin to see the variety of possibilities for organizing and the ways organizational patterns can be mixed with each other.

To reinforce your organizational sense, repeat the exercise a second and third time, each time choosing a new subject from a new column and writing about your chosen subject twice, using two different thought patterns. By the end of three classes, you will have used six patterns of organization, and you will have heard—from the rest of the class—the other patterns, and other ways of using the same patterns. You are building up your intuitive resources for organization.

All the thought patterns used in the exercise above are aids to readers. A definition makes clear a term that your reader may be unfamiliar with. Classification helps a reader sort a product or an issue into its important parts. A contrasting example helps a reader to see the subject you're focusing on more clearly. A cause-effect explanation helps a reader see *why* a certain event occurred. A narrative helps a reader see how certain issues might affect his or her life.

After this week of practice, you should be able to explain, better than a textbook can, what uses each pattern serves. You will also see that the patterns are not too complicated, and that they often overlap—that you almost always use more than one pattern in any extended piece of writing. As you listen to the sketches written by others, you'll probably also be reminded of how important details and examples are in backing up any assertions that are made.

Exercise 5-4

Any message, no matter what its length and no matter where it's posted, will, if it wishes to be clear and persuasive, be grounded in an organizational pattern. The messages on cereal box panels and matchbook covers, in junk-mail circulars, on traffic signs, in department memos and political ads, and on medicine bottles were all written by someone, and each writer, often more intuitively than consciously, used some thought pattern to organize the message. In the examples below, try to determine the author's principle of organization.

FROM A SIDE PANEL OF A BOX OF POST GRAPE-NUTS®

classification
narration
contrast

HERE'S HOW TO

GO GRAPE-NUTS®
cereal

OVER DANNON.®

½ container (½ cups) plain or vanilla-flavored DANNON® Yogurt
¼ cup POST GRAPE-NUTS® Brand Cereal
¼ cup (about) fresh, frozen or canned fruit*

Or use ½ container DANNON® Yogurt, any fruit flavor, and omit the fruit.

Spoon yogurt into dish. Top with cereal, then add fruit and serve at once. Makes 1 serving.

contrast
definition

SIGN ON A BATHROOM DOOR

MEN'S ROOM

SIGN ON A STAIRCASE DOOR

assertion
with reasons

FIRE DOOR
KEEP CLOSED AT ALL
TIMES TO PREVENT
FIRE FROM SPREADING

cause-effect
classification
building to a
climax

FROM THE SIDE LABEL ON A BOTTLE OF PEPTO-BISMOL

Caution: This product contains salicylates. If taken with aspirin and ringing of the ears occurs, discontinue use. If taking medicine for anticoagulation (thinning the blood), diabetes, or gout, consult physician before taking this product. If diarrhea is accompanied by high fever or continues more than 2 days, consult a physician.

FROM THE INSIDE COVER OF *NATIONAL GEOGRAPHIC*

definition

> The National Geographic Society is chartered in Washington, D.C., in accordance with the laws of the United States, as a nonprofit scientific and educational organization. Since 1890 the Society has supported more than 2,350 explorations and research projects, adding immeasurably to man's knowledge of earth, sea, and sky.

THE LYRICS FOR A HARRY CHAPIN SONG, "CAT'S IN THE CRADLE"

My child arrived just the other day.
He came to the world in the usual way.
But there were planes to catch and bills to pay.
He learned to walk while I was away.
And as he was talkin' 'fore I knew it, and as he grew
He'd say "I'm gonna be like you, dad,
You know I'm gonna be like you."

Refrain:

And the cat's in the cradle and the silver spoon
Little boy blue and the man on the moon
"When you comin' home dad?"
"I don't know when, but we'll get together then.
You know we'll have a good time then."

My son turned ten just the other day.
He said "Thanks for the ball dad, come on let's play."
"Can you teach me how to throw?" I said, "Not today."
"I got a lot to do." He said, "That's OK."
And he walked away, but his smile never dimmed.
And he said "I'm gonna be like him, yeah,
You know I'm gonna be like him."

Refrain

Well he came home from college just the other day
So much like a man I had to say
"Son I'm proud of you can you sit for a while?"
He shook his head and he said with a smile
"What I'd really like Dad is to borrow the car keys.
See you later, can I have them please?"

Refrain

I've long since retired. My son's moved away.
I called him up just the other day.
I said "I'd really like to see you if you don't mind."
He said "I'd love to dad if I can find the time.
You see my new job's a hassle and the kids have the flu
But it's sure nice talking to you."

narration — building to a climax, contrast between what we think "grown-up" like me means and what it does mean

> And as I hung up the phone it occurred to me—
> He'd grown up just like me.
> My boy was just like me.

Each of the messages above was organized according to some principle. And the longer the message was, the greater the chances that its organization could get out of hand. You'll begin to see, I hope, that even the brief papers you write for this class are complex documents, much in need of careful organization.

I wouldn't claim that the strategies I've listed above are a complete list, or a closed system. Every writer's list of organizational strategies differs, and many of these strategies overlap. But our inability to say "these are the only possibilities" should not lead us to despair of the strategies' usefulness. Keep your eyes open to whatever organizational strategies you find most common and most useful. If you find more useful strategies, add them to the list. In the meantime, this list is a valuable resource that you can turn to for any paper that you write.

Not being aware of these strategies for being systematic sets us back when we're writing a paper, but it sets us back most when we're trying to write an effective answer to an essay test question. When we're writing such an answer, the clarity with which we can present what we know becomes almost as important as what we know. Our instructors expect us not only to remember the course material but to be able to control it. But excitement or nervousness often leads us to write down all we remember at the moment, instead of setting time aside to try to organize an appropriate answer. A too–little–recognized part of our job in answering a test question is discovering what thought pattern the teacher is suggesting that we use.

Exercise 5-5

With the practice you gained in writing your six short organizational essays, look at the following questions—see if you can become expert at pattern spotting. For each question, decide on the principal organizational pattern expected, and mention also any secondary patterns that might be useful.

1. *History:* Compare and contrast the founding and development of the colonies of Massachusetts and Virginia. Be sure to discuss political, economic, social, and religious issues.

2. *Business:* Discuss three elements of risk that you discern in the business conduct of a public utility. Which is most serious?

3. *Biochemistry:* What are ketone bodies? Explain why and how they are formed in instances of starvation.

4. *Sociology:* How would you explain the differential earnings of men and women?

(handwritten margin notes: ⑤ narration, definition, contrast; ⑥ cause/effect, narration; definition)

5. *History:* How did the concept of equality change in the period from 1607 to 1865? Be sure to trace the change through time.

6. *History:* What were the five most critical events leading to the Civil War? Be sure to explain thoroughly what each event was and why it led to the Civil War.

You should quickly become impressed with your ability to tackle the organization of a question even when you know nothing about the subject matter being questioned.

If you become an expert pattern spotter, half your work in answering essay questions is over. Once you recognize a pattern, you can make a quick outline. Here, for example, is an outline for question 4, which I think calls for an assertion-with-reasons response:

Men earned 40 percent more than women in the United States in 1983

- Because pregnancy takes many women out of the job market during crucial years of advancement
- Because many women are in a dependent role where duties are expected of them at home
- Because young boys are brought up to expect careers, while many girls are not brought up to expect them
- Because job discrimination and job segregation conditions still exist

Each of these reasons will need details or examples to back it up, but now we are ready to start writing, *trying* to keep our minds thinking—and not just filling in the blanks—as we do.

We can use this three-step method (choosing a pattern, then building an outline, and finally supporting the outline statements with examples) in writing any paper. The method short-circuits much of the work and time usually involved in writing. But it also short-circuits some of the thinking. On a test, when we've done a lot of thinking already, and where we have (we hope) the examples readily at our disposal, this three-step method can be effective. A paper not done on the spot, though, at school or on the job, will require much more research and thinking, and the longer but more thorough writing method detailed in Chapter 10, "The Writing Process," will serve us much better if we wish to present not just our current knowledge but a helpful and thoughtful piece of work.

6

◆

Organization II:
PARAGRAPHING, INTRODUCTIONS, AND CONCLUSIONS

I can analyze a paragraph, telling you what is wrong with it and how to correct it, but I tend, even though I know the rules, to make stupid mistakes.

student

No one ever told me before that I could write the introduction last.

student

A four-page paper, as you may well know from counting yourself, contains roughly 1000 words. A thousand words of chaos? Sometimes it seems so, but usually not. The writer has given some organization to those words by ordering them into perhaps seventy-five or eighty sentences. But no writer could recall the seventy-five ordering decisions that went into arranging those sentences. Neither could a reader. However, if the piece is well organized, both writer and reader can spell out the ordering principles linking the paper's ten or twelve paragraphs. Paragraphs are the clearest, most memorable means a writer has to show a reader the steps in his or her thinking.

Exercise 6-1

People have very different ideas of what a paragraph is. Before we go any further, jot down in your notebook what *you* think a paragraph is.

Exercise 6-2

In order to test your assumptions about how paragraphs are formed, read through the following essay by Fred Reed and decide where you would begin paragraphs if you were the writer of this essay. (The sentences have been numbered to make class discussion about your choices easier.)

LEAN, HEALTHY, AND FORTY-FIVE

(1) The anti-jogging column threatens to become a mainstay of such literature as we have, perhaps replacing Watergate memoirs. (2) As I imagine it, the anti-jogging writer packs his slanderous tendencies into a briefcase and goes to a place where jogging is committed—a trail along the Potomac, say. (3) He waits. (4) A jogger thunders by in $65 waffle rubber shoes, $68 jogging suit of parachute fabric crafted to reduce wind resistance, and Navajo jogger's sweatband. (5) He carries organic dextrose pellets and several pounds of electronics—an integrated-circuit wrist pedometer, a digital blood-pressure indicator and a solar-powered pulse-counter with built-in coronary alarm. (6) The well-equipped jogger has the circuitry of a small fighter plane. (7) He also has a certain amount of philosophical baggage. (8) He is jogging to find out Who He Is, information that he might have gotten from his wife or his driver's license. (9) He is Probing the Limits of Self. (10) The writer tries to make this sound ridiculous (11) This is to misunderstand the jogger. (12) He is usually over 30, and has noticed that stairs are getting perceptibly steeper. (13) He is a bit disturbed by it, suspicious that something new has been slipped into the contract. (14) The moment of truth usually comes when he realizes they aren't really letting girls into college at age 14. (15) He looks uneasily around the office at men 10 years older. (16) They have smoker's cough, liver conditions, and look as though they are smuggling medicine balls. (17) In all important senses they are sessile. (18) At this point he acquires a deep desire to go white-water canoeing, to try rock-climbing or to go on a commando mission into

Botswana. (19) By the end of the afternoon he is persuaded that he has only a few hours to live. (20) That evening he wheezes around the block while his wife shadows him in a rented ambulance. (21) There is something noble, tragic and silly in it. (22) The jogger lives for 30 years on a diet of lard and french fries, plugging up his arteries and taking years from his life. (23) Then he jogs to expand the arteries around the lard, getting the time back. (24) The anti-jogging writer sniggers at this inconsistency, as well as at the mystical hooha that surrounds jogging—the confusion of crumbling cartilage with enlightenment, the Oneness with Nature, and the High, which is in fact indistinguishable from the onset of flu. (25) The jogger tends to be a fiercely competitive fellow who is not about to be intimidated by God, metabolism, time and destiny. (26) He persists, that being what the fiercely competitive do best, and, lo, soon he is running five miles a day. (27) The American male believes that if a thing is worth doing, it is worth overdoing. (28) The children slowly forget him ("Ma, who *is* that guy . . . ?"). (29) His knees fill with bone fragments and his kidneys begin to loosen, so he buys shoes. (30) By now he has noticed that running is work. (31) The jogger tries to conceal this behind a fraudulent jauntiness—"Yes, ran 40 miles today, just didn't have time for a good workout. (32) Usually do it on one leg." (33) Yet it is most dreadful work. (34) Worse, it is boring. (35) The body really can be brutalized into condition, after which it will go on forever. (36) To have a reasonable expectation of cardiac arrest, one must run for hours. (37) The nirvana promised after Mile 5 doesn't materialize. (38) Stir-craziness comes. (39) He still doesn't know Who He Is. (40) Nobody but a thorough-going damned fool would suffer so much without an analgesic and a reward. (41) The analgesic is toys. (42) It is fun to get a new piece of running instrumentation—preferably with LEDs, the *sine qua non* of spiritual experience. (43) He may not go faster in his new, absurdly expensive, helium-filled shoes, but it is nice to unwrap them, like having an extra birthday. (44) The reward is showing off. (45) Face it: people get very little recognition in this anthill society. (46) It's a kick to be lean, healthy and 45, to be 11 miles into a run of 20, to be bounding along at an easy lope and sticking his chest out at the high school girls. (47) They never notice—they figure a fellow of 45 belongs in the Smithsonian—but there's hope that their mothers will come along. (48) And he feels so pleasantly superior to the majority, who would collapse at anything more arduous than relaxed breathing—among whom one inevitably finds, *heh heh,* the authors of anti-jogging columns.

Once you've made your decisions, defend them—first in a small group, then with the whole class. There will probably be much disagreement. The important thing, though, is that you can explain why you thought each paragraph division should be made. Your reasons for paragraphing, taken together with the reasons given by the rest of the class, should give you a good idea of how paragraphs are formed. People choose to paragraph for such reasons as length, unity, emphasis, and tone. A new reason seems to come up every time I try the exercise.

You may want to repeat this exercise, using papers from other students in your class. Be sure, whenever you do this kind of exercise, to specify *why* you would paragraph in each place you have chosen for paragraphing.

Paragraphing is a convention of written communication. Until the seventeenth century, paper was too expensive to allow for such waste of space, but since that time, indenting has been a conventional way to avoid tiring the reader. A paragraph is a form of punctuation, but one that gives the writer much latitude. When we paragraph, we ask our readers to take this lot, to take a half-second rest, and to think about all that's been said since we last indented. Paragraphing is much like picture taking. It's a way of selecting, focusing, emphasizing. Like a photograph, a paragraph can be comprehended at a glance. Like a photograph it allows the artist to highlight. Like a photograph it shouldn't be shown to anyone but a relative until it contains something worth thinking about.

Some unskillful writers go on and on with long paragraphs. Long-paragraphers, by not making any decisions about linking, force their readers to organize the material themselves. Short-paragraphers are even harder on readers. Short paragraphs don't force a writer to do *any* linking, and thus that entire chore is left to the reader.

Your teachers have probably asked you several questions about your paragraphs when they've graded your papers. Their questions may have looked like the following:

1. What is the American Congress doing in the middle of a paragraph about the New France?

2. This seems to be a new idea. Why don't you begin a new paragraph?

3. Franklin's age certainly does not deserve a paragraph to itself.

4. One sentence doesn't make a paragraph. Doesn't this idea fit with the ideas above?

5. Does all this information belong together in the same paragraph?

6. This paragraph is very short. Can this information be combined with the information in some other paragraph?

I'm sure you know what to do, with a little thought, with comments like those above. There are other basic guidelines about paragraphs, however, that you may not be aware of. What are those basics?

1. Until paragraphing well becomes intuitive for you, it's best not to worry or think about paragraphs until you've written a complete draft. Paragraphs are more easily discovered during revision than they are composed while drafting.

2. Your reader, in pausing briefly after each paragraph, naturally focuses most on the first and last sentences of paragraphs. These sentences (during revision) should not be wasted. They represent the writer's best opportunities for emphasis.

3. The first sentence of a paragraph need not necessarily sum up the

paragraph: it is often more effective when it promises or simply piques curiosity. It might pose a problem which the writer proposes to solve, or it might be a traditional topic sentence: a topic sentence assertion can, after all, tease a reader into wanting to know the specifics that support it.

4. Perhaps more important than paragraphs themselves are the bridges between paragraphs, the guideposts that link what we've just read to what the writer would like us to read next (otherwise, there's no guarantee that we'll continue).

5. The best way, late in your drafting process, to see whether your work makes sense is to try to write a paragraph-by-paragraph summary of what you've written. Your attempt will quickly expose any irregularities in organization.

With these five guidelines in mind, you shouldn't need any paragraph "rules." Your future supervisors or printers or editors, or even the size of the paper you use, will tell you how frequently you'll be expected to paragraph.

Because we can't write paragraphs following set forms, it helps to practice paragraphing techniques until we become confident that we can control their flexibility.

Exercise 6-3

Paragraphing has a significant effect on the way we name things. Yet many of us are inept at naming things in paragraphs. In the following letter of recommendation all references to the subject of the recommendation have been removed. Reconstruct the letter by placing in each blank either the student's name, Keith Williams, or a pronoun that stands for him—*he, his,* or *him.*

Recommendation for Keith Williams

_____ was first a student in my Chem Study course during _____ sophomore year. _____ is currently in my Advanced Chemistry course. _____ has done extremely well in both courses. _____ is 2nd in a class of 17 in Advanced Chemistry and was 3rd in a class of 20 in Chem Study.

_____ is a very good student as well as a good athlete. _____ has excellent study habits and is highly motivated. _____ is a leader both on and off the field. In my courses _____ has always done outstanding work, both in the laboratory and in lecture, yet _____ perceives himself as quite average, though _____ is definitely not. _____ can apply abstract concepts to specific problems and _____ has a very logical approach to solving problems. _____ is also a self-learner. _____ works hard, enjoys the process of seeking out information, and enjoys problem solving in general. _____ also knows when _____ needs extra help and _____ seeks it out.

Some of the traits which set _____ apart from _____ peers are _____ generosity, _____ humility, and _____ quiet leadership. _____ shares _____ knowledge freely and is always willing to help other students. _____ tutors regularly.

One of *Ruth's* most unusual qualities is *his* honest humility. It is infrequent that you meet an adolescent who has a sense of himself as a part of a broader world. It is in this way that *he* seems humble. I think this is also why *he* perceives himself as an average student. *He* is simply not full of himself.

Ruth is one of the finest young men I have ever taught and I give *him* my highest recommendation.

Sincerely,

Kathleen Sweeney-Hammond

You'll find, I think, that your writing flows most smoothly if you name your subject in the first sentence of a paragraph and then use a pronoun thereafter to refer to the name. In each new paragraph you repeat the name, and when you come to your conclusion, you repeat the name a final time (that's partly how we recognize the tone of the conclusion). Occasionally, if a paragraph is long or complex, a second naming of the subject seems appropriate.

Exercise 6-4

A second exercise which will help you revise your own prose asks you to take a piece of writing and write a paragraph-by-paragraph summary of it. You can write a summary by summing up each paragraph in one sentence and considering how that paragraph serves the writer's purpose in writing the essay. Your finished summary should tell you whether the piece makes sense, and so of course you can use this technique with your own work to see whether your own writing makes sense. Do a paragraph summary of the article below:

FROM *THE SUPPER OF THE LAMB*
ROBERT FARRAR CAPON

¹ Unless you are wise in the ways of the world, you will be surprised how hard it is to find a decent kitchen knife. Not because good ones are unavailable, but because there are so many bad ones around that the odds are against you. If you take what comes to hand, the chances are you will get a knife that is too small, or the wrong shape, or that will not hold an edge. In any case, it will cost more than it is worth.

² How can that be, you wonder? How can it happen here in the land of the better mousetrap, where quality merchandise always sells and the makers of shoddy goods invariably wind up poverty-stricken? Ah, yes! I shall spare you the chapters on aesthetic principles, personal integrity, popular taste, and political mortality which a sufficient answer requires. I give you only a new category by which to examine the assumptions of your question. It is the concept of the Tin Fiddle.

³ Take the modern American bread knife. You undoubtedly own one: shining stainless steel, slightly curved blade, and *serrated edge*. They are sold, I suppose, by the millions. Yet if you remember your childhood—your grandmother's house perhaps—or if you were lucky enough to pick one up at a junk shop or a rummage sale, you have seen another, older kind of

bread knife: stained carbon steel, straight blade, and, most important of all, a *wavy* edge. Now *there* was a bread knife. It held an edge. Better yet, its long straight blade came down flush with the board for a full eleven inches. Best of all, with two wipes on a stone and six on a steel, it would slice bread fresh from the oven. (Any knife that will not cut hot bread is not a bread knife at all. If it will not let you have bread at its best, how can it be worthy of the name?)

4 Now, what happened to that knife? I own an old one: It is on its third handle. But the only modern copy of it I have ever seen was useless. It had a wavy edge, all right, but the blade was curved, the steel was hopeless, and the whole thing was too short. Why can't the vast technological resources of America bring us up at least to the level of our grandmothers? That is where the tin fiddle comes in.

5 It is as if there were a conspiracy among violin makers (for whatever reasons) to provide the public only with violins made of metal. With enough control of the market, and with advertising sufficient to arouse the public's interest, they could reach the point at which no new wooden violins were available.

6 It would meet with opposition, of course. Nobody who remembered having heard a wooden violin would think the tin one as good. No professional violinist would willingly play a tin fiddle. And there would be an active market in old wooden violins. All that notwithstanding, however, the tin ones would sell. With enough manipulation, the only thing available to the man in the street would be an instrument no professional would use: partly because some people never pay enough attention to hear any difference; but mostly because the people who really care about doing things well are not numerous enough to cut much mustard in the marketplace.

7 The serrated bread knife, therefore, is a tin fiddle, a con-job foisted off on the nonprofessional public. So too are at least half the knives on the market, as well as a good percentage of the rest of the kitchen equipment sold for home use.

8 That knives should be used on boards, and not sink or counter tops, goes without saying. Let me go further, therefore, and suggest that your cutting boards be numerous: a chopping block, if you can manage it, then a bread board, a fish board, and an onion board. Except for the chopping block, these can succeed each other in a kind of hierarchy. A new board is always a bread board; a retired bread board becomes a fish board (for filleting and skinning); and a retired fish board becomes an onion board. The principle is simple: At any given period in its life, a board will come into contact with nothing stronger than that for which it is named. A retired onion board, accordingly, becomes firewood. None of them, obviously, should ever see the inside of a dishwasher.

9 Finally, however, my protest.

10 I am against the electric knife personally, and against the electric knife sharpener absolutely.

11 To take the latter first, it is one of the greatest tin fiddles on the market. The only people who use it are people who don't care about knives. To begin with, it is not a sharpener, but a grinder. A well-treated knife, however—one kept abreast of its destiny by stone and steel—will never need

grinding. (My father had a carving knife which he kept razor-sharp for thirty-five years with nothing but a steel. There was not a scratch on the blade. My knives are as sharp as his were, but not as beautiful. We are descended, you see, from men whom we shall be lucky if we match. There were giants in the earth in those days.)

12 The electric grinder is a dull tool. Its angles are usually too steep for a long-lasting edge, it turns over a burr large enough to stop peas, and, in the hands of anyone but a genius, it will, in six short months, turn a die-straight edge into a series of gruesomely notched curves. Add to that the fact that it literally eats knives, and you have more than enough reasons for never bothering with it. Anyone who can use it well is already intelligent enough not to use it at all.

13 The electric knife, however, is a more complex problem. I grant you that there are people who carve better with one than without. So far I allow it. I would rather see a roast sliced by electricity than mangled by a clown with a dull knife: I have watched beautiful roasts dismantled by inept carvers, and I know the anguish it involves. It would be less painful—and neater—to see them kicked apart with a pointed shoe. I have also eaten Smithfield ham in great half-inch-thick slabs hacked off by a knife whose last sharpening took place at the knife factory. Anything that will spare mankind the torture of chewing its way through tough meat to searing thirst is on the side of the angels.

14 But for myself, I beg to be excused from the general stampede of progress. By one of the ironies of fate, I do in fact own an electric knife. After brief use, it was placed on permanent loan to a friend. Not that it did not do what it was supposed to do—it did; and it was admirably ingenious in the bargain. It is just that, having learned the trade from experts, I found it gross, noisy, and unnecessary. When my father or grandfather carved, knife and hand were an inseparable unity; the whole process a silent display of grace. I could as soon imagine them with wires connected to their brains, as see them wanting cords to run their knives. I grew up with *artists,* you see—with philosophers who remembered that everything new is not necessarily better than everything old. The electric carving knife, therefore, makes no more sense to me than a motor-driven palette knife or a steam-powered violin bow. When Isaac Stern changes his ways, it will be time enough for me to think about mending mine.

15 It isn't stubbornness. It's just that, once you've seen giants, you don't forget so easily.

After completing your paragraph summary, you can also note how each sentence contributes to the main idea of a paragraph by choosing one of the paragraphs above and explaining, sentence by sentence, how each sentence relates to the summarizing idea you've given for the paragraph. This task may seem complex at first, but if you force yourself to think, and if you compare your answers with those of other class members, you'll learn a great deal about how paragraphs help us structure our thinking.

Many of us are afraid that our writing within paragraphs isn't smooth enough, but we're not quite sure what *smooth* means. Clear signposts help, as in the following example (Kolb, 16):

The attorneys state that the defendant acquired additional property after the divorce hearing, and that he left a will. They further state that the court's ruling on the present motion will have a substantial effect upon the property rights of the plaintiff and the defendant's heirs. If the divorce decree is not entered, the plaintiff would take the real property as tenant by the entirety, would have widow's rights in the after acquired property, and could dissent from the will. *On the other hand,* if the divorce decree is entered nunc pro tunc, the plaintiff could have a one-half undivided interest in the real property as a tenant in common, would have no interest in the after acquired property, and could not affect the will.

Two questions are involved. First, can a successor judge enter a nunc pro tunc decree involving the action of a predecessor judge? Second, is this a proper case for the entry of a nunc pro tunc decree? The answer to both questions is yes.

The writer above used clear guideposts ("Two questions . . . First . . . Second . . ."), clear contrasts ("If . . . *On the other hand,* if . . ."), and parallel structure ("would take . . . would have . . . could dissent . . .") to make his work smooth. Smoothness only rarely requires formal connectors like *furthermore, however, moreover,* or *in conclusion.* To see how we most naturally connect our work, try the following exercise.

Exercise 6-5

Here is a set of data based on an article in the business section of a newspaper (Ross, 5). The data, though raw, is complete and is in about the right order. Shape it into a piece of efficient prose, using whatever connecting words you need and paragraphing wherever you wish. Later we will compare your result with the results of others in the class and with the original.

past decade—supermarket chains deserting inner cities in alarming numbers—residents with no cars few or no alternatives to expensive convenience stores—number in Boston, Washington, and Chicago urban areas declined 28–50% in past five years—Community Nutrition Institute—new manual—how inner cities can maintain or bring back food markets—six case studies—including Santoni's Market in southeast Baltimore—offers practical guide—establishing food co-ops, farmers' markets—independently operated supermarkets—hints—limiting food assortment to 1000 or so staple items—selling products that cater to neighborhood needs—Do food-stamp users need appliance and camera equipment counters?—Sunday hours—wine and beer sales—minibus transportation—child-care centers—urge community to lobby local government—get a low-cost lease on adjacent city-owned property—use as parking lot—resurface sidewalks—high-powered street lights—available Community Nutrition Institute—Washington, D.C.

When you finish your smooth version, circle *every* word that you've added or altered. A comparison of the choices you've made could take an entire class period. You have hundreds of options to choose from as you link, but my guess is that you'll find:

1. That your most effective link is repetition of a term or the use of a pronoun to replace that term.

2. That when you do use connective words, your best choices are simple words, like *and, but, or,* and *so.*

3. That parallel structure ("*limiting* food assortment . . . ," "*selling* products . . . ," "*avoiding* appliance counters . . . ," "*providing* minibus transportation") is one of your most useful linking devices.

4. And that only occasionally do you need big blockbuster connectors, like *moreover.*

Now you should be more conscious of the writer's techniques—paragraphing and using small connectors—that hold writing together and make it sound "smooth."

Introductions and Conclusions

Just as you guide the reader throughout the body of your paper using paragraphs, coherence, and transitions, you guide the reader at the beginning and at the end of your work with your introduction and your conclusion.

Exercise 6-6

Before you hear what I have to say about your introductions and conclusions, write in your notebook your current thinking about them:

1. What do you try to do in an introduction?

2. What do you try to do in a conclusion?

You can begin any piece of writing by introducing your credentials with a statement like:

This 500-word essay which I am about to start is based on my knowledge of and experience in high school and college.

Is that too obvious? Too dull? Perhaps you're tempted to begin by philoso-phizing:

> For everything in life we all have two choices. As we have two sides to every coin, we have two sides like positive or negative, win or lose, profit or waste. Ohio State has made my life different than I had thought it would.

Is your reader following your reverie? Perhaps not. A third alternative is just to "sort of start writing," as the student who wrote the following did:

> On July 23, 1981, I was dropped off on a desert island. I was permitted to take three things along with me. The first thing I took was a knapsack full of government books. This would enable me to keep up with my studies in school. The next product I took along.

There are better ways. You'll find many lists in textbooks of what should go into a good introduction, or what should go into a good conclusion, but I think you'll learn more by testing your own sense of what you like in an introduction or in a conclusion.

Exercise 6-7

Look over the following paragraphs. Try to decide whether each is an introductory paragraph, a concluding paragraph, or a support paragraph from the body of an essay. In the blank before each paragraph put an I if the paragraph is an introduction, an S if it is a paragraph of support, or a C if it is a concluding paragraph. Once you've made your decisions, get into a group with three or four classmates and see if you all agree. If you don't agree, give your reasons for the decisions you made about the character of the paragraphs. Then share your group's results with the rest of the class.

1. In the eighteenth century, an owler was a smuggler of sheep or wool from England to France. A few years later, the term was applied to one who sat up all night, now called a nightowl. But an owler today is one of the unusual breed of birders who do their stalking nocturnally. They often go alone, either because they prefer it that way, or because no one wants to tag along; there aren't that many people who enjoy the idea of hanging around a dim forest listening for somber owl hoots in the dead of night. (Neal Clark, "An Owling Primer," *Appalachia,* December 1981.)

2. The so-called black land drain and the plight of the black farmer have surfaced as major issues among blacks only within the last decade. During the 1950s and '60s, the focus for black equality and justice centered on such issues as voting rights and desegregation of public accommodations. Yet, during the same period, the amount of black-owned land in the South, mostly farmland, declined pre-cipitously from 12.5 million acres to 6 million acres. (Chet Fuller, "Living Off the Land," *Black Enterprise,* November 1982.)

example

___S___ 3. The rising price of land is a key factor behind the stagnation of the housing industry. In large city areas, the price of land for housing is rising by about 10 percent every year—leading to sharp increases in the price of houses, actually pushing them far beyond the reach of an average worker's purchasing power. ("The Dark Side of the Prospering Japanese Economy," *The East,* August 1982.)

topic

___I___ 4. Parenting in any setting is not an easy task. Parenting abroad offers some uniquely challenging stresses and opportunities for parents. For families recently posted to a new assignment, complaints such as "I don't want to be here . . . These people are really weird . . . This place is the pits . . . I miss my friends back home" may prevail for weeks or even months as children adjust—or fail to adjust—to their new environments. Fortunately, most children not only make a successful adjustment but benefit greatly from the experience of living abroad. There are, however, five major areas in which problems surface again and again in child-rearing when families transport themselves overseas: teaching responsibility; relations with host country nationals; family communication; peer relationships; and returning home. These deserve special attention and consideration. (Joel Wallach and Gale Metcalf, "Parenting Abroad," *Foreign Service Journal,* June 1982.)

___C___ 5. Like confident parents who believe more in bloodlines than report cards, the supporters of dispute resolution have not been discouraged by the mixed reviews of evaluating academics. They remain confident that over the years, as mediation burrows its way into the court establishment, it will reach the goals that have been expected of it. To them, dispute-resolution programs have already proven one thing—that they can provide an atmosphere rarely found in the bullpens and back benches of the urban courthouse.

summary

"The bottom line," says Royer Cook, "is that people like the way they're treated." (John J. McCarthy, "Dispute Resolution: Seeking Justice outside the Courtroom," *Corrections Magazine,* August 1982.)

stop

If your teacher lists on the board the reasons that you and your classmates have given for your various decisions, by the end of the class you'll all have a thorough list of what you as readers expect in introductions, body paragraphs, and conclusions. That list should help you decide what to put in your own.

Exercise 6-8

tip

You can learn to write better introductions or conclusions, too, by collecting some from various media to see how professionals go about that part of their business. Compare your findings with those of your classmates to see how much variety is possible. You can do this exercise by going to the library and copying out the first paragraph only of four or five of the following:

1. The preface of a psychology text
2. The first chapter of that same psychology text

3. An article in the *Wall Street Journal*

4. An article in any paper in the library's newspaper room

5. An article in *Science '85*

6. An article in the *Journal of Molecular Biology*

7. A piece of junk mail

8. A film or videotape in your library's collection (In this case, describe the introductory sequence.)

9. A fiction best-seller

10. A cookbook preface

Taking the time to copy out each of these paragraphs will teach you about paragraph length, about getting a reader's attention, and about directing writing toward the appropriate readers.

Exercise 6-9

To practice conclusions (along with the appropriate voice and the reader aware-ness that good conclusions require), close your book while your teacher reads the following student paper—or any other paper—from which the ending has been left off. As soon as you've heard the paper read through, write down your recollections about what you've just heard. Read these recollections aloud if you are called on. Then write an ending based on how you think the writer-reader relationship in this paper should conclude. After you've read aloud your version and heard several other versions, jot down some observations on what a conclu-sion can do.

¹ He was paying visits long before Jesus Christ was parting seas and healing the crippled. He will still be going strong long after our souls have been tried and sentenced. He has traveled to many a place and time. He has seen North Dakota, Wyoming and Pennsylvania, Africa, Australia and Asia. He's been through the Renaissance and the revolutions. If any men have been there he followed them closely. He is unwelcome wherever he goes, yet no man can defy, or escape, him. In times of war we expect him to be on the other side. During periods of peace we hope he visits the neighbors. One day, during the summer that I turned fourteen, he stopped on the beach in front of us to call on a short, fat, middle-aged man. It was the first time that I had seen Death. I haven't seen him since.

² I suppose the man had suffered a heart attack while swimming. He certainly advertised for it. He did not look like a fellow who had been spending time in the weight room or eating anything other than steak, potatoes and beer. It's a dog-eat-dog world out there and this man had gone back for seconds and licked the plate clean. It was respect that did him in. He respected his stomach too much to deny it; he respected the rest of his body too little to heed it. Death doesn't care for vice or virtue. He accepts all when it becomes their turn, and accepts them with a smile.

³ I had never witnessed an actual death before. The countless murders, suicides, accidents, and terminal sicknesses that I had seen on television

and in the movies had not prepared me for watching a grown man die "live." Those deaths were too far removed, safely secure within the boundaries of a screen. This wasn't a scene that could be changed by turning to a different channel, or by going to bed, and it couldn't be turned off. We were all too scared to do anything but stare at the dead man, heedless of his wife's insistence that he remain alive. She tried everything that she knew to revive him: she talked to him, she pleaded, and asked God, she rubbed his chest and she kissed his face. When it was over, all she could do was cry. The difference lies in the fact that she wasn't acting in a staged scene. The man would not get up again for anyone, not for wealth, immortality, nor love. Though the faces have faded and the names have been forgotten, the feelings that I have about that moment remain. I remember his death, unlike those that I have paid to see.

⁴ It is not hard to remember how I felt that day. I was curious, yet repulsed. After it was clear that he was dead, I stepped a little closer to view his body. I do not mean for it to sound like I had a perverted mind. I merely wanted to see what a body looked like when the soul departed: when the eyes could no longer see, the ears no longer hear, the brain no longer think. If I held up four fingers would he see? If I whistled a tune would he recognize it? If I asked him to name all fifty states would he be able to do it?

⁵ No. The dead do not rise. This was real.

⁶ The notion of death had never entered my curiosity before. I had never seriously considered what death actually stood for, until the poor man on the beach died. Death is not something that children concern themselves with. It is unimportant to the young. Death is at the root of all life; what comes from the earth will return to the earth. People no longer were just "going away"; they were also never coming back. I finally realized that everything is final. Naiveté became a luxury. I had never cared that when people die, lives change and the future is altered. The fact that I had discovered this for myself lent me further proof that I was slipping into adolescence, from the comfortable feeling of childhood. That I became curious about death was the realization that I was a little afraid of it. When one becomes afraid of dying then one is no longer a child, no longer carefree.

⁷ I was repulsed. The innocent curiosity of a child had been replaced by a feeling that something just wasn't right. A dead man that hasn't been prepared (dressed and in a coffin) is like a mannequin without any clothes; neither are meant to be viewed before they are ready. Just as nothing would ever make him rise again, nothing could ever make me touch the body of that dead man. That was all I could think about. I was afraid of falling down and touching his sweaty stomach. It was as if he had contracted a rare, contagious disease and shouldn't be touched. It was awful. It was worse than being in a room full of snakes. . . .

Your own practice with introductions and conclusions will help you most in learning to write them, of course. So expect, during the semester, to see some of your introductions or conclusions dittoed off and passed around to the class.

Introductions and conclusions, far more than any other aspects of a paper, test the writer's skill in understanding others. In an introduction you must bridge the gap between yourself and your readers. Because "shared context builds up between writer and reader as the piece proceeds, . . . the chances of losing, confusing, misleading, or frustrating a reader are at their greatest in the opening sentences" (Britton, 21). An introduction, after providing that context, might end with a "thesis," but that's not always necessary. You may prefer to raise some questions or point out some crucial issues, saving your thesis, or message, for later (see box). Whether you raise an issue, though, or state a thesis, your reader should know before long *why* you bothered to write this paper. An introduction is happy if it shows that you respect your reader and that you know what you want to talk about. A conclusion is happy if it shows that you know—and care about—the significance of what you've just done. Both introductions and conclusions are happiest in three- or four-page papers when they are short.

If you were to apply for a writing job with *Newsweek* magazine and be close to selection, you'd be given a pile of information—a correspondent's field notes—and asked to write a story based on that information. They'd judge your ability to write on the basis of the story that you came up with. That assessment technique is, I think, fair. A good writer should be able to show that she can sort information and arrange it. To become more conscious of how you sort and arrange information, finish this chapter by doing the following arrangement exercise (6-10).

On June 27, 1957, *The New York Times* ran a brief story on page 3 titled "Non-whites Strike in Johannesburg." It stated that "on June 26 about half of Johannesburg's Negro, Asian, and Colored workers stayed at home for a one-day protest strike against South Africa's racial segregation. The action also was in support of a demand for higher wages." The writer noted that "the African and Indian National Congresses have claimed the strike as a 'significant victory.'" The rest of the story was devoted to the effects of the work stoppage. Stores were closed, transportation was slowed, and coal deliveries came to a standstill. We read stories of this nature daily, believing that we now know the facts, that we have come to an understanding of what has taken place. On a second reading, however, one begins to wonder if this sense of closure is due to thorough reporting or if it is an illusion created by smooth, confident rhetoric.

—An effective introduction. It doesn't state a specific thesis, but it makes us curious about an issue the writer wants to discuss. Such a strategy can be more effective than presenting a spelled-out thesis.

Exercise 6-10

The following excerpts (parts of paragraphs) were taken from an essay by Arthur Ashe entitled "First Sign of Decline, Color Discovered." Reconstruct an essay (not necessarily Ashe's essay) in which you present this raw material as clearly and as convincingly as possible. Think particularly about how these excerpts should be grouped together in paragraphs and about which groups of excerpts you want for your introduction and for your conclusion. You may omit material which you don't think is significant enough to be included. *As you proceed, record (and list) every organizing decision you make.* In every case, explain *why* you made the decision. Then hand in your decision-and-reason list along with your cut-and-pasted version of the essay.

1. In my 25 years of playing tennis, I have signed more autographs for white kids than black kids. But it now appears that when they become old enough to economically choose between the Kennedy Center or the Capital Centre, they may opt for the performing arts or stay home.

2. The Feb. 26 issue of *Sports Illustrated* magazine says there is an "ill wind blowing" in the National Basketball Association. One owner says the decline is partly because 75 percent of the NBA is black while 75 percent of the fans are white.

3. Amateur and professional sports in the United States are open to all. And the black community is very aware of this. Why else would blacks devote so much energy to sport?

4. Johnny Dee was coaching the highly rated Irish against Michigan State. At one point, he put in five black players on the court—Austin Carr, Collis Jones, Sid Catlett, Bob Whitmore and Dwight Murphy. They were booed.

5. If it ever comes to the point that yesterday's kids avoid the Bullets because they're too black, then God help us all.

6. Two weeks ago, I watched the Southeastern Conference basketball tournament on television. It was played in Birmingham, Ala., and the game that particularly caught my attention was between Kentucky and LSU.

7. Dealing with discrimination in private life is nothing new to black communities. Getting into the best schools, getting a good job, trying to advance, making our presence felt, trying to contribute to society are perennial problems. We cope somehow.

8. Sports, after all, is entertainment. If you make over $15,000 per year we figure that you allot so much of your income for entertainment: going to see the Bullets or Redskins play means that's $10 the Kennedy Center won't get that week.

9. Judging by that contest, college basketball is healthy. The game was exciting, the teams played hard and the fans yelled and screamed.

10. And no one seemed to care that at one stage of the game eight of the players on the floor were black.

11. Some people say there already are quotas on pro teams. Should we black athletes now assume that teams have to be either 100 percent black and strictly entertainment, like the Harlem Globetrotters, or less than 45 percent black like baseball, football and hockey, so as not to arouse the subliminal ire of white America?

12. Dee, interviewed by telephone yesterday, said he felt the boos were aimed at him for inserting Whitmore, who was not playing well that day, in place of Bobby Arnzen, a popular player and the team captain. It also has to be said that the Irish fans were watching their team give a subpar performance. They lost, 71–59.

13. Other reasons given for lowered attendance figures include too long a schedule and regionalization of NBA games on television.

14. I'd like to know.

15. Don't think pro basketball wasn't warned or that baseball and football aren't now keeping tabs on the seemingly positive correlation between the "blackening" of a sport and the lowering of attendance figures.

16. But the five blacks took the booing personally and refused to play again for Notre Dame until they received a written apology from the school.

17. I often wonder why I was so "acceptable" when I was coming up. Was it because I didn't wear red shoes and purple shirts or walk around with a comb stuck in my hair? No. It was primarily because I wasn't a threat to tennis or its values.

18. One glaring example comes to mind. It happened 10 years ago in South Bend, Ind., in the field house of the most famous highly spirited, re-ligiously-affiliated university in the world — Notre Dame.

19. The black cat has been let out of the bag, it seems. So many black cats have been let out that in pro basketball, some owners and general managers don't like it.

20. They got it.

21. So, to our disappointment, in what we thought finally was an open, public and freely competitive discipline, we now face new parameters of acceptability. The comments by NBA executives are disturbing: Are we to expect rigid quotas in pro sports in the '80s?

22. How could I be a threat? I was only one player, and there didn't seem to be any more black players lined up behind me. If you think some tennis players today are vulgar, unsportsmanlike or crass, honestly now, how much would you be turned off if those players were black?

23. Little do those eight black players on the LSU and Kentucky teams realize what possibly lies ahead. They were trying to impress all those NBA scouts. Meanwhile, most NBA owners are trying to impress their white, middle-class fans.

24. But, S. I. continued, a top executive from one of the NBA's oldest teams said the gravest problem might be that "the teams are too black." In

other words, pro basketball is now viewed as a "black sport" by too many people—white people, that is.

25. But I guess our big mistake is that we thought our fellow citizens liked seeing us "do our thing" on the courts and fields across the U.S. We spent a lot of time perfecting our "moves."

26. I don't care to comment on these statements about the condition of the NBA, or whether these feelings and attitudes are correct. What matters to me is the statement it makes about American society and what America does about it.

27. Are incidents like that passé? I hope so. But if the "too-black" NBA can't amiably resolve its racial questions, there could be serious problems ahead.

28. The American dream is to make of yourself what you will, to reach for the sky, fulfill your potential. Accustomed to facing discrimination again and again in other endeavors, black people felt it was nice to finally find something like sports, where only the results mattered.

When you come to class with your decisions and your cut-and-pasted version, get into a group of three or four and compare the decisions you have made. After ten or fifteen minutes of group discussions, a class discussion can (as usual) reveal *why* you and your classmates have made the choices you have. The more *why*'s that are aired, the more you'll learn about the possible choices you can make when you organize.

7

◆

Thinking

His superiority over other learned men consisted chiefly in what may be called the art of thinking, the art of using his mind; a certain continued power of seizing the useful substance of all that he knew, and exhibiting it in a clear and forcible manner; so that knowledge, which we often see to be no better than lumber in men of dull understanding, was in him, true, evident and actual wisdom.

James Boswell, of Samuel Johnson

Writing teachers have many, many criteria for judging quality in the work of their students. A criterion we would like to use, but one which is difficult to explain, is the quality of thought per line. Are our writers investing their sentences, paragraphs, and essays with meaning? Are our writers thinking? or not? You'll find the groundwork for being a flexible thinker in the chapters preceding this one. We draw the raw material for thinking from careful observation: the basis of thinking is knowledge, so we can't get very far without the habit of useful observation. We are thinking as we select our materials, thinking as we try to be specific. We can sharpen that thoughtfulness by drawing bold inferences (and then trying to support those bold inferences with more facts). We sharpen our thoughtfulness by thinking about our readers when we write. We sharpen it as we decide on an appropriate, confident voice, as we choose among patterns of organization, and as we plan effective introductions and conclusions. But there's more, much more.

Thinking skills have been divided and subdivided, defined and redefined, in almost infinite ways, but (in addition to those mentioned already) I'd like to focus on the kinds of thinking that are most useful to writers—curiosity, reflection, and creativity—and that together result in intellectual flexibility. These are qualities we all have some of but which we too often leave untapped. You cannot acquire them simply by reading this chapter, but this chapter can provide you with some sense of direction as you try to practice them.

Curiosity

Faced with facts that we can't use immediately, we respond either with curiosity or with boredom. Curiosity inclines us to collect information which may only be useful to us sometime in the future. Boredom, on the other hand, is pleased to disregard everything but the most immediately useful. Many people in our society master the information of some special field but then decide that they are bored with subjects other than that specialty. Their plight is serious enough. But if we as yet have no specialty and have already decided to be bored with most information that comes our way, we are in big trouble. Our boredom is sometimes genuinely caused by the way another person is presenting information to us. But we ought always to examine our consciences before foisting off the blame. The people we admire, the people who've reached the top of their professions, are not lucky (and not always villainous). What they have in common, most often, is curiosity. They are constantly in search of new information, new interpretations, new solutions. When they see a new machine, they wonder how it was manufactured; when they enter an overheated classroom, they wonder what kind of heating system the campus uses; when they hear a news report about a rape or murder, they try to study what makes people commit such crimes. If you foster these tendencies in yourself, your curiosity will take you a long way—not just in this class, but in all parts of your professional and personal life. And in the short term it will help you study subjects thoroughly enough to write informative papers.

Reflection

If you become more reflective, that will help you almost as much as becoming more curious. A recent study of students writing an in-class essay found that the biggest difference between weak and good writers was that weak writers stopped often to stare out the window or around the room, while good writers, who stopped just as often, stopped to reflect on their notes or on what they'd written so far (Pianko, 275–78). Reflection makes more mature judgments possible. Your reflection is bound to improve during any writing course; the act of writing itself requires reflection. When you choose between telling and nontelling facts, you're becoming more reflective. When you interview someone and try to decide which are the telling quotations, you're becoming more reflective. When you read and decide which of the author's quotations are most telling, you're becoming more reflective. When you analyze a computer program and decide which of your results is most telling, you're becoming more reflective. Each time you read a classmate's paper and respond with advice, you're becoming more reflective. Every time you write out your thoughts at the beginning of a class, you're forcing yourself to be reflective; you're recognizing that you won't be satisfied with simply sitting passively through class.

Reflection has subskills—seeing similarities, making distinctions, qualifying extreme views, and being able to assess situations—that you can make yourself aware of by practicing a few brief exercises.

Exercise 7-1

SEEING SIMILARITIES

Invent two new sentences that imitate the structure of the original sentences below. As you do this exercise, you'll force yourself to invent two comparisons.

Original The mess hall was as usual—clouds streaming in from the kitchen and men sitting shoulder to shoulder—like seeds in a sunflower. (Alexander Solzhenitsyn)

Sample Imitation The playground seemed as usual—first-graders climbing on the monkey bars and the older kids squirting water from balloons—like elephants playing in a river.

Your Imitation _____

_____

_____

Original   The man's dead words fell like bricks around the auditorium and too many settled in my belly. (Maya Angelou)

Sample Imitation   The clown's black hands pushed like tree roots into the ground but too few noticed until his fall.

Your Imitation   _____

_____

_____

Exercise 7-2

MAKING DISTINCTIONS

Seeing comparisons is child's play compared with making distinctions. Try to explain the difference between:

> An engineer and a scientist
>
> An Arab and a Moslem
>
> A politician and a civil servant
>
> A working mother and a working father
>
> The Arctic and the Antarctic

You need some knowledge of the items being distinguished to answer these questions, so the whole class will not be equally able to make the distinctions, but in any case you will practice making such distinctions and see how important they are.

Exercise 7-3

QUALIFYING EXTREME VIEWS

A third important subskill of reflection is the ability to recognize qualifications. A quick way to practice this skill is to take proverbs in turn from a list of proverbs and try to give a specific example that shows that a proverb is not universally applicable. This exercise teaches you how to qualify, it reminds you of the vulnerability of conventional wisdom, and it makes you practice being specific.

1. Clothes make the man.

2. He who sows little reaps little.

3. Might makes right.

4. What costs nothing is worth nothing.

Exercise 7-4

ASSESSING A SITUATION

Since this is a writing course, it is appropriate to practice assessment on your own writing. After completing the assessment, compare your notes with those of your classmates.

1. What's it like to be a student writer? What would you compare it to?

2. What are you trying hardest to do when you write a composition?

3. Pick from your writing what you consider to be your best and worst pieces, and tell what parts you notice now as being particularly good or weak.

4. What rules do you use when you write?

5. How do you know when your writing has reached a satisfactory level?

Every time you write, in a library or at home, you're forcing yourself to think. That's part of what's so painful about writing. Thinking is a habit which most of us leave half developed. Your reflection will make itself evident in your writing in small ways and in large ways. Even the small ways can please a reader. A reader notes your sentences that make surprising comparisons or useful, fresh distinctions:

1. The union soldiers went about their duties with such cold efficiency that one might have thought they were *hanging their flag rather than a human being.*

2. The weekend journey across the border began for us at 16, when one of us had *secured a driver's license and, more important, a car.*

3. The many changes in our society are moving at a pace *too rapid for the elderly to keep up with and too advanced for the young to learn.*

We can see reflection in a good, self-conscious attention to words:

1. I still call Santa Barbara *home.*

2. Nadia Comaneci *warmed* the *cold* hearts of disgusted fans.

We can see it in the use of understatement:

The atom-bomb tests seemed to suggest that the closer the building was, the more damage the bomb blast would cause.

We can see it in the complexity of "although" clauses:

Although I cannot talk back to a radio, it still would give me a sense of communication while I wait on my desert island for rescue.

We can see it in the selection of telling materials:

"I had that *vivacious* disease, cancer." [From an interview.]

Writing itself is bound to improve your reflectiveness; but you can double or redouble the reflectiveness you gain from it through your attention to improving in this area.

Creativity

Creativity is the third thinking skill that it is well to try to develop during a writing class. Foolproof instructions for becoming creative are, of course, more than we can expect, but there are steps we can take in the right direction. First of all, if we want to be creative, we have to resist our tendency to imitate rather than see freshly. Robert Pirsig, in *Zen and the Art of Motorcycle Maintenance,* describes how writing became possible for one of his students only when she came to the seemingly simple recognition that she was free to start afresh. When asked to describe her college town, Bozeman, Montana, she at first couldn't think of anything to write about.

> She was blocked because she was trying to repeat, in her writing, things she had already heard. . . . She couldn't think of anything to write about Bozeman because she couldn't recall anything she had heard worth repeating. She was strangely unaware that she could look and see freshly for herself (186).

Edward Hyams, in *The Changing Face of Britain,* looked freshly at a 50-square-foot creature, "automan," which rolls past each of us hundreds of times daily but which few of us had really taken the trouble to describe:

> The cheap, private motor-car is a great boon: it gives the ordinary human being seven-league boots: in the power of movement overland he becomes a giant; but giants, of course, take up more room than people of human size. A man in movement on his feet occupies, at any given moment of time, about four square feet of surface; but an automan—that man-motor-car creature which is more or less the typical inhabitant of a modern industrial country—at any given moment occupies something like fifty square feet.
>
> To cope with the motor car explosion and its growing place in our lives we are forced to modify the shape of our cities to suit not man, but automan . . . and a town designed for automan cannot become a community of men, like a village or a small town (228).

Writers willing to look freshly and tell truths are not condemned to rehashing the same old stories, the same old issues; we have been given plenty of working room by our writing and our nonwriting ancestors. Our bookshelves (even in the so-called nonfiction sections) teem with fictions. As a nation, as human beings, we get very much used to the fictions by which we live—fictions about the family, fictions about good and evil, fictions about government, about race, about sexuality. When we write, unfortunately, we slip more readily into those fictions than we do into truth.

If we ask our readers what they want from our writing, their answer will seldom be *finesse* or *elegance* or even *clarity* but, rather, *likeness to the truth.* When a student reads his writing class a paper about the Olympics becoming an advertising event for the "official shoes," the "official beer," and the "official deodorant" of the games, the class gives the paper high praise, and when asked why they like it, they say, "Because it's true." Such praise is praise worth aiming for. Telling the truth is a service to other human beings trying to make sense of the world. For telling the truth, they'll call you creative.

Second, if we want to be creative, we must be patient: we can't too easily accept matters as they are; we can't be satisfied with solutions that work "pretty well." We must let problems remain open in our minds as long as possible so our solutions get the benefit of the most possible combining and recombining of ideas. Teaching ourselves to wait, to sift beyond the obvious, is very difficult.

Exercise 7-5

To get the feel for the patience required, try the following popular exercise (Adams, 108):

Take a blank piece of paper and list, for ten minutes, *all* the uses you can think of for a brick. Aim for fluency and flexibility of thinking.

Now swap your list with others in your class. How many uses could you think of? How flexible were the uses you suggested? (Any doorstops? water-level raisers?) Don't let your mind be satisfied with the conventional.

A second key to the time we spend sorting out problems is recognizing the conditions under which we work, the constraints, and the context. Don't assume too readily that you don't have any freedom. We often put restraints on ourselves that we think have been imposed by others.

Exercise 7-6

Draw no more than four straight lines (without lifting your pencil from the paper) which will cross through all nine dots below (Adams, 24):

This problem cannot be solved if the problem solvers limit themselves to the imaginary boundary of the nine dots. If they go slightly beyond the dots, they will find that the problem is easy to solve with four, or even three lines:

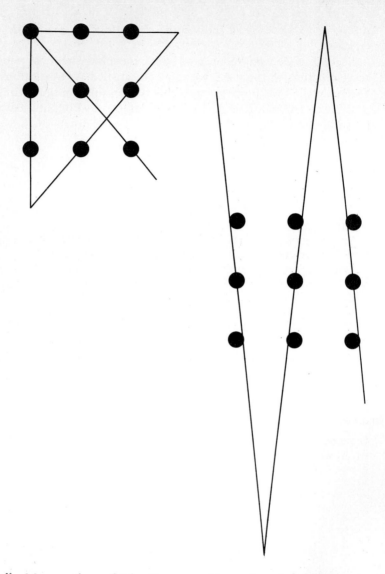

Rollo May, author of *The Courage to Create,* has charted the only path I know through the dense thicket of prerequisites for being creative: "We cannot *will* to have insights. We cannot *will* creativity. But we can *will* to give ourselves to the encounter with intensity of dedication and commitment" (May, 46). If we do commit ourselves intensively, we will occasionally be rewarded with what other people perceive as creativity. In fact, what others perceive as our creativity is our educated unconscious, our intuition, which, through our intensity of dedication, we have not allowed to go to sleep.

In most cases, we choose what kind of mind we want. We remember jokes, or we remember baseball statistics, or we remember the birthdays of all our relatives, or we let new information push out the old and we remember very little. By deciding that curiosity, reflection, and creativity are important to you and by deciding never to be satsifed with thinking that is divorced from experience (we don't want to share the fate of the retiree who lamented, "I've learned a lot in life; unfortunately, almost all of it is about aluminum"), you'll be choosing a mind that will serve you well as a writer and as a person.

Sentence Sense:

MAKING GRAMMAR YOUR ALLY

My grammar (punctuation) is not that hot, in fact it's not even warm.

student

I had grammar viciously driven into my head for eight years.

student

I find training in grammar to be quite a bore, especially with all the emphasis placed on subjects like dangling modifiers, etc., which really don't play a major role in my life in my opinion.

student

I am a good writer. Writing usually comes easy to me. I have a quality of sensitivity so the papers I write usually represent that quality. Although writing comes easily to me, grammar does not.

student

My high school training in English consisted of several poorly-taught classes and one that was well-taught. The teacher for my junior year was the head of the school's English department. She was a very strict lady who preached nothing but grammar. For most of the semester we were bombarded with pronouns, clauses, participles and more. I admit that I hated every minute of it. But now I realize she was the only teacher who took the time to concentrate on grammar. Other teachers, most likely bored by the subject, skimmed over grammar in order to do more interesting things. Even though I hated her and the course, I learned more than I did in my other high school classes. Today I am more at ease when writing because of the class.

student

Exercise 8-1

Before we begin, answer a few questions in your notebook.
When do you use:

1. A comma?

2. A semicolon?

3. A colon?

How would you define:

1. A sentence?

2. A clause?

3. A phrase?

There are about twenty-five terms you'll have to know to keep your writing under control during and after this course. You've learned five already: facts, inferences, paragraphs, introductions, and conclusions. You'll learn three more in Chapter 9: *ethos, logos,* and *pathos.* But the biggest chunk of terms will come in this chapter on grammar, sentence sense, and punctuation. Within a week, you should be comfortable writing and punctuating sentences which include all the following:

Basic parts of speech	**Sentence elements**
1. Nouns (pp. 93–95)	1. Subjects (pp. 93–94)
2. Verbs (pp. 93–96)	2. Verbs (pp. 93–96)
3. Adjectives (pp. 98)	3. Objects (pp. 94–96)
4. Adverbs (p. 98)	4. Phrases (pp. 100–103)
5. Conjunctions (pp. 96–113)	—Noun phrases (p. 100)
	—Verb phrases (p. 100)
	—Prepositional phrases (pp. 99–100)
	—Verbal phrases (pp. 102–103)
	5. Clauses (pp. 97, 99, 109–115)
	—Independent (or main) clauses (pp. 97, 109–115)
	—Dependent (or subordinate) clauses (pp. 97, 99, 109–115)

Conjunctions	**Verbals (demoted verbs)**
1. Coordinating conjunctions (p. 110)	1. Gerunds (pp. 100–103)
2. Subordinating conjunctions (pp. 96–97, 108–109)	2. Participles (pp. 100–103, 116)
3. Conjunctive adverbs (pp. 107–108, 111, 113)	3. Infinitives (pp. 100–102)
4. Conjunctive pronouns—usually called relative pronouns (p. 108)	

The two items in the above lists that most people refuse to learn are gerunds and participles, yet we use gerunds and participles almost every time we talk or write. It's time to learn what they are. Whenever, while writing, you have a question about any of these basic sentence terms, just flip back to these lists, find the appropriate pages in this chapter, and review.

The most important knowledge that you as a speaker and writer of English should have is a sense of what a sentence is. The following three collections of words are *not* sentences:

1. Knowing what you can do and cannot do.

2. A person of always good intentions.

3. Which I liked a lot, because it gives you the feeling of being in college.

The writers of these collections of words had difficulty getting their ideas across (1) because they don't know what a *subject* is, or (2) because they don't know what a *verb* is, or, most likely, (3) because they don't know that *a sentence, from the opening capital letter to the concluding period, must contain an unsubordinated subject and verb.* Perhaps you are able to see the errors in the above sentences, but still you don't know what I mean by that last phrase, "unsubordinated subject and verb." You probably wrote, in answer to the questions that open this chapter, that a sentence is a "complete thought." Well, what makes a thought "complete" (in English, and also in Swedish, Swahili, or Sanskrit) is an unsubordinated subject and verb.

Subjects and verbs are probably quite familiar to you, so we'll review them quickly before tackling the more difficult problem of "unsubordination." If you feel confident about subjects and verbs, skip ahead to Exercise 8-5.

Exercise 8-2

Say something that makes sense by adding only one word to each of the following:

Tigers _____.

Athletes _____.

Honesty _____.

Read your answers, in turn, to the rest of the class. If there are twenty students in your class, you've just heard close to sixty *verbs*.

Exercise 8-3

Now, say something that makes sense by adding a single word (capitalize it) before each word below:

_____ collapse.

_____ helps.

_____ works.

This time, as you read your answers in turn, you'll find you have sixty nouns, or _subjects_.

In English, as in most other languages, the basis of a sentence is a relation between a noun and a verb, a relation between matter and energy. Einstein's theory of relativity, $E = MC^2$, tells us that all life in this universe consists of matter, M, and energy, E. Very conveniently, sentences, too, consist of matter (a subject, or noun) and energy (a predicate, or verb). Readers don't want to hear about matter without energy, or energy without matter. They'll accept:

My baby	sleeps.
[matter]	[energy]

or

The nuclear reactor	is leaking.
[matter]	[energy]

But they won't accept:

My baby.	
[matter only]	

or

	Is leaking.
	[energy only]

Intuitively, we realize that to say something meaningful, we have to include some matter, and we must give that matter some energy. Just think of Einstein, and you'll always remember what a sentence is.

Very often, a second piece of matter is involved in a sentence, this time matter that is the receiver of the energy of the first matter.

Exercise 8-4

Again, complete the following ideas by adding a single word:

Bulldozers destroy _____.

Generosity improves _____.

Ms. Phillips teaches _____.

After hearing the responses of the rest of the class, you have sixty more nouns and pronouns, but these serve quite a different purpose in a sentence from that of the subjects. The subjects you used earlier initiate action, while the objects you've just created are receivers of the subjects' actions.

Ms. Phillips | teaches | biochemistry.

A noun (subject or object) is some "matter" we can get hold of: a _____, the _____, several _____. But included among nouns are not only things we can get a physical hold of but also things we want a mental hold of. In a divorce brief, the husband's lawyer could write, "My client resents his former wife." That's a good, solid sentence: *client* is the subject, *resents* the verb, and *wife* the object. But the lawyer might want to put an emphasis not on the antagonism between husband and wife but on the feelings of the husband. In that case he might say, "My client has resentful feelings about his former wife." *Client* is still the subject, but *has* is now the verb, and *feelings* is the object. The feelings are thus emphasized. Because they've been made into a noun, we feel almost as if we could touch them, hold them.

Verbs are more complicated than nouns. If you've ever studied a foreign language, you know that the verbs are the hardest to learn. First of all, they take many different forms:

I love.

She loves.

She loved.

Second, they often are connected to helping verbs:

I have loved.

She has loved.

He will be loved.

We can love.

We might love.

We will love.

We are loved.

The list could go on for half a page. You've studied, I'm sure, what all those forms mean. There's no need to study them again here. Intuition (without which writing would be hopelessly complex) helps us use verbs correctly almost all the time. We don't have to stop and decide whether we should say *I will love Erin* or *I have loved Erin*. The phrases trip off our tongues, and they flow from our pens. In the rare cases when they don't, we need to refer to a handbook to train or retrain our intuition.

One point about verbs should be reviewed, though, and that is that they fall into two quite different groups: *verbs of action* (all those we've mentioned so far) and *verbs of being*. Here are two common forms that sentences take:

> That man *rides* the prize-winning bull. [action verb]

> That man *is* my father. [verb of being]

There aren't many verbs of being—*is, are, was, were, am* (all forms of the verb *to be*) and sometimes *appear, grow, taste,* and *smell*. But the *is* (or *to be*) verbs are among the most commonly used verbs in our language, so sentences using *verbs of being* appear frequently in our writing.

Do verbs of being violate the principle that every sentence consists of matter and energy? No, if you can remember the distinction in physics between kinetic energy and potential energy. When a wrecking ball slams into a condemned building, it is full of kinetic (lively) energy. When that same wrecking ball is poised 10 feet above the roof of a building, it has no kinetic energy but plenty of potential energy. Verbs can, like that wrecking ball, carry either kinetic or potential energy.

> That man *rides* the prize-winning bull. [The verb has kinetic energy—it describes motion.]

> That man *is* my father. [The verb has potential energy—it describes a state ready for motion in the next sentence.]

Exercise 8-5

To see the variety of forms that good sentences can take in English, we'll need fifteen or twenty sentences from your class. To get them, we'll try the following. Write down a sentence or two about a specific doctor you know (change the name to make sure you don't spread any scandal):

_____

_____

Now compare notes with your classmates. Can you all identify your subjects? Can you all find your verbs? How many verbs are combined with helping verbs? How many of your sentences have objects? Do your verbs show kinetic energy or potential energy?

Now, I've promised that we'd get back to our original description of a sentence: *an unsubordinated subject and verb*.

Exercise 8-6

Take one of your sentences from Exercise 8-5. Mine was:

> Dr. Schulte stayed with her patient all night.

We all know that we could destroy this sentence by taking away either the subject or the verb. But can you *add* a word in front of this sentence that will destroy it as a sentence? Try.

How many examples did the class come up with? If none, then look at the following partial list of words that would work:

after	before	when
although	if	where
because	since	while

You might, for now, want to think of these words as *sentence destroyers*. In fact, they are known as *subordinating conjunctions*.

Exercise 8-7

Use a sentence destroyer at the beginning of the sentence "Dr. Schulte stayed with her patient all night," and then finish the thought in some way that satisfies you.

Read your new sentences aloud in turn. Now you may be able to see why these sentence destroyers have the name *subordinating conjunctions*. They are *conjunctions* because they *connect* things, in this case the first part of the sentence to the last part. They are *subordinating* because they make the first part of the sentence *subordinate* to, or *dependent* on, the last part of the sentence.

Exercise 8-8

From your last sentence take away your sentence destroyer and "Dr. Schulte stayed with her patient all night," and note what's left. Is what's left a sentence? Yes. Its subject and verb don't have a subordinating conjunction in front of them. They are an *unsubordinated subject and verb*. Compare your sentence with those of the rest of the class.

You now should be able to understand easily one of the most useful terms in English sentence structure: a *clause*. *Because Dr. Schulte stayed with her patient all night* is a clause. And *Mr. Schulte made breakfast for her* is also a clause. What makes a group of words a clause? A clause is a group of words that contains a subject and a verb. But clauses come in two types that are punctuated very differently. The two types are dependent (or subordinate) clauses and independent (or main) clauses. An independent clause is a complete sentence; it can stand on its own. Dependent clauses have subjects and verbs, but they also have a sentence destroyer, so they can exist only as parasites, attached to an independent clause.

One last point. Dependent, or subordinate, clauses are not necessarily subordinate in the importance of the ideas they convey. The idea in a dependent clause can be as important as, or even more important than, the idea in the independent part of the sentence. (For example: "I'll stop by to see you Friday *if I finish my paper*.") Subordinate clauses are subordinate, or dependent, only in grammatical terms, not in terms of meaning.

Next problem. I'm sure you noticed that you used words other than nouns, pronouns, verbs, and conjunctions in the sentences you've written.

Almost all of those words, and groups of words, can be classified as either adjectives or adverbs. For the moment, let us say simply that adjectives help us understand nouns, and adverbs help us understand verbs (adverbs, in fact, do more than this).

Exercise 8-9

To see what adjectives and adverbs are, let's take advantage (as we will throughout this chapter) of those among your classmates who have learned these grammatical terms before and who remember pretty well how to use them.

Take a basic sentence. I suggest:

The coach traveled.

Can you tell us something about the coach, or tell us which coach, by adding a word or a group of words to this sentence? Compare your suggestions. All your additions—whether single words, or prepositional phrases, or clauses—will be serving as adjectives.

Now return to the base sentence:

The coach traveled.

Can you tell us something about how, when, where, or why the coach traveled by adding a word or a group of words? Again, compare your suggestions. All your suggestions this time—words, prepositional phrases, or clauses—will be adverbs.

Those of you who added single-word adverbs may have noticed that most of them end in -ly. Charles Dickens spoofs writers who rely too much on adverbs in a passage from *A Tale of Two Cities* when he describes an indictment against the character Charles Darnay, who is said to have "wickedly, falsely, traitorously, and otherwise evil-adverbiously" revealed English secrets to the French king (93).

The main reason for learning the difference between adjectives and adverbs is to know whether to write *She rode smooth* or *She rode smoothly,* or *He wrote good* or *He wrote well.* In most cases, an adjective has a plain ending, while the adverb with a similar meaning ends in -ly.

Adjective	Adverb
happy	happily
sure	surely

But in one very common case, that of the adjective *good,* the form changes entirely:

Adjective	Adverb
good	well

Because so many people don't know the difference between adjectives and adverbs, we often hear on television, "He pitches good in relief" or "She skates good under pressure."

In adding adjectives and adverbs to our base sentence, some of you, instead of adding single words or phrases, probably added whole clauses, such as *when the season ended* or *because she needed a left-handed pitcher*.

Exercise 8-10

Now all of you should try to add a clause.

The coach traveled . . .

Compare your answers. What, again, is the definition of a clause?

Exercise 8-11

I'm sure that some of your adjectives and adverbs in Exercise 8-9 were neither clauses nor single words but prepositional phrases, like "in the car" or "past the pub" or "after the game." To make sure that you *all* know how to use prepositional phrases, add any one you please (a new one if you used one last time) to our base sentence:

The coach traveled . . .

How many different prepositions did the class come up with? There are forty or so in all; a good list, with sample objects attached, follows:

about the winner	*beyond* hope	*on* the plate
above the garage	*by* the farmer	*outside* the tavern
across the pond	*concerning* your father	*over* the hedge
*after breakfast	*down* the sewer	*past* the sign
against the brick	*during* the heat wave	**since* the war
along the street	*except* vegetables	*through* the woods
among the players	*for* your uncle	*to* Arkansas
around the corner	*from* your aunt	*toward* the clock tower
at the game	*in* a box	*under* the sink
*before dinner	*inside* the chest	**until* Saturday
behind the house	*into* the pool	*up* the hill
below the high-water mark	*like* her husband	*upon* demand
beneath the window	*near* the cliffs	*with* my friend
	of the plumber	*within* an hour
	off the chimney	*without* any worry

Exercise 8-12

You may have noted that some prepositions (*after, before, since,* and *until*— marked with an asterisk above) can also be used as sentence destroyers (that is, subordinating conjunctions). How can you tell, in a given sentence, whether a word like *before* or *after* is a preposition or a subordinating conjunction?

Prepositional phrases have a nice ring to them: *under the table, without regret, during the play*. Prepositional phrases are not clauses because they have no verb—just a preposition, an object, and often an adjective or two modifying the object. Prepositional phrases play a peripheral role in a sentence: they help explain nouns and verbs; they don't act themselves.

The _purpose_ of the rule _is_ to protect the committee's members.
    subject   verb
            prepositional phrase

The _success_ of my plans _depends_ on you.
    subject   verb
        prepositional phrase

Also, prepositions desperately need their objects. Prepositions and their objects are so closely connected that it wasn't until the thirteenth century that prepositions were separated from their objects when people wrote. A twelfth-century writer, if he used modern spelling, would have written "inthetree" or "behindthebush."

Prepositional phrases are the most common of several kinds of _phrases_ in English sentence structure. A phrase is a group of words not easily separated that _does not include a subject-verb pair._

A noun with its modifiers is sometimes called a _noun phrase:_

The old school will be torn down.

A good leader could solve our problems.

A verb with its helping verbs is often called a _verb phrase:_

Refugees _have been helped._

Victory _might be achieved._

John _can be bribed._

These helping verbs (and combinations of them) can be used along with the main verb of a sentence to form a _verb phrase:_

_am_	_has_	_could_
_is_	_have_	_will_
are	_had_	_would_
was	_should_	_shall_
were	_may_	_do_
_be_	_might_	_does_
being	_must_	_did_
been	_can_	

Participles, gerunds, and infinitives also introduce phrases, but we need to review them before we look at their phrases. Steel yourself while we look first at those common but strangely named grammatical animals, participles and gerunds. There are two bizarre paradoxes in sentence structure. One, you've already seen, is that you can add a word to a complete sentence and by doing so make the sentence incomplete. The second paradox is that you can take a verb's "verbness" away from it by adding -*ing*. Watch.

Exercise 8-13

_____ing, Gary left for the park.

Fill in the blank with any word you choose.
   When you compare your suggestions, you'll find that every word you suggested is a verb but that each new word you created—*running* or *laughing* or *coughing,* for example—is clearly not the verb in the sentence. *Left* is the verb. Your newly created word is an adjective modifying *Gary*. Thus a *present* participle (there are *past* participles too) is a base verb plus -*ing* which acts as an adjective.

Exercise 8-14

Past participles differ from present participles only in their ending—usually -*ed* or -*en* rather than -*ing*. Fill in the following blank with any word you choose.

   The _____ed mother looked out the window.

Again, comparing suggestions, you'll find that you filled in the blank with a verb but that your newly created -*ed* word is an adjective (a past participle) modifying *mother*.

   Gerunds, unfortunately, look just like present participles. They also are made up of a basic verb plus -*ing*.

Exercise 8-15

Fill in the blank with any word you like.

_____ing pays off in the long run.

Compare your answers. You all filled in a verb, but you wound up with a subject for your sentence.

   Gerunds are frequently used as subjects of sentences:

   Swimming exercises every muscle in the body.

   Writing is less difficult when you write regularly.

You might remember the difference between participles and gerunds by remembering that a gerund is a verbal noun and that a participle is a verbal adjective.
   Now you know—once a verb has -*ing* added to it, it's not a verb anymore. (Actually, that last sentence is not entirely correct: *is riding, was riding,* and *will be riding* are all verbs. A helping verb from the *is* family—*is, are, been, be, was, were, am*—combined with an -*ing* verb is a perfectly good

verb for a sentence. But often, the *-ing* ending on what used to be a verb is a signal that the verb is no longer a verb.)

Exercise 8-16

To give you some idea of how versatile these *-ing* forms are, try returning to your base sentence:

> The coach traveled.

Now, convert the verb into a participle modifying the coach and add a new verb to the sentence. Compare your sentence with those of your classmates. Then convert the verb into a gerund and make a statement about the coach: e.g., Traveling is a coach's curse.

Just to make sure that you can recognize when a verb plus *-ing* is still a verb, take our base sentence and alter the verb so that it contains an *-ing* form that is still a verb.

Participles and gerunds are both called *verbals*—not verbs but *verbals*. A verbal is a sort of verb that has been demoted to noun or adjective status. There is one other kind of verbal, the *infinitive*. Compared to participles and gerunds, infinitives are easy. They're marked with an extra word, *to: to knit, to see, to travel*. Like the other verbals, infinitives cannot serve as *the* verb in a sentence.

> I <u>want</u> <u>to study</u>.
>   *verb infinitive object*

> <u>To breathe</u> freely <u>is</u> a sign of health.
> *infinitive subject   verb*

Exercise 8-17

To practice just for a moment, take our original sentence, convert *travel* into an infinitive, and add a new verb.

Note how the verb ending changes. Try another example:

> The mayor of Atlanta attends many dinners.

Now alter this sentence to indicate that the mayor only plans to be at these dinners:

Again, note how the verb ending on *attends* changes. Also note the ending on *plans*. The practice of adding an *-s* ending to a verb attached to a third-person-singular subject doesn't apply to an infinitive because an infinitive is not the verb in the sentence.

While the verbals—participles, gerunds, and infinitives—have been demoted from main-verb status in the sentence, they still retain some of the characteristics of verbs: they are often accompanied by direct objects or modified by adverbs or adverb phrases:

> At Lodi, near Medea, fifteen rebels attacked workers
> <u>repairing</u> <u>the railway.</u>
> *participle*   *and its object*

> A conference of specialists in <u>cultivating</u>   <u>rice</u>
>   *gerund*   *and its object*
> will be held Tuesday in Calcutta.

> <u>Decisively</u> <u>defeated</u> <u>in the New Hampshire primary,</u>
> *its adverb*   *participle another adverb, this one a prepositional phrase*
> Howard Baker was forced to withdraw as a candidate for the presidency.

A verbal with its adverbs or objects is called a *verbal phrase.*

If you feel that all we've done so far is a fog, you'll need to get a grammar workbook and go through it step by step. But if you've followed this chapter most of the way, don't worry. You don't need to know *everything* about grammar.

The exercises that you've just completed will help you write with more variety in your sentence structure. You should now be able to see many, many options that you have when you write your sentences. But sentence variety is not as important as it is sometimes said to be in writing; in fact, sentence similarity, or similarity of sentence patterns, is an often neglected virtue. Repetitive, or parallel, structure within and among sentences is one of the writer's principal tools for achieving coherence, clarity, and a pleasing rhythm. Few of the devices available to the writer are as helpful, as frequently applicable, as strengthening to style as parallel structure. The ease with which the English language doubles its subjects, its verbs, or its phrases or clauses makes parallel structure a fluid way to write.

Exercise 8-18

If you practice imitating parallel structures in the writing of others, the rhythm of parallel writing will soon come naturally to you.

Model The town stopped noticing National Suicide Day because they had absorbed it into their thoughts, into their language, into their lives. (Toni Morrison)

Sample Imitation The boys stopped practicing basketball because they had pushed sports out of their afternoons, out of their summers, out of their concerns.

Your Imitation _____

_____

_____

Model   Her blindness has limited her to puttering in the garden, walking to the mailbox, and listening to the radio.

Your Imitation _____

_____

_____

Model   Without the mitochondria in our cells, we would be unable to move a muscle, to drum a finger, to think a thought. (Lewis Thomas)

Your Imitation _____

_____

_____

Punctuation

With a knowledge of the basic elements of grammar, you can learn all the important rules for punctuation. Punctuation is your readers' best friend. It helps words on a page sound as much as possible like the human voice. So you owe it to your readers to punctuate as clearly as possible. Erratic punctuation distracts a reader the same way that backstage stage-crew voices distract an audience at a play. In both cases the "noise" is clearly unprofessional, and it prevents the listener from concentrating on the main event.

Exercise 8-19

To quickly review your abilities and preferences in punctuation, try to reintroduce the punctuation into the following passage, from which all punctuation has been removed (McPhee, *The Pine Barrens*, 11–12):

I asked Fred what all those cars were doing in his yard and he said that one of them was in running condition and that the rest were its predecessors the working vehicle was a 1956 Mercury each of the seven others had at one time or another been his best car and each in turn had lain down like a sick animal and had died right there in the yard unless it had been towed home after a mishap elsewhere in the pines Fred recited with affection the history of each car of one old Ford for example he said I upset that up to Speedwell in the creek and of an even older car a station wagon he said I busted that one up in the snow I met a car on a little hill and hit the brake and hit a tree one of the cars had met its end at a narrow bridge about four miles from Hog Wallow where Fred had hit a state trooper head-on

Fred apologized for not having a phone after I asked where I would have to go to make a call later on he said I don't have no phone because I don't have no electric if I had electric I would have had a phone in here a long time ago he uses a kerosene lamp a propane lamp and two flashlights

You may be able to punctuate the above passage correctly even if you don't know many rules of punctuation. Your ear will help you punctuate if you are a frequent reader. But if you do make some mistakes, or if you find your ear unreliable, you can only learn punctuation if you learn the rules. So whether you need them or whether you just want a quick review, here are the rules for punctuation in English, each introduced in connection with a common writing problem.

Common Problems in Punctuation

A. In my experience the most common grammatical fault in our writing is the so-called *comma splice*. No wonder we all have trouble with it; we don't really know what *splice* means. *Splice* is a word used regularly only by sailors, fishers, and Boy Scouts. To splice is to join, usually to join two pieces of rope. Here's a rope splice:

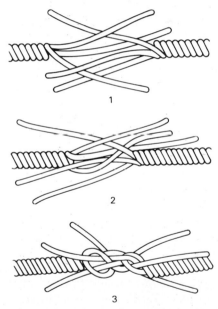

Sequence of steps in making a short splice

A comma splice is the use of a comma rather than a semicolon or a period to join two complete sentences.

I haven't decided how many kids to have, there are a lot of factors to consider when we decide to have kids.

She is capable of doing the work, that is what is so puzzling.

In New York, Philadelphia, and Baltimore, the sugar refineries ran out of raw sugar, this led to the layoff of 15,000 workers.

Sentences, of course, shouldn't be joined by a comma. If there's a complete sentence on both sides of a comma, the comma should be replaced by a semicolon:

She is capable of doing the work; that is what is so puzzling.

Or the comma should be replaced by a period and a capital letter:

She is capable of doing the work. That is what is so puzzling.

A comma is only useful in sorting things out within a sentence. It has no use between sentences.

Occasionally, ill-informed writers join two sentences without using even a comma.

I am glad I chose this school it is now my home.

Such a sentence is called a *fused sentence*. *Fused*, like *splice*, is a technical term. When two wires from separate electrical circuits come too close to each other, the heat generated can melt the wires and join them together so that the circuits are no longer distinct and useful. Similarly, in a fused sentence the two distinct sentences are damaged because they are brought so close together that readers can't tell them apart.

Comma splices and fused sentences are both often called *run-on sentences*. But *run-on sentence* is a much misunderstood—and feared—term. When you write a long sentence and worry about whether it's a "run-on," you're usually worrying needlessly. *Run-on* is a technical term for the error of joining two complete sentences with no punctuation, or a mere comma. There's nothing wrong with a long sentence as long as it's punctuated correctly.

In New York, Philadelphia, and Baltimore, the sugar refineries ran out of raw sugar; this led to the layoff of 15,000 workers.

When a sentence is finished, shut it up with a period or a semicolon. Don't leave its gates wide open (with no punctuation) or even half open (with a comma).

B. You may not feel quite confident yet about your ability to locate and avoid comma splices and fused sentences, but I want to discuss one more common problem before trying to clear up all three. This problem is the sentence fragment; it is much easier to understand. *Fragment* is a more common word than *splice* or *fused*. A fragment is a broken part of something—a part of a broken vase, part of a broken hammer, part of a broken sentence. Here are some common fragments:

Because each person's definition of success is different.

Something I could be proud of.

All of which is prepared by the infamous hospitality crew.

Perhaps you can see that comma splices and fragments are related errors. A comma splice is too much of a good thing (a grammatical sentence *is* a good thing); a fragment is too little of a good thing. In both cases, inexperienced writers usually go wrong because they don't know which connectors—often pronouns—are grammatically independent and which are grammatically dependent. Let's see whether I can make the distinction clear.

1. Personal pronouns—he, she, it, they, etc.—do not make a sentence dependent.

    Jeff is a bum. *He* stole my football yesterday.

    The sense of the second sentence does depend on the first sentence having been there, but the second sentence is grammatically independent. It is not wholly independent in meaning, but it's a rare sentence in any piece of writing whose meaning is *wholly* independent of what comes before and after. Punctuation decisions must be based not on meaning independence but on grammatical independence.

2. So-called *demonstrative* pronouns, pronouns that point out (this, that, these, those), are like personal pronouns (he, she, it, they) in that they do not make a sentence dependent.

    Perry left home yesterday. *This* was fine with me.

3. *There* and *here,* in the constructions *there are* and *here are,* also leave a sentence independent.

    I have six brothers. *There* are four living right here in Portland.

4. Many connecting words—specifically those that are conjunctive adverbs—also leave a sentence independent.

also	likewise	then
besides	immediately	therefore
consequently	moreover	similarly
finally	instead	thus
first	nevertheless	still
otherwise	now	on the other hand
on the contrary	meanwhile	in fact
furthermore	sometimes	
however	indeed	

I won the mile. *Now* I feel that I can quit racing anytime.

Business is booming. *Still* I worry about our loans.

For all but the shortest conjunctive adverbs, like *now* and *still* above, a comma is normally used to separate the conjunctive adverb from the body of the sentence:

> *Finally,* our rosebush is blooming. The petunias, *however,* won't bloom for another week.

Conjunctive adverbs get their name because they act as adverbs—they tell *how, when, where,* or *why*—while at the same time they serve as conjunctions, making connections clear.

5. There are two kinds of connectors that *do* make a clause dependent. They really must be memorized so you can distinguish them from conjunctive adverbs.

Subordinating conjunctions		Conjunctive (or relative) pronouns
Common	**Less common**	who
after	though	whom
although	even though	which
because	whereas	that
before	as	
if	whenever	
since	till, until	
when	unless	
where	as if	
while	as though	
	as much as	
	as long as	
	in order that	
	so that	
	wherever	
	how	
	whether	

Elizabeth is home *because there was a fire at the library*.

I know a lawyer *who works every Saturday in a Boulder legal aid clinic*.

To see what these sentence destroyers can do, compare the following examples:

> When caffeine ($C_8H_{10}N_4O_2$) is burned in a limited supply of O_2, the products are CO, H_2O, and NO; all are gases.

When caffeine ($C_8H_{10}N_4O_2$) is burned in a limited supply of O_2, the products are CO, H_2O, and NO, all *of which* are gases.

Which is a sentence destroyer. Even *of which* will do the trick, and so "all of which are gases" can't stand alone. It must be connected to a whole sentence with a comma.

These conjunctions are often given little respect. We love good nouns, verbs, adjectives, and adverbs. But the connectors, the conjunctions, are the keys to clear punctuation, and we don't usually pay them enough mind. The common definition of a sentence as a "complete thought" doesn't help us much in punctuating. But when we keep in mind that a sentence is an "unsubordinated subject and verb," our understanding of how to punctuate improves rapidly.

OK, now you see that recognizing clauses, independent and dependent, is the key to punctuation. When clauses are linked, and most sentences link clauses, they are linked in very predictable ways.

Independent Clause	;	Independent Clause
Dependent Clause	,	Independent Clause
Independent Clause	o	Dependent Clause

Let me give several examples of each:

1. IC;IC

    I like pizza; Kathy likes hot dogs.
    I wonder where our neighbors found the money; perhaps they've been robbing banks.

    Of course, you can always use a period and a capital letter in the place of a semicolon.

2. DC,IC

    When Errol paints his house, we'll celebrate.
    Unless he loses, Jack will still be arrogant.

    In sentences of this type, the comma serves as a sort of warning that now the independent (or main) clause is coming.

3. ICoDC

    We'll celebrate when Errol paints his house.
    Jack will still be arrogant unless he loses.

    In these sentences no comma is necessary because the independent clause, having come first, is already clear.

C. If you now have the punctuation of independent and dependent clauses straight, you've learned the most important part of this chapter. If you feel pretty secure, I'd like to introduce a less frequent but still common punctuation problem: punctuation with *and*.

I've said that IC;IC is correct. And, of course, IC.IC is correct. But there is a third way of connecting independent clauses—that is, with a comma and a so-called *coordinating conjunction* (this is the last conjunction that you'll meet). The coordinating conjunctions are *and, but, or, nor, for, yet*, and *so*, but the most common by far are *and* and *but*. These conjunctions (connecting words) are called *coordinating* rather than *subordinating* conjunctions because they do not subordinate. They leave the two things they connect grammatically equal.

> John loves Abby, *and* Abby loves John.
> The government gives, *and* the government takes away.
> I like pizza, *but* it doesn't like me.

Exercise 8-20

And, of course, can be used to connect many things other than independent clauses. To give you some idea of the variety possible, finish, with the rest of your class, the following sentence:

George bought a hammer and . . .

When you've finished completing the sentence, decide whether you should put a comma after *hammer.* When you compare your answer with your classmates' answers, you'll see how easily any of the grammatical parts of our sentences can be doubled. Some of you doubled the object *(hammer),* some the verb plus the object *(bought a hammer),* and some the subject, verb, and object. Only in the last case do you need a comma before the *and. Only when* and *is connecting two entire independent clauses do you need to put a comma before it.*

So, our earlier rule is revised:

IC⊙IC *or* IC⟨ and ⟩IC

Here's another way to look at it:

verb	⟨and⟩	verb
phrase	⟨and⟩	phrase
object	⟨and⟩	object
	but	
IC	⟨, and⟩	IC

D. Next problem. How many times have teachers or editors told you that you must use a comma both *before* and *after* a certain word, or phrase, or clause. Do you know why? You will soon.

You've seen that the principal use of commas (e.g.: DC,IC) is to highlight the independent clause in a sentence. And that's the same reason why you use a comma before and after any *interrupter* of the independent clause.

INDEPENDENT, INTERRUPTER, CLAUSE
Peter, *however,* is the one you can depend on.
Jessica, *you may remember,* was our first choice.

The rule might be stated as follows: "Use a pair of commas to set off material that adds information without affecting the meaning of the rest of the sentence" (Raymond and Goldfarb, 49). Using one comma but not both is a common mistake:

WRONG: The prison system, he believes attempts to be fair.
WRONG: Barbara soon made friends, or at least acquaintances of her own age.

Deciding where to put the second comma depends on our being able to pick out the sentence's independent clause. The second comma follows the interrupter; it comes just before the flow of the independent clause resumes.

CORRECT: The prison system, he believes, attempts to be fair.
CORRECT: Barbara soon made friends, or at least acquaintances, of her own age.

There are a number of kinds of interrupters:

1. Single-word comments, including conjunctive adverbs

   The Kangfu Textile Company in Shanghai will, *incidentally,* start production in November of medical elastic stockings.

2. Nouns, with their modifiers, giving further information (called *appositives*)

   El Arish, *the main depot for Egyptian forces in the Sinai peninsula,* was the last bastion to be attacked.

3. Participial phrases

   Raiders of the Lost Ark, written and produced by George Lucas and Stephen Spielberg, offered the same appealing adventure as the 1973 movie *The Sting.*

4. Adjective clauses

   The Jordanian fighter plane, *which was built in Seattle, Washington,* was intercepted while flying in international air space.

5. Alternative words

> A new hat is an extra, *if minor,* responsibility.

6. Long prepositional phrases

> Will the Soviets now try, *under cover of the world's preoccupation with Middle Eastern events,* to reassert their sway over Hungary?

A problem that many writers take to their graves is being unsure of which phrases and clauses are interrupters and which are not. For example, consider this common maxim:

> People who live in glass houses shouldn't throw stones.

The clause *who live in glass houses* is not set off by commas. Why? Because the independent clause, the main part of the sentence, doesn't have the same meaning if that clause is eliminated:

> People shouldn't throw stones.

We need the clause *who live in glass houses* to know what people the writer is talking about. Note the contrast in the following sentence:

> Bill, who spent last year in Thailand, plans to begin study at the University of Wyoming in the fall.

This sentence makes sense without the interrupting clause. The clause is not necessary to our knowing who Bill is. Therefore, it is a genuine interrupter and merits two commas. The difference between noninterrupting and interrupting clauses goes by several names—*restrictive* versus *nonrestrictive,* for example, and *defining* versus *commenting*—but I like best the distinction *identifying* versus *supplementary. Identifying* clauses make it possible for us to know exactly who or what the noun preceding them is. *Supplementary* clauses give interesting information, but not information necessary for identifying the noun that they follow.

Identifying phrases and clauses should not be separated from their main clauses with any punctuation. *Supplementary* words, phrases, and clauses, by contrast, need two commas to show that they are supplementary, to acknowledge that they are interrupters. To see how the two are commonly used and to make yourself confident of the way they are punctuated, try the following exercise.

Exercise 8-21

Make the following statements more specific by adding an appropriate phrase or clause in each of the blanks. Decide whether your additions should be separated from the main clause by commas.

Women _____ have power _____.
The Exxon station _____ ordered a sign _____.
The veteran _____ raised a flag _____.
An earthquake _____ killed 700 persons _____.

When your clauses are *supplementary,* when they *interrupt* the main flow, they'll have been set off by two commas. When your clauses *identify* the nouns they follow, they'll fit right in without any punctuation.

If you've understood the IC;IC and DC, IC and IC ○ DC rules, and if you've understood the "interrupter" rules, you should from now on be able to punctuate that troublesome word *however*.

> The list, *however,* didn't include the rest of the family: Mary, Louis, Carol, Ralph, and Theresa.
> I ran out of gas; *however,* a passing motorist quickly gave me a ride.

However is surrounded by commas when it interrupts a single independent clause. But when it introduces a second independent clause, it will have a semicolon before it, dividing the two independent clauses, and a comma after it, separating the *however* from its own independent clause.

E. Next problem: introducing a quotation. You may think that this is easy, but it requires some subtlety. Once again, the key to understanding what punctuation is appropriate is understanding where the independent and dependent clauses begin and end.

When punctuating a lead-in to a quotation, you have three choices: a comma, a colon, or nothing.

> He summarized his views on revision in this way: "A writer's principal work is rewriting."
> He summarized his views on revision by saying "A writer's principal work is rewriting."
> He said, "A writer's principal work is rewriting."

What's the difference? Why the need for different punctuation? Sentence structure. In the first example, the grammatical sentence is complete before the quotation begins. The colon says, "Wait, there's more, even though the grammatical sentence is complete." In the second example, the structure of the sentence before the quotation is not complete. We must add an object for *saying*. *Saying* what? Since the gerund *saying* needs an object to be completed, we can't pause, so we use no punctuation. The quotation serves as the object of the gerund *saying*. (A quotation always serves as a noun in a sentence.)

What about the third example? The use of the comma in the third sentence is a matter of convention. *She said* or *he said* is so common in English that it gets its own rules. To be precise we should say:

He said that "The writer's principal work is rewriting."

That the writer's principal work is rewriting is a noun clause, a clause which is acting as a noun, the object in the sentence. But the expression is so common that we save ourselves trouble and skip the *that*. When we do, we replace it with a comma.

Review:

1. When the sentence structure is complete before the quotation, use a colon to introduce it.
2. When the sentence is continuing, particularly when the quotation is the object of a preposition, or a participle, or a gerund, no punctuation is needed.
3. When a *that* is skipped after *said*, use a comma to replace the *that* and introduce the quotation.

Note: The same rule that governs the use of colons in quotations governs their use elsewhere too. We all "know" that a colon introduces a list, but not every list needs a colon. What about the following?

The Rossborough Inn is used by faculty, staff, and alumni for: conferences, luncheons, banquets, cocktail parties, and wedding receptions.

The colon here is intrusive. It blocks the path from a preposition (*for*) to its objects (*conferences,* etc.). The structure of the sentence is not complete at *for*. A colon would be appropriate if *for* were given the object *the following*.

The Rossborough Inn is used by faculty, staff, and alumni for the following: conferences, luncheons, banquets, cocktail parties, and wedding receptions.

So, here are the punctuation rules and guidelines.

1. IC;IC
2. DC,IC
3. IC○DC
4. I, int., C
5. IC, and IC
6. A colon builds anticipation. Use a colon to introduce a quotation or a list *if* the structure of the sentence is already complete.
7. The key to punctuation is locating the sentence's independent clause.
8. The purpose of most commas is to highlight the main clause of a sentence. A comma is also used to separate in

lists of three or more items (e.g.: apples, oranges, and bananas). And it is used to indicate a pause for emphasis (e.g.: John, I want you home by 3:00).

Punctuation conventions have shifted many times in history as writers and publishers have tried to find the most flexible system for making their meanings clear. When Thomas More wrote in the early sixteenth century, he simply used a virgule (/) any time he wanted his reader to pause:

> First yf he have cause to fere / yet fereth he more than he nedeth / For their is no devill so diligent to destry him / as god is to preserve hym / nor no devill so nere hym to do hym harme / as god is to do hym good / nor all the divelles in hell so strong to invade & assawte hym / as god is to defend hym / yf he distrust hym not but faythfully put his trust in hym / (153)

Within a hundred years, though, the virgule was replaced by a four-part breathing system: a comma (,) meant a short breath, a semicolon (;) a slightly longer breath, a colon (:) an even longer breath, and a period (.) a full stop. Our current uses of these four marks are partly related to the sixteenth-century breathing standard, but in the eighteenth century, their uses were firmly tied to sentence structure. The eighteenth century has bequeathed us the rules we've worked through above, such as IC;IC and DC,IC. But the virgule, or a new form of it, the dash, is coming back. Even in the eighteenth century it could be found in the novel *Tristram Shandy* by Lawrence Sterne:

> —My mother, who was sitting by, looked up,—but she knew no more than her backside what my father meant,— but my uncle, Mr. Toby Shandy, who had been often informed of the affair,—understood him very well. (3)

Sterne used the dash to reinforce commas, which we no longer do. The wonderful thing about the modern dash is that it is so flexible. I can use it to substitute for a period:

> You may say that this business of marking books is getting in the way of your reading. It probably will—that's one of the reasons for doing it.

For a colon:

> Consider some of the things the blues are about—work, love, death, floods, lynchings.

For a semicolon:

> One day I absentmindedly started crossing the street without looking up or down—the street was empty.

For a comma:

> In order to communicate with the dying, we must ourselves understand—and try to feel—the process of dying.

For opening and closing parentheses:

> So I walked on and on—horses were too expensive—until I had wandered beyond railways, beyond stage lines, to a land of "varmints" and rattlesnakes.

When you're not sure how to punctuate, try a dash. It may not win you any prizes, but it won't get you into any trouble either. Then head back to this chapter for a quick review of the more sophisticated comma, semicolon, colon, and period.

The final two grammatical problems I'll review here are not related to punctuation, but they are frequent sources of trouble.

F. Omitted *-ed* endings.

> I read an article call "Trouble for Dad."

Your ear probably tells you that *call* above should be *called*. But it may not. And you probably don't know why it should be *called*. *Called* is not the subject of the sentence; *I* is. It's not the verb; *read* is. It's not the direct object; *an article* is. *Called* is a participle, one of those verbs demoted to adjectives. It is easy to recognize *-ing* participles, *present* participles like *driving* in the phrase *a driving rain*. But equally important, though a little harder to recognize, are *past* participles.

> a *crumbled* brick
> a *renewed* contract
> a *broken* twig

We talk about a *washing* machine, a machine in the act of washing, but we also speak of *washed* clothes, where the washing is already completed.

Most past participles end in *-ed*. But some end in *-en*, and a few are very irregular. (Common past participles which don't end in *-en* or *-ed* are *bent, bet, hit, held, hurt, lost, made, rung, sung, strung, struck,* and *taught*.) All have the same form of the verb (called the third principal part) that you use when you say "I have *fixed*," or "I have *broken*," or "I have *run*," or "I have *joked*." Past participles are frequently used in English:

> Ruth bought 60 acres of *cultivated* land.
> The stone structures in London, *blackened* by coal soot in the nineteenth century, are now being cleaned.

Here are a few common errors related to the use of the past participle (or its identical twin, the verb form that follows the helping verb *have*):

WRONG: The college buildings were in the *old-fashion* design.
WRONG: Here in college I have been *force* to study more.
WRONG: I've *notice* some changes in myself.

If you make similar errors, try to check over your writing, after you have everything else straight, to see whether some of your participles, and verbs following *have,* aren't missing their *-ed.*

G. Problem G, the apostrophe. The apostrophe is often confusing to people who write infrequently because we don't need it when we talk, so we are careless about learning it for when we write. One of the apostrophe's uses is simple. It fills in for missing letters in contractions:

it's for *it is*
you're for *you are*
let's for let us

The second use is equally simple. When a noun is converted to an adjective (as *Tom* is in the phrase *Tom's pipe*), *'s* is added to the noun. If the word already ends in *s (boys, gloves),* a simple apostrophe is added to make the word possessive (i.e., to make it an adjective): *boys', gloves'.*

One of the most frequently made errors is using *'s* to indicate the plural when a simple *s* will do.

I was at San Francisco State for two year's.
There were 300 student's in my first college class.

The other case where writers tend to use an unnecessary apostrophe involves the possessive pronoun *its.* This word has no apostrophe in it. But because it indicates possession, we just itch to put an apostrophe in it: we want to write *it's* or even *its'.* Resist the urge. You don't have the urge to put an apostrophe in *his* or *her* or *our* or *their,* do you? Well, *its* is in the same family.

her house   our house   its house
his house   their house

Its needs an apostrophe no more than *his* or *her* or *their* or *our* does. *Its* is a good clean word without any little squiggles above the line. Save your apostrophes for converted nouns that need them.

Here's a review of some of the rules in this chapter, courtesy of William Safire (16):

The fumblerules of grammar

Avoid run-on sentences they are hard to read.

Use the semicolon properly, always use it where it is appropriate; and never where it isn't.

Reserve the apostrophe for it's proper use and omit it when its not needed.

No sentence fragments.

Proofread carefully to see if you any words out.

Avoid commas, that are not necessary.

Write all adverbial forms correct.

Don't string too many prepositional phrases together unless you are walking through the valley of the shadow of death.

The survey of grammar in this chapter is by no means complete. Nor it is 100 percent reliable (the very mention of the word *grammar* triggers the association: *exceptions*). But it is intended to be practical: it covers the grammar you need to know to punctuate correctly, and it is brief enough so that you shouldn't be afraid of coming back to it any time your confidence needs a boost.

9

◆

Persuasion:
WRITING WITH AUTHORITY

The argument paper was the hardest because you couldn't just do research and write down a lot of facts. You really had to convince the reader that you were right.

student

Newspapers, television, movies, advertisements, parents, and friends, all, at one time or another, attempt to persuade you to accept a particular point of view. Theirs. If you are aware of the basic argumentative techniques, you may either use them to persuade others, or analyze how someone else has used them in an attempt to persuade you.

Joyce Middleton,
writing teacher

Unless you settle first the questions that are on your readers' minds, they won't listen to a thing you want to say.

Hubert Miller,
Nuclear Regulatory Commission

Most of us have very little faith that we are capable of changing another person's opinion or affecting another person's action. We have very little faith because we have no strategies in mind for influencing people. As a result, when we are asked to argue, we talk or write without thinking, and we produce something as muddled as this excerpt from a lab report of an eighth-grade student trying to persuade her teacher that the melting point and the freezing point of a substance will be two different temperatures.

> Personally I think that, when a substance has a freezing point and/or a melting point in its graph measurements, that they don't equal each other. In other words, the heating points and melting points do not equal each other (their answers are different). The reason I think this is because when something freezes it pretty much always has air bubbles and when a substance melts it is a solid. So when weighing the substance the freezing point is heavier plus the freezing point is colder and the melting point is hot and they both can't be heated and melted at the same time, plus there is no movement in the frozen substance, but there is movement in a melted substance, so there is no way a freezing point and a melting point can equal each other.

(In fact, the melting point and the freezing point of a substance are identical—for water, for example, both are 32°F).

This student is floundering, partly because she is ill-informed, but partly because she is intimidated by the great knowledge gulf she sees as separating herself from her teacher. In order to persuade people, we must overcome that feeling of intimidation, and we do so by becoming well-informed, not only about our subject but about methods of persuading. It's up to you to become well-informed about your subjects, but I can help you a bit with the chief methods of persuading: *ethos, logos,* and *pathos* (I'll explain these terms shortly).

Persuasive writing is a form of selling. We in school sometimes pretend that we are above selling things, but just as Skippy peanut butter would be off the shelf in five years if Best Foods stopped advertising it, so, too, would our ideas be lost if we stopped speaking and writing in their behalf. So let's take a few pages out of the advertiser's book of strategy.

Exercise 9-1

How do the ads on the following pages try to get you to buy the products? Write out the strategies you notice, or discuss them during class.

The appeals made by these ads can all be categorized as stemming from *ethos* (appealing to us through the "character" of the product or its manufacturer), from *logos* (appealing to us through logic, usually with facts), or from *pathos* (appealing to our emotions). I challenge you to think of any strategy used by any seller that can't fit into one of those three categories of appeal.

capitol

"LION" HATS
The Right Hat for Real Men

YOU find Lion Hats on the heads of men who do things. Men who are leaders. The kind of men who demand the best. But whose time is too valuable to be wasted in endless shopping, picking and choosing.

Perhaps one reason why they like Lion Hats is because all they need to do is to go to a good hat shop, ask for the size they wear and look for the Lion Seal on the inner band.

You will be quickly pleased—and have the satisfaction of knowing that there is nothing better.

LANGENBERG HAT CO.
St. Louis, Mo., U.S.A.
ESTABLISHED 1860
Manufacturers of Lion Hats, Caps and Gloves

Rather emotional appeal - ither character of product

A Bushel of Food

In a Package of Quaker Oats
And At One-Tenth the Cost

A 35-cent package of Quaker Oats contains 6221 calories—the energy measure of food value.

You would buy a bushel of ordinary mixed foods to equal that calory value. And that bushel would cost you ten times 35 cents.

Here is what it would take of certain good foods to furnish you 6221 calories:

To Supply 6221 Calories			
In Quaker Oats . .	1 Pkg.	In Potatoes	21 Lbs.
In Round Steak . .	7 Lbs.	In Hubbard Squash .	65 Lbs.
In Hens' Eggs . . .	7 Doz.	In Young Chicken	20 Lbs.
In Cabbage	55 Lbs.	In String Beans . .	36 Lbs.

And here is what those calories would cost at this writing in some necessary foods:

Cost of 6221 Calories			
In Quaker Oats . . .	35c	In Hens' Eggs . . .	$3.12
In Round Steak . . .	$2.06	In Fish about . . .	2.25
In Veal or Lamb . . .	3.12	In Potatoes	65c

Consider these facts in your breakfasts. The oat is the greatest food that grows. It is almost a complete food—nearly the ideal food. It supplies essentials which most foods lack.

At least once a day use this supreme food to cut down your table cost.

57 Cents
Per 1000 Calories

5½ Cents
Per 1000 Calories

50 Cents
Per 1000 Calories

Quaker Oats

Only 10 Pounds From a Bushel

Get Quaker Oats for exquisite flavor. They are flaked from queen grains only—just the rich, plump, flavory oats. We get but ten pounds from a bushel.

When such an oat dish costs no extra price it is due to yourself that you get it.

15c and 35c per Package
Except in the Far West and South

Packed in Sealed Round Packages with Removable Cover

3191

"— and Jim, don't worry about us"

"We're fine, really we are. The children are growing so fast. You'll be as proud of them when you come home as they are proud of you.

"As for those 'civilian shortages' you ask about—don't worry about us! If you could see me this minute, you'd know I'm simply basking in luxury. I'm writing this in bed—all tucked in under one of those beautiful Kenwood blankets Mother gave us when we were married. They are as soft and lovely as they were that exciting day when we opened our gifts. Remember?"

IF YOU, TOO, ARE FORTUNATE enough to own Kenwoods, take good care of them. They are more precious than ever now. You won't buy new blankets, of course, unless you *need* them...but if you do, don't assume you can't get Kenwoods until you have tried. Like other blanket manufacturers, we are largely engaged in war work. But we are making some blankets for the home.

Ask your favorite fine store to show you the new Kenwoods in all their fresh beauty, rich with soft, luxurious warmth. Their long-lasting satisfying service will make them treasured possessions through the years. **KENWOOD MILLS, Albany, New York**

Kenwood Blankets

123

"WHERE, OH WHERE DID MY BENDIX GO ♪ OH WHERE, OH WHERE 🎵 CAN IT BE-E-E...

♪ IT'S WASHING CLOTHES IN A U.S.O. ♪ FOR SOLDIERS INSTEAD OF FOR ME!"

"I waited too long. My dealer didn't have a single Bendix Automatic Home Laundry left when I tried to buy one. And the factory had converted to war work.

"So I didn't get a Bendix. But I found that many I might have bought, had I inquired earlier, were serving Uncle Sam.

."They're scattered far and wide, by now—from this one in a USO club 'somewhere in Alaska' to the 55 on duty at the Maritime Training Station, Sheepshead Bay, N. Y. Not doing a *fighting* job, of course,

but washing, rinsing and damp-drying *fighting clothes* at the turn of a single dial.

"So here's what I decided: If the Bendix I didn't get is serving boys in service, the dollars I didn't spend for it should be serving, too.

"And they *are* serving. I invested them in WAR BONDS—*extra* War Bonds in *addition* to those we buy each payday. Why not do the same—*all* you folks who *would* be buying Bendix Automatic Home Laundrys through these war years if they were available?"

★ **TO MORE THAN 300,000 BENDIX OWNERS:**
If your Bendix should need repair or servicing, call an authorized Bendix Automatic Home Laundry dealer or serviceman listed in the classified section of your phone book, or write **BENDIX HOME APPLIANCES, INC.**, South Bend, Ind. *The People who Pioneered and Perfected the Automatic "Washer."*

OUT TO WAR—BACK LATER!

BENDIX
AUTOMATIC HOME LAUNDRY

The Changing Face of South Africa

South Africa is changing. Creating opportunities for all her peoples. In her social, political and economic life, reform is a reality.
A new constitutional framework is in the making. And positive results are emerging from the ongoing consultations between Government and the leaders of all groups.

This is further evidence that the leaders of this multi-ethnic society are willing to work together to provide opportunity and achieve peace and prosperity.
As a nation committed to the free enterprise system, South Africa has a lot to offer and a lot you can profit from.

So take a look at the changing face of South Africa.
If you require any further information regarding progress and development in South Africa, do not hesitate to write to: The Minister (Information), South African Embassy, 3051 Massachusetts Ave. N.W., Washington, D.C. 20008.

Republic of South Africa-Looking forward to the future.

de Villiers & Company 79120/US/1

That's why it's good to know *Mr.* Goodwrench.

I get fast service from Mr. Goodwrench. To begin with, he greets me promptly when I bring in my van. But, above all, he knows I want my van back by the time he promises to get it back. That matters.

Mr. Goodwrench has GM training. And he works on GM cars every day. It stands to reason that he's the mechanic I should go to when I need service on my GM van or my car. Mr. Goodwrench is committed to reasonable prices that are competitive with those of other places I've gone to around here for service.

I want genuine GM parts and I know that Mr. Goodwrench seems to have a good supply of the parts I need. So whenever my van needs service, I watch for a Mr. Goodwrench sign. It's at more than 5,000 GM dealers. Across America.

Let's have disposable retirement income, not disposable retirees.

Despite $700 billion in pension funds today, tomorrow could be less than golden.

More men and women are retiring, often years earlier, and

living to collect checks longer.[1] While inflation's share of those checks keeps increasing.

Can Social Security prevent disaster? At best, it's a partial answer. At worst, it may go broke unless its bite on salaries goes *much* deeper or its provisions change drastically.[2]

The burden is on private pensions. And we at Ætna Life & Casualty are convinced private pensions can help shoulder it.

Employers can't pull dollars out of thin air. So let's change tax laws that discourage small businesses from setting up pensions in the first place.[3]

Let's also give employees incentives to put a little extra into their company pension or savings plan. And — especially important for today's mobile work force — improve their pension vesting.

Neither last nor least, pensions should be better designed to stave off the munching of inflation. Ætna's acutely aware of this problem, and we're working on it.[4]

If you don't want the American dream of retirement to be permanently retired, use *your* influence with the powers that be — as we are trying to use ours.

Ætna
wants retirement to be affordable.

[1]America is crossing over to what's been called "the other side of the baby boom." The median age is shifting upwards, and with it the proportion of over-65's to the general population. In 1979 there were 5.4 workers to every retiree, as opposed to 7.5 to 1 in 1950, and by 2030 the ratio will be about 3 to 1.

[2]Social Security was never *intended* to be more than a basic system supplemented by private pensions and individual savings. The price for forgetting this has been high and promises to get higher: combined employer/employee FICA taxes on our grandchildren's salaries could reach 25%. Of course, there are alternatives. Social Security could increase the official retirement age, pay benefits based on government-determined need, or simply *...reduce benefits in general!*

[3]Two-thirds of small businesses surveyed in 1978 offered no pension plans at all. One reason: Typically, big employers can write off 46¢ in taxes for every pension dollar they contribute, while most small ones can only write off about 20¢. In some cases, they can't write off anything.

[4]Our real estate and participating mortgage separate accounts, for example, are designed to offer larger returns in the face of double-digit inflation. We've also helped fund the Pension Research Council's study of pensions and inflation.

LIFE & CASUALTY

Ætna Life & Casualty.
151 Farmington Avenue.
Hartford, CT 06156.

The party begins.

I can drive when I drink.

2 drinks later.

I can drive when I drink

After 4 drinks.

I can drive when I drunk.

After 5 drinks.

I can drin when I drin

7 drinks in all.

I can drunken drunk

The more you drink, the more coordination you lose. That's a fact, plain and simple.

Still, people drink too much and then go out and expect to handle a car.

When you drink too much you can't handle a car. You can't even handle a pen.

The House of Seagram

For reprints please write Advertising Dept. SI-782, The House of Seagram, 375 Park Ave., N.Y., N.Y. 10152. © 1973 The House of Seagram

The same limits apply to writing. Every writer who succeeds does so by using *ethos, logos,* and *pathos* (Greek terms suggested by Aristotle)—presenting a trustworthy character, substantiating all claims, and influencing the reader's emotions.

Perhaps we should talk first about *logos,* or logic, since most people are afraid that they aren't competent in this area. People often use the term *logic* very loosely—when they complain that we're not being "logical," they usually mean that we're not being systematic, that we haven't followed a common thought pattern like those in Chapter 5. Being systematic does help convince people, but speaking strictly, there are *only two* logical forms of persuasion: *induction* (arguing from specific examples to a general conclusion) and *deduction* (applying a general principle to a specific case). You've been practicing induction ever since Chapter 3—induction is drawing reliable inferences from a set of examples. Here's a brief review. If I were a Laplander who arrived in St. Louis and watched, for a few weeks, the way people worked and the way they were paid, I might notice the following: that doctors work hard and that they are paid handsomely; that judges work hard and that they are paid handsomely; that construction workers work hard and that they are paid handsomely. I'd surely draw the inference that Missourians who work hard are paid handsomely. I might check my inference, my inductive thinking, by looking at trash collectors. Since they work hard and are paid handsomely, I'd begin to think that my logic was foolproof. But if I then turned to shoe repairers, or mothers, or administrative assistants, I'd be very confused. Or if I were a well-schooled Laplander, I'd just realize that induction is never foolproof. Induction is our most common method of reasoning. And several examples are often enough to convince. But neither writers nor readers can ever be certain that a counterexample won't turn up.

I doubt whether you've heard the term *induction* very often, even though it describes the most frequently used way we think. If I said "deduction," though, I'd guess you'd think immediately of detectives, perhaps of Sherlock Holmes or of Columbo, who often speak of making "simple deductions" from facts. These so-called *deductions* are, in fact, inferences, the products of inductive thinking. Genuine deduction is quite a different matter.

Deduction is more rarely used than induction, but it can be very helpful. It is based on a logical device called the *syllogism.* A syllogism has three parts: a general principle (or common assumption), a specific example of that principle, and finally a conclusion.

GENERAL PRINCIPLE: All human beings die.

SPECIFIC APPLICATION: My father is a human being.

CONCLUSION: Therefore, my father will someday die.

If you use this method of reasoning and your general principle is foolproof, then your conclusion is foolproof. Deduction looks like a powerful tool, eh? But there's a catch. Very few general principles are as certain as the one—"All human beings die"—that I began the sample syllogism with. There aren't many principles (assumptions) that you can be sure your audience will share. Most human issues belong to the realm of the probable rather than the certain. When I try to think of general principles that no one could disagree with, I fail again and again:

"All people have a right to respect." (response: Even criminals?)

"A human being, to be ethical, must regard people as intrinsically more valuable than animals." (response: Does this mean that we can kill and eat animals without qualms?)

Any such statement that I make *I* will call a general principle. *You* are more likely to call the same statement my assumption. If you make such a statement, *you'll* consider it a principle, while *I'll* call it your assumption. Deduction is beginning to look a little shaky.

Let's look at a few more examples. Suppose I wanted to argue that women should be drafted. The syllogistic structure of my argument might look like this:

GENERAL PRINCIPLE: Men and women are equal.

SPECIFIC APPLICATION: Men are subject to the U.S. draft.

CONCLUSION: Therefore, women should be subject to the U.S. draft.

This one, like most attempts at deductive argument, is complicated. A reader might at first agree with my general principle, but once he saw my conclusion, he might go back, fairly, and ask me to define *equal*. Another reader might not want to listen because she feels that not even men should be subject to a draft. I'm stopped in my tracks because my readers will not accept my assumptions. Deduction is therefore fraught with risks: readers can ignore your whole train of thought if they disagree with your assumptions. Still, deduction is useful for writers in fields like engineering or the law, where fixed codes exist, that is, where decisions are often based on "first principles."

GENERAL PRINCIPLE: Those guilty of second-degree murder should serve eight to ten years in prison.

SPECIFIC APPLICATION: Donald Hyde has been found guilty of second-degree murder.

CONCLUSION: Therefore, Donald Hyde should serve eight to ten years in prison.

Deduction is also helpful when you can find some assumption that is shared by the person you want to persuade. If I, for example, wanted the principal of my daughter's junior high school to require three years of language study, and the principal was opposed to language study because he had never "used" the French he had learned but was also worried because the students in his school were having difficulty with English grammar and vocabulary, I might argue as follows:

> GENERAL PRINCIPLE: Any study which improves students' grammar and vocabulary ought to be encouraged.
>
> SPECIFIC APPLICATION: The study of other languages improves students' mastery of English grammar and vocabulary.
>
> CONCLUSION: Therefore, the study of languages other than English ought to be encouraged.

Since I had found for the basis of my deduction a general principle on which we both agreed, the principal would have to think twice.

You can review the strengths and weaknesses of induction and deduction most easily, I think, by being aware of the vulnerability of inferences drawn from single facts. If, for example, I note that a robin has appeared in my backyard, I might infer that it's spring and that the last frost has passed. But I might be wrong to draw that inference. To make my inference less vulnerable, I need either more facts—the forsythia is blooming, worms are starting to appear in the grass, tree buds are all over the sidewalk (in which case I'd be arguing inductively)—or a general principle—Washington, D.C., has never had a frost after the arrival of the first robin (in which case I'd be arguing deductively). Logic, for writers, is largely a matter of being able to substantiate, with general principles or with further facts, the inferences we draw.

The two attempts to persuade below are letters to the editor of the *Los Angeles Times* responding to a court case in which the federal government attempted to force the parents of a child born with severe birth defects and brain damage to agree to have partially corrective surgery attempted. One writer uses deduction, one writer induction:

Deduction	Induction
Inference backed by general principles (assertion with reasons)	Inference backed by facts (assertion with examples)
The intervention of the U.S. surgeon general in the case of severely retarded and paralyzed Baby Jane Doe must be condemned quickly and completely.	The government lawyer says "what the family wants is not the issue here." Why? Will he take over Baby Doe's care? Who does he expect to care and love this poor suffering creature? Will society in its callous way take the place of caring parents?
By what right does Dr. C. Everett Koop presume to involve himself in the tragedy of this family? Is he a close friend or relative? Does he bear the cost of the child's care? Does he share the heartbreak of these parents?	I had a sister—born two years before me. She was made brain damaged by blood poisoning (before 5 years of age) when the scab of her

No! Yet, he comes into their lives unasked, to challenge a decision that they have made with the help of their doctors, their family and their God. I pray that the courts will not allow Koop's unjustified, self-serving interference to continue.

smallpox vaccination was pulled off by a rusted suit button of a caring and loving uncle who was playing with her. She was confined to the Wrentham State Hospital in Waltham, Mass. for 35 years.

She knew little family love after that.

At first we had no transportation, and with seven others to care for, not the time. Did she know? We will never know. The state cared for her through the many convulsions—keeping her a prisoner in her room (for her own sake). She never roamed the beautiful grounds. Her care was protective and skillful. But there was a vacuum of life around her; she was not a contributor to society—just sick and alone and jailed. She mercifully died at 40 years. Not a life of my choosing certainly.

Baby Doe will have 100 times the agony my sister Pearl survived.

As I write this I am listening for the telephone to ring—announcing the birth of our second grandchild. I would *hate* for "our Lawyer" to intrude in this child's life.

Arguing inductively (with several examples) or deductively (starting from a common assumption), we may well influence our listeners, but we must remember that our conclusion is never going to be certain. "Proofs" are not possible in writing. We all know the vulnerability of inductive arguments: no matter how many examples we include, a counterexample can embarrass our argument. With deductive arguments, our assumptions are vulnerable. Advertisers can't "prove" that their products are best; similarly, we can't "prove" that our ideas or our proposals are best. Since *logos,* then, is always vulnerable, since it can't "prove" anything, we see why there's plenty of room for *ethos* and *pathos* to play significant roles in our efforts to persuade.

Ethos (the Greek word for "character") is our most powerful tool in writing. Every writer must employ logic, *logos,* before we'll trust him. But much of our trust comes not from a writer's logic but from other, less tangible qualities. Just as a musician wins a competition not only by playing the correct notes but by giving the musical phrasing "character," just as a salesclerk who is both knowledgeable and friendly earns more substantial commissions than one who is merely knowledgeable, so a writer with both a command of the material and a clear enjoyment of writing succeeds when a plodding writer doesn't.

A strong *ethos* does not come easily; you cannot fake an *ethos*. Everything you read, everything you write, every conversation you have, every trip you take contributes to the *ethos,* the voice, the character that is available to you when you write. You may do these things to enjoy yourself or perhaps to increase your ability to make friends and to find someone who'll want to spend a lifetime with you. But you're also working on your writing *ethos*. If your *ethos* building succeeds, some letter you write when you are 24 may get you the job you want; some memo you write when you are 34 will get you a promotion; some report you write when you're 44 will make you a well-respected leader. But thousands of hours of curiosity, and learning, and conversation will go into building the phrase, the sentence, the tone that will later come naturally at a time when you'll need it. If you can come through in your writing as a person of intelligence, integrity, confidence, and goodwill, you have done everything that *ethos* is capable of.

Whenever we write, we reveal ourselves—our intelligence or lack of it, our care or lack of it, our honesty or lack of it. When we revise and look at the "character" that emerges in an early draft, we can make adjustments in the way we wish to present ourselves. But we can't, once we hand in a finished copy, avoid responsibility for the character that comes through. Building up a trustworthy *ethos,* a trustworthy writer's character, is the biggest challenge we face as writers.

Pathos (often thought of simply as an appeal to the emotions) does not have a great reputation. We're glad to acknowledge that we respect writers who are logical and writers whom we can trust. But we don't like to admit that writers succeed by making emotional appeals to us. *Pathos,* though, is not simply the raising of violent emotions in a reader. A writer can make an emotional appeal to the audience's sense of integrity, as John Kennedy did with his famous sentence, "Ask not what your country can do for you; ask what you can do for your country." But a writer needn't even be that dramatic to make good use of *pathos*. If we can reduce the reader's irritation and increase the reader's pleasure, we have employed *pathos* effectively. By not writing down to a reader, we make the reader more comfortable. By acknowledging the reader's point of view, we make the reader more ready to listen to ours. By using standard grammar and punctuation, we allow the reader to enjoy reading the substance of what we have to say.

While you try to use *ethos, logos,* and *pathos* in your own writing to make it effective, you should be becoming increasingly aware of the ways in which others, or you in your early drafts, misuse them. Misuses of *ethos, logos,* or *pathos* are usually called *fallacies* or *attempts to deceive,* although we often commit fallacies without intending to do so. Some of the more common writers' fallacies are the following:

1. Hasty generalization (weak induction; not enough facts considered)
   Example: "I can't write. I got D's on my first two papers."
2. Debatable unstated assumptions (devious deduction; not stating the first principles of your arguments)
   Example: "We can't hire her. She's too pretty."
3. Undefined key terms (weak or devious deduction; carelessness about whether the audience really knows what you mean)
   Example: "Work ten hours a week and earn thousands in your spare time."
4. Inappropriate comparisons or analogies (weak or devious deduction; unstated general principle is that the two items compared are essentially alike)
   Example: "Since Napoleon made France strong again by attacking Austria and Italy, we should make the U.S. strong again by attacking Canada."
5. Unsubstantiated cause-effect claims (weak or devious deduction; unstated general principle is that your cause caused your effect)
   Example: "The English are a morose people because their weather is so cloudy."
6. The citing of illegitimate authorities (devious induction; use of an authority's opinion as a fact to establish an inference you want to make, when that authority's opinion is suspect)
   Example: "Dick Butkus and Bubba Phillips think this beer tastes great."
7. A claim that there are only two choices (weak or devious deduction; unstated general principle is that there are only two possibilities)
   Example: "Either fight communism wherever it rears its head, or live in a world in which we have no friends."
8. Ignoring the point at issue (absence of *logos;* not constructing arguments that are to the point)
   Example, from a paper on nuclear power plant safety: "A hydrogen bomb could destroy half of Connecticut."
9. The hurling of insults (misuse of *pathos;* trying to get readers emotional about irrelevant matters)
   Example: "You're not going to trust the word of a bureaucrat!"
10. Appeal to irrelevant emotions (misuse of *pathos;* this one is often very difficult to decide)
    Example: "No one who loves children can fail to put $25 in an envelope and send it to P.O. Box 47, New York, New York."
11. Exaggeration (abuse of *ethos;* readers won't trust a writer who overreacts)
    Example: "'You can't judge a book by its cover' is a very familiar saying, and probably the best one yet."

These are several of the many ways that you can annoy your reader or lose your reader's trust. The fallacies can be attributed to failures in *ethos, logos,* or *pathos,* but ultimately, all weaken *ethos.* They all weaken the reader's trust in the writer, and thus they weaken also the reader's willingness to take the action that the writer was hoping for in writing.

A great number of problems in argument are problems of definition. When I said earlier that I thought men and women were "equal," I should, if I wanted any real communication to take place, have explained what I meant by *equal:* equal in strength? equal in dignity? equal in opportunity? When I said that "spring" had arrived, what did I mean by *spring?* The sun passing the vernal equinox? Green grass? Temperature permanently above 32°F? Much of what passes for careful reasoning can be shown to be shallow if a few definitions are questioned.

Exercise 9-2

Read, for example, this exchange between Socrates and Hermogenes in Plato's dialogue *The Cratylus* (1.332) *undefined key term*

SOCRATES: How would you answer, if you were asked whether the wise or the unwise are more likely to give correct names?

HERMOGENES: I should say the wise, of course.

SOCRATES: And are the men or the women of the city, taken as a class, the wiser? *only 2 choices*

HERMOGENES: I should say, the men.

SOCRATES: And Homer, as you know, says that the Trojan men called him Astyanax (king of the city); but if the men called him Astyanax, the other name of Scamandrius could only have been given to him by the women.

HERMOGENES: That may be inferred.

SOCRATES: And must not Homer have imagined the Trojans to be wiser than their wives? *debatable unstated assumption*

HERMOGENES: To be sure.

SOCRATES: Then he must have thought Astyanax to be a more correct name for the boy than Scamandrius?

HERMOGENES: Clearly.

What "fallacies" of argument does Plato employ? Compare your answers with those of other students in the class.

Exercise 9-3

Referring back to the list above if you need to, note what bothers you about each of the following attempts to persuade.

1. I feel I can honestly say that motorcycles, in some instances, are safer than cars. How many motorcycle accidents have you heard of in which

hasty generalization — inappropriate comparison

the driver went through the windshield or was speared by the steering column? In some motorcycle accidents the driver flies clear of the object he hit, as I did when I struck that woman's car.

2. Fidel Castro says that communism is the best form of government.
3. Birth control clinics are the cause of increased teenage sex.
4. If a thing can be produced without art or preparation, much more can it be produced with the help of art and care. (Aristotle)
5. If a thing is possible for inferior, weaker, less intelligent people, it is more so for people who are superior, stronger, and more intelligent. (Aristotle)
6. Buy Giant Panda hot dogs.
7. The virtues and corresponding works of a man are nobler than those of a woman. (Aristotle)
8. Those things are good which are one's own, possessed by no one else, and exceptional. (Aristotle)
9. It's time we take notice. The trend is now unmistakable. You need to understand *what it means*! Suddenly the United States no longer enjoys the highest per capita income of any nation. Sweden has now risen above us. The United States' world's highest living standard has *started on the way down.*
10. Most of the advanced nations of the free world—many of which are critical of America as supreme leader of the West—are suffering from faltering and divided leadership, lack of purpose, and lack of will to act unitedly against onrushing crises.
11. A letter to the editor:

   With a great show of moral indignation, it was recently revealed that 67 percent of Garfield College students "cheated" on quizzes, prelims, and examinations. Since then, readers of the *Bulletin* have been deluged with pious commentaries. Isn't it about time someone asked whether our modern Puritans aren't being overly righteous in this matter? A little giving or taking of information on an examination or the use of a few crib notes is not as bad a thing as some prudish minds would have us believe. The very fact that so many loyal Garfield students indulge in this is evidence that it can't be very wrong.

   On the contrary, copying or the use of crib notes seems quite predictable and pardonable in many courses. In a course which requires remembering a lot of facts, why not use crib notes? It's only a difference in degree between using them and using some elaborate system for memorizing facts. Both are artificial means to help you remember.

   If we view the problem from another angle, we can see that what is so smugly denounced as "dishonesty" may actually reveal foresight—which is certainly a praiseworthy trait. If you were going into an unknown wilderness, you would take along the things you knew were needed for survival, wouldn't you? Taking crib notes into the unknown territory of an examination shows the same foresight. Now suppose also that one of your companions on this expedition desperately needed water or food or help of some sort. You'd do what you could to help him, wouldn't you? Helping someone on an exam is no different.

   To put the question another way, suppose we define *charity* as

(handwritten marginal notes:)

2. citing of illegitimate authorities
3. unsubstantiated cause/effect claim
4. undefined key terms — same as #4
5. illegitimate authorities
6. undefined
7. key terms — same as #7
8. exaggeration
9. appeal to irrelevant emotions — undefined — key terms #6
   others — #6
10. undefined — key terms — exaggeration
11. almost all — insults

faulty analogy

language = put-down

undefined

[handwritten marginalia: faulty analogy]

[handwritten marginalia: undefined terms]

"giving to a person in need." Isn't one, therefore, performing an act of charity during an examination when one gives some "needy" person the desired information? The fact that one isn't giving money or food does not make the act less charitable.

[handwritten marginalia: No facts]

[handwritten marginalia: name-calling]

If we inquire *who* is stirring up this fuss over alleged "cheating," we find it's the faculty—in other words, the persons who have their selfish interests to protect. Obviously, they flunk students to make them repeat the course and thus to keep the course filled.

[handwritten marginalia: evid.? exaggeration]

Finally, to take a long-range view, why should colleges get all excited over what they choose to call "cheating" when there are much more urgent things for them to worry about? When the very existence of our democracy is being threatened by communism, why should we fret about the source of Johnny's information on an ancient history exam?

[handwritten marginalia: avoiding issue]

Exercise 9-4

In order to ensure that you understand the ways in which you can easily offend, I suggest that you try to write a brief, persuasive letter of complaint using *as many fallacies as possible.* Your letter will be given to other members of the class and rated according to how bad you've been able to make it.

In this chapter, I may seem to have assumed that persuasive writing is a distinct kind of writing. If there are distinctions among various "kinds," I think those kinds could be listed as follows:

Exploratory writing—writing to try to figure something out (a scientist's doodlings, or a teenager's diary). Exploratory writing is not really intended for others.

Expressive writing—writing primarily about one's own feelings and ideas (some poetry and literary prose). With expressive writing it is assumed that the writer is interesting enough to have his or her thoughts, feelings, and language studied by others.

Informative writing—writing to help others learn what you know (reports, newspaper articles, radio and television news spots, letters, how-to books, much literature, bread-and-butter writing).

Scientific writing—writing to convince others that your ideas are correct (most academic writing, reports from national think tanks, philosophy).

Persuasive writing—writing designed to change people's attitudes or ideas or even actions (editorials, political speeches, commercials, sermons, proposals for action, lawyers' briefs).

While it helps to be able to see the differences above, most writers don't specialize in one form or another. The principles of good writing—well-chosen facts, thoughtful inferences, clear organization, correct grammar and punctuation—apply as readily to one form as to another (the first form, exploratory writing, is perhaps an exception, but exploratory writing is not intended for a reader). Moreover, the distinction between the various kinds is often blurred. All four kinds (again, excepting exploratory) must be informative—persuasion won't succeed unless it includes reliable information, and even expressive writing provides information about the writer. All four public kinds also intend to be persuasive—scientific writing tries to convince readers that the writer's interpretation of the facts is correct, informative writing wants readers to believe that the information is worth spending time on, and expressive writing wants readers to agree that the writer's thoughts are significant. *Ethos, logos,* and *pathos* will be useful to you in any kind of writing (not just persuasive writing). Similarly, you can judge the quality of any piece of writing—whether a formal speech by Martin Luther King or a quick letter from your mother—by evaluating its *ethos, logos,* and *pathos.* But they are most useful as tools, of course, when they are most necessary—that is, when your expected audience is indifferent or hostile, when you must fully employ all your writing resources.

Planning to use *ethos, logos,* and *pathos* impressively may seem, at this point, to be a hopelessly complex task. But as you plan a persuasive paper, you can generally reduce your concerns to three: (1) to collect all the information you can about the subject (an aspect of *logos*); (2) to get to understand as best you can how those opposed to you would think (an aspect of both *ethos* and *pathos*); and (3) to screw up the courage to take a firm stand (an aspect of *ethos*).

First, information, not cleverness, is your best ally. (Information includes facts, statistics, examples, the writer's own experience, and the opinions of authorities.) What facts do you know or can you find out about this issue? When writers want something, their temptation is to attack, to get their passions roused, to tick off their arguments fast and furiously. If we agree, we are often seduced into considering such pleas good writing. But anyone even mildly opposed is repelled by such tactics. As psychologist Carl Rogers has noted, readers have a natural tendency to judge rather than listen (284–89). We give our opponent much less opportunity to judge rather than listen if we refrain from judging ourselves and if we stick to specifics. John McPhee, one of the most admired current writers in nonfiction, has successfully but implicitly argued for the preservation of several wilderness areas, including New Jersey's Pine Barrens, by simply describing life as it is lived in those areas. When we fail to be specific, readers with views opposite to ours usually stop listening, as when we assert, for example, that Carter had a better foreign policy than Reagan. Specificity reduces the readers' opportunities to rush to judgment, thus allowing for some real communication, even if differences of opinion do continue to exist.

Second, to quote one of my students, "one cannot tell his reader that he is totally right and doesn't care how the reader feels." A reader whose beliefs or values are being threatened won't listen. Learning to write is (far more than we might expect) learning to understand other people. As John Stuart Mill paraphrases Aristotle, "He who knows only his side of the case, knows little of that" (36). Before you begin your own argument, try to write out a one-page argument from your reader's point of view. Then think in terms of values you might agree on. See whether you can find an assumption you share, as in the example of the uses of foreign language instruction a few pages back. What values make you most committed to your position? What values does your reader hold most dearly to (often money, or the desire not to have to work too hard)? Are there other values in your reader to which you can appeal? Even if the reader knows the facts, he or she still needs nudging in your direction, usually because money or work is involved.

Third, most of us are timid about making judgments, and therefore we don't write much in the margins of our books or say much in class, or in bull sessions, or to our elected representatives in government. It takes some courage not to let current matters stand. In order to have courage to make judgments, we first need plenty of information. But then we also need the courage to risk displaying our judgments—in discriminating between good work and bad, the correct and the incorrect, the moral and the immoral. We're all very careful (and we should be) to substantiate our assertions, but we should also encourage ourselves to be willing to stick our necks out, to make assertions. One of your goals for this semester should be to become "opinionated"—not in the sense that you come up with opinions without any facts, but in the sense that you try to find enough facts to justify expressing well-founded opinions.

10

◆

The Writing Process

English has always been a difficult subject, in that words get lost between the mind and the hand.

student

Books always amaze me, due to the fact that so many people can express themselves in writing without much difficulty.

student

The fun is not in writing; the fun is in HAVING WRITTEN.

Gene Olson

Writing is easy. All you do is stare at a blank sheet of paper until drops of blood form on your forehead.

Gene Fowler

I now write my first drafts like an optimist, assuming that people are interested in anything I have to say. I revise like a pessimist who figures that none of my ideas will get through.

student

Now when I know I have to write, I don't feel the task is against me, but on my side.

student

Exercise 10-1

For your notebook, before we begin:

1. What do you hate most about writing?

2. What are the main differences you imagine between a professional writer and yourself?

I don't know anyone who thinks he or she has found the most efficient way to write. In fact, most of us are a little embarrassed about the way we go about it, procrastinating often and being irrationally attached to a Parker pen or a yellow legal pad or a clean desk on the fourth floor of the library. Most of all, we hate to admit how much we hate facing a blank page.

Exercise 10-2

The most effective way to get over a fear of writing is to admit it, and to admit it in complete detail. Think of something you've written that you're proud of—a report from high school, a poem, a paper from this course, a letter, anything. Think about *how* you went about writing. What did you do while preparing for and writing it? What problems did you have? Record both the physical and the emotional steps you went through from the time you first thought about writing to the time you gave your work to someone. If you've never written anything you're proud of, make a record of how you went about writing some piece that you hated doing. Save your results, and keep them in mind as you read this chapter.

Your writing process may seem annoyingly complex to you, but that process will seem miraculously simple if you compare it with the filming process that any director is faced with. Here is Satyajit Ray, the most prominent Indian filmmaker, explaining the process of creating one short scene for *Pather Panchali:*

> To me it is the inexorable rhythm of its creative process that makes film-making so exciting in spite of the hardships and the frustrations. Consider this process: you have conceived a scene, any scene. Take the one where a young girl, frail of body but full of some elemental zest, gives herself up to the first monsoon shower. She dances in joy while the big drops pelt her and drench her. The scene excites you not only for its visual possibilities but for its deeper implications as well: that rain will be the cause of her death.
>
> You break down the scene into shots, make notes and sketches. Then the time comes to bring the scene to life. You go out into the open, scan the vista, choose your setting. The rain clouds approach. You set up your camera, have a last quick rehearsal. Then the "take." But one is not enough. This is a key scene. You must have another while the shower lasts. The camera turns, and presently your scene is on celluloid.
>
> Off to the lab. You wait, sweating—this is September—while the ghostly negative takes its own time to emerge. There is no hurrying

this process. Then the print, the "rushes." This looks good, you say to yourself. But wait. This is only the content, in its bits and pieces, and not the form. How is it going to join up? You grab your editor and rush off to the cutting room. There is a grueling couple of hours, filled with aching suspense, while the patient process of cutting and joining goes on. At the end you watch the thing on the moviola. Even the rickety old machine cannot conceal the effectiveness of the scene. Does this need music, or is the incidental sound enough? But that is another stage in the creative process, and must wait until all the shots have been joined up into scenes and all the scenes into sequences and the film can be comprehended in its totality. Then, and only then, can you tell—if you can bring to bear on it that detachment and objectivity—if your dance in the rain has really come off. (Geduld, 269–70)

Most beginning writers want to skip this patient "editing" stage that is so important to the success of a film. They feel that "planning" and "shooting" a paper is the most they should be expected to do.

Another art closely related to writing is sculpture—listen to these descriptions of the French sculptor Auguste Rodin at work:

Nothing in Rodin's surroundings resembles the society studios of fashionable sculptors; no knick-knacks, no art objects calculatingly displayed for sale. Everything here reminds one of the craftsman, wearing wooden shoes, with dust and smears of clay on his garments.

Rodin always carried some clay and something to draw with in his pocket and never seemed to spend more than five minutes, even while talking or eating, without either sketching or modeling some shape with his busy fingers.

Rodin appeared to work slowly. When in 1898 he had to part with his *Balzac* to meet the Salon's deadline (he had put off the delivery of the statue as long as he could) he felt he was being hurried and was greatly upset. "They're snatching the work out of my hands," he grumbled, as the statue was removed from the Dépôt des marbres. "When will those idiotic officials understand that in order to turn out something good, one must have time to forget it?" (Descharnes and Chabrun, 236, 238)

You'll begin to see, now, as you read accounts of how John McPhee (*Coming into the Country, The Pine Barrens*) and John K. Galbraith (*The Affluent Society, The New Industrial State*) go about writing, that writing is not all that different.

J. K. Galbraith:

In my own case there are days when the result is so bad that no fewer than five revisions are required. However, when I'm greatly inspired, only four revisions are needed before . . . I put in that note of spontaneity which even my meanest critics concede. (103)

William Howarth, writing about McPhee:

When he starts to hear the same stories a third time, McPhee stops interviewing, returns to Princeton, and begins the tortuous process of composition. His working methods vary according to a project, but some steps are fairly constant. He first transcribes the notebooks, typing entries in order, occasionally adding other details or current thoughts as he goes. He likens this process to a magnet's attraction of iron filings; as the notes take shape, they draw from him new ideas about placement, phrasing, or possible analogies. When finished, he may have a hundred typed sheets of notes, enough to fill a large spring binder. He makes a photocopy of the original set and shelves it for later use. He then reads and rereads the binder set, looking for areas he needs to flesh out with research and reading at Firestone Library. The reading produces more notes, the notes more typed pages for his binder. Finally, he reads the binder and makes notes on possible structures, describing patterns the story might assume.

While its structure is forming, or when he senses how the story may end, McPhee often writes out a first draft of "the lead," a term journalists use to describe openings. In newspaper writing the lead is usually a single-sentence paragraph, designed to impart the classic who-what-where particulars of a story. In McPhee's work the lead is longer (fifteen hundred to two thousand words), more dramatic, yet rather more oblique. It establishes a mood, a setting, and perhaps some main characters or events, but not in order to put the story in a nutshell or even to hint at its full dimension. . . .

Having read the lead via telephone to an editor at *The New Yorker*, he goes back to the binder and begins to code it with structural notes, using titles like "Voyageurs" "Loons" or acronyms—"GLAT," "LASLE." These are his topics, the formal segments of narrative, which he next writes on a series of index cards. After assembling a stack, he fans them out and begins to play a sort of writer's solitaire, studying the possibilities of order. Decisions don't come easily; a story has many potential sequences, and each chain produces a calculus of desired and undesired effects, depending on factors like character and theme. When he has the cards in a satisfactory arrangement, he thumbtacks them to a large bulletin board. The shade of Mrs. Olive McKee, his high school English teacher, smiles upon this array. McPhee defines the outline that finally emerges, in deference to her training, as "logical," but its logic is of no ordinary, abecedarian variety, A to Z or 1 to 10.

Cards on the board, committed to their structure, he next codes the duplicate set of notes and then scissors its sheets apart, cutting large blocks of paragraphs and two- or three-line ribbons. In a few hours he has reduced the sheets to thousands of scraps, which he sorts into file folders, one folder for each topical index card on the bulletin board. These folders are precompositional skeletons of the narrative segments he will refine when writing a first draft. With the folders squared away in a vertical file, he is ready to write. A large steel dart on the bulletin board marks his progress. He stabs the dart under an index card, opens a folder, further sorts scraps and ribbons until this segment also has a "logical" structure. Then, without invoking the muse, he begins to type his first draft, picking up where the lead ends. When he finishes a folder, he moves the dart, gets the next folder, sorts it out, and continues to type.

Outlined in this fashion, McPhee's writing method may seem excessively mechanical, almost programmatic in his sorting and retrieval of data bits. But the main purpose of this routine is at once practical and aesthetic: it runs a line of order through the chaos of his notes and files, leaving him free to write on a given parcel of work at a given time. The other sections cannot come crowding in to clutter his desk and mind; he is spared that confusion by the structure of his work, by an ordained plan that cannot come tumbling down. The strategy locks him in, gives him no easy exits from the materials at hand, which he must confront with that humorless partner, the typewriter. (xiv–xv)

Exercise 10-3

Now look at the accounts of the writing process that you and your classmates turned in. Any universal truths? Any new ideas? Compare your own fears and strategies with those of the professionals and of your classmates.

In the rest of this chapter, I'd like to give you some general advice about writing strategies gleaned from the descriptions I've read by my students and colleagues over the past few years. Some of this advice is repeated elsewhere in this book, but I've made it all available, too, in this single chapter to which you can return. The writing process is never as neat and orderly as a cookbook process, but it can be thought of in terms of useful stages. Every writing teacher will give you a different version of these stages. Their versions are more or less specific (four are shown below), and their categories overlap, but you'll find many different versions useful.

Richard Gebhardt ("The Writing Process," 21)	Kenneth Dowst (4.2, 4.14)
1. generating and focusing 2. drafting 3. revising	1. invention-writing 2. revision-writing

Michael Adelstein (120)	Sharon Pianko (275–78)
1. worrying (15%) 2. planning (10%) 3. writing (25%)	1. pre-writing 2. planning 3. composing

4. revising (45%)
5. proofreading (5%)

4. writing
5. pausing
6. rescanning
7. re-reading
8. stopping
9. contemplating the finished product
10. handing in the finished product

This variety should remind us that even in this chapter, we should be looking not for a single writing strategy but, rather, for "workable strategies." Every writing assignment and every writing situation is slightly different; no advice about the writing process can give us ironclad, step-by-step instructions. All we can say of even the best advice is that it is *often* fruitful.

1 Collecting and Selecting

Everyone seems to agree that a person can't just start writing: writing requires preparation. But what that preparation should be is a matter of some dispute. Many student writers have been scared or misled by the rhetorical term for prewriting: *invention*. How am I to "invent" a whole five-page paper out of nothing? But *invention* (from the Latin verb *invenire*) means "to find, to discover." Our task is more manageable if we realize that we only have to *find* things. We are all capable of doing that. Or are we? If we have to find *ideas*, that's still a mystical task.

In many traditional writing courses, you practiced that mysticism, finding a topic (finding a topic meant finding the right-size topic) and then choosing a pattern of organization to "develop" that topic. But this mysticism is quite unnecessary. Prewriting should begin not with topic analysis but with information. It then continues with interpretation of the information we want to pass on. Once we "find" the information, our creativity, our "invention," comes into play as we draw inferences from the information we have.

Once you've been given a problem or area to research, then, "invention" begins with observation, with a search for telling details. Writing is not worth reading if its subject has not been carefully observed. Why should any of us, even if we are teachers, go to the trouble of reading a piece by a writer who doesn't know his or her subject? The search for details may begin with a careful look at a place, with an interview, with the underlining of passages in books, or with note-taking in a library. No matter where this fact collecting takes place, though, the writer will have along the tools of our trade—a pen (or pencil) and plenty of paper—to note whatever facts (details, statistics, quotations) seem pertinent. When drafting time comes, a fact on solid paper is worth ten in the writer's leaky memory. While collecting facts, a writer should also note down *any* ideas about those facts which come to mind. Ideas are even more slippery than facts we observe—they fly out of the head as fast as they fly in—so they must be noted down. (This crucial step probably must be practiced, for it isn't often natural—we're not used to listening to ourselves think.) If we later decide that an idea is harebrained or exaggerated, we can always discard or qualify it. Once we have maybe twenty-five telling details and maybe six or seven good ideas, we have the foundation for a three- to four-page paper, and we can consider beginning to write.

Such note-taking requires starting early—no one can write an information-rich paper the night before it's due. As often as possible, you should start your work early enough so that you can bring your notes—not even a draft—to class and have them discussed for their value. Which of your notes would the teacher and other students like to see in a paper? Which would elicit a check mark of praise in a final paper—"Ah! New information" or "Ah! Well thought through"? If you bring no raw material that's provoking to this session, no amount of coherence will glue a decent paper together by the due date.

Once you've taken some notes, you may want to try some timed writing like that you practiced in Chapter 4 to see what direction your writing might take. Setting a timer forces you to get a page or two or three written, and you may well discover in this kind of writing new aspects of your subject that you'd like to explore. Writing with a timer often allows us to see what we really want to say about a subject—and not just what we think we should say. Observing freshly, trying to tell the truth, can make this first part of writing much easier. Most of us are stymied when we try to begin those form letters which are required to accompany applications—for example, "Explain in 500 words why you want to be a lawyer." Usually, we're blocked by the idea that the admissions committee must be looking for "fine," clever writing. Writing quickly but honestly on this or any other kind of subject temporarily frees our conscious minds from social restraints which cause us to fall into patterns rather than make a mark for ourselves. Later on, we may not be satisfied with what we've drafted, but we now have some raw material that we can work with.

After either timed writing or note-taking, a writer should look over the chaos of facts and ideas on the page and consider her first step well done. We can't begin unless we have some chaos to work with, as we're reminded by Mary Shelley, the author of *Frankenstein:* "Invention, it must be humbly admitted, does not consist in creating out of a void, but out of chaos" (7).

From this chaos we may proceed to make a list, or a rough outline, or a test draft—our job is to derive somehow some order out of our chaos:

> The aim of composing is not to tolerate chaos for its own sake but to learn to put up with it while you discover ways of emerging. That can be less difficult than generating chaos in the first place because, for one thing, the mind doesn't like chaos; ordering is its natural activity. (Berthoff, 65)

The writer should now find, among the facts and ideas, the kernels she likes, and she should then ask some questions. For any specifics in the paper, she ought to anticipate a reader's asking "So what?" For any ideas or generalizations, she ought to anticipate a reader's asking "For instance?" Short written answers to these questions should (when combined with the original notes) start giving shape and density to the paper.

2   Incubation (Waiting)

Fortunately, not all our writing decisions need to be conscious. After doing some spadework for an essay, we can go play ball, do housework, or just go to sleep without feeling guilty, because we are allowing our subconscious mind to take its turn while the conscious mind goes fishing. Both our conscious and our subconscious minds have plenty to contribute. A paper written by choosing a thesis, writing an outline, and filling out the paragraphs is completed entirely by the conscious mind—the paper may be good, and time limits may make this way of writing necessary, but it is not the best we can do.

Donald Murray, a Pulitzer-prize-winning writer, has shown how we can put our intuitive strengths to work when we write. When we begin to see a shaping idea for a paper, we should pull away from it for a while, partly to see how new evidence that we come across fits with that idea, but partly just to await the ordering process of our mind, as it sifts and resifts the data we've collected in the light of this new "idea." We don't immediately make judgments about the idea—we test it, half consciously, half unconsciously. The temptation, of course, is to let this part of the process go on indefinitely: "writing which can be delayed, will be" ("Write," 375). Research is more fun than sharing research. It's a great pleasure to have a head full of ideas, but it doesn't do anyone any good but yourself. Murray suggests that at this point only force—a waiting audience or an approaching deadline—can make a writer write, can pull the writer out of this very satisfying state ("Write," 376). I do think *ego* will also do it; fortunately, our egos want credit for the ideas they have. Of all the kinds of force, though, deadlines are the most effective. Don't curse them. They are there to bring out the best in you. Satisfaction doesn't come until late in the writing process—though the pleasures of research come early. Without a deadline, most writers would prefer to bask in the early pleasure of learning—but when we allow ourselves to do so, we deny ourselves the opportunities for the genuine satisfaction that comes from presenting what we've found to others.

3   Ordering

Let's assume now that we're faced with a writer's dream—we have plenty of notes, and we've stopped for a day or two to think about them. What are we going to do with the information now that we have it? How are we going to organize it? The next steps we take are going to commit us in ways that are difficult to retrace, so it may be time to make sure of our own commitment. I find it most useful to make, at this point, a statement of commitment:

I plan to [aim] for [readers] by [methods].

This statement sets our tone, our pace, our level of difficulty, and the question of whether we want to inform, judge, or persuade. It should help us see the direction in which further research can take us. But if we have completed the necessary research, we can now simply sort through the information we've collected and see what categories it can fall into, categories, that is, that will be useful for our intended readers. A brief breakdown of the categories can then serve as a provisional outline, which is all we want at this stage. The outlines we form now should only be rough sketches—outlines will play a larger part later in the writing process when we check our draft to see whether we've been systematic and whether we've kept our sense of proportion.

The structure we create in this way should not be considered a complete map of our finished paper. Much will be added during the actual writing. But if the structure seems only half or less than half complete, a writer might refer to some list of common organizing principles, or ways of filling out the plan:

1. Do I have enough information in each category?
2. Have I drawn as many inferences as I can safely draw from my information? Are my inferences bold enough? thoughtful enough?
3. Are there any contrasts that might highlight my subject?
4. Would some analogy make any of my points clearer to my intended readers?
5. Would my readers appreciate a historical context?
6. Do any of my key terms need defining?
7. Have I answered the readers' questions—Who? What? When? Where? (these four are important, but rapidly answered) and, more important, Why? and How?

Thus, the "invention" process continues, and it is perhaps more imaginative at this point than it is in the beginning of our work on a paper. By considering (and often rejecting) these options, we not only may stumble onto an organizing principle which solves all our problems; we also may discover what we don't yet know about our subject.

Planning at this point increases efficiency. An utterly unplanned draft may take so long to sort out that its value as "something on paper" is more than offset by the revision time it requires. A plan reduces the load on our memories, leaving our minds free to deal with each sentence as it comes.

4   Drafting

With rare exceptions, all of us would rather do anything than begin to write: no matter how many times a person has written and succeeded before, each time he starts, he faces a fear that nothing of quality will come out this time. In the face of this fear, our best ally is determination: we must make ourselves do what we have to do, when it ought to be done, whether we like it or not. But when we have done all the gathering and planning mentioned in the previous few pages, summoning the determination to begin is much less traumatic. We face no blank page. All we have to do is transfer information from papers on the left side of our desk to papers on the right side of our desk. Three other things can help. First, we must realize that there is *no* rule in writing that can't be broken. Our materials, our purpose, our intended readers may require a strategy that we've never heard of. It can't hurt to try. We can always revise later. Second, as we write out our first draft, we must not even consider perfection—"decent" is all we want; "playful," perhaps, but "decent" will do. We shouldn't allow ourselves to be slowed down by an attempt to find the "perfect" word or by a worry over a matter of grammar or spelling. Third, we need a deadline— if the teacher won't impose it, then we must impose one ourselves. Unless we're in the position of having an audience waiting for our results, we won't very often start without a deadline. Flexible deadlines are, I would guess, the greatest cause of writer's block on our college campuses.

The other cause of writer's block is a fear that "style"—indeterminate, indefinable "style"—is what makes or breaks a paper. It's very difficult to write when we don't understand the grounds on which we might be judged. If we feel secure, though, that the quality of a piece of writing depends primarily on the quality of the facts selected and the quality of the inferences drawn from those facts, then much of the quality of a paper is established before the first draft begins to appear on the page—the first draft has thus shrunk to its proper dimensions.

Once writer's block has been shuttled aside, drafting becomes one of the easiest steps in the writing process. We should allow ourselves *some* revision during this stage. One good sentence often produces better sentences after it. One good paragraph often produces better paragraphs following. But it is important to remember that this is "only" a draft, so let's make sure that the clear voice of a writer enjoying writing comes through; let's take some risks (revision is always back there, prudently waiting to rescue us). And let's be willing to write much more than we will eventually need (thus letting the reviser in us choose the better from the worse). As we write, we must keep in mind not only our subject but the questions our readers will have for us and about our subject. The difficulties we can expect while drafting are that we'll have to start earlier than we want to, that our hands and fingers will get tired, that our ideas will tend to come faster than we can express them, and, worst of all, that we'll get discouraged because we'll lose faith that our work is original or that anyone will want to read it. All four difficulties are normal: but when we expect them, they don't hurt so much.

We should think seriously about completing this drafting step at a typewriter or word processor, if at all possible. Many writers disagree with me here. Paul Theroux, author of *The Great Railway Bazaar,* argues that writing by hand is slow and thus allows for surprise. Many writers (not journalists, though) say they can think better with pen and paper than they can at the typewriter. But many writers grew up before every college student had a typewriter, before college papers were required to be typed. Technology has changed: journalists have moved on to word processors; the rest of us should join them as soon as we can afford word processors. The advantages of working at a word processor (or even a typewriter) are numerous, unless a person really can't "think" at either of those machines, in which case she'd best stay with pen and paper. A typed or processed draft is much easier to read objectively, much easier to make changes on while still remaining readable. When we write in longhand and use the typewriter only as a "finishing machine" for producing a final draft, we become almost superstitious about revising that draft, which is a shame, since that type-written draft gives us our first opportunity to really read our work care-fully. Starting on a typewriter (or a word processor) will save you much time now, and you will be able to develop better writing habits (primarily the willingness to revise) for your use in your future professions.

The most important thing to note about a draft, though, is not whether it's typed or written but whether the mind is engaged while it's coming into being. Donald Murray says that "the most accurate definition of writing, I believe, is that it is the process of using language to discover meaning in experience and to communicate it ("Internal Revision," 86). Thus he calls the first draft a "discovery draft," a very useful term. The writer has a plan before beginning that "discovery draft," but she is open to new ideas as she executes it, and she is disappointed if she hasn't "discovered" something as she's worked her way through it. We need room to breathe while writing. We begin with a sense of direction, yes, but we rarely know our final intention before we have finished the paper. If a writer doesn't learn much in writing a paper, the reader isn't likely to learn much from reading it.

5   Revising (Making the Work Readable)

> When I say writing, O believe me, it is rewriting I have chiefly in mind.
>
> Robert Louis Stevenson

Revising begins almost as soon as a paper is first conceived, with the writer's first shift in ideas about what to include in or how to organize the paper. It continues with changes in the writer's first written sentence and with pauses for reflection and rereading as the draft is taking shape. But concentrated revising, beginning *after* a first draft, is the point at which a work either comes to life or falls dead. All the preceding steps of writing are relatively easy; the hard work begins here. The British writers Robert

Graves and Alan Hodge tell us that "there should be two main objects in ordinary prose writing: to convey a message, and to include in it nothing that will distract the reader's attention or check his habitual pace of reading" (154). Collecting, selecting, waiting, and drafting focus on coming up with a message; revising focuses on getting that message, as clearly as possible, to the reader. Only when we have gathered and written out some worthwhile information are we willing to go through this final process, which demands (admittedly) that we become a little fanatic about perfection. (It may seem that as writers we spend a very long time to gain a very small end, but we might compare our efforts with those of filmmakers. How many thousands of hours do they spend to give us just two hours of entertainment?) Most people equate revising with cleansing, with seeing to it that what is written conforms to the conventions and rules, so that the written piece can be received and judged by the reader without the distraction of faulty punctuation, poor spelling, or other errors. Such cleansing is important, but revising is a much broader process. Seldom do we write down exactly what we meant to say. Only when we read through our papers can we judge whether our points have come out the way we thought they did. Once we've adjusted our draft so that it says what we meant to say, we must check also to see whether there are any points on which we've changed our minds since we started writing. And finally, once we are reasonably sure of what we mean, revising also entails reading to see whether we've made our meaning clear to others.

To revise successfully, a writer must first break away (we writers love breaks). A day is good, and an hour is essential, for the writer needs time to take off the writer's cap and put on the reader's cap. A writer's assumptions and background are necessarily different from those of any reader, and the writer must therefore try to read from that alien perspective. Much of revising lies in the writer's ability to read his writing as though he were an interested but uninformed reader. His job is much easier if he can get an honestly critical friend or relative or expert to read his paper. The foremost question that each of these readers should be asking is a question suggested by Aristotle: Have I learned easily? If not, why not? These readers' comments are often very helpful. But even if they aren't directly helpful, they may indirectly trigger new ideas for the writer. We all become fond of our own words and ideas (much as parents become fond of their own children, because they have gone to so much trouble to bring them up), but our ideas, like our children, still need to be disciplined into shape. Outsiders don't share our uncritical fondness, and they can help us sort out the best in our writing from the unnecessary.

If no reader is available, the writer should at least read her own work aloud until she is satisfied with the way it sounds. In ancient Greece, "all literature was written to be heard, and even when reading to himself a Greek read aloud" (Kennedy, 4). Therefore, Aristotle took it for granted that "a composition should be easy to read or—which is the same thing—easy to deliver" (195). We, in the twentieth century, seem to have forgotten that words are written to be heard. But if, when we read our work aloud, we find ourselves halting or embarrassed, we should consider that embarrassment an invitation to revise:

1. We may see several places where we have hinted at, rather than specified, our meaning.

2. We may find that we need more details.

3. We may see that a briefer introduction or conclusion would better use our reader's time.

4. We may think of an introduction or conclusion which would make our intentions clearer.

5. We may see that our main point—the something that we wanted to achieve when we began—isn't clear (we may want to add an explicit thesis).

6. We may see that our coverage of issues isn't balanced and that some important matter needs more explanation.

7. We may find that a paragraph is too long and needs to be split or that several are too short and might well be combined.

8. We may find sentences that are clumsy or ungrammatical.

9. We often find that some of our sentences are not linked together well.

10. We may find that we've written lies or half-lies which we have to correct.

11. We may find clutter that distracts the reader from our message.

12. We may find that we've put our most important points in places where they'll receive little emphasis.

13. We may want to rewrite sentences to achieve a better sound or rhythm.

14. We ought to write a paragraph-by-paragraph outline to see whether the draft makes sense, and perhaps we need to add some direction-indicating sentences that will make reading easier.

15. Most important, we ought to check to make sure that a real author comes through clearly to the reader.

In short, we "must read with an eye to alternatives in content, form, structure, voice, and language" (Murray, "Internal Revision," 95). When we're finished, we should have few qualms about handing this piece to a reader.

6 Publishing

Only now are we ready to check spelling, punctuation, grammar, and neatness. We can forget, finally, what we've said; we can make sure (with a dictionary) that the words we're not sure of are spelled right, check (using the techniques of Chapter 8) our punctuation, and look over the whole paper to make sure it looks clean. We don't want to leave in our work any unnecessary distractions from what we're trying to say.

Ways to Cheat on the Writing Process We don't always spend all the time suggested here and go through all these stages as we write papers for school or reports outside school. As our writing intuitions develop, many of these steps will take place more quickly. But even with highly developed intuitions, writing is never easy, and it requires several blocks of uninterrupted time to be completed. And even with several blocks of uninterrupted time, time limits prevent our writing from being as solid as we'd like it to be. Most of the papers you'll write in this course will be conceived, researched, and written in less than three weeks. With some papers you will do everything suggested here; with others you'll be able to cut corners—to make the process as efficient as possible for yourself. After all, we do have other things to do besides writing. We want writing to become an efficient, not an overwhelming, part of our lives. When we're confident that our audience is sympathetic, for example, we can rely on memory rather than research to substantiate some of our assertions. When we're not writing for publication, we can sometimes omit standard footnote forms and simply note to our readers what our sources are. With a short paper, we can often revise while we write so that our first draft (though messy) is ready for final typing. When a paper comes due, we can hand in a "deadline draft," even if we know that we could do more to improve it. And when we simply don't have time to write, we can often just call on the telephone and use our notes.

John Muir has said that the great thrill of exploring is that "we find more than we seek." That's the same thrill of the writing process, and that's what so often leaves us satisfied after so much work.

11

◆

Revision

By many directors, editing—which can be described very simply as the assembling and joining of selected pieces of film—is regarded as the creative peak of the entire film-making process, the preliminary shooting being largely a matter of collecting together the necessary materials to be assembled into a coherent whole.

Ivan Butler

Writing is committed speech—speech we are willing to polish, fix, and vouch for.

Dennis Drabelle

Exercise 11-1

Before you begin reading, write in your notebook what you mean by the term *revision*.

Exercise 11-2

Select from your notebook a free-writing piece you did in Chapter 4. Read through it, and decide what you'd want to do with it before you'd want anyone to read it. Then, psychologically disown the piece so that you don't mind giving it to someone (perhaps you should write "Disowned" at the top of the paper). Pass the free writing, unaltered, to a neighbor, and ask the neighbor to revise it. After ten or fifteen minutes, all the members of the class can discuss the kinds of revisions that they each decided to make.

Or write a brief essay (spend about twenty minutes) on the effect that being the ___th child in your family has had on your development. Consider the paper a draft; you may make changes by crossing out, substituting words or phrases, rearranging paragraphs—anything you like. When your teacher stops you, sit back and compare your classmates' answers with your own responses to the following questions:

1. Did you have a difficult time getting started? Why?
2. How did you decide on your focus?
3. Did you reject specific focuses?
4. Did you change anything? What kinds of changes did you make?
5. Did you think of something and decide not to include it?
6. Have you thought of something you would like to include since you stopped writing?
7. How do you feel about what you have written?
8. Would you like to hand it in now for a grade? Why not?

We spent some time on revision in the previous chapter, but revision—not just changing a few words and fixing some punctuation, but looking back *(re-vision)* and making changes in what we've thought or written—is so important that it deserves a chapter to itself. Any piece of writing that you write straight out in one session is the product of one person; a piece that you write out and then consciously revise becomes the work of two people, and it's often twice as good—the difference between a C and a B, between a B and an A. During a first draft, a "discovery" draft, we are most curious to find out how much we have to say (and how well we can substantiate what we say) on the issue we've chosen to work with. We revise even here as we change major ideas to minor ones and shift our original plans, and we occasionally change sentences, phrases, and words if they don't sound the way we want to sound or if they don't say what we want to say. But most successful writers take special pains during a first draft to ignore back-of-their-mind questions about words or sentences or even whole sections, special pains to suppress the reviser in them so that they can concentrate on finding the most interesting and appropriate facts and on interpreting those facts thoughtfully. But then as a deadline approaches, because they want to get their message across as clearly as possible and because they want to avoid embarrassment, they get very careful (even ruthless) not only about their facts, their inferences, and their introductions and conclusions but about their sentences and even their words.

Several recent politicians have tried to take their words back by saying that they "misspoke." But I haven't yet heard any writers excuse themselves by saying that they "miswrote." We can't take our writing back. Filmmakers, who know they can't take their films back ("I misfilmed?"), routinely spend six months editing until they have revised a film into the precise form that they want it to take. Of course, the filmmaker is hoping to make $20 million on a film, and you're only trying to please yourself, some of your classmates, and your teacher, so you may (understandably) decide to give less than six months to the task.

Revising, like the other facets of writing, is a skill that improves with practice. At first, you'll probably feel awkward and unworthy of making judgments. If you're like most of us, you'll start by criticizing surface problems, like short, choppy sentences.

> This is a real story. It happened six years ago. I had a very close circle of friends. One day somebody proposed to climb a mountain. Actually a volcano. I was sure I was going to get lost. It was a terrible day and night for me.

Or an awkward repetiton of words:

> When junior high school *started, I started* getting my first taste of real discipline.

Or poor grammar, word choice, or spelling:

> *Santity* depends mainly on the way one *discipline* himself.
>
> I could *dare* his bet.

These things do matter, but it takes practice to break away from judging words, which is comparatively easy, and to start to judge the thought that went into your paper (the draft review work sheets in this chapter are designed to help you do that). Learning to see the whole picture of what you are trying to say is one of the most difficult habits that you'll try to acquire during this course.

Student writers (including myself) have a history of revising very little. Our habit of starting late often leaves too little time for revision, but even when we have the time, we change very little (1) because it's too much trouble to make changes, since a substantial change in one part of the paper often requires changes elsewhere, (2) because we've used all the lines on our paper with our draft, and there's no room to insert changes even if we want to make them, and (3) because even when we read over our work and are puzzled by a sentence or a paragraph, rather than change it we decide that we must have had a reason for including it the first time.

Let's stop kidding ourselves. First, it's not difficult to allow time for revision. If we believe in its value, we will make time for it. Second, we have to develop a strategy for leaving room for legible revisions. *Trying* to leave margins doesn't work for me (they get smaller and smaller as I go along). Writing on every second or third line doesn't work either (it distracts me from what I'm saying). What does work is a suggestion by Roger Garrison (24) that a writer draw a line down the middle of each page and draft only to the right of that line, thus allowing plenty of space on the left for questions, comments, and readable revisions. (See example on opposite page.) Third, we're fools if we wholly trust the self that wrote our first draft, figuring "we must have had a reason." At this point we need some help from a person who is less uncritically fond of our work than we are.

By the time a paper has reached the clean draft stage and is ready for full-time revision, the writer is not always the best person to do the critical reading necessary to decide what should stay, what should go, and what should be added. The reading of a classmate, or teacher, or friend is fresher and will often help more because that reader has not become fond of ideas or phrases, as the writer has. When I submitted a draft of this book to editors at McGraw-Hill, they sent the draft out to six reviewers, all of whom sent me five to ten pages of compliments, criticism, and suggestions. Those reviewers were trying not just to "fix" my work but to help me say best what I was trying to say. Some of their comments hurt when I first read them, but all the comments, particularly those that hurt, helped me to improve the final draft.

In this chapter, you'll have an opportunity to learn how the assistance of a reviewer can improve your work, and you will be able to practice being a reviewer yourself so that you ultimately become a better reviewer of even your own work.

Exercises 11-3 to 11-10

Included are eight sample papers, each of which was written in response to one of the suggested assignments in Chapter 15. I recommend that you review each of these papers, using the accompanying draft review work sheet, at the point in the course where you are working on the same or a similar assignment yourself. Reviewing will be easier if you make notes to yourself on the paper as you read. And be sure to add your own questions to the draft review work sheets if they don't ask the questions you think are most important.

After you practice on each of these papers, you'll be well prepared to spend a class day, before each paper is due, trading your draft with those of classmates, and making constructive suggestions based on the questions on the work sheets. Using the suggestions of your reviewers, and the experience you gain reviewing the papers of others, you should be able to make substantial improvements in your final drafts.

Add the section I now have later in the chapter on "revising improves with practice."

Also add the two paragraphs I wrote up for the department handout on the Harrison method of drawing a line down the middle of the page.

precise form that they want it to take.
Of course, the filmmaker is hoping to make
$20 million on a film, and you're only
trying to please yourself, some of your
classmates, and your teacher, so you may
(understandably) decide to give less than
six months to the task.

By the time a paper ~~is ready for~~ has reached the
revision, the writer is not always the
best person to do the ~~pruning. The~~ critical reading necessary to decide
~~opinion of a potential reader—class-~~ what should stay, what should go, and what should
or   or
~~mate,~~ teacher, friend, is fresher and be added. The reading of a classmate,
will often help more because that
reader has not become fond of ideas or
phrases, as the writer has. In this
chapter, I will call this collaborator,
this reader, your reviewer.

clean draft stage and is ready for full-time

Explain this in practical detail. What kinds of people serve as "reviewers"? What do they do?

1-3

Type it to give it to the writer

DRAFT REVIEW WORK SHEET
Description of a Curious Place

Writer: _____   Reviewer: _____

1. Can you picture the place that the writer has described? What detail best helps you picture it? Note two or three sentences or words that are too vague to call up a picture. *Vague - too broad.*

2. Are there enough facts here to make you glad you read this paper? What kinds of facts do you feel are missing?

3. Does the writer seem to have a genuine interest in the place and a good grasp of information about the place? *- Many varied details*

4. Note every point in the paper where you were temporarily confused. Explain two such places here. *switches topics*

dominant impression

5. After reading this paper, do you feel that you understand the character of the place described? What character do you think the author intended to express? *poverty -*

6. Are there any changes you would suggest in punctuation, grammar, or spelling?

7. How has reading this paper given you a new perspective on the paper you are working on yourself?

LIFE IN THE GHETTO

¹ Living in the ghetto, especially in Washington, D.C., is a great struggle for many families, but they know that it will be an even greater fight to survive.

² When a stranger enters this area, the first thing that he notices is that all of the buildings are four stories high and the color is a drab, old and dingy brick red, trimmed in a pale green. They extend from Burns Place, Southwest, to Minnesota Avenue, Northeast. Two of the buildings are completely boarded up, because of two fires set by arsonists, which claimed the lives of two young children.

³ There are two posters nailed to the boards, one advertising protest against the Alan Baake decision and the other campaigning for the election of three government officials, who are Marion Barry, Walter Fauntroy and Mayor Walter E. Washington.

⁴ On the right side of one of the buildings is a rusty twenty-gallon garbage can, that was overfilled. When you walk past the garbage can, your nostrils pick up a distinct odor of rotted vegetables, molded bread and dead rodents. This odor is something that your stomach cannot adjust to. It creeps through cracks in the door, while you try to enjoy a good breakfast consisting of fatback, fried potatoes, grits and biscuits.

⁵ The buildings are so badly infested with roaches and rats, you can sometimes hear them in the basement at night, rumbling through the trash. The plumbing is so inadequate, many families go for days without hot water. When they complain to the rentoffice for months at a time, they receive no response.

⁶ In the back yard there are two broken washers. One washer has a blue dull color with paint scraped off the side to spell out a dirty word, and the other washer is pink with the lid torn completely off. There are sixty-seven trees surrounding the entire area, all of which are pine. The residents complain, because it looks like part of Fort Dupont Park.

⁷ Parked on the curb is a 1969 brown Skylark, with the front window broken completely out. The car was abandoned for two months by a young boy, who hot wired it and went on a joy ride.

⁸ On Friday and Saturday nights, the air is filled with the sounds of recording artists such as Ashford and Simpson, Peabo Bryson and Parliament, singing their gold record hits, as the neighbors tune in their radios to OK100. The sounds of arguing families make you an informed listener. It also keeps you from getting a good night sleep. The smoke of a freshly lit joint fills the lungs of dope users, as they get a "contact high."

⁹ During the Fourth of July, when you stand on the rooftops, you can see the fireworks being shot off from the monument grounds.

¹⁰ The homes were built at the start of World War One. They were used as off-base housing for military families. There is a sixty-foot pole in the backyard, which was used to hang flags on, by American soldiers. One section was used as a graveyard, but it is covered by bricks.

[11] Four years ago, ground breaking ceremonies were held by Mayor Washington for the building of the first recreational center in the southeast area. There are five outdoor basketball courts, a football field and three tennis courts. Two years ago, when a thunderstorm flooded the tennis courts up to the nets, the neighborhood kids went swimming in the water.

[12] The area itself is ninety-nine percent black, but there is one white man living in the ghetto. Jack Macy is forty-three years old with stringy brown hair, a broad nose and a protruding chin. He considers himself black, and if you challenged him, he would probably curse you out.

[13] Every first of the month, Jack gets dressed up in his burgundy colored polyester suit, cashes his check and gets drunk. When he returns home staggering drunk, he carries a brown paper bag tucked safely under his arm. The bag contains two six packs of Miller and Schlitz beer. Upon entering his apartment, he plays the only record that he owns, which is his Fats Domino record. Although Jack is a drunk, he is mechanically inclined. He is able to repair television sets, refrigerators and radios.

DRAFT REVIEW WORK SHEET

Audience Analysis of Two Newspapers

Writer: _____   Reviewer: _____

1. Does the writer tell you enough about the newspapers so that you get a good sense of what the papers are like? Does the writer sound as though he or she knows the papers well?

2. Does the writer quote from the newspapers? Do the quotations help you sense the "flavor" of the newspapers?

3. Describe the writer's organizational strategy paragraph by paragraph. Is there any point where the structure becomes unclear?

4. Does the paper contain a clear thesis statement? If not, is the writer's final judgment about the newspapers clear?

5. Note every point in the paper where you were temporarily confused. Explain two such places here.

6. What changes in spelling, grammar, or punctuation would you suggest?

7. What is your most important suggestion for revision?

NEWSPAPER COMPARISON PAPER

¹ What is the first thing about newspaper that catches your eye? Is it the title, the pictures or the front headline? In choosing my seconf newspaper for this report it happened to be all three. "The Sun" happened to hit me as an uplifting title. One of the first headlines read, "Boogieing with the Bird", corresponding with a color picture of the Oriole mascot dancing with one of the cheerleaders.

² Another picture was one of a dirty little boy with a sad look on his face, standing next to an older sad looking man. This was also in color. Both had enough pathoes in them to make anyone want to read the articals which were found on the next page.

³ This is an example of how the editors figure that they will sell the paper. They definitly want to catch attention through the appeal of pictures. It seems to me that the editors believe that it is pictures that sell the paper, being that the two pictures on the front page are the only colored ones in the whole newspaper. To go on, the fact that there thirty-seven photographs, more than half the number of articles, we could assume that the editors also believe that pictures tell a better story. The pictures show and tell quite a bit about the story. There are detailed shots of what the story behind them is about.

⁴ In compairing this to another newspaper, the Seattle Post Intellegencer, this is quite the opposite. This paper has a total of sixty-three articles to a mere twenty-three photographs, which out of all, only has one colored picture in the last section. Maybe the editors of the Intellegencer believe that a paper should be just what the title suggests, to intelligize the readers, "cutting the crap" and getting straingt to the point.

⁵ This assumption can also be pointed out through the big difference of advertisements and coupons in both papers. The Sun has a total of 105 advertising ads, almost twice as many as the Intellegencer, with a total of sixty. In spite of this difference though, there is no way that anyone looking through these ads could not possibly notice that computors are the most popular item on the market today.

⁶ Computor ads rank highest of all other, especially in the business and finance section, which happens to be the thickest section in The Sun. There are nineteen articles in this paper which out does the Intelligencer by ten articles. Besides the nineteen articles, there are four pages of stock information. I would say that Baltimore is a much more business orientated city than Seattle just by the amount of information that is put in the paper. Also I find it interesting that the food and liesure section of The Sun, is considerably thinner than the same section in the Intellegencer. In this paper, there are only five articles and the rest of the pages are coupons and advertising. The Intellegencer's section is the thickest of all the other sections. The only colored picture in the paper is on the front page of this section. It has twenty articles consisting of cooking tips, recipes, and a few articles on

cooking traditions in other countries. I think this is very interesting and shows a treat deal just where the people of Seattle, Wash. and the people of Baltimore, Md. place their interests.

7 As far as the sports go, I think every newspaper has sufficient information and more on our beloved sports. The Sun only has six more articles than the Intellegencer has. Both only cover very local information on local teams. The reason for more articles in The Sun, might account for the success that the Maryland Baltimore Oriols have had in past seasons. Also the fact that one-fourth of the sports page was the Business section, limits the amount of space that the sports can use.

8 Local reports in Maryland are also half as much higher than in the Seattle paper. This is most likely the case because Baltimore is an industrial and highly populated city. It is understandable that there be alot of local information. In Seattle education seems to be a prime matter being that three out of eight articles deal with Seattle public schools. One could assume without knowing anythin about Seattle, that it is a small city. If it weren't for the classified ads in this section, Local would be a single sheet of paper. (The classified ads are six pages of cars and other items for sale including one and a half pages of job openings. This fact can also lead to saying that Seattle is a smaller, less populated, and less business orientated city than Baltimore with nine pages of classified ads and four of those being job openings, mostly for conputor processors and programmers.)

9 This now leaves us with world political issues which range just about the same in both of the papers. This topic in the front page section of the papers seems to have less articles that any other section. The current topics are brief but well covered. I did notice, though that not one of the articles, in either of the papers, was put as as headline. This tells me that these papers are both basically local papers cobering limited amount of matters outside their own territory.

10 Just by examing the style and content of the papers it can become a little obvious that they are from two cities in two different parts of the country. One, Seattle, being from the Northwestern part, where leisure time, food, and sports, seems to be the main interest of the people, and Baltimore, the home of the Orioles and the dwelling of the big businesses.

DRAFT REVIEW WORK SHEET

Audience Analysis of a Magazine

Writer: _____   Reviewer: _____

1. What does the writer attempt to do in the introduction to the paper? Does the introduction provide the background you need to understand the analysis that follows? *#1 Discussing book - no*
#2 - Describe aud. yes
#3 Describes purpose - yes

2. Do the facts and quotations cited help you sense the "flavor" of the magazine? Which quotation captures the flavor best? What single piece of information in the paper are you most likely to remember a week from now?
#1 - no quotes - somewhat
#2 - many quotes - details - fillers
#3 many quotes - war info

3. Did the writer draw at least four distinct inferences from the facts found in the magazine? List the inferences you find.
#1 yes -
#2 yes -
#3 yes

4. What is the writer's overall opinion of the magazine? How do you know?
#1 Not clear
#2 Same as writers
#3 Interesting - details / inferences Thoughtful

5. Does your reading get tedious at any point? Specify where.

6. Do you have any suggestions for improving spelling, punctuation, or grammar?

7. How has reading this paper given you a new perspective on the paper you are working on yourself?

1 Think of a boat that goes sixty miles an hour, reads depth level, P. H. content, oxygen level, and water temperature. It is a sleek, streamlined boat with cushioned seats high on pedestals, wall to wall carpeting and aerated live-wells to keep fish alive. It sounds like a biologist's dream, but actually it is a modern day bass fisherman's boat.

2 I found that today's bass fisherman has to be a fairly intelligent individ-ual. Many articles describe how to use different gauges and contour maps to paint a precise picture of a lake in scientific terms. Moon phases and barometric pressure must also be considered. Tables show oxygen level, water temperature and P.H. level that bass prefer. Learning and knowing these things among others they suggest, will greatly increase your catch.

3 There seems to be an ever growing number of professional bass fisher-man, some of whom make over fifty thousand a year. These men fish two or three day tournaments which are held by the organization who publishes this magazine. These tournaments are featured in the magazine with the writer describing how every fish was caught.

4 Other articles describe new artificial lures, boating products and fishing rods. One soft plastic lure is described as being mushy and flexible like a frog, fooling the bass into holding the lure and enabling the fisherman to set the hook. Another lure is computerized, has a battery pack and runs on its own on top of the water like an injured minnow.

5 Bass fisherman seem to be away from home quite a bit pursuing the sport of fishing. In every edition of the magazine, there is a story on the escapades of two fictitious characters named Harry and Charlie. They are two die-hard bass fisherman who are "good ole boys" from the South. Their wives are always nagging them to stay home. It seems their every free moment is spent fishing or making plans to sneak out and go fishing. On one occasion, they are in the local beer joint after unsuccessfully trying to launch their boat because of a large crowd at the boat ramp. At the beer joint, they connive a plan to get their "old ladies" to let them go away to a secluded fishing spot. While chewing tobacco and drinking beer, they realize they are going to have to bring the "old ladies" along. They decide to tell them it is a second honeymoon. As things turn out, Harry's wife catches a huge bass and puts Harry to shame. Stories with Harry and Charlie of this nature are in every issue. I suppose most bass fishermen identify with these stories.

6 Bass fishermen, in general, are somewhat intelligent and spend quite a deal of money on fishing and boating equipment. If they are exceptionally good at fishing, they can make a lot of money. Above all, they must stay flexible, innovative and try new lures and techniques. They must also make fairly good money since the average boat seems to cost around six thousand dollars. However, there are ways to bass fish without a great deal of invest-ment. One might consider buying a small, inexpensive aluminum boat or even fishing off of the bank of the lake or river. Less area can be covered like this but this is precisely how many young children get started.

7 In conclusion, one thing all fishermen have in common is that they spend a great deal of their time fishing because it is a time consuming sport by nature.

DRAFT REVIEW WORK SHEET

Study of a Historical Issue

Writer: _____   Reviewer: _____

1. A writer promises to do something. What does the writer promise to do in this piece of writing? Where is the promise made? Does the writer keep the promise?

2. Read over the introductory paragraph again. Does it introduce the subject adequately? Does it attract your interest? How? Read over the concluding paragraph. What emotion does the writer try to leave you with? Can you make any suggestions for improving either the introduction or the conclusion?

3. Describe the paper's organizational strategy, paragraph by paragraph. Is there any point where the structure becomes unclear?

4. Does the writer use quotations well? How well do they contribute to and support the thesis of the paper? Do any sections of the paper need more quotations for support? Where would you like more information?

5. Can you recognize the writer's voice, the writer's *ethos,* throughout the paper? In which sections does the writer sound more like an encyclopedia?

6. Are there any changes you would suggest in spelling, punctuation, or grammar?

7. After reading this paper, what thoughts do you, as an intelligent, caring reader, have about this topic? How has reading this paper affected your thoughts?

JOHN KENNEDY

[1] Presidential candidates are often charged with changing faces in different parts of the country. This was a major accusation of Jimmy Carter during his run for the Presidency. I am going to focus on four speeches given by Senator Kennedy during his campaign against Vice President Nixon.

[2] Kennedy—on vacation after the Democratic convention nominated him as their Presidential candidate—chose three men to head top slots in the campaign, Byron R. White, John M. Bailey, and J. Leonard Reinsch. Kennedy and his staff were planning campaign schedules, trying to decide if they should open the campaign on Labor Day with a speech in Cadillac Square, Detroit, as other Democratic Presidential nominees had done (New York Times, July 21, 1960).

[3] Kennedy did open his campaign with a Labor Day speech in Cadillac Square, Detroit (New York Times, September 6, 1960). The crowd was enthusiastic and his first phrase would label the theme of his administration the new frontier, "I have come today from Alaska, America's last frontier, to Michigan to state the case for America's new frontier." He mentions his endorsement from the A.F. of L.-C.I.O. and asks labor for their support. While he was discussing the economy he brought up a figure dealing with car production, in this car producing city of Detroit. He stated that the President had said, on August 10, that we had a fine year in automobile sales even though a few years ago we produced 1,500,000 more cars than this year.

[4] In this speech, given on November 1, in Philadelphia's Convention Hall there was a confident Kennedy speaking (New York Times, November 2, 1960). During this campaign, Kennedy and Nixon held four television debates in which Kennedy appeared as an able and capable leader. Today these debates are considered major turning points for Kennedy. He started this speech with this comment, "This, unfortunately, is not the fifth debate, but I am glad to be here and have a chance to express my views on this occasion, and I wish the Vice President could have arranged his schedule to do likewise tonight." He went on with promises for School Equality and for Fair Farm Prices. This was to try to get votes from strong Republican midwestern States. He warned Americans that Russia was spreading communism through Asia and Africa by sending diplomats well versed in the language and customs of the country they were being sent. He said in 1958 our ambassador to Moscow was the only United States ambassador to a communist country who knew the language of the country to which he was assigned. He brought the idea of the Peace Corps, young men and women trained in skills and taught the language and customs of the country they will be assigned. Kennedy was emhasizing the importance of learning foreign languages, in his speech he quoted Goethe, "A man who is ignorant of foreign languages is ignorant of his own." This emphasis on language

was peculiar because Kennedy did not speak foreign languages. In <u>Conversations</u> <u>with</u> <u>Kennedy</u> Ben Bradlee noted that once during a French embassy dinner at the White House talk around the table was all French and he had a difficult time. Bradlee said that Kennedy spoke French with a Cuban accent.

5 In his last two speeches in San Francisco and Chicago had the similar promises of the first two (<u>New</u> <u>York</u> <u>Times</u>, November 3 and November 5, 1960). In San Francisco he again attacked the administration for letting the United States fall behind Russia. In Chicago he told the audience that Mr. Nixon was running not Mr. Eisenhauer. He urges for Social Security with a Medical Care Plan taoted on. The farming issue came up again with Kennedy stating that the administration had driven income down and this caused nearly 11,000 people to lose work in Illinois.

6 Speeches during a Presidential election don't have much substance. Their purpose is to gain votes and stir emotion. Senator Kennedy did give moving speeches, his most memorable speech was his inaugural address. The debates served a greater service to voters than individual speeches. The two answered the same questions and the public could decide which was the most capable. The speeches bring an old cliche, easier said than done.

DRAFT REVIEW WORK SHEET
Character Sketch

Writer:_____   Reviewer:_____

1. Does the interview you just read make the person interviewed seem simple or complex? Too simple? Too complex? Explain.

2. The most effective interviewers let their subjects tell their stories in their own words. Which quotation in this paper best helps you understand the personality of the person interviewed. Point out any sections of the paper where the writer needs to add quoted material.

3. Does the writer include enough commentary and background information to show that he or she is in control of the material? Or has the writer allowed the person interviewed to do all the talking?

4. Has the writer grouped material into paragraphs of reasonable length? Find a paragraph that you think is either too long or too short, and explain why you think so.

5. How does the writer's introduction convince you that the person interviewed is worthy of your attention? How does the writer conclude? What is your last impression of the person interviewed, and does it seem consistent with the writer's point of view?

6. Are there any questions that you think the writer should go back and ask the person interviewed?

7. Do you have any suggestions for improving grammar or punctuation?

8. What is your most important suggestion for revision?

INTERVIEW WITH JOHN MORQUAY

1 He wasn't much to look at. In fact, if there was any athletic ability in this aging man, it was very difficult to detect. He was a jockey, or still is, depending on who you are talking to. A small man of about fifty who grew up around the track and made horse racing his life. His name is John Morquay.

2 John was born of Hispanic origin, but raised in America. The deep South to be exact. He was raised in an impoverished environment where his father worked some 12 hours a day at a local racetrack. John's father had a big influence on his son. Often he would say, "You will have it better than me, John. Cleaning stables is no life for a son of mine." It was hard for a young boy like John to see his father working so hard for nothing. When he would accompany his father to the track, he would notice all the jockeys in their fine satin riding suits. This is when he decided that racing was to be the life for him.

3 As he grew older, he moved from exercise boy to apprentice rider. He was a small boy, but very agile and learned to be aggressive when he rode. "This," he said, "was what owners and trainers liked to see. A rider who was aggressive but who also knew when to be patient in a race." These skills John acquired quickly and with his knowledge he soon became well-liked. All that was left for him was to finish his apprenticeship. At the age of 18 he was a full fledged jockey at the racetrack near where he grew up.

4 The next 10 years of John's life were spent riding the circuit in Florida, South Carolina, North Carolina, and Georgia. This is the period in his life that he says is the most important. He grew up not only physically, but mentally as well. He saw the hardships and realities of life. Moralistic values were set and he found himself maturing to the point where he was his own man. He mentioned morals specifically because John was an honest man and looked with disfavor on corruption. Corruption, however, is what he saw. It would be no great surprise to be told of races being fixed or horses being drugged to make them run faster. These illegal activities surprisingly shocked John very much. John's father protected him from seeing these things when he was younger, but this sheltering proved harmful as he became older. Now he had to make a choice. There was good money to be made by fixing a race, but on the other hand, there were many risks involved. John heard of jockeys losing their licenses to race and even going to jail. He knew he could not participate in these shadey operations because for the first time in his life, he was going to plan for his future, to look ahead.

5 At the age of 26, John had taken a wife. He fathered two children, a girl and a boy. Having saved a good deal of money, he decided to move up North. He did not want his children growing up in the same environment as he did. It was time for a change. New York was the place to go. Bigger tracks, more money, and greater exposure were also some reasons for moving.

6 Some twenty years later it happened. What John likes to call his midlife crisis. That fear of getting old. His racing ability was slipping. He now had to rely on his cleverness and years of experience to combat the physical powers of younger jockeys. To compound his troubles there was a divorce. As with all separations of marriage there are many feelings and emotions that need to be dealt with. Since his children had already grown up and left home, he decided to get away, to take a year off from racing and collect himself. Well, one year grew to another and he had not raced in all this time. He had some money saved, but was growing bored with the apathetic life he was now leading. He needed the thrill of racing again, the competition, the danger. But how could he get his now soft body back into racing shape, and if he could, did he still have what it takes to win? These are questions he still asks himself.

7 It is hard to say whether he can do it or not. Sitting here talking with him, I get the feeling he will try, that he's not a quitter, that there's still fight left in him. It will be interesting to see whether he makes it or not. As for myself, I am <u>betting</u> on it.

Good conclusion

Topic too broad — narrow conclude more quotes

DRAFT REVIEW WORK SHEET

Film Evaluation

Writer:_____   Reviewer:_____

1. Can you tell from the introduction of this paper whether the writer considers the film an effective, persuasive film or not?

2. Does the writer examine the film's *logos, ethos,* and *pathos*? Which is examined most superficially?

3. Is there enough evidence in the paper to substantiate the writer's opinion? Which evidence of the writer's do you find most persuasive?

4. Describe the paper's organizational strategy, paragraph by paragraph. Is there any point where the structure becomes unclear?

5. Do you feel you understand the film better now than you did before you read this paper? What is the most interesting thing you learned about film technique?

6. Do you have any suggestions for improving grammar or punctuation?

7. How has reading this paper given you a new perspective on the paper you are working on yourself?

FUTURE SHOCK

[1] Future shock, according to the film, is the disorientation of society, with respect to its values and customs, caused by too much change occurring too quickly. The film also calls this the premature arrival of the future. Some important questions are raised. Where is society headed? What will happen to our family structure? Will we be able to cope with having to choose between an increasing number of alternatives?

[2] Orson Welles, dressed conservatively in a dark suit and overcoat, is in contrast to the idea of the film. He stands out as permanent and reassuring in a film that depicts society as transcient and chaotic. The film begins by showing two people walking through a park. This scene is intermittently interrupted by flashes of riot, war scenes, and anguished faces, immediately capturing the viewer's imagination. The two lovers are but robots as seen when the telescopic lens of the camera sucks their eyes into the screen. They are not eyes but silicon chips.

[3] Welles appears in the next scene, looking sober and reassuring, to drop the bombshell. We are experiencing future shock. Throughout the film he is dressed like a priest on Sunday evening and he delivers the same message. Damnation. There is no escape for we have to maintain our technological growth. Everyone else moves hurriedly while Welles takes deliberately slow strides. He remains alarmingly calm, and this strikes me as strange. With all the chaos around, riots of the 1960's and anti-war demonstrations, he is too unconcerned. If he was caught up in this rush the film would have been even more believable.

[4] The film exploits contrasts well. Welles is shown at his friend's country home which represents tranquility while he talks of our doom. In the end a baby's face is followed by an old man's, depicting our susceptibility to the element time. This film makes us lean in favor of its point of view.

[5] The film has some valid arguments that it exaggerates to prove that future shock exists. It may be true that we cannot comprehend all the new facts scientists present to us. We are shown a parallel view of a few books then an upward view and finally one that is almost vertical that makes us feel overwhelmed.

[6] Society is projected as having lost its admiration for permanence. A little girl is shown trading her old doll for a new one that talks. The family is shown moving and the new doll is left behind once again.

[7] The film shows a couple arguing and this is blamed on the stress placed on them by a technologically advancing world. The film never shows loving times between these two people. What can our good times be attributed to? Surely not the stress. For this and other reasons the argument is slanted. There are millions of people who cope with and enjoy the changes brought about by technology. I, for one, enjoy not having to do tedious manual calculations, thanks to my affordable calculator.

DRAFT REVIEW WORK SHEET
Proposal

Writer: _____   Reviewer: _____

1. Does the writer make you feel that the problem is significant? What examples, illustrations, or statistics does he or she use to convince you? If there are not enough facts, how could the writer research this issue more thoroughly?

2. Will the author's suggested solution work? Why or why not? What is one way it might break down?

3. What about the writer's *ethos*? Is the writer an "expert" on the subject? Has the writer been fair to the other side?

4. What are two possible objections that the writer has not taken into consideration? If you were in the position of power, would this proposal make you take action? What priority would you give it?

5. Describe the paper's organizational strategy, paragraph by paragraph. Is there any point where the structure becomes unclear?

6. What is your most important suggestion for revision?

To Whom It May Concern:*

¹ This letter is written in behalf of myself, a personal property owner in Huntington Village since 1968, although its contents may affect most of the other 308 owners, who I suspect will not wish maltreatment in the callous and unethical manner that I was. I request—no, I demand—the opportunity to appear at the Huntington Village Community Association Board of Directors next meeting to present my grievance and receive answers to my questions. I provide the following details in advance so that you may reasonably prepare your responses, a consideration that was denied me.

² On 24 March 1982 an employee of your nursery contractor ruthlessly and effectively cut off at the ground seven mature and living but dormant butterfly bushes that paralleled the rear fence of my property. He was merely executing orders and I have no grievance with that man. In my effort to determine responsibility, however, that night the Architecture Committee chief confided that she was the one responsible. I pursued several direct questions, to which I insist I am entitled to a reasonable answer. The first question was why my bushes were cut down. I was informed that, in accordance with the publicized Herald of September/October 1981, they were not "my" bushes if they were outside the fence. I do not challenge that technical point further at this time, but I suggest it has suspect legality. Proceeding on, I asked why these particular bushes were removed; she provided three plausible reasons. First, home owners have been planting on common ground bushes and trees that are not compatible with Huntington Village decor and that violate public and personal rights; this assessment is a factual one but it is inapplicable in my case, since my bushes were planted there by the Huntington Village developer in 1968, with some frail bushes subsequently having been replaced by me. The second reason given was that many bushes in Huntington Village are eyesores and detract from the community decor; if that be the case, and I seriously doubt that it is the sole reason, why then has it taken thirteen years for someone (?) to decide their unacceptability? And why were mine the only offensive butterfly bushes? (More on this subject later.) The third reason given was that some overhanging bushes interfere with the mowing of lawns by contractor personnel; in my humble opinion, anyone who endorses that it is right to destroy living plants for the convenience of lawnmowing or other similar activity has a peculiar sense of values. I STILL DO NOT KNOW WHY MY BUSHES WERE DESTROYED. My second question was what would now be done to correct the horrible eyesore created by the removal of the bushes; you are invited to examine the ugly brown fence (standard for Huntington Village, when not partially hidden by foliage), the dead grassed area and the tree stumps which were previously hidden. The initial answer was that nothing more will be done;

---

* This time I've included a letter written by a condominium owner rather than a student paper because it offers so much to comment on.

eventually, though, she acknowledged that sod may be brought in and the stumps removed. My third question pertains to an aspect of this entire experience that is by far the most distressing. Why was this heinous act perpetuated without even the decency to notify me that something was allegedly unacceptable and that corrective action was imminent? She will have to provide you her own rationale, since I do <u>not</u> want to misquote what she told me.

³ In my subsequent inspection of Huntington Village, and you can believe I have made a thorough one, I found that the dormant butterfly bushes to the rear of my fence and two of them across the roadway at the playground (along Clover Road) were decapitated on 24 March. I found that <u>green</u> bushes along Clover Road were <u>not</u> touched. I found a proliferation of dormant butterfly bushes along other property in Oxford and Cambridge Courts which were <u>not</u> touched. I have found <u>no</u> other evidence of "corrective surgery." I come to the inescapable conclusion that for some reason I have been selected for discrimination, and I don't really appreciate it one bit!

⁴ I do not deny the need for community standards, nor do I challenge the Board's responsibilities and rights for correction of deficiencies and nuisances. In the discharge of those functions I would trust that my Board would perform in a reasonable and legal and professional manner.

⁵ The following facts apply:

1. I have incurred damages, both tangible and intangible. The destruction of the bushes, whoever's they may have been, constitutes a loss in immediate resale value of my property. The eyesore newly created has a deleterious effect on all Huntington Village property, for that matter. The removal of the bushes denies my family the degree of privacy formerly provided by those bushes blocking the spaces in the alternately-slatted fence. This whole unsavory and uncompassionate experience has caused extreme mental anguish to my family.

2. This entire experience, with all applicable acts, has been highly selective in nature and prejudicial against one person: me.

3. Common and uncommon criminals such as Charles Manson and John Hinckley are accorded rights that insure they be confronted by their accusers, be informed of alleged indiscretions, be properly judged and then, and only then, be punished if found guilty. I have been deprived of comparable rights. I am waiting for someone to inform me of my alleged indiscretions (property nuisance features, if that be the case) that have warranted the premature and unwarned corrective/destructive action against me, for which the Board is responsible.

⁶ Lastly, I will not tolerate a recurrence of this selective maltreatment, nor do I wish to witness similar wanton actions against my fellow neighbors.

DRAFT REVIEW WORK SHEET

Persuading a Classmate to Consider an Issue Further

Writer: _____   Review: _____

1. What, judging from this paper, is the point of view of the classmate whom this writer is trying to persuade? What is the point of view of the writer? If you are the person to whom this paper is directed, has the writer succeeded in changing your mind at all?

2. Does the writer use a variety of sources of information? Does the writer seem well-informed about the issue? Note here some remark made that seems to be superficial.

3. Describe the paper's organizational strategy, paragraph by paragraph. Did you get lost anywhere as you read? Note every point in the paper where you were temporarily confused. Explain two such places here.

4. How would you characterize this writer's *ethos*. Cite examples from the paper to explain your characterization.

5. What uses does the writer make of *pathos*? Do you find them effective?

6. Do you have any suggestions for improving grammar or punctuation?

7. How has reading this paper given you a new perspective on the paper you are working on yourself?

PERSUASION PAPER: ABORTION

1 During my interview with Bridgette Duncan I became immediately aware that she was Pro-Abortion. It seems as though she views abortion as a legal matter instead of a moral issue. Bridgette feels emotionally that "If a law was passed making abortion illegal, I feel it would take away control of myself." Intellectually she feels, "That the individual should have complete freedom over her body, a government cannot dictate rules over a person." She feels threatened to lose other personal choices, she does'nt want to lose her freedom (control over her body).

2 Bridgette feels abortion should remain legal due to its tie with individual choice. She gets most of her information from television news programs, and an author named Ayn Rand who publishes books on individualism. Being an Atheist she is not swayed either way by religion. Medically she is not sure of the point of viability, but she assumes it begins at birth. She argues for the rights of women believing that the fetus is merely a part of the woman's body, the body which she is free to control.

3 Wanting the freedom to control one's body is understandable. Yet do women really control their own bodies? If a woman could actually control her bodily functions she would not be faced with the dilemma of unwanted pregnancy. A thought which probably runs through the minds of these women is quoted:

> This is somehow unthinkable if you have not planned to be pregnant, and especially if you've never been pregnant before. It is YOUR body, known, familiar; you realize in an almost abstract way that it is equipped for pregnancy, but the idea that it should suddenly begin to function in this strange and unfamiliar way without your willing or intending it seems utterly unreasonable. How can it happen to you?[1]

4 A woman who is unexpectedly pregnant has three options. She can have the baby and keep it, she can have it and surrender it—temporarily to foster care or permanently to adoption. Getting a legal abortion is a relatively new option for most women in the U.S. But it has been defined specifically as a right by the U.S. Supreme Court in 1973.

5 The three methods are: D&C, vacuum aspiration and saline method. Up to the twelfth week of pregnancy a D&C short for dilation and curettage can be performed. The process includes dilating the cervix wide enough to accept a curette, a rod shaped instrument with a sharp spoon edge. The doctor then scrapes the walls of the uterus. A new method called vacuum aspiration is more widely used. A small tube which connects with a vacuum aspirator is inserted to empty the uterus. Both procedures take less than ten minutes and books say they are painless. On the contrary women I've spoken with report that local anesthetics do not work, and the procedure can be painful. Complications do occur. For instance, many times after examining the fetal tissue not all parts are located and the procedure must be performed consecutively until all parts are identified. The other method available is for aborting a fetus. A saline abortion, commonly known as

salting out, is performed between the sixteenth and twentieth weeks of pregnancy. A saline abortion must be performed in a hospital, it carries seven times more risk than an early abortion and is unquestionably more expensive. With a long hypodermic needle the doctor removes some amniotic fluid and replaces it with a saline solution. Sometime after, between five hours and two days the uterus begins to contract as in labor and the contractions continue until the uterus pushes out the fetal and placental material.

6 Saline abortions are extremely expensive and dangerous. A friend of mine experienced this horrible encounter. She was put into a private hospital and ended up staying there five days due to complications. The doctor first attempted a D&C but soon realized she was too far gone. He then induced labor with a saline solution. Complications arose, the patient needed blood transfusions and remained under close watch for five days. That was the first in a series of abortions for her. Why young women torture themselves along with the baby inside them is beyond me. Birth control is widely available, but rarely used.

7 Contraception and premarital sex are no longer taboo. Sex education is provided in most public schools and there are 188 Planned Parenthood affiliates in 43 states and the District of Columbia plus they operate some 700 clinics. Their help and consultation is free.[2]

8 Although contraception helps to prevent pregnancies it is not infallible. Unplanned pregnancies do occur. Abortion is now one alternative, yet many others do exist. Being a moral issue, abortion is a very controversial topic. Yet it has legal aspects. Who should play God? Should we have enough legal rights concerning our own bodies to do away with the living fetus within? The point of viability is yet to be discovered, but a child is recognizable early in the embryonic tissue.

9 Besides abortion there are the other choices such as adoption. Statistics show that it is very hard to adopt. For each baby available there are fifteen to twenty applicants who must wait anywhere from five to seven years.[3] Adoption benefits all three parties; the mother, baby and adopting parents.

10 For years we managed without legalizing abortion. If birth control use would rise and those fighting for the right to control their bodies in fact learned to control themselves, perhaps the rate of unplanned pregnancies would drop and along with it the need for legal abortions.

ENDNOTES

[1] Planned parenthood, Abortion: A Women's Guide (New York: Abelard-Schuman LTD., 1973.)

2 "   "

[3] Bates & Zawadski, Criminal Abortion (Springfield, Illinois, Charles C. Thomas, 1964.)

Also, two personal interviews.

Reviewing the sample papers above is designed to prepare you for reviewing the papers of your classmates. Reviewing each other's work can be done in at least two very useful ways.

The first is to have writers read their drafts aloud to each other. (Reading aloud makes a writer aware of changes she'd like to make even before her readers suggest any.) Reviewers should listen carefully and then:

1. Simply explain to the writer what they think she did in her paper.

2. Tell the writer one or two things from her paper that they're likely to remember a week from now.

3. Give the writer two or three pieces of advice about improving the paper. The writer wants to think that she's finished, but she knows in her heart that she's not.

After trying this technique the first time, each writer should explain to the reviewer what she thinks about, and how she feels about, the advice she's been given. This exchange is often awkward the first time, but if it's not done, reviewers don't learn to judge whether their comments are being helpful or hurtful to the writers. Your comments should soon become helpful if you remember that a reviewer's job is to be a *generous* critic. The reviewer's aim is to help make the writer's final work be the best it can be.

The second kind of reviewing is both quicker and more thorough, though it lacks one important advantage: it doesn't require writers to read their work aloud. In this second method of review, you work with your classmates' drafts much as you worked with the sample papers in this chapter. On an assigned day, you bring a draft to class and exchange drafts with a classmate. Using a draft review work sheet, you read through the paper and make comments which will help the writer improve. If time permits, you can repeat this process with two or three papers, and your own paper will get two or three readings. You'll probably get several ideas for your own paper just by reading the papers of others, and you'll also be able to take home two or three pages of comments which you can consider as you revise.

Of course, you're not bound to take all the advice that you get. *You* are responsible for your final decisions, and you may have reasons for disagreeing with some of the advice that you get. But even if you disagree, the comments from your reviewers will aid you in rethinking your paper, which is the purpose of revision. And ultimately, the goal of all this reading and rereading is not only to give you sources of advice but to make you a better reviewer of your own work—now, later in college, and as you write in your profession. Having become someone else's reviewer, someone else's reader, you should now be readier to become your own.

*   *   *   *   *

Guidelines for Revision

When you revise, you attend not only to the major issues—adequacy of facts, thoughtfulness of inferences, clarity of organization, helpfulness of the introduction and conclusion—mentioned in the work sheets but also to many "smaller" points that will help you to cleanse and clarify your work, often improving your work from solid to distinguished. The items listed below (roughly in order of importance) are items that you'll want to check each time you revise. In fact, you won't think about them every time (you won't have the chance), but many of them will become part of your intuitive revising process.

1. Make reading as easy as possible for your reader by organizing your work clearly.

   - Make sure your introduction makes clear your sense of direction and your conclusion answers the question "So what?"

   - Check your organization by doing a paragraph outline of your paper to see whether it moves systematically.

   - Check the opening sentences in your paragraphs. Not all paragraphs need a topic sentence, but the first sentence should at least hint at the paragraph's direction of movement.

   - Give your reader the results of your research, not a record of it. Take out references to what you are doing. Just do it. Skip words like those underlined below:

     > There is a distinct difference between *professional* and *amateur*. First of all, I will give you my definitions for *professional* and *amateur*. A professional is a person that . . .

     > I'm reporting on a movie that real movie hawks will enjoy the technical effects of.

     > The best inference I can think of is that Baton Rouge parents care about their children.

   - Check that you've used all your inferences to make worthwhile comments. Don't waste your reader's time or lose your reader's respect with inferences like that underlined below:

     > Forty-five percent of the voters polled felt that the worst possible punishment for a crime is the death penalty. Fifty-five percent felt that a life sentence without parole is an even worse punishment than death. These opinions vary to some extent.

   - Read through your draft to make sure that it reads "smoothly." (Recall Exercise 6-5.)

- Parallel structure makes any similar set of ideas easier for a reader to comprehend.

Confused	Clear
Keith, my nephew, was only 13, skied like he was born on the slopes, fast, fluid, and he never fell.	Keith, my 13-year-old nephew, skied as if he was born on the slopes—he was fast, he was fluid, and he never fell.
The happiest moments in my life were getting married and having two kids, then see my two kids graduated from high school and college.	The happiest moments in my life were getting married, having two kids, and seeing my two kids graduated from high school and college.

- Make sure you've made your transitions in thought clear to your reader—often a simple "but" can help signal a contrast and make reading your work easier.

2. Identify for your reader the people, terms, and times that you want to talk about.

- Don't leave your reader stranded in time or space. Specify, near the beginning of your work, where and when the events you are talking about took place.

Confused	Clear
John Llewellen Lewis dominated the United Mine Workers for half the union's life.	John L. Lewis, an Iowa and Illinois miner, dominated the United Mine Workers from 1933 to 1960, more than half the union's life.

- Identify any wars or speeches or documents or organizations you refer to.

Confused	Clear
Chiang Kai-shek led the Kuomintang.	Chiang Kai-shek led the Kuomintang, a party founded by Dr. Sun Yat-sen in 1911 and challenged by the Communist party only after 1930.

- Define terms that the reader may be unfamiliar with.

Confused	Clear
Dr. Sun's party didn't appeal to Chinese peasants because	Dr. Sun's party didn't appeal to Chinese peasants because

most of his lieutenants were from Canton.	most of his lieutenants were from Canton, a rich coastal province with several large cities.

- Don't define terms that readers can be expected to understand. There is no need, for example, in an article for adults about birth control practices, to stop and define *conception*.

- Use a person's name the first time you refer to him or her in any paragraph. After that, you can switch to a short form of the name or to *he* or *she*.

Confused	Clear
In 1966, *he* gained new popularity in *his* party, and *he* entered the bid for the 1968 presidential nomination. To alter *his* reputation as a political loser, *Nixon* countered with a strategy aimed at settling the nomination in a series of presidential primaries. *He* won the first victory in New Hampshire easily. After *Nixon* had won most of the primaries, Governors Nelson Rockefeller of New York and Ronald Reagan of California entered the contest, but it was too late.	In 1966, *Nixon* gained new popularity in *his* party, and *he* entered the bid for the 1968 presidential nomination. To alter *his* reputation as a political loser, *he* countered with a strategy aimed at settling the nomination in a series of presidential primaries. *He* won the first victory in New Hampshire easily. After *he* had won most of the primaries, Governors Nelson Rockefeller of New York and Ronald Reagan of California entered the contest, but it was too late.

3. Be specific.
   - Don't leave details to the readers' imaginations.

     When stopped at the light at the intersection of Quesada and Dodge Streets, a driver could see <u>all kinds of interesting things going on</u> through the open windows of the hotel.

   Often in revision you'll see that you need more details. You may have written an error-free paper, but you haven't given us a clear picture of your subject.

   - Even when you're generalizing, make sure your statements are specific enough to be comprehensible.

     <u>It's funny how many different kinds of things there are of one thing.</u>

> Keats achieves this by organizing the subject matter in a certain order and comparing it with something else.

> Working at the Jersey City Medical Center was certainly an experience in itself.

More thought is all that's necessary to make these phrases more specific. Many writers, for example, have a fondness for unfocused words like the pronoun *this* or the noun *thing*:

> The thing of it is, if you're onto a thing, it becomes a priority.

When you're tempted to use the word *thing,* remember the following advice:

> The Thing was a movie made in the 1950s, starring James Arness as a monster with the cellular structure of a giant carrot. Only use the word thing to refer to the carrot or to the movie (in which case it is capitalized and underlined). If you use the word thing in your papers, your teacher will substitute the word carrot. If the sentence then makes sense, you are correct. (King)

• Make your verbs as specific as you can. There are quite a few "easy" verbs in English—*go, make, have, do,* for example—that don't tax the writer's mind when they're used and that don't, therefore, engage the reader's mind. When you search for a stronger verb, you're in fact searching for a more specific verb.

> books we did in class

> books we read in class [more specific]

> books we studied in class [still more specific]

• Learn the names for items you want to talk about. If you start talking to me about "the object blocking the tube when the tube was shaken" and you're really talking about a *cork,* I'm going to lose interest in the way you write. We all should be working constantly to expand our vocabularies, not so much to SAT words like *ineffable* and *callow* as to the names of everyday objects. Do you know what a mullion is, or a sill, a baseboard, a wainscot, or a socket? Do you know that a leather hat with a "thing sticking out" is a leather hat with a *visor*? Do you know the difference between asphalt tile and cedar shingles? between macadam and an oiled road? between elms and oaks and hickories?

• Not all specifics are interesting. Details from which no useful or appropriate inferences can be drawn lie heavy on the page if they appear in too much abundance.

The scoreboard can also be seen from any part of the field and keeps the time, the score, the down, the quarter, time-outs, the number of yards to go, and what yard the ball is on.

These are boring, not telling, facts; the reader asks, So what? But because our tendency to generalize is so strong, it is rare that we go wrong like this when trying to write specifically.

4. "Tighten" your writing until only the important words, phrases, and sentences remain.

Loose	Tight
There is a certain unfairness in that.	That's unfair.
A waiter can tell by the customers' actions and body language that they are impatient.	A waiter can tell by the customers' body language that they are impatient.

Every word, phrase, and sentence must earn its place, usually with the meaning it adds, but sometimes also by how it helps emphasis, rhythm, or grace. One way to get yourself to be more careful when you revise is to force yourself to cut by one-quarter, or one-third, or some other arbitrary figure (*this doesn't mean cutting out telling details*). Often your boss or your editor will do this cutting for you. It's excellent discipline, and it will lead you to making many qualitative, not just quantitative, decisions.

The following is an outstanding exercise in tightening, adapted from Ken Macrorie's *Telling Writing* (60).

Exercise 11-11

Strengthen the following paragraph by cutting it in half. You may rearrange the ideas if you wish. Think about what might make a good beginning and what might provide a sense of closure for the conclusion.

Hands, did you ever notice how many different kinds of hands there are? I first began to notice hands when I found that all men's hands were not as large as my Dad's hands. They were large, strong, and forceful, yet always gentle like the man. His hand encompasses mine even now when he takes it gently yet firmly, as though providing it with a cover of protection against the outside world. But he has always been like that, strong and protective, yet gentle. When those hands hold a baby, the baby stops crying and is quiet as though calmed by their strength and gentleness. When those hands take a pencil and draw an idea, the lines are firm and confident. Other men seem to respond when they shake his hand to the friendliness and strength behind the handshake.

You see here that you've been forced not only to omit words but to rethink organization, to consider using parallel structure, and to decide what you most want to say. Tightening shows respect for the meaning of words and respect for our readers' time. It also helps us to specify, without unnecessary noise, the essence of what we want to say. Tightening teaches us one of the most useful writing skills: being selective—giving the reader not all, but the best.

5. Don't let yourself be satisfied with words that are only *close* to the meaning you want.

• Check the meanings of words you're not quite sure of.

> Ms. Winston is not sparing in the use of *acrimonious vituperations* against certain mental health practitioners; and in her case, this is *justifiably understandable*.

The writer here, in an attempt to impress the reader with multi-syllabic words, has achieved the reverse. How are *vituperations* different when they are *acrimonious*? Not at all. What does *understandable* gain by being modified by *justifiably*? Nothing. The writer isn't trusting the meaning of her words. She's trying to bowl us over with the mere sound of them. Her carelessness weakens her *ethos*.

One of the most common carelessly used words is *revolve,* which must sound impressive to us, because it doesn't mean much and yet it is used frequently.

> This essay will <u>revolve around</u> answering the question of whether studying at the University of Texas has been a positive or negative experience for me.

> The world <u>revolves around</u> the word *survival*.

What is this writer trying to say? What do the words say? If you catch yourself using larger words than you want, you can use a thesaurus to find simpler words. You could change, for example, *approximately* to *roughly*. If you do use simpler words, your writing may achieve the same virtue that the Canon 35-mm camera claims to have: so advanced, it's simple.

• Remember that words have not only their strict meaning (called the *denotative* meaning) but also emotional colorations (called their *connotative* meanings). Even the names of cities—Paris, New York, Montreal, Liverpool, Dallas—call up emotions at the same time that they specify a place. We rarely make mistakes in connotation. We all know the difference in connotation, for example, between cheap and inexpensive. We all know the difference between crafty and intelligent. What we need to pay attention to during revision, though, is whether a word for which we have one connotation might have another connotation for our reader. I might think that *smart* has positive connotations, but some people don't, so I may well, in revision, when talking about my reader's favorite president, substitute *intelligent* for *smart*. Making such a change is attending carefully to the *pathos* I'm using to persuade my reader.

- Finally, look for differences between spoken English and written English as you review your final draft. *Really* should always be replaced. *Got* is often suspect. Even *this* must sometimes be questioned. When we're telling a story, we frequently say, "We went down *this* road for miles." *This* is pointing to a specific road in the speaker's mind, but to a reader *this road* is only *a* road. The correct form in writing, unless the road has already been identified, is *a road*.

6. Check your punctuation.

   - Review the rules for IC;IC and DC,IC and IC○DC in Chapter 8, and check that you've followed them in your paper.

   - If you have trouble writing complete sentences, read through your paper backward, sentence by sentence. When you read backward, you're less likely to miss fragments that don't sound too bad when they follow a good sentence.

7. Make revisions on the basis of your understanding of how English grammar can best serve your meaning.

   - Check whether you've accidentally switched back and forth in your verb tenses (between present and past, for example) without any desire to change the time that you are referring to.

   - Strike out adjectives and adverbs that steal impact from your nouns and verbs.

     Many questions ~~still~~ remain unanswered.

   - Often you can strengthen your prose by making the subject you're writing about the grammatical subject of your sentence.

Foggy	Clear
To relieve academic pressures and personal problems one may encounter was another purpose of the Nyumburu Center being formulated.	The Nyumburu Center was established to help students relieve academic pressures and talk through personal problems.

   - Likewise, it often helps to make your verb active when you're describing an action.

Foggy	Clear
The pleasures of canoeing *were described* by John McPhee.	John McPhee *described* the pleasures of canoeing.

• Check that each pronoun you use refers directly to some noun that appears before it. (A writer often doesn't notice whether pronouns agree with their antecedents until revision.)

Foggy	Clear
He may use whatever *methods* he wants as long as *it* is effective.	He may use whatever *methods* he wants as long as *they* are effective.

8. Listen to the sounds of our language.

• Note the meaningless repetition of sounds.

His *marks* improved *markedly*.

Many people are bothered by the repetition of sounds when they read through their own writing. Are there good reasons to avoid repeating a word or a sound? There are. A similar sound makes it seem to readers, if only for a moment, that they have come across a similar meaning. Then if the meaning is not similar, they have to sort out both meanings, and this takes time, if only a moment. But repetition is not necessarily an evil. Often, not only is it not awkward, but it serves your purpose.

The best guide to repetition is the end of Lincoln's Gettysburg Address (Macrorie, 27):

> government of the *people*
> by the *people*
> and for the *people*
>   shall not perish from the earth

Lincoln chose to repeat *people,* his main idea. We'd think he was too much concerned with his own role as President if he had said:

> *government* of
> *government* by
> and *government* for
>   the people shall not perish from the earth

If repetition is justified by your ideas, by all means use it. If it is only confusing, rethink your expression. Above all, don't make matters worse by going to a thesaurus for synonyms. Don't, in a paper about the actor Errol Flynn, call him Don Juan, then Casanova, then Romeo, then "the deceiver," then "Mr. Insatiable." Such "elegant variation" doesn't fool anybody. In fact, it calls more attention to the word we're repeating. Instead of looking for another term, what we should do is examine our thinking that has led to so much repetition. If you're repeating a reference to a person and that person is the subject of your paper, you should expect to be making repeated references to that person. If you're repeating an idea and the idea is worth repeating, it should stay in. If it is not worth repeating, perhaps some large-scale revision is needed.

9. Check to see that you've placed your emphasis where you want it.

- The principal place of emphasis is the end—the end of a sentence, the end of a paragraph, the end of a paper. When we read a poor ending, we have a strong sense of anticlimax:

> The audience of the eighteenth-century *Gentleman's Magazine* was intelligent gentry and merchants, although there were some exceptions.

The reason why a thesis seems to fit so well at the end of the first paragraph of a paper is that the end of a paragraph is an obvious point of emphasis. If you'd written the following introductory paragraph, you'd probably want to revise it.

> *Vietnam Tien-Phong,* a very popular magazine back in my country, has continued its progress after 1975 in America and it has become the most sought-after bi-weekly magazine in the Viet community everywhere in the world. The reporters and editors serve the Vietnamese well with serious political views as well as with entertainment like novels, anecdotes, and jokes. The reporters work very hard. The magazine starts with a full page resume of the world's events.

Sentences have the same emphasis pattern. Linguists have recently—and tentatively—suggested that the easiest sentence pattern for a reader to follow is this one: given information first, new information last. Thus a skilled writer begins a sentence with a word or a phrase already familiar to the reader and then continues by adding something new about the subject:

> When Ted Taylor was growing up, in Mexico City in the nineteen-thirties, he had three particular interests, and they were music, chemistry, and billiards. His father had been a widower with three sons who married a widow with a son of her own, so Ted had four older half brothers—so much older, though, that he was essentially raised an only child, in a home that was as quiet as it was religious. His maternal grandparents were Congregational missionaries in Guadalajara. His father, born on a farm in Kansas, was general secretary of the Y.M.C.A. in Mexico. His mother was the first American woman who ever earned a Ph.D. at the National University of Mexico. Her field was Mexican literature. (McPhee, *Curve,* 8–9)

The circled words keep the reader on familiar territory, while the rest of each sentence moves on to new information. This pattern is by no means always necessary. But it *does* make the reader comfortable at the beginning of the sentence, and it leaves the reader free to *notice* what comes at the end, in the emphatic position.

- Emphasis also falls on the verb.

> She spends her days sewing patchwork quilts and blankets.

This sentence puts the emphasis on *spends,* not on the *sewing.* This version makes her work seem boring. An alternative— "She *sews* patchwork quilts and blankets"—calls more attention to her artistry.

10. Check over your paper to see what it looks like.

    - Revise with an eye to emptiness and fullness. If you have a brief paragraph, you may want to add details to it, combine it with another paragraph, or remove it entirely. If you have a paragraph that fills a whole page, you may want to eliminate weak sections of it or find places to divide it into two or three paragraphs of more readable length.

11. Check the spelling of any words you're not sure of. For this purpose, a speller's dictionary is far better than an ordinary dictionary, because you can look a word up *the way you spelled it,* and the dictionary will provide the correct spelling right after your spelling. Two good spellers' dictionaries are *The Misspeller's Dictionary,* by Peter and Craig Norback (Quadrangle Books, 1974), and *The Bad Speller's Dictionary,* by Joseph Krevisky and Jordon L. Linfield (Random House, 1967).

12. Check that the "style" that comes through in your work is the one that you'd like to come through. Efforts to inject some "style" by adding words or phrases usually backfire, but we should be concerned, as we revise, about the tone of voice that comes through. One alteration in tone that many inexperienced writers ought to consider is making their writing slightly stronger, slightly more confident than they're actually feeling. In a few cases this will lead to artificial haughtiness, but in most cases the alteration will reflect the confidence that the writer deserves but doesn't yet have. Inexperienced writers can easily find themselves hedging at every opportunity:

    > An amateur *is thought of* as not knowing as much as a professional *to an extent.*

When we write something, we should legitimately think of ourselves as challenging our readers. A reader of the sentence above is left with nothing to think about. Most readers like to meet strength with strength. Unless they meet a strong writer, they don't want to give a work a strong reading.

13. Give your work a title that it deserves.

• Let me quote an expert on this matter (and many others), Harry Crosby, who sees a "high correlation between the quality of a written composition and its title" (387–91):

> I have long believed that the shuttlecock process of finding an appropriate title stimulates creativity, unity, and significance. The writer starts out with a working title, writes a few pages, and then pauses to tinker with the title to make it fit what he has written. This helps him go back to writing with a sharper focus on what he is really trying to say. This back-and-forth process continues. If a good title emerges, the writer has evidence that he or she is developing a significant message expressed in a unified manner. If no title is possible, something is wrong.

Crosby notes several kinds of titles, among them:

> Clever titles:
> "Two Cheers for Democracy"—E. M. Forster
> "The Scrutable Japanese"—Craig Spence

> Titles which announce the thesis:
> "We Scientists Have the Right to Play God"—Edmund F. Leech
> "This Thing Called Love Is Pathological"—Lawrence Cusler

> Titles which indicate the controlling question:
> "What Is a Classic?"—Charles Augustin Sainte-Beuve
> "What Does a Tune-Up Include?"—Charlotte Slater

> Titles which indicate a specific topic:
> "Desegregating Sexist Sports"—Harry Edwards
> "Substitutes for Violence"—John Fisher

> Titles which announce the general subject:
> "On the Middle Class"—Steve Slade
> "Historical Lessons About Great Leaders"—Arnold Toynbee

The first three types are admirable, and type four and type five get gradually weaker, but many student titles wouldn't even reach the bottom of this list. A good number of students use, as their title, the title of the assignment: "Description of a Curious Place"; "Persuading a Classmate to Consider an Issue Further." Another good number use no title at all. Look over the titles of the sample essays in this chapter; you'll probably be embarrassed for the authors. Then think before you write a title; give your work a title that it deserves.

MICHAEL BERHEIDE'S BRIEF GUIDE TO REVISION

1. Avoid redundancy. It should be avoided. It is repetitive and redundant; that is, redundancy should not be used. So stay away from redundancy and repetitiveness.

2. Personally attacking the proponent of an argument does not refute the argument, you idiot.

3. There are two types of people in the world: those who continually divide the people of the world into two types, and those who do not. Try to belong to the latter type, and avoid "overclassification."

4. Always check for spelin erors.

5. Try to keep, somewhere near the predicate of your sentence, so the reader does not have to look all over for it, your object.

6. I really don't think that your personal feelings should be used as if they were arguments—it just doesn't seem right.

7. It is not advisable to ever split infinitives.

8. I really don't know whether to tell you to be "wishy-washy" or not. Some say yes, others say no. Who's to decide?

9. If you had not made your verb tenses agree, you will have wished that you do.

10. Fragmented sentences: no good. And this sentence no verb.

11. Some people think that simply stating the converse of an argument refutes it, but this is not true.

12. Don't you think that asking lots of rhetorical questions is silly?

13. One should assiduously strive to disencumber an exposition of obfuscatory and vestigial verbiage.

14. Colloquialisms and trite expressions should be avoided like the plague. And it is not hip to use slang, either.

15. Avoid redundancy. It should be avoided. It is repetitive and redundant, so avoid it.

 In class Thurs.

Exercise 11-12

To be read on the day you hand in a paper. You may have thought when you typed up your paper last night that you were typing a "final draft." But no draft is ever final. A draft that we hand in is only a "deadline draft." We can't keep our work forever; a deadline forces us to quit. But that doesn't mean we could not have done better.

This time you're going to get one more chance not only to proofread but also to revise so that we can compare notes on what last-minute revisions people make.

First, take ten minutes just to proofread your paper, that is, to check for typing errors, spelling errors, and obvious errors in punctuation. When you finish, compare notes with the class on what you've changed. Check whether your habits are similar to those of your classmates. Which of you has the best strategy?

Next, take ten minutes to revise any parts of your paper you can without making major rearrangements (if a major rearrangement might be desirable, you can make a note to that effect at the end of your paper). Again, when you've finished, discuss with the class the kinds of changes you've made, and listen carefully to the kinds your classmates made.

12

◆

Reading

Reading is not simply a matter of gathering data, but also, and simultaneously, a matter of going through a sequence of moves which the writer has controlled for the purpose of leading the reader to assent. The skill of critical reading, it goes without saying, is one of understanding when one's assent has been earned.

John T. Gage

Writing is both knowing conventions and knowing where to flaunt them. Reading is knowing conventions and knowing how to recognize when, how, and why they have been broken.

Alan C. Purves

I have been told that reading helps.

student

Exercise 12·1

Before you begin this chapter, answer the following question in your notebook: When you pick up a book or a magazine casually, what is it that makes you keep reading?

Whenever we read, we expect our writer to take us a step beyond our current situation. (When we're writing, of course, we should keep the same in mind—that we are trying to take *our* readers a step beyond *their* current situation.) Reading, like writing, is a naturally reflective activity. Rarely do we just soak in something that we're reading. Most of the time we implicitly comment on what we read while we read. Of course, when we're distracted or tired, our eyes may cover the pages, but we're not really reading.

Your reading has been becoming more thoughtful throughout this course. Back in Chapter 1, you read the work of some professionals, and you wrote down your sense of what was strong or what was weak in that writing. In Chapter 11, you've been reading and judging several sample essays. On draft review day, you've been reading and judging the work of your classmates. And throughout the course you've been reading and judging your own work as you revise. In addition, you may frequently have been asked to write in class about your reading assignments. Perhaps you've even kept a journal of notes on what intrigued or puzzled you about the works that you've read during the semester. All these exercises have helped to make you a more active reader. In this chapter, though, we'll try to become more self-conscious of what we do when we read thoughtfully.

Any piece you pick up to read will consist primarily of facts (selected by the writer) and inferences (made by the writer).

> *Fact* (in the following article): "[Ants] farm fungi, raise aphids as livestock, launch armies into wars, use chemical sprays to alarm and confuse enemies, capture slaves."

> *Inference* (in the following article): "Ants are so much like human beings as to be an embarrassment."

As readers, we can simply take all this in, adding the facts to our memories and accepting the inferences as helpful insights. *Or* we can do our own thinking, our own drawing of *secondhand inferences* about the facts and inferences as we read. Our inferences are secondhand not because they show less intelligence than those of the writer but because we are making observations and inferences not about the author's subject but about the author. The author's fact and inference above become, for the reader, two facts about the author.

Fact 1	Reader's secondhand inference 1
The author selected little-known information about the living habits of ants to use as evidence.	The author knows ants well. Perhaps I'll trust his judgment when he draws conclusions about them.

Fact 2	Reader's secondhand inference 2
The author thinks we'll be embarrassed that ants live so much like we do.	The author understands human nature well: he knows we'll be embarrassed when we realize that a so-called *lesser* species resembles us.

Exercise 12-2

gives facts + inferences

An active reader draws a large number of secondhand inferences while reading. See if you can draw ten secondhand inferences as you read the following article. Bring your list to class. You and your classmates can compare lists—either in small groups or as a class. You should be able to refer to sentences, words, or phrases in the article to back up your inferences.

ON SOCIETIES AS ORGANISMS (1971)
Lewis Thomas

1 Viewed from a suitable height, the aggregating clusters of medical scientists in the bright sunlight of the boardwalk at Atlantic City, swarmed there from everywhere for the annual meetings, have the look of assemblages of social insects. There is the same vibrating, ionic movement, interrupted by the darting back and forth of jerky individuals to touch antennae and exchange small bits of information; periodically, the mass casts out, like a trout-line, a long single file unerringly toward Childs's. If the boards were not fastened down, it would not be a surprise to see them put together a nest of sorts.

2 It is permissible to say this sort of thing about humans. They do resemble, in their most compulsively social behavior, ants at a distance. It is, however, quite bad form in biological circles to put it the other way round, to imply that the operation of insect societies has any relation at all to human affairs. The writers of books on insect behavior generally take pains, in their prefaces, to caution that insects are like creatures from another planet, that their behavior is absolutely foreign, totally unhuman, unearthly, almost unbiological. They are more likely perfectly tooled but crazy little machines, and we violate science when we try to read human meanings in their arrangements.

3 It is hard for a bystander not to do so. Ants are so much like human beings as to be an embarrassment. They farm fungi, raise aphids as livestock, launch armies into wars, use chemical sprays to alarm and confuse enemies, capture slaves. The families of weaver ants engage in child labor, holding their larvae like shuttles to spin out the thread that sews the leaves together for their fungus gardens. They exchange information ceaselessly. They do everything but watch televison.

4 What makes us most uncomfortable is that they, and the bees and termites and social wasps, seem to live two kinds of lives: they are individuals, going about the day's business without much evidence of thought for tomorrow, and they are at the same time component parts, cellular elements, in the huge, writhing, ruminating organism of the Hill, the nest, the hive. It is because of this aspect, I think, that we most wish for them to be something foreign. We do not like the notion that there can be collective

societies with the capacity to behave like organisms. If such things exist, they can have nothing to do with us.

5 Still, there it is. A solitary ant, afield, cannot be considered to have much of anything on his mind; indeed, with only a few neurons strung together by fibers, he can't be imagined to have a mind at all, much less a thought. He is more like a ganglion on legs. Four ants together, or ten, encircling a dead moth on a path, begin to look more like an idea. They fumble and shove, gradually moving the food toward the Hill, but as though by blind chance. It is only when you watch the dense mass of thousands of ants, crowded together around the Hill, blackening the ground, that you begin to see the whole beast, and now you observe it thinking, planning, calculating. It is an intelligence, a kind of live computer, with crawling bits for its wits.

6 At a stage in the construction, twigs of a certain size are needed, and all the members forage obsessively for twigs of just this size. Later, when outer walls are to be finished, thatched, the size must change, and as though given new orders by telephone, all the workers shift the search to the new twigs. If you disturb the arrangement of a part of the Hill, hundreds of ants will set it vibrating, shifting, until it is put right again. Distant sources of food are somehow sensed, and long lines, like tentacles, reach out over the ground, up over walls, behind boulders, to fetch it in.

7 Termites are even more extraordinary in the way they seem to accumulate intelligence as they gather together. Two or three termites in a chamber will begin to pick up pellets and move them from place to place, but nothing comes of it; nothing is built. As more join in, they seem to reach a critical mass, a quorum, and the thinking begins. They place pellets atop pellets, then throw up columns and beautiful, curving, symmetrical arches, and the crystalline architecture of vaulted chambers is created. It is not known how they communicate with each other, how the chains of termites building one column know when to turn toward the crew on the adjacent column, or how, when the time comes, they manage the flawless joining of the arches. The stimuli that set them off at the outset, building collectively instead of shifting things about, may be pheromones released when they reach committee size. They react as if alarmed. They become agitated, excited, and then they begin working, like artists.

8 Bees live lives of organisms, tissues, cells, organelles, all at the same time. The single bee, out of the hive retrieving sugar (instructed by the dancer: "south-southeast for seven hundred meters, clover—mind you make corrections for the sundrift") is still as much a part of the hive as if attached by a filament. Building the hive, the workers have the look of embryonic cells organizing a developing tissue; from a distance they are like the viruses inside a cell, running off row after row of symmetrical polygons as though laying down crystals. When the time for swarming comes, and the old queen prepares to leave with her part of the population, it is as though the hive were involved in mitosis. There is an agitated moving of bees back and forth, like granules in cell sap. They distribute themselves in almost precisely equal parts, half to the departing queen, half to the new one. Thus, like an egg, the great, hairy, black and golden creature splits in two, each with an equal share of the family genome.

all during
amoebic form

9 The phenomenon of separate animals joining up to form an organism is not unique in insects. Slime-mold cells do it all the time, of course, in each life cycle. At first they are single <u>amebocytes</u> swimming around, eating bacteria, aloof from each other, untouching, voting straight Republican. Then, a bell sounds, and acrasin is released by special cells toward which the others converge in <u>stellate</u> ranks, touch, fuse together, and construct the slug, solid as a trout. A splendid stalk is raised, with a fruiting body on top, and out of this comes the next generation of amebocytes, ready to swim across the same moist ground, solitary and ambitious.

10 Herring and other fish in schools are at times so closely integrated, their actions so coordinated, that they seem to be functionally a great multi-fish organism. Flocking birds, especially the seabirds nesting on the slopes of offshore islands in Newfoundland, are similarly attached, connected, synchronized.

11 Although we are by all odds the most social of all social animals— more interdependent, more attached to each other, more inseparable in our behavior than bees—we <u>do not feel our conjoined intelligence</u>. Perhaps, however, we are linked in circuits for the storage, processing, and retrieval of information, since this appears to be the most basic and universal of all human enterprises. It may be our biological function to build a certain kind of Hill. We have access to all the information of the <u>biosphere</u>, arriving as elementary units in the stream of <u>solar photons</u>. When we have learned how these are rearranged against randomness, to make, say, springtails, quantum mechanics, and the late quartets, we may have a clearer notion how to proceed. The circuitry seems to be there, even if the current is not always on.

12 The system of communications used in science should provide a neat, workable model for studying mechanisms of information-building in human society. Ziman, in a recent *Nature* essay, points out, "the invention of a mechanism for the systematic publication of *fragments* of scientific work may well have been the key event in the history of modern science." He continues:

> A regular journal carries from one research worker to another the various . . . observations which are of common interest. . . . A typical scientific paper has never pretended to be more than another little piece in a larger jigsaw—not significant in itself but as an element in a grander scheme. *This technique, of soliciting many modest contributions to the store of human knowledge, has been the secret of Western science since the seventeenth century, for it achieves a corporate, collective power that is far greater than any one individual can exert* [italics mine].

13 With some alternation of terms, some toning down, the passage could describe the building of a termite nest.

14 It is fascinating that the word "explore" does not apply to the searching aspect of the activity, but has its origins in the sounds we make while engaged in it. We like to think of exploring in science as a lonely, meditative business, and so it is in the first stages, but always, sooner or later, before the enterprise reaches completion, as we explore, we call to each other,

communicate, publish, send letters to the editor, present papers, cry out on finding.

Lewis Thomas is very careful in the above article to explain what he thinks are the implications of the facts he presents. As readers, we can draw our own inferences, but if we do, we must compare them with his. Other authors prefer to engage their readers more actively by using telling facts (usually in narrative or descriptive form) and allowing the readers to draw their own inferences.

Exercise 12-3

See how many inferences you can draw about the family described in the passage below, the opening pages of Richard Wright's *Native Son.* Again, bring your list of inferences to class, and compare your results with those of your classmates. As always, be prepared to point to the evidence for your inferences (you may want to underline such evidence).

FROM *NATIVE SON* (1940)
Richard Wright

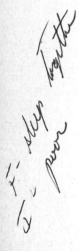

1 Brrrrrrriiiiiiiiiiiiiiiiiiiinng!

2 An alarm clock clanged in the dark and silent room. A bed spring creaked. A woman's voice sang out impatiently:

3 "Bigger, shut that thing off!"

4 A surly grunt sounded above the tinny ring of metal. Naked feet swished dryly across the planks in the wooden floor and the clang ceased abruptly.

5 "Turn on the light, Bigger."

6 "Awright," came a sleepy mumble.

7 Light flooded the room and revealed a black boy standing in a narrow space between two iron beds, rubbing his eyes with the backs of his hands. From a bed to his right the woman spoke again:

8 "Buddy, get up from there! I got a big washing on my hands today and I want you-all out of here."

9 Another black boy rolled from bed and stood up. The woman also rose and stood in her nightgown.

10 "Turn your heads so I can dress," she said.

11 The two boys averted their eyes and gazed into a far corner of the room. The woman rushed out of her nightgown and put on a pair of step-ins. She turned to the bed from which she had risen and called:

12 "Vera! Get up from there!"

13 "What time is it, Ma?" asked a muffled, adolescent voice from beneath a quilt.

14 "Get up from there, I say!"

15 "O.K., Ma."

16 A brown-skinned girl in a cotton gown got up and stretched her arms above her head and yawned. Sleepily, she sat on a chair and fumbled with her stockings. The two boys kept their faces averted while their mother and sister put on enough clothes to keep them from feeling ashamed; and the mother and sister did the same while the boys dressed. Abruptly, they all paused, holding their clothes in their hands, their attention caught by a light tapping in the thinly plastered walls of the room. They forgot their conspiracy against shame and their eyes strayed apprehensively over the floor.

17 "There he is again, Bigger!" the woman screamed, and the tiny one-room apartment galvanized into violent action. A chair toppled as the woman, half-dressed and in her stocking feet, scrambled breathlessly upon the bed. Her two sons, barefoot, stood tense and motionless, their eyes searching anxiously under the bed and chairs. The girl ran into a corner, half-stooped, and gathered the hem of her slip into both of her hands and held it tightly over her knees.

18 "Oh! Oh!" she wailed.

19 "There he goes!"

20 The woman pointed a shaking finger. Her eyes were round with fascinated horror.

21 "Where?"

22 "I don't see 'im!"

23 "Bigger, he's behind the trunk!" the girl whimpered.

24 "Vera!" the woman screamed. "Get up here on the bed! Don't let that thing *bite* you!"

25 Frantically, Vera climbed upon the bed and the woman caught hold of her. With their arms entwined about each other, the black mother and the brown daughter gazed open-mouthed at the trunk in the corner.

26 Bigger looked round the room wildly, then darted to a curtain and swept it aside and grabbed two heavy iron skillets from a wall above a gas stove. He whirled and called softly to his brother, his eyes glued to the trunk.

27 "Buddy!"

28 "Yeah?"

29 "Here; take this skillet."

30 "O.K."

31 "Now, get over by the door!"

32 "O.K."

33 Buddy crouched by the door and held the iron skillet by its handle, his arm flexed and poised. Save for the quick, deep breathing of the four people, the room was quiet. Bigger crept on tiptoe toward the trunk with the skillet clutched stiffly in his hand, his eyes dancing and watching every inch of the wooden floor in front of him. He paused and, without moving an eye or muscle, called:

34 "Buddy!"

35 "Hunh?"

36 "Put that box in front of the hole so he can't get out!"

37 "O.K."

38 Buddy ran to a wooden box and shoved it quickly in front of a gaping hole in the molding and then backed again to the door, holding the skillet ready. Bigger eased to the trunk and peered behind it cautiously. He saw

nothing. Carefully, he stuck out his bare foot and pushed the trunk a few inches.

39 "There he is!" the mother screamed again.

40 A huge black rat squealed and leaped at Bigger's trouser-leg and snagged it in his teeth, hanging on.

41 "Goddamn!" Bigger whispered fiercely, whirling and kicking out his leg with all the strength of his body. The force of his movement shook the rat loose and it sailed through the air and struck a wall. Instantly, it rolled over and leaped again. Bigger dodged and the rat landed against a table leg. With clenched teeth, Bigger held the skillet; he was afraid to hurl it, fearing that he might miss. The rat squeaked and turned and ran in a narrow circle, looking for a place to hide; it leaped again past Bigger and scurried on dry rasping feet to one side of the box and then to the other, searching for the hole. Then it turned and reared upon its hind legs.

42 "Hit 'im, Bigger!" Buddy shouted.

43 "Kill 'im!" the woman screamed.

44 The rat's belly pulsed with fear. Bigger advanced a step and the rat emitted a long thin song of defiance, its black beady eyes glittering, its tiny forefeet pawing the air restlessly. Bigger swung the skillet; it skidded over the floor, missing the rat, and clattered to a stop against a wall.

45 "Goddamn!"

46 The rat leaped. Bigger sprang to one side. The rat stopped under a chair and let out a furious screak. Bigger moved slowly backward toward the door.

47 "Gimme that skillet, Buddy," he asked quietly, not taking his eyes from the rat.

48 Buddy extended his hand. Bigger caught the skillet and lifted it high in the air. The rat scuttled across the floor and stopped again at the box and searched quickly for the hole; then it reared once more and bared long yellow fangs, piping shrilly, belly quivering.

49 Bigger aimed and let the skillet fly with a heavy grunt. There was a shattering of wood as the box caved in. The woman screamed and hid her face in her hands. Bigger tiptoed forward and peered.

50 "I got 'im," he muttered, his clenched teeth bared in a smile. "By God, I got 'im."

51 He kicked the splintered box out of the way and the flat black body of the rat lay exposed, its two long yellow tusks showing distinctly. Bigger took a shoe and pounded the rat's head, crushing it, cursing hysterically:

52 "You sonofa*bitch*!"

53 The woman on the bed sank to her knees and buried her face in the quilts and sobbed:

54 "Lord, Lord, have mercy. . . ."

55 "Aw, Mama," Vera whimpered, bending to her. "Don't cry. It's dead now."

Some writers, especially those who have come to be regarded as authorities, use fewer facts than you've noticed in the two previous readings. A writer who has become an authority (by showing in earlier work a command of facts) tends to rely more on judgments based on experience and often on the clever use of language. As readers, when we read such writers, we should be alert for assumptions that are not explicitly written down and for words used in ways that we are not accustomed to. By noting these words and by discovering these assumptions, we can better understand the writer's point and make a better-informed decision about whether or not we agree.

Exercise 12-4

Read the following editorial by Ellen Goodman of the *Boston Globe*. Circle all the words that are used in an unusual way, and when you've finished, try to explain, for each circled word, the difference between the usual meaning of the word and the meaning implied by the author. Also, try to locate any assumptions the author has about relations between men and women that are not stated but that clearly influence the author's point of view. Bring your notes to class, and compare your results with those of your classmates.

WHEN GRATEFUL BEGINS TO GRATE (1979)
Ellen Goodman

1 I know a woman who is a grateful wife. She has been one for years. In fact, her gratitude has been as deep and constant as her affection. And together they have traveled a long, complicated road.

2 In the beginning, this young wife was grateful to find herself married to a man who let her work. That was in 1964, when even her college professor said without a hint of irony that the young wife was "lucky to be married to a man who let her work." People talked like that then.

3 Later, the wife looked around her at the men her classmates and friends had married and was grateful that her husband wasn't threatened, hurt, neglected, insulted—the multiple choice of the mid-'60s—by her job.

4 He was proud. And her cup overran with gratitude. That was the way it was.

5 In the late '60s, when other, younger women were having consciousness-raising groups, she was having babies and more gratitude.

6 You see, she discovered that she had a Helpful Husband. Nothing in her experience had led her to expect this. Her mother was not married to one; her sister was not married to one; her brother was not one.

7 But at 4 o'clock in the morning, when the baby cried and she was exhausted, sometimes she would nudge her husband awake (wondering only vaguely how he could sleep) and ask him to feed the boy. He would say sure. And she would say thank you.

8 The Grateful Wife and the Helpful Husband danced this same pas de deux for a decade. When the children were small and she was sick, he would take charge. When it was their turn to carpool and she had to be at work early, he would drive. If she was coming home late, he would make dinner.

9 All you have to do is ask, he would say with a smile.

10 And so she asked. The woman who had minded her p's and q's as a child minded her pleases and thank yous as a wife. Would you please put the baby on the potty? Would you please stop at the store tonight for milk? Would you please pick up Joel at soccer practice? Thank you. Thank you. Thank you.

11 It is hard to know when gratitude first began to grate on my friend. Or when she began saying please and thank you dutifully rather than genuinely.

12 But it probably began when she was tired one day or night. In any case, during the car-time between one job and the other, when she would run lists through her head, she began feeling less thankful for her moonlighting job as household manager.

13 She began to realize that all the items of their shared life were stored in her exclusive computer. She began to realize that her queue was so full of minutiae that she had no room for anything else.

14 The Grateful Wife began to wonder why she should say thank you when a father took care of his children and why she should say please when a husband took care of his house.

15 She began to realize that being grateful meant being responsible. Being grateful meant assuming that you were in charge of children and laundry and running out of toilet paper. Being grateful meant having to ask. And ask. And ask.

16 Her husband was not an oppressive or even thoughtless man. He was helpful. But helpful doesn't have to remember vacuum cleaner bags. And helpful doesn't keep track of early dismissal days.

17 Helpful doesn't keep a Christmas-present list in his mind. Helpful doesn't have to know who wears what size and colors. Helpful is reminded; helpful is asked. Anything you ask. Please and thank you.

18 The wife feels, she says, vaguely frightened to find herself angry at saying please and thank you. She wonders if she is, indeed, an ingrate. But her wondering doesn't change how she feels or what she wants.

19 The wife would like to take just half the details that clog her mind like grit in a pore and hand them over to another manager. The wife would like someone who would be grateful when she volunteered to take *his* turn at the market or *his* week at the laundry.

20 The truth is that after all those years when she danced her part perfectly, she wants something else. She doesn't want a helpful husband. She wants one who will share. For that, she would be truly grateful.

Exercise 12-5

In all your reading thus far in this chapter I've told you what to look for. But each of us reads in an individual way, based on past reading experience and on past experience in general. Consequently, each of us draws unique inferences (you might prefer the term *insights*) from any work we read with care. While reading the following article, underline whatever *you* think is important, and make at least five comments in the margins. Emphasize anything you like. In class, then, compare your comments with those of your classmates in terms of variety and quality. What did you underline? Why did you underline what you did?

contrast - game
real life

THE SEARCH FOR MARVIN GARDENS (1975)
John McPhee

telling facts

1 Go. I roll the dice—a six and a two. Through the air I move my token, the flatiron, to Vermont Avenue, where dog packs range.

2 The dogs are moving (some are limping) through ruins, rubble, fire damage, open garbage. Doorways are gone. Lath is visible in the crumbling walls of the buildings. The street sparkles with shattered glass. I have never seen, anywhere, so many broken windows. A sign—"Slow, Children at Play"—has been bent backward by an automobile. At the lighthouse, the dogs turn up Pacific and disappear. George Meade, Army engineer, built the lighthouse—brick upon brick, six hundred thousand bricks, to reach up high enough to throw a beam twenty miles over the sea. Meade, seven years later, saved the Union at Gettysburg.

3 I buy Vermont Avenue for $100. My opponent is a tall, shadowy figure, across from me, but I know him well, and I know his game like a favorite tune. If he can, he will always go for the quick kill. And when it is foolish to go for the quick kill he will be foolish. On the whole, though, he is a master assessor of percentages. It is a mistake to underestimate him. His eleven carries his top hat to St. Charles Place, which he buys for $140.

4 The sidewalks of St. Charles Place have been cracked to shards by through-growing weeds. There are no buildings. Mansions, hotels once stood here. A few street lamps now drop cones of light on broken glass and vacant space behind a chain-link fence that some great machine has in places bent to the ground. Five plane trees—in full summer leaf, flecking the light—are all that live on St. Charles Place.

5 Block upon block, gradually, we are cancelling each other out—in the blues, the lavenders, the oranges, the greens. My opponent follows a plan of his own devising. I use the Hornblower & Weeks opening and the Zuricher defense. The first game draws tight, will soon finish. In 1971, a group of people in Racine, Wisconsin, played for seven hundred and sixty-eight hours. A game begun a month later in Danville, California, lasted eight hundred and twenty hours. These are official records, and they stun us. We have been playing for eight minutes. It amazes us that Monopoly is thought of as a long game. It is possible to play to a complete, absolute, and final conclusion in less than fifteen minutes, all within the rules as written. My opponent and I have done so thousands of times. No wonder we are sitting across from each other now in this best-of-seven series for the international singles championship of the world.

6 On Illinois Avenue, three men lean out from second-story windows. A girl is coming down the street. She wears dungarees and a bright-red shirt, has ample breasts and a Hadendoan Afro, a black halo, two feet in diameter. Ice rattles in the glasses in the hands of the men.

7 "Hey, sister!"

8 "Come on up!"

9 She looks up, looks from one to another to the other, looks them flat in the eye.

10 "What for?" she says, and she walks on.

11 I buy Illinois for $240. It solidifies my chances, for I already own Kentucky and Indiana. My opponent pales. If he had landed first on Illinois,

the game would have been over then and there, for he has houses built on Boardwalk and Park Place, we share the railroads equally, and we have cancelled each other everywhere else. We never trade.

12 In 1852, R. B. Osborne, an immigrant Englishman, civil engineer, surveyed the route of a railroad line that would run from Camden to Absecon Island, in New Jersey, traversing the state from the Delaware River to the barrier beaches of the sea. He then sketched in the plan of a "bathing village" that would surround the eastern terminus of the line. His pen flew glibly, framing and naming spacious avenues parallel to the shore—Mediterranean, Baltic, Oriental, Ventnor—and narrower transsecting avenues: North Carolina, Pennsylvania, Vermont, Connecticut, States, Virginia, Tennessee, New York, Kentucky, Indiana, Illinois. The place as a whole had no name, so when he had completed the plan Osborne wrote in large letters over the ocean, "Atlantic City." No one ever challenged the name, or the names of Osborne's streets. Monopoly was invented in the early nineteenthirties by Charles B. Darrow, but Darrow was only transliterating what Osborne had created. The railroads, crucial to any player, were the making of Atlantic City. After the rails were down, houses and hotels burgeoned from Mediterranean and Baltic to New York and Kentucky. Properties—building lots—sold for as little as six dollars apiece and as much as a thousand dollars. The original investors in the railroads and the real estate called themselves the Camden & Atlantic Land Company. Reverently, I repeat their names: Dwight Bell, William Coffin, John DaCosta, Daniel Deal, William Fleming, Andrew Hay, Joseph Porter, Jonathan Pitney, Samuel Richards—founders, fathers, forerunners, archetypical masters of the quick kill.

13 My opponent and I are now in a deep situation of classical Monopoly. The torsion is almost perfect—Boardwalk and Park Place versus the brilliant reds. His cash position is weak, though, and if I escape him now he may fade. I land on Luxury Tax, contiguous to but in sanctuary from his power. I have four houses on Indiana. He lands there. He concedes.

14 Indiana Avenue was the address of the Brighton Hotel, gone now. The Brighton was exclusive—a word that no longer has retail value in the city. If you arrived by automobile and tried to register at the Brighton, you were sent away. Brighton-class people came in private railroad cars. Brighton-class people had other private railroad cars for their horses—dawn rides on the firm sand at water's edge, skirts flying. Colonel Anthony J. Drexel Biddle—the sort of name that would constrict throats in Philadelphia—lived, much of year, in the Brighton.

15 Colonel Sanders' fried chicken is on Kentucky Avenue. So is Clifton's Club Harlem, with the Sepia Revue and the Sepia Follies, featuring the Honey Bees, the Fashions, and the Lords.

16 My opponent and I, many years ago, played 2,428 games of Monopoly in a single season. He was then a recent graduate of the Harvard Law School, and he was working for a downtown firm, looking up law. Two people we knew—one from Chase Manhattan, the other from Morgan, Stanley—tried to get into the game, but after a few rounds we found that they were not in the conversation and we sent them home. Monopoly should always be *mano a mano* anyway. My opponent won 1,199 games, and so

did I. Thirty were ties. He was called into the Army, and we stopped just there. Now, in Game 2 of the series, I go immediately to jail, and again to jail while my opponent seines property. He is dumbfoundingly lucky. He wins in twelve minutes.

17 Visiting hours are daily, eleven to two; Sunday, eleven to one; evenings, six to nine. "NO MINORS, NO FOOD, Immediate Family Only Allowed in Jail." All this above a blue steel door in a blue cement wall in the windowless interior of the basement of the city hall. The desk sergeant sits opposite the door to the jail. In a cigar box in front of him are pills in every color, a banquet of fruit salad an inch and a half deep—leapers, co-pilots, footballs, truck drivers, peanuts, blue angels, yellow jackets, redbirds, rainbows. Near the desk are two soldiers, waiting to go through the blue door. They are about eighteen years old. One of them is trying hard to light a cigarette. His wrists are in steel cuffs. A military policeman waits, too. He is a year or so older than the soldiers, taller, studious in appearance, gentle, fat. On a bench against a wall sits a good-looking girl in slacks. The blue door rattles, swings heavily open. A turnkey stands in the doorway. "Don't you guys kill yourselves back there now," says the sergeant to the soldiers.

18 "One kid, he overdosed himself about ten and a half hours ago," says the M.P.

19 The M.P., the soldiers, the turnkey, and the girl on the bench are white. The sergeant is black. "If you take off the handcuffs, take off the belts," says the sergeant to the M.P. "I don't want them hanging themselves back there." The door shuts and its tumblers move. When it opens again, five minutes later, a young white man in sandals and dungarees and a blue polo shirt emerges. His hair is in a ponytail. He has no beard. He grins at the good-looking girl. She rises, joins him. The sergeant hands him a manila envelope. From it he removes his belt and a small notebook. He borrows a pencil, makes an entry in the notebook. He is out of jail, free. What did he do? He offended Atlantic City in some way. He spent a night in the jail. In the nineteen-thirties, men visiting Atlantic City went to jail, directly to jail, did not pass Go, for appearing in topless bathing suits on the beach. A city statute requiring all men to wear full-length bathing suits was not seriously challenged until 1937, and the first year in which a man could legally go barechested on the beach was 1940.

20 Game 3. After seventeen minutes, I am ready to begin construction on overpriced and sluggish Pacific, North Carolina, and Pennsylvania. Nothing else being open, opponent concedes.

21 The physical profile of streets perpendicular to the shore is something like a playground slide. It begins in the high skyline of Boardwalk hotels, plummets into warrens of "side-avenue" motels, crosses Pacific, slopes through church missions, convalescent homes, burlesque houses, rooming houses, and liquor stores, crosses Atlantic, and runs level through the bombed-out ghetto as far—Baltic, Mediterranean—as the eye can see. North Carolina Avenue, for example, is flanked at its beach end by the Chalfonte and the Haddon Hall (908 rooms, air-conditioned), where, according to one biographer, John Philip Sousa (1854–1932) first played when he was twenty-two, insisting, even then, that everyone call him by his entire name. Behind these big hotels, motels—Barbizon, Catalina—crouch.

strip show's
wooden

France
Germany

telling
facts

Marvin
Gardens

Between Pacific and Atlantic is an occasional house from 1910—wooden porch, wooden mullions, old yellow paint—and two churches, a package store, a strip show, a dealer in fruits and vegetables. Then, beyond Atlantic Avenue, North Carolina moves on into the vast ghetto, the bulk of the city, and it looks like Metz in 1919, Cologne in 1944. Nothing has actually exploded. It is not bomb damage. It is deep and complex decay. Roofs are off. Bricks are scattered in the street. People sit on porches, six deep, at nine on a Monday morning. When they go off to wait in unemployment lines, they wait sometimes two hours. Between Mediterranean and Baltic runs a chain-link fence, enclosing rubble. A patrol car sits idling by the curb. In the back seat is a German shepherd. A sign on the fence says, "Beware of Bad Dogs."

22 Mediterranean and Baltic are the principal avenues of the ghetto. Dogs are everywhere. A pack of seven passes me. Block after block, there are three-story brick row houses. Whole segments of them are abandoned, a thousand broken windows. Some parts are intact, occupied. A mattress lies in the street, soaking in a pool of water. Wet stuffing is coming out of the mattress. A postman is having a rye and a beer in the Plantation Bar at nine-fifteen in the morning. I ask him idly if he knows where Marvin Gardens is. He does not. "HOOKED AND NEED HELP? CONTACT N.A.R.C.O." "REVIVAL NOW GOING ON, CONDUCTED BY REVEREND H. HENDERSON OF TEXAS." These are signboards on Mediterranean and Baltic. The second one is upside down and leans against a boarded-up window of the Faith Temple Church of God in Christ. There is an old peeling poster on a warehouse wall showing a figure in an electric chair. "The Black Panther Manifesto" is the title of the poster, and its message is, or was, that "the fascists have already decided in advance to murder Chairman Bobby Seale in the electric chair." I pass an old woman who carries a bucket. She wears blue sneakers, worn through. Her feet spill out. She wears red socks, rolled at the knees. A white handkerchief, spread over her head, is knotted at the corners. Does she know where Marvin Gardens is? "I sure don't know," she says, setting down the bucket. "I sure don't know. I've heard of it somewhere, but I just can't say where." I walk on, through a block of shattered glass. The glass crunches underfoot like coarse sand. I remember when I first came here—a long train ride from Trenton, long ago, games of poker in the train—to play basketball against Atlantic City. We were half black, they were all black. We scored forty points, they scored eighty, or something like it. What I remember most is that they had glass backboards—glittering, pendent, expensive glass backboards, a rarity then in high schools, even in colleges, the only ones we played on all year.

23 I turn on Pennsylvania, and start back toward the sea. The windows of the Hotel Astoria, on Pennsylvania near Baltic, are boarded up. A sheet of unpainted plywood is the door, and in it is a triangular peephole that now frames an eye. The plywood door opens. A man answers my question. Rooms there are six, seven, and ten dollars a week. I thank him for the information and move on, emerging from the ghetto at the Catholic Daughters of America Women's Guest House, between Atlantic and Pacific. Between Pacific and the Boardwalk are the blinking vacancy signs of the

Aristocrat and Colton Manor motels. Pennsylvania terminates at the Sheraton-Seaside—thirty-two dollars a day, ocean corner. I take a walk on the Boardwalk and into the Holiday Inn (twenty-three stories). A guest is registering. "You reserved for Wednesday, and this is Monday," the clerk tells him. "But that's all right. We have *plenty* of rooms." The clerk is very young, female, and has soft brown hair that hangs below her waist. Her superior kicks her.

24 He is a middle-aged man with red spiderwebs in his face. He is jacketed and tied. He takes her aside. "Don't say 'plenty,'" he says. "Say 'You are fortunate, sir. We have rooms available.'"

25 The face of the young woman turns sour. "We have all the rooms you need," she says to the customer, and, to her superior, "How's that?"

26 Game 4. My opponent's luck has become abrasive. He has Boardwalk and Park Place, and has sealed the board.

27 Darrow was a plumber. He was, specifically, a radiator repairman who lived in Germantown, Pennsylvania. His first Monopoly board was a sheet of linoleum. On it he placed houses and hotels that he had carved from blocks of wood. The game he thus invented was brilliantly conceived, for it was an uncannily exact reflection of the business milieu at large. In its depth, range, and subtlety, in its luck-skill ratio, in its sense of infrastructure and socioeconomic parameters, in its philosophical characteristics, it reached to the profundity of the financial community. It was as scientific as the stock market. It suggested the manner and means through which an underdeveloped world had been developed. It was chess at Wall Street level. "Advance token to the nearest Railroad and pay owner twice the rental to which he is otherwise entitled. If railroad is unowned, you may buy it from the Bank. Get out of Jail, free. Advance token to nearest Utility. If unowned, you may buy it from Bank. If owned, throw dice and pay owner a total ten times the amount thrown. You are assessed for street repairs: $40 per house, $115 per hotel. Pay poor tax of $15. Go to Jail. Go directly to Jail. Do not pass Go. Do not collect $200."

28 The turnkey opens the blue door. The turnkey is known to the inmates as Sidney K. Above his desk are ten closed-circuit-TV screens—assorted viewpoints of the jail. There are three cellblocks—men, women, juvenile boys. Six days is the average stay. Showers twice a week. The steel doors and the equipment that operates them were made in San Antonio. The prisoners sleep on bunks of butcher block. There are no mattresses. There are three prisoners to a cell. In winter, it is cold in here. Prisoners burn newspapers to keep warm. Cell corners are black with smudge. The jail is three years old. The men's block echoes with chatter. The man in the cell nearest Sidney K. is pacing. His shirt is covered with broad stains of blood. The block for juvenile boys is, by contrast, utterly silent—empty corridor, empty cells. There is only one prisoner. He is small and black and appears to be thirteen. He says he is sixteen and that he has been alone in here for three days.

29 "Why are you here? What did you do?"

30 "I hit a jitney driver."

31 The series stands at three all. We have split the fifth and sixth games.

We are scrambling for property. Around the board we fairly fly. We move so fast because we do our own banking and search our own deeds. My opponent grows tense.

32 Ventnor Avenue, a street of delicatessens and doctors' offices, is leafy with plane trees and hydrangeas, the city flower. Water Works is on the mainland. The water comes over in submarine pipes. Electric Company gets power from across the state, on the Delaware River, in Deepwater. States Avenue, now a wasteland like St. Charles, once had gardens running down the middle of the street, a horse-drawn trolley, private homes. States Avenue was as exclusive as the Brighton. Only an apartment house, a small motel, and the All Wars Memorial Building—monadnocks spaced widely apart—stand along States Avenue now. Pawnshops, convalescent homes, and the Paradise Soul Saving Station are on Virginia Avenue. The soul-saving station is pink, orange, and yellow. In the windows flanking the door of the Virginia Money Loan Office are Nikons, Polaroids, Yashicas, Sony TVs, Underwood typewriters, Singer sewing machines, and pictures of Christ. On the far side of town, beside a single track and locked up most of the time, is the new railroad station, a small hut made of glazed firebrick, all that is left of the lines that built the city. An authentic phrenologist works on New York Avenue close to Frank's Extra Dry Bar and a church where the sermon today is "Death in the Pot." The church is of pink brick, has blue and amber windows and two red doors. St. James Place, narrow and twisting, is lined with boarding houses that have wooden porches on each of three stories, suggesting a New Orleans made of salt-bleached pine. In a vacant lot on Tennessee is a white Ford station wagon stripped to the chassis. The windows are smashed. A plastic Clorox bottle sits on the driver's seat. The wind has pressed newspaper against the chain-link fence around the lot. Atlantic Avenue, the city's principal thoroughfare, could be seventeen American Main Streets placed end to end—discount vitamins and Vienna Corset shops, movie theatres, shoe stores, and funeral homes. The Board-walk is made of yellow pine and Douglas fir, soaked in pentachlorophenol. Downbeach, it reaches far beyond the city. Signs everywhere—on windows, lampposts, trash baskets—proclaim "Bienvenue Canadiens!" The salt air is full of Canadian French. In the Claridge Hotel, on Park Place, I ask a clerk if she knows where Marvin Gardens is. She says, "Is it a floral shop?" I ask a cabdriver, parked outside. He says, "Never heard of it." Park Place is one block long, Pacific to Boardwalk. On the roof of the Claridge is the Solarium, the highest point in town—panoramic view of the ocean, the bay, the saltwater ghetto. I look down at the rooftops of the side-avenue motels and into swimming pools. There are hundreds of people around the rooftop pools, sunbathing, reading—many more people than are on the beach. Walls, windows, and a block of sky are all that is visible from these pools—no sand, no sea. The pools are craters, and with the people around them they are countersunk into the motels.

33 The seventh, and final, game is ten minutes old and I have hotels on Oriental, Vermont, and Connecticut. I have Tennessee and St. James. I have North Carolina and Pacific. I have Boardwalk, Atlantic, Ventnor, Illinois, Indiana. My fingers are forming a "V." I have mortgaged most of these

properties in order to pay for others, and I have mortgaged the others to pay for the hotels. I have seven dollars. I will pay off the mortgages and build my reserves with income from the three hotels. My cash position may be low, *clue.* but I feel like a rocket in an underground silo. Meanwhile, if I could just go to jail for a time I could pause there, wait there, until my opponent, in his inescapable rounds, pays the rates of my hotels. Jail, at times, is the strategic place to be. I roll boxcars from the Reading and move the flatiron to Community Chest. "Go to Jail. Go directly to Jail." *characteristic of given long.*

34 The prisoners, of course, have no pens and no pencils. They take paper napkins, roll them tight as crayons, char the ends with matches, and write on the walls. The things they write are not entirely idiomatic; for example, "In God We Trust." All is in carbon. Time is required in the writing. "Only humanity could know of such pain." "God So Loved the World." "There is no greater pain than life itself." In the women's block now, there are six blacks, giggling, and a white asleep in red shoes. She is drunk. The others are pushers, prostitutes, an auto thief, a burglar caught with pistol in purse. A sixteen-year-old accused of murder was in here last week. These words are written on the wall of a now empty cell: "Laying here I see two bunks about six inches thick, not counting the one I'm laying on, which is hard as brick. No cushion for my back. No pillow for my head. Just a couple scratchy blankets which is best to use it's said. I wake up in the morning so shivery and cold, waiting and waiting till I am told the food is coming. It's on its way. It's not worth waiting for, but I eat it anyway. I know one thing when they set me free I'm gonna be good if it kills me." *life*

35 How many years must a game be played to produce an Anthony J. Drexel Biddle and chestnut geldings on the beach? About half a century was the original answer, from the first railroad to Biddle at his peak. Biddle, at his peak, hit an Atlantic City streetcar conductor with his fist, laid him out with one punch. This increased Biddle's legend. He did not go to jail. While John Philip Sousa led his band along the Boardwalk playing "The Stars and Stripes Forever" and Jack Dempsey ran up and down in training for his fight with Gene Tunney, the city crossed the high curve of its parabola. Al Capone held conventions here—upstairs with his sleeves rolled, apportioning among his lieutenant governors the states of the Eastern seaboard. The natural history of an American resort proceeds from Indians to French Canadians via Biddles and Capones. French Canadians, whatever they may be at home, are Visigoths here. Bienvenue Visigoths! *Goths invaded Rome* *plane of curr*

36 My opponent plods along incredibly well. He has got his fourth railroad, and patiently, unbelievably, he has picked up my potential winners until he has blocked me everywhere but Marvin Gardens. He has avoided, in the fifty-dollar zoning, my increasingly petty hotels. His cash flow swells. His railroads are costing me two hundred dollars a minute. He is building hotels on States, Virginia, and St. Charles. He has temporarily reversed the current. With the yellow monopolies and my blue monopolies, I could probably defeat his lavenders and his railroads. I have Atlantic and Ventnor. I need Marvin Gardens. My only hope is Marvin Gardens.

37 There is a plaque at Boardwalk and Park Place, and on it in relief is the leonine profile of a man who looks like an officer in a metropolitan bank— *char. of lion*

"Charles B. Darrow, 1889–1967, inventor of the game of Monopoly." "Darrow," I address him, aloud. "Where is Marvin Gardens?" There is, of course, no answer. Bronze, impassive, Darrow looks south down the Boardwalk. "Mr. Darrow, please, where is Marvin Gardens?" Nothing. Not a sign. He just looks south down the Boardwalk.

38 My opponent accepts the trophy with his natural ease, and I make, from notes, remarks that are even less graceful than his.

39 Marvin Gardens is the one color-block Monopoly property that is not in Atlantic City. It is a suburb within a suburb, secluded. It is a planned compound of seventy-two handsome houses set on curvilinear private streets under yews and cedars, poplars and willows. The compound was built around 1920, in Margate, New Jersey, and consists of solid buildings of stucco, brick, and wood, with slate roofs, tile roofs, multimullioned porches, Giraldic towers, and Spanish grilles. Marvin Gardens, the ultimate outwash of Monopoly, is a citadel and sanctuary of the middle class. "We're heavily patrolled by police here. We don't take no chances. Me? I'm living here nine years. I paid seventeen thousand dollars and I've been offered thirty. Number one, I don't want to move. Number two, I don't need the money. I have four bedrooms, two and a half baths, front den, back den. No basement. The Atlantic is down there. Six feet down and you float. A lot of people have a hard time finding this place. People that lived in Atlantic City all their life don't know how to find it. They don't know where the hell they're going. They just know it's south, down the Boardwalk."

When you write a paper, or an essay exam, about something you've read, your responsibility is to draw inferences about what you've read (to make judgments about it), and not simply to summarize it. In your paper, the material you include from your source will be the *facts* from which you've drawn your inferences; these facts serve to substantiate your points. The originality in your paper derives from the inferences you've made as you read—the comments, in effect, that you've made in the margins. In a longer paper, you will need an introduction and a conclusion, and you'll have to qualify some of the strong statements you want to make, but at the heart of critical writing is selecting telling facts from your reading and then specifying the inferences that you think those facts tell.

In completing the exercises in this chapter, you will see more clearly what you value when you read, and you will begin to discover what other readers look for. Compare what you look for with what your classmates look for and with what your teacher looks for. Are some ways of reading better than others?

As you continue to read, for school and on your own, consciously or unconsciously you'll consistently increase your ability to judge the value of what you read by applying the standards you've developed or refined in this course:

Ethos	Logos	Pathos
1. Is the writer intelligent?	1. Are the facts used relevant?	1. Does the writer show a concern for the needs of the reader?
2. Well-informed?	2. Are the author's inferences justified by the facts?	
3. Fair?		2. Does the writer make a skilled use of emotional appeal?
4. A person of goodwill?	3. Are the author's assumptions justifiable?	
	4. Is the piece well-organized?	
	5. Is its purpose clear?	

Your textbooks, your mail, and everything else you "read" (including ads, films, political speeches, and popular songs) can be judged by the same standards. If you'd like further practice (or just some good reading), try the pieces in the remainder of this chapter.

FROM *THE ROAD TO WIGAN PIER* (1937)

George Orwell

Our civilization . . . *is* founded on coal, more completely than one realizes until one stops to think about it. The machines that keep us alive, and the machines that make the machines, are all directly or indirectly dependent upon coal. In the metabolism of the Western world the coal miner is second in importance only to the man who ploughs the soil. He is a sort of grimy caryatid upon whose shoulders nearly everything that is *not* grimy is supported. For this reason the actual process by which coal is extracted is well worth watching, if you get the chance and are willing to take the trouble. . . .

It is impossible to watch the "fillers" at work without feeling a pang of envy for their toughness. It is a dreadful job that they do, an almost superhuman job by the standards of an ordinary person. For they are not only shifting monstrous quantities of coal, they are also doing it in a position that doubles or trebles the work. They have got to remain kneeling all the while—they could hardly rise from their knees without hitting the ceiling—and you can easily see by trying it what a tremendous effort this means. Shoveling is comparatively easy when you are standing up, because you can use your knee and thigh to drive the shovel along; kneeling down, the whole of the strain is thrown upon your arm and belly muscles. And the other conditions do not exactly make things easier. There is the heat—it varies, but in some mines it is suffocating—and the coal dust that stuffs up your throat and nostrils and collects along your eyelids, and the unending rattle of the conveyor belt, which in that confined space is rather like the rattle of a machine gun. But the fillers look and work as though they were made of iron. They really do look like iron—hammered iron statues— under the smooth coat of coal dust which clings to them from head to foot. It is only when you see miners down the mine and naked that you realize what splendid men they are. Most of them are small (big men are at a disadvantage in that job) but nearly all of them have the most noble bodies: wide shoulders tapering to slender supple waists, and small pronounced buttocks and sinewy thighs, with not an ounce of waste flesh anywhere. In the hotter mines they wear only a pair of thin drawers, clogs and knee-pads; in the hottest mines of all, only the clogs and knee-pads. You can hardly tell by the look of them whether they are young or old. They may be any age up to sixty or even sixty-five, but when they are black and naked they all look alike. No one could do their work who had not a young man's body, and a figure fit for a guardsman at that; just a few pounds of extra flesh on the waistline, and the constant bending would be impossible. You can never forget that spectacle once you have seen it—the line of bowed, kneeling figures, sooty black all over, driving their huge shovels under the coal with stupendous force and speed. They are on the job for seven and a half hours, theoretically without a break, for there is no time "off." Actually they snatch a quarter of an hour or so at some time during the shift to eat the food they have brought with them, usually a hunk of bread and dripping and a bottle of cold tea. The first time I was watching the "fillers" at work I put my hand upon some dreadful slimy thing among the coal dust. It was a chewed quid of tobacco. Nearly all the miners chew tobacco, which is said to be good against thirst.

Probably you have to go down several coal mines before you can get much grasp of the processes that are going on round you. This is chiefly because the mere effort of getting from place to place makes it difficult to notice anything else. In some ways it is even disappointing, or at least is unlike what you have expected. You get into the cage, which is a steel box about as wide as a telephone box and two or three times as long. It holds ten men, but they pack it like pilchards in a tin, and a tall man cannot stand upright in it. The steel door shuts upon you, and somebody working the winding gear above drops you into the void. You have the usual momentary qualm in your belly and a bursting sensation in the ears, but not much sensation of movement till you get near the bottom, when the cage slows down so abruptly that you could swear it is going upward again. In the middle of the run the cage probably touches sixty miles an hour; in some of the deeper mines it touches even more. When you crawl out at the bottom you are perhaps four hundred yards under ground. That is to say you have a tolerable-sized mountain on top of you; hundreds of yards of solid rock, bones of extinct beasts, subsoil, flints, roots of growing things, green grass and cows grazing on it—all this suspended over your head and held back only by wooden props as thick as the calf of your leg. But because of the speed at which the cage has brought you down, and the complete blackness through which you have traveled, you hardly feel yourself deeper down than you would at the bottom of the Piccadilly tube.

What *is* surprising, on the other hand, is the immense horizontal distances that have to be traveled underground. Before I had been down a mine I had vaguely imagined the miner stepping out of the cage and getting to work on a ledge of coal a few yards away. I had not realized that before he even gets to his work he may have to creep through passages as long as from London Bridge to Oxford Circus. In the beginning, of course, a mine shaft is sunk somewhere near a seam of coal. But as that seam is worked out and fresh seams are followed up, the workings get farther and farther from the pit bottom. If it is a mile from the pit bottom to the coal face, that is probably an average distance; three miles is a fairly normal one; there are even said to be a few mines where it is as much as five miles. But these distances bear no relation to distances above ground. For in all that mile or three miles as it may be, there is hardly anywhere outside the main road, and not many places even there, where a man can stand upright.

You do not notice the effect of this till you have gone a few hundred yards. You start off, stooping slightly, down the dim-lit gallery, eight or ten feet wide and about five high, with the walls built up with slabs of shale, like the stone walls in Derbyshire. Every yard or two there are wooden props holding up the beams and girders; some of the girders have buckled into fantastic curves under which you have to duck. Usually it is bad going underfoot—thick dust or jagged chunks of shale, and in some mines where there is water it is as mucky as a farmyard. Also there is the track for the coal tubs, like a miniature railway track with sleepers a foot or two apart, which is tiresome to walk on. Everything is gray with shale dust; there is a dusty fiery smell which seems to be the same in all mines. You see mysterious machines of which you never learn the purpose, and bundles of tools slung together on wires, and sometimes mice darting away from the beam of the lamps. . . .

At the start to walk stooping is rather a joke, but it is a joke that soon wears off. I am handicapped by being exceptionally tall, but when the roof falls to four feet or less it is a tough job for anybody except a dwarf or a child. You have not only got to bend double, you have also got to keep your head up all the while so as to see the beams and girders and dodge them when they come. You have, therefore, a constant crick in the neck, but this is nothing to the pain in your knees and thighs. After half a mile it becomes (I am not exaggerating) an unbearable agony. You begin to wonder whether you will ever get to the end—still more, how on earth you are going to get back. Your pace grows slower and slower. You come to a stretch of a couple of hundred yards where it is all exceptionally low and you have to work yourself along in a squatting position. Then suddenly the roof opens out to a mysterious height—scene of an old fall of rock, probably—and for twenty whole yards you can stand upright. The relief is overwhelming. But after this there is another low stretch of a hundred yards and then a succession of beams which you have to crawl under. You go down on all fours; even this is a relief after the squatting business. But when you come to the end of the beams and try to get up again, you find that your knees have temporarily struck work and refuse to lift you. You call a halt, ignominiously, and say that you would like to rest for a minute or two. Your guide (a miner) is sympathetic. He knows that your muscles are not the same as his. "Only another four hundred yards," he says encouragingly; you feel that he might as well say another four hundred miles. But finally you do somehow creep as far as the coal face. You have gone a mile and taken the best part of an hour; a miner would do it in not much more than twenty minutes. Having got there, you have to sprawl in the coal dust and get your strength back for several minutes before you can even watch the work in progress with any kind of intelligence. . . .

It may seem that I am exaggerating, though no one who has been down an old-fashioned pit (most of the pits in England are old-fashioned) and actually gone as far as the coal face, is likely to say so. But what I want to emphasize is this. Here is this frightful business of crawling to and fro, which to any normal person is a hard day's work in itself; and it is not part of the miner's work at all, it is merely an extra, like the City man's daily ride in the tube. The miner does that journey to and fro, and sandwiched in between there are seven and a half hours of savage work. I have never traveled much more than a mile to the coal face; but often it is three miles, in which case I and most people other than coal miners would never get there at all. This is the kind of point that one is always liable to miss. When you think of a coal mine you think of depth, heat, darkness, blackened figures hacking at walls of coal; you don't think, necessarily, of those miles of creeping to and fro. There is the question of time, also. A miner's working shift of seven and a half hours does not sound very long, but one has got to add on to it at least an hour a day for "traveling," more often two hours and sometimes three. Of course, the "traveling" is not technically work and the miner is not paid for it; but it is as like work as makes no difference. It is easy to say that miners don't mind all this. Certainly, it is not the same for them as it would be for you or me. They have done it since childhood, they have the right muscles hardened, and they can move to and fro underground with a startling and rather horrible agility. A miner puts his head down and *runs,* with a long swinging stride, through places where I can only stagger. At the workings you see them on all fours, skipping round the pit props almost like dogs. But it is quite a mistake to think that they enjoy it. I have talked about this to scores of miners and they all admit that the "traveling" is hard work; in any case when you hear them discussing a pit among themselves the "traveling" is always one of the things they discuss. It is said that a shift always returns from work faster than it goes; nevertheless the miners all say that it is the coming away, after a hard day's work, that is especially irksome. It is part of their work and they are equal to it, but certainly it is an effort. It is comparable, perhaps, to climbing a smallish mountain before and after your day's work.

When you have been down two or three pits you begin to get some grasp of the processes that are going on underground. (I ought to say, by the way, that I know nothing whatever about the technical side of mining: I am merely describing what I have seen.) Coal lies in thin seams between enormous layers of rock, so that essentially the process of getting it out is like scooping the central layer from a Neapolitan ice. In the old days the miners used to cut straight into the coal with pick and crowbar—a very slow job because coal, when lying in its virgin state, is almost as hard as rock. Nowadays the preliminary work is done by an electrically driven coal-cutter, which in principle is an immensely tough and powerful band-saw, running horizontally instead of vertically, with teeth a couple of inches long and half an inch or an inch thick. It can move backward or forward on its own power, and the men operating it can rotate it this way and that. Incidentally it makes one of the most awful noises I have ever heard, and sends forth clouds of coal dust which make it impossible to see more than two or three feet and almost impossible to breathe. The machine travels along the coal face cutting into the base of the coal and undermining it to the depth of five feet or five feet and a half; after this it is comparatively easy to extract the coal to the depth to which it has been undermined. Where it is "difficult getting," however, it has also to be loosened with explosives. A man with an electric drill, like a rather smaller version of the drills used in street-mending, bores holes at intervals in the coal, inserts blasting powder, plugs it with clay, goes round the corner if there is one handy (he is supposed to retire to twenty-five yards distance) and touches off the charge with an electric current. This is not intended to bring the coal out, only to loosen it. Occasionally, of course, the charge is too powerful, and then it not only brings the coal out but brings the roof down as well.

After the blasting has been done the "fillers" can tumble the coal out, break it up, and shovel it on to the conveyor belt. It comes out at first in monstrous boulders which may weigh anything up to twenty tons. The conveyor belt shoots it on to tubs, and the tubs are shoved into the main road and hitched on to an endlessly revolving steel cable which drags them to the cage. Then they are hoisted, and at the surface the coal is sorted by being run over screens, and if necessary is washed as well. As far as possible the "dirt"—the shale, that is—is used for making the roads below. All that cannot be used is sent to the surface and dumped; hence the monstrous "dirt-heaps," like hideous gray mountains, which are the characteristic scenery of the coal areas. When the coal has been extracted to the depth to which the machine has cut, the coal face has advanced by five feet. Fresh props are put in to hold up the newly exposed roof, and during the next shift the conveyor belt is taken to pieces, moved five feet forward and re-assembled. As far as possible the three operations of cutting, blasting, and extraction are done in three separate shifts, the cutting in the afternoon, the blasting at night (there is a law, not always kept, that forbids its being done when there are other men working near by), and the "filling" in the morning shift, which lasts from six in the morning until half-past one. . . .

Watching coal miners at work, you realize momentarily what different universes different people inhabit. Down there where coal is dug it is a sort of world apart which one can quite easily go through life without ever hearing about. Probably a majority of people would even prefer not to hear about it. Yet it is the absolutely necessary counterpart of our world above. Practically everything we do, from eating an ice to crossing the Atlantic, and from baking a loaf to writing a novel, involves the use of coal, directly or indirectly. For all the arts of peace coal is needed; if war breaks out it is needed all the more. In time of revolution the miner must go on working or the revolution must stop, for revolution as much as reaction needs coal. Whatever may be happening on the surface, the hacking and shoveling have got to continue without a pause, or at any rate without pausing for more than a few weeks at the most. In order that Hitler may march the goosestep, that the Pope may denounce Bolshevism, that the cricket crowds may assemble at Lord's, that the Nancy poets may scratch one another's backs, coal has got to be forthcoming. But on the whole we are not aware of it; we all know that we "must have coal," but we seldom or never remember what coal-getting involves. Here am I, sitting writing in front of my comfortable coal fire. It is April but I still need a fire. Once a fortnight the coal cart drives up to the door and men in leather jerkins carry the coal indoors in stout sacks smelling of tar and shoot it clanking into the coal-hole under the stairs. It is only very rarely, when I make a definite mental effort, that I connect this coal with that far-off labor in the mines. It is just "coal"—something that I have got to have; black stuff that arrives mysteriously from nowhere in particular, like manna except that you have to pay for it. You could quite easily drive a car right across the north of England and never once remember that hundreds of feet below the road you are on the miners are hacking at the coal. Yet in a sense it is the miners who are driving your car forward. Their lamp-lit world down there is as necessary to the daylight world above as the root is to the flower.

It is not long since conditions in the mines were worse than they are now. There are still living a few very old women who in their youth have worked underground, with a harness round their waists and a chain that passed between their legs, crawling on all fours and dragging tubs of coal. They used to go on doing this even when they were pregnant. And even now, if coal could not be produced without pregnant women dragging it to and fro, I fancy we should let them do it rather than deprive ourselves of coal. But most of the time, of course, we should prefer to forget that they were doing it. It is so with all types of manual work; it keeps us alive, and we are oblivious of its existence. More than anyone else, perhaps, the miner can stand as the type of the manual worker, not only because his work is so exaggeratedly awful, but also because it is so vitally necessary and yet so remote from our experience, so invisible, as it were, that we are capable of forgetting it as we forget the blood in our veins. In a way it is even humiliating to watch coal miners working. It raises in you a momentary doubt about your own status as an "intellectual" and a superior person generally. For it is brought home to you, at least while you are watching, that it is only because miners sweat their guts out that superior persons can remain superior. You and I and the editor of the *Times Lit. Supp.*, and the Nancy poets and the Archbishop of Canterbury and Comrade X, author of *Marxism for Infants*—all of us *really* owe the comparative decency of our lives to poor drudges underground, blackened to the eyes, with their throats full of coal dust, driving their shovels forward with arms and belly muscles of steel.

NO NO SMOKING (1976)

Russell Baker

I have nothing against people who don't smoke. I stopped smoking myself for five years once and it didn't do me any noticeable harm. If people want to sit around not smoking, it doesn't offend me in the least. I certainly wouldn't bully them and try to make them feel absolutely terrible about not taking up the habit.

If I were a cab driver, I wouldn't dream of pasting a sign in my taxi that said: "Smoke!" And even if I did and somebody got in my cab and didn't light up, I would never turn around and say, "There is no nonsmoking in this cab."

If I invited somebody to dinner who didn't smoke, it would never occur to me to embarrass and humiliate her, or even him, by saying, "If you're not going to smoke, will you please go outside where it doesn't irritate the other guests?"

As a smoker, I feel no sense of moral superiority whatever. I don't even feel self-righteous about smoking. Not even when I am in a crowded room with 15 or 20 nonsmokers. After all, I might want to give up smoking again one of these days, and if I do I don't want smokers looking down their noses at me.

Being of this turn of mind, I am baffled by the growing intolerance among so many people who don't smoke. Not long ago, I was severely put down by a New York cab driver for lighting up in his machine. It was puzzling. He was offended by my smoking, yet I wasn't in the least offended by his not smoking.

What was behind his eagerness to oppress me? Was it a tyrannical concern for my health? Not likely. As a pedestrian, I know from long experience that New York cab drivers are utterly indifferent to my physical longevity.

Was it a concern for his own health? Some fear that my used smoke would filter under the filthy plastic barrier which separated us and shorten his years? This made no sense at all. He was, after all, spending his life running an internal-combustion engine whose poisonous fumes surrounded him during all his working hours.

Such minute quantities of my used smoke as he might inhale were negligible compared to the vast clouds of sulphur and carbon gases in which he had voluntarily chosen to spend his life. Moreover, both shock absorbers and springs had long ago disappeared from his cab and he was willingly submitting to the risk of grave spinal damage by spending hours every day jolting and crashing through an endless series of uncushioned collisions with New York's thousands of potholes.

On the floor of the rear seat there was sundry garbage, including what I later discovered to be some fairly typical New York dog droppings. A man concerned about his health would scarcely live in such constant proximity to burgeoning bacterial colonies. Obviously, it wasn't health that had turned him into a tyrant. Some subtler factor was at work. Something had persuaded him that the smokers of the world were an inferior class who had to be elevated, brutally if necessary, by society's better people, its nonsmokers.

This is a fairly new attitude among nonsmokers, and I believe it results from the diminishing number of people in this country whom one can treat with intolerance and contempt without risk of being called a bigot. Until very recently, there were dozens of classes of people to whom one could safely feel superior. Nowadays, you can't even tell a Polish joke without being hailed before the Committee for Stamping Out Bigotry. The list of people who can safely be pushed around, which used to include "ethnics"— whatever they are—and blacks, Jews, women, Catholics, Dixiecrats, Californians, fundamentalists, homosexuals, professors and poets—has been so diminished by the forces of uplift that there is scarcely anybody left.

Smokers, I suspect, are being used to replace them by people who can't make it through the day without having an inferior class to feel superior to. Already, the airlines—the buses of the late 20th century—force smokers to ride in the back of the plane. Some restaurants have already begun to segregate smokers from other diners. In New York City, where breathing the municipal air is equivalent to smoking two packs of cigarettes a day, smokers are subject to criminal punishment for smoking in many stores while city buses puff gales of exhaust fumes with legal impunity.

Smokers have historically been tolerant of their nonsmoking compatriots. Too tolerant perhaps. It may be time for us to go on the attack and start accusing the nonsmokers of bigotry. If we put on enough heat, we can give them such guilty consciences that they will never again be able to refuse to light up after dinner without explaining that some of their best friends are smokers.

PROFESSIONAL TRAVELING (1983)

Jewell Parker Rhodes

Business travel can be treacherous when you're female and black. Sooner or later, in neon script, the double whammy of racism and sexism hits.

One morning in Saratoga, I was nibbling a cantaloupe for breakfast when a white colleague cracked a watermelon joke. "I thought y'all preferred to pick seeds," he said. A white couple at an Ivy League Club in New York mistook me for a maid and asked me to clean their room—despite the fact that my hair was neatly pinned, I carried a briefcase, and wore my "intellectual" glasses and my three-piece pinstripe suit. A fellow professor at a convention in Detroit assumed I was a local black hooker. Why? I wasn't near a bar. On one excursion South, I eschewed a conference cafeteria lunch in favor of a hamburger diner; over relish and onions, an ancient white man offered me five dollars if I took a trip to his house: "Just for an hour." (He must have been recalling pre-inflation days.) Needless to say, my professional performance lacked luster when I delivered my paper during the afternoon conference session.

Like an innocent or a fool, I begin each trip with optimism, still determined that race and sex not impede my performance and acceptance. My pretensions get depressed.

How potent is the subliminal irritation of being the only woman on the businessman's shuttle between New York and Washington? Of being the only minority at a professional meeting? Each trip represents for me a lesson in alienation. Yet because I'm conducting business, "networking," and trying to promote a career, I can't afford feeling alien since it engenders mistrust and withdrawal. So each trip I'm vulnerable anew.

Why *can't* business travel be pleasurable? I've read all the books and articles on "how to dress for success." Wind me up and I conduct myself with adequate charm. But after following all the advice, I find myself still belittled—*and* rendered less effective—due to the emotional and psychological assaults.

Articles and books don't tell you how to deal with the loneliness of being the only visible minority in a Midwestern town, or in an airport, or at a meeting. Once I walked through a community for hours and never saw another face with the slightest hint of brown. I did, however, spend my evenings being interrogated by "well-intentioned" liberals who wanted my opinion on every civil rights issue since the Civil War. Willy-nilly, I am a spokesperson for my race.

Articles and books also don't tell you how to deal with sexual assaults beyond "carry a book to dinner." My rage gets dissipated only in a Howard Johnson's hotel room, alone, with room service.

It becomes doubly hard to ward off sexual invitation when you feel intense loneliness because nowhere else in the conference, the hotel, or the lounge, is there anyone who in the least resembles your sex or color. One loneliness begets another. Yet ward off sexual invitations you must—since the macho, conquering male abounds at professional meetings and since men compound their sexism with racist awe regarding your color. Any nonwhite characteristics can be viewed as exotic plumes.

Once, in the District of Columbia following a conference dinner, my white male colleague and escort was nearly attacked by three black youths. Only a police officer delayed their action. Do you honestly believe I was at my professional peak the next day? And there also have been predominantly black conferences where sexist attitudes angered me so intensely I could barely function. I recall the time in Ohio when an African colleague called me in my hotel room at 1:30 in the morning so we could "discuss" improved relations between his country and mine. The rest of the night I didn't sleep.

In Atlanta, I spent a whole day shunning a black male's advances. The bathroom provided my sole measure of peace. At dinner, I was enjoying my conversation with an author on my right when my ego-bruised pursuer shouted, "I'm a man too!" I groaned. I wanted to hide beneath the table. I'd forgotten that any public conversation between a male and female is seen as sexual.

What are the strategies for negotiating the sexist and racist trails of professional meetings? I honestly don't know. A business suit doesn't necessarily serve as armor. A book doesn't shield one from all sexual encounters. I've tried wearing makeup and no makeup. I've tried dressing up and dressing down. I've tried the schoolmarm's bun and also the thick-rimmed glasses. Still sexism abounds. Superficial transformations don't negate discrimination. About my color, I can do nothing (nor would I want to if I could).

The best one can do is try to prevail with dignity. When I've been the only woman at a conference, I search for minority colleagues—shared interests and shared culture sometimes bind. When I've been the only black, I search for women—women hug you when you're down and encourage you in your work. When I've been the only black *and* the only woman, I call long distance to reach out and touch a friend.

Sometimes humor helps. One year I dressed severely to compensate for my baby face. I wore high heels to compensate for my lack of height. I felt every inch the professional. Yet at the academic convention registration, I was brusquely pulled aside. "Can't you read the signs? Student registration is to the right."

If they don't get you for race and sex, they get you for something else.

AIRPORT: A TAKEOFF ON A POEM (1980)

E. Ethelbert Miller

sitting in the airport
for about two hours
i finally landed a conversation
with an old white lady who looked
mulatto
she asked me if i was a student
at the university
i told her no
she asked me what i did
i told her i wrote poetry
she asked me what i wanted to do
i told her i had always
wanted to kill a large number of people
i told her of my desire to climb into
clocktowers and be a sniper
i told her that i had missed the draft
and was too proud to enlist
i told her about all the audie murphy
films i had ever seen
i told her that i was the type
that carried bombs inside luggage
when making short trips
i watched the old mulatto lady
turn white
there was no mistaking it now
she was a white lady and i . . .

well i have been sitting in this
airport for over two hours more
listening to the soft ticking sounds
coming from the case i carry my poems in

NOTES ON PUNCTUATION (1979)

Lewis Thomas

There are no precise rules about punctuation (Fowler lays out some general
advice (as best he can under the complex circumstances of English prose (he
points out, for example, that we possess only four stops (the comma, the
semicolon, the colon and the period (the question mark and exclamation
point are not, strictly speaking, stops; they are indicators of tone (oddly

enough, the Greeks employed the semicolon for their question mark (it produces a strange sensation to read a Greek sentence which is a straightforward question: Why weepest thou; (instead of Why weepest thou? (and, of course, there are parentheses (which are surely a kind of punctuation making this whole matter much more complicated by having to count up the left-handed parentheses in order to be sure of closing with the right number (but if the parentheses were left out, with nothing to work with but the stops, we would have considerably more flexibility in the deploying of layers of meaning than if we tried to separate all the clauses by physical barriers (and in the latter case, while we might have more precision and exactitude for our meaning, we would lose the essential flavor of language, which is its wonderful ambiguity)))))))))))).

The commas are the most useful and usable of all the stops. It is highly important to put them in place as you go along. If you try to come back after doing a paragraph and stick them in the various spots that tempt you you will discover that they tend to swarm like minnows into all sorts of crevices whose existence you hadn't realized and before you know it the whole long sentence becomes immobilized and lashed up squirming in commas. Better to use them sparingly, and with affection, precisely when the need for each one arises, nicely, by itself.

I have grown fond of semicolons in recent years. The semicolon tells you that there is still some question about the preceding full sentence; something needs to be added; it reminds you sometimes of the Greek usage. It is almost always a greater pleasure to come across a semicolon than a period. The period tells you that that is that; if you didn't get all the meaning you wanted or expected, anyway you got all the writer intended to parcel out and now you have to move along. But with a semicolon there you get a pleasant little feeling of expectancy; there is more to come; read on; it will get clearer.

Colons are a lot less attractive, for several reasons: firstly, they give you the feeling of being rather ordered around, or at least having your nose pointed in a direction you might not be inclined to take if left to yourself, and, secondly, you suspect you're in for one of those sentences that will be labeling the points to be made: firstly, secondly and so forth, with the implication that you haven't sense enough to keep track of a sequence of notions without having them numbered. Also, many writers use this system loosely and incompletely, starting out with number one and number two as though counting off on their fingers but then going on and on without the succession of labels you've been led to expect, leaving you floundering about searching for the ninethly or seventeenthly that ought to be there but isn't.

Exclamation points are the most irritating of all. Look! they say, look at what I just said! How amazing is my thought! It is like being forced to watch someone else's small child jumping up and down crazily in the center of the living room shouting to attract attention. If a sentence really has something of importance to say, something quite remarkable, it doesn't need a mark to point it out. And if it is really, after all, a banal sentence needing more zing, the exclamation point simply emphasizes its banality!

Quotation marks should be used honestly and sparingly, when there is a genuine quotation at hand, and it is necessary to be very rigorous about the words enclosed by the marks. If something is to be quoted, the *exact* words must be used. If part of it must be left out because of space limitations, it is good manners to insert three dots to indicate the omission, but it is unethical to do this if it means connecting two thoughts which the original author did not intend to have tied together. Above all, quotation marks should not be used for ideas that you'd like to disown, things in the air so to speak. Nor should they be put in place around clichés; if you want to use a cliché you must take full responsibility for it yourself and not try to job it off on anon., or on society. The most objectionable misuse of quotation marks, but one which illustrates the dangers of misuse in ordinary prose, is seen in advertising, especially in advertisements for small restaurants, for example "just around the corner," or "a good place to eat." No single, identifiable, citable person ever really said, for the record, "just around the corner," much less "a good place to eat," least likely of all for restaurants of the type that use this type of prose.

The dash is a handy device, informal and essentially playful, telling you that you're about to take off on a different tack but still in some way connected with the present course—only you have to remember that the dash is there, and either put a second dash at the end of the notion to let the reader know that he's back on course, or else end the sentence, as here, with a period.

The greatest danger in punctuation is for poetry. Here it is necessary to be as economical and parsimonious with commas and periods as with the words themselves, and any marks that seem to carry their own subtle meanings, like dashes and little rows of periods, even semicolons and question marks, should be left out altogether rather than inserted to clog up the thing with ambiguity. A single exclamation point in a poem, no matter what else the poem has to say, is enough to destroy the whole work.

The things I like best in T. S. Eliot's poetry, especially in the *Four Quartets,* are the semicolons. You cannot hear them, but they are there, laying out the connections between the images and the ideas. Sometimes you get a glimpse of a semicolon coming, a few lines farther on, and it is like climbing a steep path through woods and seeing a wooden bench just at a bend in the road ahead, a place where you can expect to sit for a moment, catching your breath.

Commas can't do this sort of thing; they can only tell you how the different parts of a complicated thought are to be fitted together, but you can't sit, not even take a breath, just because of a comma,

WHY BEING SERIOUS IS HARD (1978)

Russell Baker

Here is a letter of friendly advice. "Be serious," it says. What it means, of course, is, "Be solemn." The distinction between being serious and being solemn seems to be vanishing among Americans, just as surely as the distinction between liberty and making a mess.

Being solemn is easy. Being serious is hard. You probably have to be born serious, or at least go through a very interesting childhood. Children almost always begin by being serious, which is what makes them so entertaining when compared to adults as a class.

Adults, on the whole, are solemn. The transition from seriousness to solemnity occurs in adolescence, a period in which Nature, for reasons of her own, plunges people into foolish frivolity. During this period the organism struggles to regain dignity by recovering childhood's genius for seriousness. It is usually a hopeless cause.

As a result, you have to settle for solemnity. Being solemn has almost nothing to do with being serious, but on the other hand, you can't go on being adolescent forever, unless you are in the performing arts, and anyhow most people can't tell the difference. In fact, though Americans talk a great deal about the virtue of being serious, they generally prefer people who are solemn over people who are serious.

In politics, the rare candidate who is serious, like Adlai Stevenson, is easily overwhelmed by one who is solemn, like General Eisenhower. This is probably because it is hard for most people to recognize seriousness, which is rare, especially in politics, but comfortable to endorse solemnity, which is as commonplace as jogging.

Jogging is solemn. Poker is serious. Once you can grasp that distinction, you are on your way to enlightenment. To promote the cause, I submit the following list from which the vital distinction should emerge more clearly.

(1) Shakespeare is serious. David Susskind is solemn.

(2) Chicago is serious. California is solemn.

(3) Blow-dry hair stylings on anchor men for local television news shows are solemn. Henry James is serious.

(4) Falling in love, getting married, having children, getting divorced and fighting over who gets the car and the Wedgewood are all serious. The new sexual freedom is solemn.

(5) Playboy is solemn. The New Yorker is serious.

(6) S. J. Perelman is serious. Norman Mailer is solemn.

(7) The Roman Empire was solemn. Periclean Athens was serious.

(8) Arguing about "structured programs" of anything is solemn. So are talking about "utilization," attending conferences on the future of anything, and group bathing when undertaken for the purpose of getting to know yourself better, or at the prescription of a swami. Taking a long walk by

ithas — ① *no faulty arguments*
② *shows that his claims are justified*
③ *compassionate* — *defense of human rights*
④ *free from self-interest*

yourself during which you devise a foolproof scheme for robbing Cartier's is serious.

(9) Washington is solemn. New York is serious. So is Las Vegas, but Miami Beach is solemn.

(10) Humphrey Bogart movies about private eyes and Randolph Scott movies about gunslingers are serious. Modern movies that are sophisticated jokes about Humphrey Bogart movies and Randolph Scott movies are solemn.

Making lists, of course, is solemn, but this is permissible in newspaper columns, because newspaper columns are solemn. They strive, after all, to reach the mass audience, and the mass audience is solemn, which accounts for the absence of seriousness in television, paperback books found on airport bookracks, the public school systems of America, wholesale furniture outlets, shopping centers and American-made automobiles.

I make no apology for being solemn rather than serious. Nor should anyone else. It is the national attitude. It is perfectly understandable. It is hard to be Periclean Athens. It is hard to be Shakespeare. It is hard to be S. J. Perelman. It is hard to be serious.

And yet, one cannot go on toward eternity without some flimsy attempt at dignity. Adolescence will not do. One must at least make the effort to resume childhood's lost seriousness, and so, with the best of intentions, one tries his best, only to end up being vastly, uninterestingly solemn.

Writing sentences that use "One" as a pronoun is solemn. Making pronouncements on American society is solemn. Turning yourself off when pronouncements threaten to gush is not exactly serious, although it shows a shred of wisdom.

— *recalls Declaration of Independence idea of freedom* — *democracy* —

I HAVE A DREAM (1963)

Martin Luther King, Jr.

Gettysburg address

imaginary pathos

Five score years ago, a great American, in whose symbolic shadow we stand, signed the Emancipation Proclamation. This momentous decree came as a great beacon light of hope to millions of Negro slaves who had been seared in the flames of withering injustice. It came as a joyous daybreak to end the long night of captivity.

FACTS

But one hundred years later, we must face the tragic fact that the Negro is still not free. One hundred years later, the life of the Negro is still sadly crippled by the manacles of segregation and the chains of discrimination. One hundred years later, the Negro lives on a lonely island of poverty in the midst of a vast ocean of material prosperity. One hundred years later, the Negro is still languishing in the corners of American society and finds himself an exile in his own land. So we have come here today to dramatize an appalling condition.

pathos — *appeal to our sense of injustice*

In a sense we have come to our nation's Capitol to cash a check. When the architects of our republic wrote the magnificent words of the Constitution and the Declaration of Independence, they were signing a promissory note to which every American was to fall heir. This note was a promise that all men would be guaranteed the unalienable rights of life, liberty, and the pursuit of happiness.

It is obvious today that America has defaulted on this promissory note insofar as her citizens of color are concerned. Instead of honoring this sacred obligation, America has given the Negro people a bad check; a check which has come back marked "insufficient funds." But we refuse to believe that the bank of justice is bankrupt. We refuse to believe that there are insufficient funds in the great vaults of opportunity of this nation. So we have come to cash this check—a check that will give us upon demand the riches of freedom and the security of justice. We have also come to this hallowed spot to remind America of the fierce urgency of *now*. This is no time to engage in the luxury of cooling off or to take the tranquilizing drug of gradualism. *Now* is the time to make real the promises of Democracy. *Now* is the time to rise from the dark and desolate valley of segregation to the sunlit path of racial justice. *Now* is the time to open the doors of opportunity to all of God's children. *Now* is the time to lift our nation from the quicksands of racial injustice to the solid rock of brotherhood.

It would be fatal for the nation to overlook the urgency of the moment and to underestimate the determination of the Negro. This sweltering summer of the Negro's legitimate discontent will not pass until there is an invigorating autumn of freedom and equality. 1963 is not an end, but a beginning. Those who hope that the Negro needed to blow off steam and will now be content will have a rude awakening if the nation returns to business as usual. There will be neither rest nor tranquillity in America until the Negro is granted his citizenship rights. The whirlwinds of revolt will continue to shake the foundations of our nation until the bright day of justice emerges.

But there is something I must say to my people who stand on the warm threshold which leads into the palace of justice. In the process of gaining our rightful place we must not be guilty of wrongful deeds. Let us not seek to satisfy our thirst for freedom by drinking from the cup of bitterness and hatred. We must forever conduct our struggle on the high plane of dignity and discipline. We must not allow our creative protest to degenerate into physical violence. Again and again we must rise to the majestic heights of meeting physical force with soul force. The marvelous new militancy which has engulfed the Negro community must not lead us to a distrust of all white people, for many of our white brothers, as evidenced by their presence here today, have come to realize that their destiny is tied up with our destiny and their freedom is inextricably bound to our freedom. We cannot walk alone.

And as we walk, we must make the pledge that we shall march ahead.

concession
somewhat

We cannot turn back. There are those who are asking the devotees of civil rights, "When will you be satisfied?" We can never be satisfied as long as the Negro is the victim of the unspeakable horrors of police brutality. We ① can never be satisfied as long as our bodies, heavy with the fatigue of travel, cannot gain lodging in the motels of the highways and the hotels of the ② cities. We cannot be satisfied as long as the Negro's basic mobility is from a smaller ghetto to a larger one. We can never be satisfied as long as a Negro in Mississippi cannot vote and a Negro in New York believes he has ③ nothing for which to vote. No, no, we are not satisfied, and we will not be satisfied until justice rolls down like waters and righteousness like a mighty stream.

I am not unmindful that some of you have come here out of great trials and tribulations. Some of you have come fresh from narrow jail cells. Some of you have come from areas where your quest for freedom left you battered by the storms of persecution and staggered by the winds of police brutality. You have been the veterans of creative suffering. Continue to work with the faith that unearned suffering is redemptive.

Go back to Mississippi, go back to Alabama, go back to South Carolina, go back to Georgia, go back to Louisiana, go back to the slums and ghettoes of our northern cities, knowing that somehow this situation can and will be changed. Let us not wallow in the valley of despair.

I say to you today, my friends, that in spite of the difficulties and frustrations of the moment I still have a dream. It is a dream deeply rooted in the American dream.

I have a dream that one day this nation will rise up and live out the true meaning of its creed: "We hold these truths to be self-evident; that all men } FACT are created equal."

I have a dream that one day on the red hills of Georgia the sons of former slaves and the sons of former slaveowners will be able to sit down together at the table of brotherhood.

I have a dream that the state of Mississippi, a desert state sweltering with the heat of injustice and oppression, will be transformed into an oasis of freedom and justice.

I have a dream that my four little children will one day live in a nation where they will not be judged by the color of their skin but by the content of their character.

I have a dream today.

I have a dream that the state of Alabama, whose governor's lips are presently dripping with the words of interposition and nullification, will be transformed into a situation where little black boys and black girls will be able to join hands with little white boys and white girls and walk together as sisters and brothers.

I have a dream today.

I have a dream that one day every valley shall be exalted, every hill and mountain shall be made low, the rough places will be made plain, and the

negro is
a man
therefore
creation
equal
deserves
equality

crooked places will be made straight, and the glory of the Lord shall be revealed, and all flesh shall see it together.

This is our hope. This is the faith with which I return to the South. With this faith we will be able to hew out of the mountain of despair a stone of hope. With this faith we will be able to transform the jangling discords of our nation into a beautiful symphony of brotherhood. With this faith we will be able to work together, to pray together, to struggle together, to go to jail together, to stand up for freedom together, knowing that we will be free one day.

This will be the day when all of God's children will be able to sing with new meaning

My country, tis of thee
Sweet land of liberty,
Of thee I sing:
Land where my fathers died,
Land of the pilgrims' pride,
From every mountainside
Let freedom ring.

And if America is to be a great nation this must become true. So let freedom ring from the prodigious hilltops of New Hampshire. Let freedom ring from the mighty mountains of New York. Let freedom ring from the heightening Alleghenies of Pennsylvania!

Let freedom ring from the snowcapped Rockies of Colorado!

Let freedom ring from the curvacious peaks of California!

But not only that; let freedom ring from Stone Mountain of Georgia!

Let freedom ring from Lookout Mountain of Tennessee!

Let freedom ring from every hill and molehill of Mississippi. From every mountainside, let freedom ring.

When we let freedom ring, when we let it ring from every village and every hamlet, from every state and every city, we will be able to speed up that day when all of God's children, black men and white men, Jews and Gentiles, Protestants and Catholics, will be able to join hands and sing in the words of the old Negro spiritual, "Free at last! free at last! thank God almighty, we are free at last!"

HANDS (1919)

Sherwood Anderson

Upon the half decayed veranda of a small frame house that stood near the edge of a ravine near the town of Winesburg, Ohio, a fat little old man walked nervously up and down. Across a long field that had been seeded for clover but that had produced only a dense crop of yellow mustard weeds, he could see the public highway along which went a wagon filled with berry pickers returning from the fields. The berry pickers, youths and maidens, laughed and shouted boisterously. A boy clad in a blue shirt leaped from the wagon and attempted to drag after him one of the maidens, who screamed and protested shrilly. The feet of the boy in the road kicked up a cloud of dust that floated across the face of the departing sun. Over the long field came a thin girlish voice, "Oh, you Wing Biddlebaum, comb your hair, it's falling into your eyes," commanded the voice to the man, who was bald and whose nervous little hands fiddled about the bare white forehead as though arranging a mass of tangled locks.

Wing Biddlebaum, forever frightened and beset by a ghostly band of doubts, did not think of himself as in any way a part of the life of the town where he had lived for twenty years. Among all the people of Winesburg but one had come close to him. With George Willard, son of Tom Willard, the proprietor of the New Willard House, he had formed something like a friendship. George Willard was the reporter on the *Winesburg Eagle* and sometimes in the evenings he walked out along the highway to Wing Biddlebaum's house. Now as the old man walked up and down on the veranda, his hands moving nervously about, he was hoping that George Willard would come and spend the evening with him. After the wagon containing the berry pickers had passed, he went across the field through the tall mustard weeds and climbing a rail fence peered anxiously along the road to the town. For a moment he stood thus, rubbing his hands together and looking up and down the road, and then, fear overcoming him, ran back to walk again upon the porch on his own house.

In the presence of George Willard, Wing Biddlebaum, who for twenty years had been the town mystery, lost something of his timidity, and his shadowy personality, submerged in a sea of doubts, came forth to look at the world. With the young reporter at his side, he ventured in the light of day into Main Street or strode up and down on the rickety front porch of his own house, talking excitedly. The voice that had been low and trembling became shrill and loud. The bent figure straightened. With a kind of wriggle, like a fish returned to the brook by the fisherman, Biddlebaum the silent began to talk, striving to put into words the ideas that had been accumulated by his mind during long years of silence.

Wing Biddlebaum talked much with his hands. The slender expressive fingers, forever active, forever striving to conceal themselves in his pockets or behind his back, came forth and became the piston rods of his machinery of expression.

The story of Wing Biddlebaum is a story of hands. Their restless activity, like unto the beating of the wings of an imprisoned bird, had given him his name. Some obscure poet of the town had thought of it. The hands alarmed their owner. He wanted to keep them hidden away and looked with amazement at the quiet inexpressive hands of other men who worked beside him in the fields, or passed, driving sleepy teams on country roads.

When he talked to George Willard, Wing Biddlebaum closed his fists and beat with them upon a table or on the walls of his house. The action made him more comfortable. If the desire to talk came to him when the two were walking in the fields, he sought out a stump or the top board of a fence and with his hands pounding busily talked with renewed ease.

The story of Wing Biddlebaum's hands is worth a book in itself. Sympathetically set forth it would tap many strange, beautiful qualities in obscure men. It is a job for a poet. In Winesburg the hands had attracted attention merely because of their activity. With them Wing Biddlebaum had picked as high as a hundred and forty quarts of strawberries in a day. They became his distinguishing feature, the source of his fame. Also they made more grotesque an already grotesque and elusive individuality. Winesburg was proud of the hands of Wing Biddlebaum in the same spirit in which it was proud of Banker White's new stone house and Wesley Moyer's bay stallion, Tony Tip, that had won the two-fifteen trot at the fall races in Cleveland.

As for George Willard, he had many times wanted to ask about the hands. At times an almost overwhelming curiosity had taken hold of him. He felt that there must be a reason for their strange activity and their inclination to keep hidden away and only a growing respect for Wing Biddlebaum kept him from blurting out the questions that were often in his mind.

Once he had been on the point of asking. The two were walking in the fields on a summer afternoon and had stopped to sit upon a grassy bank. All afternoon Wing Biddlebaum had talked as one inspired. By a fence he had stopped and beating like a giant woodpecker upon the top board had shouted at George Willard, condemning his tendency to be too much influenced by the people about him. "You are destroying yourself," he cried. "You have the inclination to be alone and to dream and you are afraid of dreams. You want to be like others in town here. You hear them talk and you try to imitate them."

On the grassy bank Wing Biddlebaum had tried again to drive his point home. His voice became soft and reminiscent, and with a sigh of content- ment he launched into a long rambling talk, speaking as one lost in a dream.

Out of the dream Wing Biddlebaum made a picture for George Willard. In the picture men lived again in a kind of pastoral golden age. Across a green open country came clean-limbed young men, some afoot, some mounted upon horses. In crowds the young men came to gather about the feet of an old man who sat beneath a tree in a tiny garden and who talked to them.

Wing Biddlebaum became wholly inspired. For once he forgot the hands. Slowly they stole forth and lay upon George Willard's shoulders. Something new and bold came into the voice that talked. "You must try to forget all you have learned," said the old man. "You must begin to dream. From this time on you must shut your ears to the roaring of the voices."

Pausing in his speech, Wing Biddlebaum looked long and earnestly at George Willard. His eyes glowed. Again he raised the hands to caress the boy and then a look of horror swept over his face.

With a convulsive movement of his body, Wing Biddlebaum sprang to his feet and thrust his hands deep into his trousers pockets. Tears came to his eyes. "I must be getting along home. I can talk no more with you," he said nervously.

Without looking back, the old man had hurried down the hillside and across a meadow, leaving George Willard perplexed and frightened upon the grassy slope. With a shiver of dread the boy arose and went along the road toward town. "I'll not ask him about his hands," he thought, touched by the memory of the terror he had seen in the man's eyes. "There's something wrong, but I don't want to know what it is. His hands have something to do with his fear of me and of everyone."

And George Willard was right. Let us look briefly into the story of the hands. Perhaps our talking of them will arouse the poet who will tell the hidden wonder story of the influence for which the hands were but fluttering pennants of promise.

In his youth Wing Biddlebaum had been a school teacher in a town in Pennsylvania. He was not then known as Wing Biddlebaum, but went by the less euphonic name of Adolph Myers. As Adolph Myers he was much loved by the boys of his school.

Adolph Myers was meant by nature to be a teacher of youth. He was one of those rare, little-understood men who rule by a power so gentle that it passes as a lovable weakness. In their feeling for the boys under their charge such men are not unlike the finer sort of women in their love of men.

And yet that is but crudely stated. It needs the poet there. With the boys of his school, Adolph Myers had walked in the evening or had sat talking until dusk upon the schoolhouse steps lost in a kind of dream. Here and there went his hands, caressing the shoulders of the boys, playing about the tousled heads. As he talked his voice became soft and musical. There was a caress in that also. In a way the voice and the hands, the stroking of the shoulders and the touching of the hair were a part of the schoolmaster's effort to carry a dream into the young minds. By the caress that was in his fingers he expressed himself. He was one of those men in whom the force that creates life is diffused, not centralized. Under the caress of his hands doubt and disbelief went out of the minds of the boys and they began also to dream.

And then the tragedy. A half-witted boy of the school became enamored of the young master. In his bed at night he imagined unspeakable things and in the morning went forth to tell his dreams as facts. Strange, hideous accusations fell from his loose-hung lips. Through the Pennsylvania town went a shiver. Hidden, shadowy doubts that had been in men's minds concerning Adolph Myers were galvanized into beliefs.

The tragedy did not linger. Trembling lads were jerked out of bed and questioned. "He put his arms about me," said one. "His fingers were always playing in my hair," said another.

One afternoon a man of the town, Henry Bradford, who kept a saloon, came to the schoolhouse door. Calling Adolph Myers into the school yard he began to beat him with his fists. As his hard knuckles beat down into the frightened face of the schoolmaster, his wrath became more and more terrible. Screaming with dismay, the children ran here and there like disturbed insects. "I'll teach you to put your hands on my boy, you beast," roared the saloon keeper, who, tired of beating the master, had begun to kick him about the yard.

Adolph Myers was driven from the Pennsylvania town in the night. With lanterns in their hands a dozen men came to the door of the house where he lived alone and commanded that he dress and come forth. It was raining and one of the men had a rope in his hands. They had intended to hang the schoolmaster, but something in his figure, so small, white, and pitiful, touched their hearts and they let him escape. As he ran away into the darkness they repented of their weakness and ran after him, swearing and throwing sticks and great balls of soft mud at the figure that screamed and ran faster and faster into the darkness.

For twenty years Adolph Myers had lived alone in Winesburg. He was but forty but looked sixty-five. The name of Biddlebaum he got from a box of goods seen at a freight station as he hurried through an eastern Ohio town. He had an aunt in Winesburg, a black-toothed old woman who raised chickens, and with her he lived until she died. He had been ill for a year after the experience in Pennsylvania, and after his recovery worked as a day laborer in the fields, going timidly about and striving to conceal his hands. Although he did not understand what had happened he felt that the hands must be to blame. Again and again the fathers of the boys had talked of the hands. "Keep your hands to yourself," the saloon keeper had roared, dancing with fury in the schoolhouse yard.

Upon the veranda of his house by the ravine, Wing Biddlebaum continued to walk up and down until the sun had disappeared and the road beyond the field was lost in the grey shadows. Going into his house he cut slices of bread and spread honey upon them. When the rumble of the evening train that took away the express cars loaded with the day's harvest of berries had passed and restored the silence of the summer night, he went again to walk upon the veranda. In the darkness he could not see the hands and they became quiet. Although he still hungered for the presence of the boy, who was the medium through which he expressed his love of man, the hunger became again a part of his loneliness and his waiting. Lighting a lamp, Wing Biddlebaum washed the few dishes soiled by his simple meal and, setting up a folding cot by the screen door that led to the porch, prepared to undress for the night. A few stray white bread crumbs lay on the cleanly washed floor by the table; putting the lamp upon a low stool he began to pick up the crumbs, carrying them to his mouth one by one with unbelievable rapidity. In the dense blotch of light beneath the table, the kneeling figure looked like a priest engaged in some service of his church. The nervous expressive fingers, flashing in and out of the light, might well have been mistaken for the fingers of the devotee going swiftly through decade after decade of his rosary.

13

◆

Research

The assignments were interesting, but involved a very lot of work and research for some of them.

student

I learned the most from my research assignment because 1) it taught me how to use the microfilm, 2) it helped in my organization problems, and 3) it helped me to take advantage of the libraries.

student

Exercise 13-1

Before you begin this chapter, write a few sentences in your notebook about what you think research is.

Research is *not* looking into the encyclopedia and copying out some information appropriate to your topic. It is *not* taking twenty books out of the library and picking out pieces of each to pull together into a term paper. It is *not* "changing" the words of your sources into your own words so that you can hand in a paper. Research is bringing the knowledge of the past to bear on problems of the present. It is delving into libraries and other storehouses of information to find facts from which *you* draw inferences. If and when you become a professional researcher, it will be very important that you find *all* the important facts and *all* the important sources of information before you begin to write. The purpose of professional research is to arrive at the soundest possible judgments based on the best information available.

But while you're an undergraduate, you will be assigned research papers because your teachers value curiosity, reflection, and creativity, and they know that you can only increase those skills if you practice them. Thus when you search a subject, it's important for you to find representative facts, but by no means all of them. Your teachers will be most interested not in your command of the subject you've studied but in the curiosity, reflection, and creativity with which you draw inferences from the facts you find. The facts you'll find are of several kinds.

1. The fact that something happened:

   In February 1965, President Lyndon Johnson ordered the first bombing raids into North Vietnam. [Doris Kearns, *Lyndon Johnson and the American Dream* (New York: Harper & Row, 1976), 261.]

2. The fact that someone said something:

   Sir Thomas Browne, a seventeenth-century father of eleven: "I could be content that we might procreate like trees, without conjunction, or that there were any way to perpetuate the world without this trivial vulgar way of union: it is the foolishest act a wise man commits in all his life." [Sir Thomas Browne, *The Religion of a Doctor* (New York: Dutton, 1969), 79.]

3. Statistical facts:

   The population of Kenosha, Wisconsin, in 1970 was 78,805. [*Encyclopaedia Britannica,* 15th ed. (Chicago: University of Chicago Press, 1974), 5, 760.]

4. The fact that some authority interpreted a given fact in a given way:

   Eleanor Roosevelt thought early in 1952 that Adlai Stevenson would make a good president, but she doubted whether he could get the Democratic nomination. [Joseph P. Lash, *Eleanor: The Years Alone* (New York: Norton, 1972), 206.]

The sources for all four kinds of facts must be acknowledged, as I've done above. What can't be acknowledged, because they can't be borrowed, are the inferences you draw from these facts. Your paper will be shaped by these inferences. *You* are the thinker (and the selector) at work in the history of information and ideas. When you finish a research paper, you will understand a situation much better than you did when you began, partly because you've found so much more information, but primarily because you've been forced to draw so many inferences, to make so many judgments, about the facts that you've found. If you're afraid to draw inferences (because you're underinformed), that will come through in the hesitant or dependent voice you project in your paper. On the other hand, if you report your interpretations with confidence, your readers will quickly recognize your success in making sense of the material you've worked with.

Though the term *research paper* usually means "library research paper," library research isn't, of course, the only way to locate information. When you do research, you are looking for firsthand information, and libraries are only one source of it. Other sources include:

1. Interviews.
2. Corporation records.
3. Court records.
4. City, state, or federal records.
5. Museum holdings.
6. Letters in your grandparents' attic.
7. Films, television videotapes, and radio tapes or transcripts.
8. Old copies of *Farmer's Almanac* or *National Geographic,* or old cookbooks in secondhand stores.
9. Computerized data bases with clever names, like NEXIS, for business information, or BIOSIS, for information in the biological sciences. (A data base is a huge computer-memory collection of information. You can select data for examination by typing in the key words you're interested in.)

Looking at a videotape of the June 5, 1953, *CBS Evening News* or at a January 1918 edition of the *San Francisco Chronicle* makes you feel like you're reliving history and (often) makes you feel like writing about what you feel so that you can share the feeling with others. The thrill just isn't there when you look up "World War I" or "McCarthyism" in the encyclopedia.

When you are asked to write, to write anything, the first thing that should pop into your head is *research*—you have to search somewhere for the facts from which you will draw your inferences. That research can often be completed without the help of a library. When a student decides to write about the Campus Health Center, he goes there to see what he can see, to collect any facts about it that are telling. When a book reviewer reads through a book she's just been sent by a publisher, she underlines passages that strike her as good, or bad, or unusual, and then when she starts writing, she looks back at her carefully observed underlinings to find "telling" quotations to use in her review. When a journalist interviews the owner of a successful racehorse, he observes carefully how the person acts and what is said or unsaid. Your purpose in practicing this research, this patient, thoughtful observation (besides that of learning more for yourself), is, most often, to help your teacher and classmates understand the subject of your research a little better than they did before.

Research, wherever it starts, though, often takes a writer to a library, simply because so much of our history—documents, newspapers, magazines, audiotapes, videotapes, books, academic studies—is deposited in libraries. I know you've been told before that there are "treasures" in your library, but most of us don't believe that line because what we've found—encyclopedias, summaries, and thirdhand accounts with all the human details removed—hasn't made us eager to return. General encyclopedias are useful for looking up people, places, and terms with which we're not at all familiar—"Heraclitus," perhaps, or "Odessa." They help us learn, but they rarely offer an invitation to study or to think. Many of the encyclopedia and other thirdhand accounts are dull, not just because they're thirdhand stories, but because writers so often write badly. If you were to spend a day reading randomly in the library, you'd probably spend five out of seven hours with bad—or at best mediocre —writing. But during the other two hours you might also find:

1. A firsthand account of World War II (or the 1929 stock market crash) in *Time* magazine.

2. Social thinking about birth control in 1911 in *The Yale Review*.

3. *National Geographic* articles about Iran dated 1975, 1968, 1960, 1953, 1947, 1943, and 1932.

4. Poems by Australian or African poets.

5. Firsthand accounts of life in prison, or in Colorado, or in El Salvador.

6. Local, national, and international newspapers, on microfilm, dating well back into the nineteenth, and occasionally even the eighteenth, century.

7. Microfilmed document collections—e.g., in my library, *The Archives of George Allen and Company, 1893–1915,* or *Contemporary Newspapers of the North American Indian,* or *Records and Briefs in the United States Cases Decided by the Supreme Court.*

8. Videotapes of 1940s detective films. (Films and videotapes in libraries are—perhaps surprisingly—underused, because they're not

easy to return to for patient examination; books—thanks to libraries—are easy to find and use, so they get most of the attention.)

If you get interested in Americans in Paris in the 1920s, you can probably find sixty books in your library on the subject, some to be flipped to the side quickly, others so absorbing that you won't want to leave.

You'll do yourself a great favor if you make your local library a familiar resource. Take the library tour at your library to learn its main features, but stick around after the tour is over and watch a few tapes, look over some old documents, browse through some old magazines. You may feel, once school starts, that you're too busy to "shop" in the library, but you can always procrastinate on a paper or on anything else you're doing in the library by finding your favorite shelf and taking down a book or a magazine.

Because libraries collect so much chaotic information, useful and seemingly useless, well written and poorly written, they need a system to organize it and make it possible for users to find what they're looking for. The Chinese, who formed libraries as early as the sixth century B.C., divided their collections into "classics," "history," "philosophy," and "literature." Our modern libraries are fuller, and therefore our classification systems are more complex. Almost all United States libraries organize their collections using either the Library of Congress classification system or the Dewey decimal classification system.

The Library of Congress (LC) system uses letters of the alphabet to classify holdings, and the Dewey decimal system uses three-digit numbers:

The Library of Congress System

A	General Works
B	Philosophy, Psychology, Religion
C	History and Auxiliary Sciences
D	History and Topography (except North and South America)
E–F	History: North and South America
G	Geography and Anthropology
H	Social Sciences: Economics, Sociology, Statistics
J	Political Science
K	Law
L	Education
M	Music
N	Fine Arts: Architecture, Painting, Sculpture
P	Language and Literature
Q	Science
R	Medicine

S   Agriculture

T   Technology

U   Military Science

V   Naval Science

Z   Bibliography and Library Science

The Dewey Decimal System

000–099   General Works

100–199   Philosophy

200–299   Religion

300–399   Social Sciences

400–499   Language

500–599   Pure Science

600–699   Technology (Applied Science)

700–799   The Arts

800–899   Literature

900–999   General Geography and History

These systems were developed during the 1870s—the Dewey by Melvil Dewey for the Amherst College Library, the Library of Congress by Charles Cutter for the Library of Congress—and although both systems have proved useful enough to last more than a century, neither is *so* good that it has driven out the other. Today you'll find that most college libraries use the Library of Congress system and that most public libraries use the Dewey system. The systems are used to classify a library's holdings not only in books but in magazines, films, tapes, and microforms as well. Thus the call number for the book *Cosmos,* by Carl Sagan, in the LC system is as follows:

```
QB44.2
.5235
```

The call number for the videotaped television series of the same name is this:

```
VIDEO CASSETTE
QB 981
.c83
```

And a related journal, *Space Sciences Review,* has this call number:

```
Q81
.577
```

More important than trying to remember what call numbers are associated with what subject is becoming familiar with your library's principal rooms. These vary from library to library, but in general you'll find that you want to know:

1. The catalog (until recently almost always a *card* catalog, now increasingly on microfiche).
2. The book stacks.
3. The reference room.
4. The periodicals room.
5. The nonprint media room.

To get a sense of the layout of these rooms in your own library, you might try the following exercises (or similar exercises specific to your library). If you are stumped at any point, ask a librarian for help. Librarians know well how complex a research task can be, and they welcome the opportunity to teach us how to use the library efficiently.

The Catalog and the Book Stacks

Exercise 13-2

A. Recall that the catalog contains not only title cards and author cards (or microfiche notes) but also subject cards. Find the call number for a book about United States agriculture written during the 1920s (try the 1950s if that's impossible).
B. Locate your book in the stacks, and write down the floor and the shelf where you found it. (If you don't find it, ask a librarian how you can find out where it might be, and explain to your class what you learned by asking.)

The Reference Room

Exercise 13-3

A. Go to the reference section of your library, and browse to see what's available. Find a book in the reference section that you'd like to spend more time with, or one that leads you to an interesting book or magazine elsewhere in the library. In class the next day, identify and describe the book that helped you so that others will realize that it's available. Also mention at least two other books from the reference section, perhaps less intriguing, but at least useful.

B. What is the call number and location in the reference section of *The New York Times Index?* of the *Readers' Guide to Periodical Literature?* What is the earliest date for which each is available?

C. By using *The New York Times Index,* identify two articles written for *The New York Times* in 1964 about inflation.[1] Give the dates and a brief description of each (the *Index* will give you all this information).

The Periodicals Room

Libraries use the term *periodical* to refer to newspapers, magazines, journals, and any other kinds of reports that are published "periodically," at regular intervals.

Exercise 13-4

A. The list of what periodicals are available in your library is usually called the *serials list.* (*Serials* is a term that includes all periodicals, as well as reports and journals that come out not periodically, but irregularly.) Using the serials list, find the call number of *Time* magazine and note the date of the earliest *Time* that is owned by your library.

B. Look up (on microfilm) *The New York Times* from the day that one of your parents was born. In class the next day, describe, using two or three examples, the world into which your parent was born.

C. Introduce yourself to *The Yale Review,* a magazine that is still published, but perhaps one that was in its glory from 1911 to 1920. During those years, *The Yale Review* contained articles on everything you could think of, from homosexuality to real estate holdings by railroads to new discoveries in radiation. Look at the library's serials list to see where *The Yale Review* is located in the library. Once you find it on the shelves, leaf through one of the 1911–1920 volumes (or the earliest volume your library has), and read an article that catches your interest. (If your library does not carry *The Yale Review,* try some other magazine published during the 1930s or earlier.) While you read, take some notes, including at least the following:

    1. The author's main point

    2. Two or three assumptions that the author makes

    3. Five to ten fact-inference pairs that the author uses

    4. The *ethos* that the author presents

When you're finished with this article, stop in the reference room and check the *Readers' Guide to Periodical Literature* to see if you can find at least one other article by the author of your article, or at least one other article written on the same subject during the same decade. After finding this second article and reading it, note briefly the difference between the two articles. In class the next week, compare your notes with those taken by others in your class.

[1] *Note:* Before using any reference book, save yourself time and confusion by reading the preface, in which its methods, aims, and abbreviations are explained.

The Nonprint Media Room

Exercise 13-5

Browse through the separate nonprint catalog, if there is one, or the central catalog, if not, and pick out a videotape that you've never seen before. Check it out, watch it, and note whether the tape was fiction or nonfiction, persuasive or informative, well-made or ill-made. Compare your results with those of your classmates.

* * * * *

You may already have written research papers that you've learned from and been proud of. If so, you know that an invitation to write another library research paper is an opportunity to learn yet another subject well. On the other hand, you may never have written a research paper, or you may have written several that you didn't much care for. If you are in this "other hand," let's start fresh this time and make the most of the opportunity.

First, it helps to recognize that any long paper is not written through the use of only one or two skills. There are many constituent skills in research-paper writing. Let's consider several of these one at a time.

1. *Following a Curiosity Trail*   When you start work on a research paper and your subject has not been specified for you, indirection can often serve you as well as direction. As I was preparing this chapter, for example, I decided that I wanted to use as an example an opinion by Eleanor Roosevelt. I'm not sure why I chose her; I suppose it was because I've always admired her. I liked the *Eleanor and Franklin* show on television, and I knew there was a book of the same name, so I thought I'd look the book up in the card catalog. First, though, I wondered whether I could find an opinion of hers more easily in the *Encyclopaedia Britannica* (which I could look at in the reference room, on the same floor I was on). The very brief article there on Eleanor Roosevelt didn't tell me much (it didn't mention any of her opinions), but it recommended two books by Joseph Lash, *Eleanor and Franklin* and *Eleanor: The Years Alone*. Now I felt more confident going to *Eleanor and Franklin* because I could be more sure that it was a respectable source. So I headed for the card catalog (still on the second floor) and looked up Joseph Lash. He had written several books on Mrs. Roosevelt during the 1960s and 1970s, and he had also made a cassette or two (held by our library) talking

about the books. I copied out the call numbers $\left(\begin{array}{ccc} E807.1 & E807.1 & E807.1 \\ .R572 & .R573 & .R574 \end{array} \right)$ I might be able to use, but I also noticed that Lash was born in 1909 and that

he had written a book back in 1936 called *War Our Heritage:* $\boxed{\begin{array}{c} JX\ 1953 \\ .L33 \end{array}}$. That sounded like a pacifist book by a very young man, and I've long been intrigued by the philosophical passions Americans of the thirties seem to have had—I've seen nothing like them in my lifetime: the passions I knew during the sixties were more political than philosophical. So after I picked up a couple of E807s on the fourth floor, I stopped on the third floor to pick up the JX book. Before I looked at *Eleanor and Franklin,* I paged through *War Our Heritage.* Sure enough, it was a pacifist argument, with a preface by a World War I–era pacifist, much older, who explained how he thought pacifism had changed since his youth. If I were responsible for a research paper later this term, I'd have had the beginnings of an idea for a paper—a comparison of the pacifist attitudes of 1930s students with those of 1910s students. I'd look into the preface writer, Bruce Bliven, to see whether he'd written anything else. I'd note anybody else whom Lash mentioned or footnoted in his book. But mostly I'd look into my favorite sources— newspapers and magazines, of 1915, say, and 1935 (using *The New York Times Index* and the *Readers' Guide* to look up "Pacifism")—and find some contemporary thought on the subject.

The only difficulty in following a curiosity trail is starting it. The trails don't begin very easily in your own brain, even if you're a naturally curious person. Suggested Assignment 4 in Chapter 15 starts you with the issue of *The New York Times* published on the day of your birth. But you can start a curiosity trail almost anywhere in the library—in an article about the effects of railroads on Chicago's urban planning that you find in a book in the reference room called *The Encyclopedia of Urban Planning* (Arnold Whittich, McGraw-Hill, 1974), in an article about acid rain in Norway from a magazine that you pick up in the periodicals room called *Research in Norway,* in a short videotape that you find lying around in the nonprint media room called *Basic Film Terms.* Once you pick up a book or a magazine or a tape, you've started on your curiosity trail, and you can follow the trail in whatever direction you like. Make your research a genuine search, a search which heads in a direction that fascinates you.

2. Finding Information Systematically This search strategy is much more thorough and direct than following a curiosity trail. A systematic search begins not at the card catalog, but in the reference room. Welcome to the world of indexes. It seems at first forbidding, but you'll soon appreciate what it can do for you.

I'd like to introduce you here to two reference books for looking up current issues, two reference sources for looking up historical issues, and one very useful source for background information on any subject. Once you've located and used these books and checked into the books near them on the reference shelves, you'll leave any sketchy advice I can offer far behind you.

When you have a paper assignment that requires you to study a topic of current controversy, two excellent books you'll probably want to turn to are *Public Affairs Information Service Bulletin* (New York: Public Affairs Information Service, Inc., published yearly) and *Bibliographic Index* (New York: H. W. Wilson, published yearly). *PAIS* is most useful when you're looking for statistics or when you're writing on an issue with public policy implications, for it indexes articles, books, and pamphlets in all fields, as long as they bear on public policy decisions. Here's a typical excerpt (521):

Public relations

† Maddalena, Lucille A. A communications manual for nonprofit organizations. '81 222p bibl il chart index (LC 80-67965) (ISBN 0-8144-5606-5) $17.95—*Am mgt assns*

INSTRUCTIONAL MATERIALS. See Education - Instructional materials.

INSULATION

Hirst, Eric and Raj Talwar. Reducing energy consumption in low-income homes: evaluation of the weatherization program in Minnesota. bibl tables *Evaluation R 5:671-85 O '81*

Smith, Gaines. Stormy weatherization: billed as models for the rest of the nation, mandatory insulation programs in Oregon are models of special-interest politicking. *Reason 13:31-9 F '82*

United States. House. Com. on Small Bus. Subcom. on Antitrust and Restraint of Trade Activities Affecting Small Bus. EPA [Environmental Protection Agency] proposed rulemaking on chlorofluorocarbons (CFCs) and its impact on small business: hearing, July 15, 1981. '81 iv+202p bibl tables chart (97th Cong., 1st Sess.) pa—*Washington, DC 20515*
　　Synthetic compounds used widely in the refrigeration industry and in insulation.

INSURANCE
　　See also
　　Annuities.

I learn here (after checking abbreviations in the abbreviation key at the front of the volume) that I can find information on insulation policy in *Evaluation Review,* Volume 5 (October 1981), pages 671 to 685, in *Reason: Free Minds and Free Markets,* Volume 13 (February 1982), pages 31 to 39, and in a published 202-page July 15, 1981, hearing of a congressional subcommittee entitled "EPA Proposed Rulemaking on Chlorofluorocarbons and Its Impact on Small Business" (which should be available in my library's government documents collection). Perhaps one of these sources will prove valuable and interesting; perhaps this source, or one of the others, will mention another possible source or even include a bibliography of further sources.

A second current-issues index, probably more valuable than *PAIS,* is the *Bibliographic Index,* which lists any bibliography (with more than fifty citations) published during a current year either separately or as part of a book, pamphlet, or periodical. If you find an entry here, it may well lead you to a single article or book that can give you your entire list of possible sources, and thus you will have more time for your note-taking and writing. I imagined that my subject was Argentina, for example, and looked up "Argentina" in the 1982 *Bibliographic Index* and found (33):

ARECUNA Indians
Thomas, David John. Order without government; the soc. of the Pemon Indians of Vene-
zuela. (Ill. studies in anthropology, no 13)
Univ. of Ill. press '82 p250-6

ARGENTINA
History
Walter, R. J. Argentina; 1862-present. Hist
Teach 14:313-26 My '81

Politics and government
Rodríguez, Celso. Lencinas y Cantoni; el po-
pulismo cuyano en tiempos de Irigoyen. Editorial de Belgrano '79 p345-67 annot

ARGENTINE painting. See Painting, Argentine
ARGUMENTATION. See Oratory
ARHAR. See Pigeon pea

ARID regions
See also
Deserts

ARID regions agriculture
See also
Dry farming

ARIDIZATION of land. See Desertification

ARISTOCRACY in literature
Stanton, Domna C. Aristocrat as art; a study
of the honnête homme and the dandy in 17th
and 19th cent. French literature. Columbia
univ. press '80 p279-300

ARISTOTLE, 384-322 B.C.
Hardie, William Francis Ross. Aristotle's ethical
theory. 2nd ed Oxford univ. press '80 p430-7
Sober, E. Evolution, population thinking, and
essentialism. Philos Sci 47:382-3 S '80

---

about

Aristoteles. La poétique; le text grec avec une
traduction et des notes de lecture par Roselyne
Dupon-Roc et Jean Lallot; pref. de Tzvetan
Todorov. Seuil '80 p463-5

Warterlow, Sarah. Nature, change, and agency

I don't read Spanish (a considerable handicap when trying to write about
Argentina), so I'll have to ignore Celso Rodríguez's article, but I will expect
to find a considerable list of sources of Argentinian history, 1862 to the
present, in *History Teacher* magazine (I decoded "Hist Teach" by looking it
up at the beginning of the *Index*), Volume 14 (May 1981), pages 313 to 326.

When you're trying to locate historical events or historical attitudes
toward issues, the most efficient indexes to turn to are *The New York Times
Index* and the *Readers' Guide to Periodical Literature. The New York Times
Index* notes every article that appeared in *The New York Times* during a
given period. As I glanced through the July to September 1916 *Index,* I came
upon "Georgia," and the entries there, though only briefly described,
would seem to offer the beginnings of a cultural history of sex, ethnic, and
political relations of the period (152):

GEORGE, V., King of England (continued)—
success, Sept. 7, I., 1:8; issues proclamation with regard to property of British
subjects in enemy countries, Sept. 9, 3:5.

GEORGE, Charles E.—wife applies for ali-
mony and counsel fees pending her suit
for divorce, July 9, I., 6:8.

GEORGE, John Valance—death, Aug. 17,
11:3.

GEORGE, E. WARREN (freighter,) *see*
SHIPBUILDING.

GEORGIA—Editorial on passage of bill per-
mitting women to practice law, July 31,
8:4; Atlanta Journal charges that T. E.
Watson is in a scheme with Louisville &
Nashville R. R. to capture State Govt. in
primaries and support H. M. Dorsey for
Gov., Sept. 11, 3:7; Dorsey attacks ex-
Gov. Slaton and charges that Jews have
raised a fund to defeat him because of
Frank case, Sept. 12, 3:3; Dorsey nominated for Gov., Sept. 13, 1:4; editorial,

> Sept. 14, 6:3; letter by ex-Gov. Slaton re-
> plying to charges of Dorsey, Sept. 16,
> 10:6; final returns give large majority to
> Dorsey, statement by Gov. Harris, Sept.
> 20, 5:4.
>
> GERARD, (Amb.) James Watson—letter to
> A. von Briesen of Amer. Physicians' Ex-
> pedition Committee commending work of
> hospital in Germany, July 9, I., 14:1;
> plans to take rest in Scandinavia, July 11,

These entries are quite easy to read. The first editorial on women practicing law can be found, the *Index* says, in the July 31 (1916) *Times* on page 8, starting in column 4. Although *The New York Times Index* only locates articles in *The New York Times,* the dates of its articles often indicate where information can be found in other papers. Here, for example, I would expect that an editorial on women practicing law could be found in *The Atlanta Constitution* on or near July 31, 1916. I'd be curious to compare the perspective in the two editorials.

To get further historical information from weekly and monthly maga-zines, our best source is the *Readers' Guide to Periodical Literature,* which indexes articles in by no means all our periodicals, but in about 200 of our most popular and most respected ones. *Readers' Guide* entries look much like the entries in the other indexes, as you can see in this example from the March 1957–February 1959 volume (1610):

> RAILROADS, Toy
> For after-Christmas railroading. il Sunset 120:
> 54 Ja '58
> Now you see it, now you don't. J. C. Gon-
> zalez. il diag Am Home 59:94-5 D '57
> Roll away blackboard and train table. R. G.
> Smith, jr. il Workbench 14:18-20 N '58
> Toymaker puts a new train on the tracks.
> il Bsns W p 116-17+ Je 29 '57
>   *See also*
> Railroad models
>
> RAILROADS and state
>   United States
> Can technology solve our railroad problems?
> address, May 5, 1958. A. E. Perlman. Vital
> Speeches 24:565-8 Jl 1 '58
> Make room for competition. Farm J 82:86 Ag
> '58

Railroads: from overlord to underdog. R.
Bendiner. Reporter 19:19-24 Ag 7 '58
Railroads: the track ahead. il Newsweek 51:
78-80 Ja 20 '58
Things are looking up for the railroads. il
U S News 45:73-4 Ag 1 '58
See also
Railroads—Federal aid

RAILS (birds)
Clapper rail. H. M. Hall. il Audubon Mag 60:
72-5 Mr '58
Singing wood-rail. A. F. Skutch. il Audubon
Mag 61:20-1 Ja '59 (to be cont)

RAILTON, Arthur R.
Detroit listening post. See issues of Popular
mechanics magazine

RAILWAY express agency
Express stop? Bsns W p 18 Ja 3 '59
Expressman's burden. Newsweek 53:53 Ja 5
'59

One of these articles (in *The Reporter,* Volume 19, pages 19 to 24, August 7, 1958) indicates that railroads are declining, another (in *U.S. News & World Report,* Volume 45, pages 73 to 74, August 1, 1958) that their future is looking up. Here, again, is the beginning of a problem I could investigate. If I wanted to find out what more thorough studies (longer than two to five pages) of the railroads suggested in 1958, I'd turn first to *PAIS* from that year or to the *Bibliographic Index* of that year. I'd soon have plenty of material to try to interpret. If I wanted a current update on railroads, I could turn to *PAIS* or the *Bibliographic Index* for the most recent year, or I could perhaps decide to pay for a computer search (most computer search services combine the resources of several indexes), using *railroad* and perhaps *future* as my key words. A librarian will be happy to teach you how to do a computer search and will help you decide on key words most appropriate to your needs.

The reference sources I've recommended so far plunk you down in the middle of a problem and trust you to interpret ("inference") your way out of it. If and when you feel lost, you can probably gain great comfort from some item you'll find in the last reference source I'd like to mention: Eugene P. Sheehy's *Guide to Reference Books* (Chicago: American Library Association). Unlike the indexes we've been talking about, this book isn't an alphabetic list of people, places, and subjects, but a field-by-field guide to helpful reference books. When I looked up "Canada" in Sheehy, two of the items I found listed were *The Oxford Encyclopaedia of Canadian History* and a book by William Matthews called *Canadian Diaries and Autobiographies* (Berkeley: University of California Press, 1950), which is said to list 1276 published and unpublished works. When I looked up "Biochemistry," I

found, among other things, *The Encyclopedia of Biochemistry,* for nonspecial-
ists, that might help me find my bearings.

Too much time spent in the reference room makes me desperate to find a
book with a story that continues from one page to the next. On the other
hand, too much time in a week of issues of *The New York Times* makes me
want a reference book to help me put what I've read into some kind of
perspective. Your search strategy will depend on your subject, but you
should plan to be moving back and forth between the reference room, the
catalog, and the stacks where your books and magazines are. The step you'll
be tempted to skip is visiting the reference room, so I recommend that you
leave your jacket and your papers in the reference room to make sure you
keep coming back.

3. Note-Taking   Writers are sorters. The quality of your work will depend to a
great extent on your ability to decide what is worth noting and what is not.
The notes you take reflect your intellectual achievement as a sorter.

As you read, you'll begin to see facts you'll want to use, quotations
you'll want to use, opinions of others you'll want to use and comment on.
Each time you finish copying out a fact, a quotation, or an opinion, ask
yourself, "So what?" Your answers to that question will begin to build
your stock of inferences. Many writing instructors suggest that you note
these facts and quotations and comments on 3- by 5-inch or 4- by 6-inch
note cards. They might be right. Note cards can easily be arranged and
rearranged. But they are also heavy. And they are difficult to carry under
your arm. And I never have them sitting around my room. So I prefer to
use paper—full-size paper. I keep all my notes—facts, quotations, opinions,
references—on a series of loose-leaf papers that might be termed a "research
log." Instead of buying note cards, I've bought a scissors and some paper
clips. So when I want to arrange and rearrange my notes, I cut my large
paper, shift pieces of it from stack to stack, and clip slips of related notes
together.

Reference notes, those separate notes detailing information for endnotes
("footnotes" gathered together at the end of your paper) or your "works
cited" list, can easily get out of hand as a writer proceeds with research. I've
often been advised to copy out a complete bibliographic entry, for example,

> Lash, Joseph P. *Eleanor: The Years Alone.* New York: W. W. Norton,
> 1972.

for every book I look at so I won't be missing any information when the
paper is completed and it's time to type up the endnotes or list of works
cited. That recommended method is thorough, and it is necessary in preparing a scholarly work like a dissertation, but I found as an undergraduate,
and still find now, that it saps my energy and my curiosity. I like to move
fast while I'm researching, flipping from book to book to journal to
magazine to newspaper. So I use a shortcut which I recommend, with

caution, to you. When I decide that I'll probably use a quotation, I copy it out, and I put only a brief reference after it, as follows:

> Eleanor Roosevelt's comment on John Kennedy in 1960:
>
> > "Here is a man who wants to leave a record (perhaps for ambitious personal reasons as people say) but I rather think because he really is interested in helping people of his own country and mankind in general."
>
> (Lash, p. 298)

I may never use the quotation in my paper. If I don't use it, I won't have wasted time copying out all the information, such as the full title and the publisher's name. If I do use it in my final draft, then after I complete the final draft, I can return to the book (if I still have it) or to the library's card catalog (if I don't) and look up the information I need to put in my endnote list or my list of works cited. I have found this method much more efficient and less wasteful than the usually recommended method.

If any class time can be made available, you should bring twenty or twenty-five notes to class on a specified day well before your paper is due and compare with your classmates the kinds of notes you've taken and your reasons for taking the notes you have. You'll get several useful tips from your classmates.

4. Keeping the Subject Covered to a Reasonable size   Only time and experience will help you do this. It is obviously difficult to cover the war in Vietnam or the life of Margaret Mead in three to ten pages. But that doesn't mean that you have to restrict yourself to the battle of Khe Sanh from 12:00 to 4:00 p.m. on February 25, 1968. You can write about large events or whole lives by discussing them through typical events or representative examples. You could look, for example, at criticism of our war in Vietnam in your 1965 student newspaper, in the 1970 *Times* (of London), and in the 1975 debates in Congress published in the *Congressional Record*. Similarly, you could look at Margaret Mead on her first trip to Samoa in 1925, as a prominent professor of anthropology in 1957, and as a television personality in 1965. Almost any large issue or whole life can be brought within a reasonable compass if you examine three or four representative examples.

5. Evaluating Your Sources   As a student, you can't always tell whether the sources you quote from are reliable or not. The fact that they've been published and the fact that they've been bought by your library help establish their reliability, but these facts are no guarantee of either accuracy or sophistication of judgment. Looking up reviews in a review journal from the field you're investigating might help, but reviews can often have racist, sexist, patriotic, or "old boy network" biases. As you get to know certain fields (black history, for example, or computer design), you'll gradually come to realize whom you can trust and whom you can't in those fields. Do try to get to know the political conditions in the fields you write about, but because papers are due early and often, you'll often, in the meantime, just have to use your own judgment of the *ethos, logos,* and *pathos* employed by the authors you're reading when you try to assess their value.

6. *Ensuring That Your Work Is Your Own*   The point of doing a research paper is to arrive at *your* interpretation of events or people or productions that we all are aware of (or could be aware of, if we kept ourselves informed). You fail to achieve that interpretation if you rely heavily on someone who has already interpreted the same events. When we read a persuasive interpretation of some event, it's difficult in most cases to form an alternative interpretation, so the best defense against borrowing the ideas of others is not to read them. Look as much as possible at firsthand sources of information, not at later interpretations. Try, as often as possible, to work with periodicals rather than books. Inevitably, though, you will come across some interpretations (even in newspaper accounts); just remember that "_____ thinks _____" is, to you, just another piece of evidence, a fact that you must in turn draw your own inference from.

You know you can't use any opinions of others, word for word, as if they were your own. For example, suppose you were writing a paper about ecology and you came across the following passage:

> Nature is, above all, profligate. Don't believe them when they tell you how economical and thrifty nature is, whose leaves return to the soil. Wouldn't it be cheaper to leave them on the tree in the first place? (Annie Dillard, *Pilgrim at Tinker Creek,* p. 65.)

In most schools, if you turned in a paper which used the words above without a note and without quotation marks, you'd fail your course and be put on academic probation. You'd be just as guilty, though, if you wrote the following, in an attempt to "change a few words":

> Nature is wasteful. Just because its leaves return to the soil doesn't make it economical and thrifty. Wouldn't it be cheaper if the tree just kept its leaves all year round?

In order to avoid danger, and in order to force yourself to do the thinking that a research paper is supposed to elicit from you, you should (if you want to use this passage) do one of the following:

1. Quote it all, acknowledge your source (with a note or a parenthetical reference), and then comment on the quotation from your own point of view.

or

2. Summarize the quotation in one sentence, acknowledge your source, and use the summary as part of your evidence.

A research paper requires a serious investment of time and thinking. There are no legitimate shortcuts. Shortcuts like plagiarism short-circuit learning, and they are a breach of trust.

7. *Acknowledging Sources*   Sometimes students get the impression (not, I'm afraid, far from the truth in some cases) that the purpose of writing research papers is to learn the forms for footnotes and bibliographies. It is not. Students are assigned research papers so that they can practice investigating a mass of material, determining what is important in that material (a crucial skill), coming to a conclusion about the material, and organizing the selected material to help a reader. Learning accepted forms for acknowledging sources is far less important than these four skills, but you should nevertheless become aware of the basic conventions for acknowledgment.

Conventions for acknowledging sources have been shifting significantly this past decade, and they may well continue to shift during your writing career. Footnotes rarely appear at the bottom of a page anymore. In books, they usually appear after each chapter or near the back of the book; in students' papers, they are usually accepted at the end of the paper (and thus are called *endnotes*). If you include a list of endnotes, there should be no need to rearrange each of these notes to compose a separate bibliography—the endnotes are easy enough to read.

Endnotes themselves will soon be an endangered species. In most fields, note numbers referring the reader to endnotes are being replaced by parenthetical references referring the reader to a final list of "Works Cited." This "Works Cited" list (or "Reference List" as it is called in the social sciences) is similar in form to, and in effect has replaced, our old bibliographies. A writer now, instead of writing "mind is an assumption." [1], writes "mind is an assumption" (Adcock, 15). When you see such a reference, you can be sure that a book or article by Adcock is part of a reference list, or list of "Works Cited," at the end of the piece you're reading. The *15* after *Adcock* means that the words *mind is an assumption* appeared on page 15. This method of acknowledging sources, sometimes called the *author-date method,* or the *Harvard method,* has much to recommend it. It allows a writer to make quick references (e.g., Thomas, 147) when taking notes for a paper and then to use those references directly when writing out the paper. If you're quoting from two books by Maya Thomas, you can distinguish them by date of publication (Thomas, 1975, 3 and Thomas, 1980, 110) or by abbreviated title (Thomas, *Heartbreak,* 3 and Thomas, *Rebirth,* 110). Then, when you've finished your paper, you make a list of all the works you've cited, get all the bibliographic information you need, and make up, in alphabetic order by authors' last names, your list of "Works Cited." If there are several books that you've consulted and that have influenced you but that you did not include in citations, you may want to add a list of "Works Consulted" in the same form. But this addition is usually not necessary.

If I had written this book fifteen years ago, I could have told you *exactly* how you should print out your notes and your bibliography. Most publishers, editors, and teachers at that time agreed to follow the guidelines of Kate Turabian's University of Chicago *Manual for Writers*. Some publishers still follow the guidelines in this manual, but the special needs of various fields of study have resulted in alternative guides—the *Publication Manual of the American Psychological Association* (2nd edition, Washington, D.C., 1974) for social science subjects; the *Council of Biology Editors Style Manual* (1972) for sciences; and the *Modern Language Association Handbook* (a new edition of which, that ceases to recommend footnoting, is due out in the fall of 1984) for humanities subjects. Many questions we have about citing references have answers that differ from style guide to style guide: Which words should be capitalized? Should *p.* be used before the page number? Should Roman or Arabic numerals be used? Should names of states or months be abbreviated? In what order should I place my information?

The discrepancies between guidelines from one field to another are not arbitrary nor are they purposefully confusing. In the sciences and social sciences, for example, the date of a work figures prominently in references because recent work builds on previous work and is consequently of most interest. In the arts and in fields like literature, history, or philosophy, ideas are less cumulative and the most recent work is much less certain to be the best informed. Therefore the date figures less prominently and the title of the work more prominently.

Where does all this logic, though, leave a student in a writing course? As I see it, you have three sensible alternatives for citing references in your papers for this course:

1. Follow some specific set of guidelines recommended by your teacher.

2. Follow the guidelines of the chart at the end of this chapter. The endnote forms are in keeping with the *Modern Language Association Handbook* (New York, 1977), and the "Works Cited" forms are in keeping with the forthcoming revision of that *Handbook*.

3. Use, with your teacher's permission, a system of references that makes sense for the scope and type of paper you are writing. You'll note that the students whose work appears in this book have selected several different styles of citing references. Many are quite clear, though they don't conform to any specific guide.

As we live through this period of shifting guidelines, it is well to remember the reason that we develop conventions for acknowledging sources. References allow us to acknowledge help where we've found it and to give our readers enough information to find more information in our original sources. The charts in this book and in the APA, CBE, and MLA manuals all help, but no chart can foresee all the possible complications in sources that you'll run into. When you're stuck, just try to serve your reader by being clear, convenient, and concise.

8. *Incorporating Quotations* One of the recurrent worries of writers of research papers is how to handle quotations: we worry about what to quote, about taking quotations out of the author's context, and about blending quotations into our own writing. The principal guidelines to follow are that you should use your quotations as evidence, not as a continuation of your own argument, that you should identify every quotation, and that you should follow up each quotation by explaining its significance.

Exercise 13-6

To practice the mechanical rules for introducing quotations in your work, answer the questions below, and compare your answers with those of your classmates. Perhaps your teacher can put a couple of answers for each question on the board.

1. How would you punctuate your sentence if you were using endnote style and you wanted to quote from page 296 of Ralph Ellison's *Shadow and Act,* where he says that in Harlem "it is possible for talented youths to leap through the development of decades in a brief twenty years"?

2. How would you punctuate this same quotation if you were using not endnotes but parenthetical references with a "List of Works Cited" at the end?

3. If you want to quote the words "this is no dream" from page 296, and you know that "this" refers to Harlem but your reader doesn't, how can you make it clear to the reader?

4. If you want to quote the line "a world so fluid and so shifting that often within the mind the real and the unreal merge, and the marvelous beckons from behind the same sordid reality that denies its existence" from page 296, but you think the quotation is too long, and you don't think that the part about the real and the unreal merging is so important, how can you shorten your quotation?

5. If you wanted to quote Robert Capon's whole paragraph about the electric knife sharpener (Chapter 6, page 70), how would you place it on the page?

We consider our writing finished, and we begin to feel genuine pride in it, when we are confident of our inferences, confident, that is, of our interpretations. It is those thoughtful interpretations, and the well-selected information on which we have based our interpretations, that make the difference between drudgery (halfhearted term papers) and challenging intellectual work.

	Acceptable footnote or endnote form	Acceptable form for bibliography or "Works Cited" list
BOOKS		
One Author	1 John McPhee, *Basin and Range* (New York: Farrar, Straus, and Giroux, 1981), pp. 91–108.	McPhee, John. *Basin and Range.* New York: Farrar, Straus, and Giroux, 1981.
Two Authors	2 James Raymond and Ronald Goldfarb, *Clear Understandings* (New York: Random House, 1982), p. 49.	Raymond, James, and Ronald Goldfarb. *Clear Understandings.* New York: Random House, 1982.
Editor	3 Lane Cooper, ed., *The Rhetoric of Aristotle* (New York: Appleton, Century, Crofts, 1932), p. 195.	Cooper, Lane, ed. *The Rhetoric of Aristotle.* New York: Appleton, Century, Crofts, 1932.
Author and Editor	4 Henry Fielding, *Tom Jones,* ed. Sheridan Baker (New York: Norton, 1973), p. 275.	Fielding, Henry. *Tom Jones.* Ed. Sheridan Baker. New York: Norton, 1973.
No Author Identified	5 *College Park Grammar Review Worksheets* (Raleigh, North Carolina: Contemporary Publishing Company, 1980), p. 10.	*College Park Grammar Review Worksheets.* Raleigh, N.C.: Contemporary Publishing Company, 1980.
Second or Later Edition	6 William Strunk and E. B. White, *The Elements of Style,* 3rd ed. (New York: Macmillan, 1981), p. 15.	Strunk, William, and E. B. White. *The Elements of Style.* 3rd ed. New York: Macmillan, 1981.
One of Several Volumes	7 Helen Rex Keller, *The Dictionary of Dates* (New York: Macmillan, 1934), II, 79.	Keller, Helen Rex. *The Dictionary of Dates.* 2 vols. New York: Macmillan, 1934.
Article That Is Included in a Book	8 Irving Babbitt, "Burke and the Moral Imagination," in *The Burke-Paine Controversy,* ed. Ray B. Browne (New York: Harcourt, Brace, & World, 1963), p. 152.	Babbitt, Irving. "Burke and the Moral Imagination." In *The Burke-Paine Controversy.* Edited Ray B. Browne. New York: Harcourt, Brace, & World, 1963.
MAGAZINES AND NEWSPAPERS		
Signed Magazine Article	9 Richard Gebhardt, "Imagination and Discipline in the Writing Class," *English Journal,* Dec. 1977, p. 31.	Gebhardt, Richard. "Imagination and Discipline in the Writing Class." *English Journal,* December 1977, 26–32.
Unsigned Magazine Article	10 "A Fighter Pilot Turned Negotiator," *Time,* 10 Oct. 1983, p. 35.	"A Fighter Pilot Turned Negotiator." *Time,* 10 Oct. 1983, 35.
Signed Newspaper Article	11 William Zinsser, "Why Johnny's Teachers Can't Write," *The New York Times,* 12 Nov. 1978, Sec. VI, p. 30.	Zinsser, William. "Why Johnny's Teachers Can't Write." *The New York Times,* 12 Nov. 1978, 6, 30.

	Acceptable footnote or endnote form	Acceptable form for bibliography or "Works Cited" list
Unsigned Newspaper Article	[12] "Another Icy Blast Moves In," *Houston Chronicle*, 19 Jan. 1984, Sec. 1, p. 1.	"Another Icy Blast Moves In." *Houston Chronicle*, 19 Jan. 1984, 1.1.
Newspaper Editorial	[13] "Politics of Earth, Air, Water," Editorial, *The Christian Science Monitor*, 30 Jan. 1984, p. 13.	"Politics of Earth, Air, Water." Editorial. *The Christian Science Monitor*, 30 Jan. 1984, 13.
Book Review	[14] Harry Rosenfeld, review of *O Albany*, by William Kennedy, *The Washington Post Book World*, 29 Jan. 1984, p. 1.	Rosenfeld, Harry. Review of *O Albany*, by William Kennedy. *The Washington Post Book World*, 29 Jan. 1984, 1.
ENCYCLOPEDIA ARTICLES		
Signed Article	[15] R. J. Thorn, "Solid-State Chemistry," *McGraw-Hill Encyclopedia of Science and Technology*, 1982 ed.	Thorn, R. J. "Solid-State Chemistry." *McGraw-Hill Encyclopedia of Science and Technology*, 1982 ed.
Unsigned Article	[16] "Lipid," *The Encyclopedia Americana*, 1982 ed.	"Lipid." *The Encyclopedia Americana*, 1982 ed.
UNPUBLISHED MATERIALS		
Doctoral Dissertation or Master's Thesis	[17] Mary Kay Jordan, "The Effects of Peer Review on College Students Enrolled in a Required Advanced Technical Writing Course," Diss. Maryland, 1983.	Jordan, Mary Kay. "The Effects of Peer Review on College Students Enrolled in a Required Advanced Technical Writing Course." Diss. Maryland, 1983.
Photocopy	[18] Mark Walsh and Martha Walsh, "The Farm," unpublished manuscript, 1969.	Walsh, Mark, and Martha Walsh. "The Farm." Unpublished manuscript, 1969.
Lecture	[19] Ralph Ellison, "A Writer's Life," University of Notre Dame, 4 Apr. 1968.	Ellison, Ralph. "A Writer's Life." University of Notre Dame, 4 Apr. 1968.
Interview	[20] Personal interview with Kathleen Miller, The Stencil Box, Inc., 17 Jan. 1984.	Miller, Kathleen. Personal Interview. 17 Jan. 1984.
Television or Radio Program	[21] Pat Robertson, "The 700 Club," 5 Feb. 1984.	Robertson, Pat. "The 700 Club." 5 Feb. 1984.

14

◆

Interviewing

At first I was scared, but I enjoyed interviewing someone. It made me and him feel important.

student

Nothing so animates writing as someone telling what he thinks or what he does—in his own words.

William Zinsser

Exercise 14-1

Answer the following question in your notebook:

What qualities would you expect to find in a good interviewer?

In most kinds of writers' research, the first steps are the easiest: browsing through books related to your topic, sitting back to watch a movie through the first time before you review it, walking through a farmers' market watching the customers and the sellers while jotting notes in a notebook. But when your writing is to be based on an interview, the hardest step comes first—asking a stranger to set aside an hour to sit and talk with you. (Asking for the first interview of your life is also harder than asking for any later ones.) Once you've screwed up your courage to ask for an interview, though, the interview itself and writing the paper will come more easily. The interview, if you have well-prepared questions, is almost always more enjoyable than you would have guessed, and writing the paper involves, as usual, selecting the best material, searching for a focus and organization, testing your ideas in a first draft, and revising that draft until it makes good sense.

Before you ask for an interview, stop to ask yourself whether you have picked up some bad habits without even having started writing. First of all, most published interviews are interviews of "famous" people, and as readers we're not very demanding about what we're willing to listen to from them. If an interviewer can get Richard Pryor to say anything, we'll probably pay money to read it. The writer doesn't have to ask skillful questions or select very carefully what she'll print and what she'll edit out. Writers of interviews with famous people often earn their salaries more for their abilities in "getting" interviews than for their abilities to write or edit them well. The person you interview for this class will *not* be famous, so you'll have to ask good questions, and you'll have to select very carefully what to present your readers with. You'll have to both interview and write well.

The second bad habit you may have picked up is the laziness of printing an interview as a disjointed set of questions and answers, as in the following excerpt from an interview with British novelist E. M. Forster (Cowley, 28):

> INTERVIEWERS: While we are on the subject of the planning of novels, has a novel ever taken an unexpected direction?
>
> FORSTER: Of course, that wonderful thing, a character running away with you—which happens to everyone—that's happened to me, I'm afraid.
>
> INTERVIEWERS: Can you describe any technical problem that especially bothered you in one of the published novels?
>
> FORSTER: I had trouble with the junction of Rickie and Stephen. [The hero of *The Longest Journey* and his half brother.] How to make

them intimate, I mean. I fumbled about a good deal. It *is* all right once they are together. . . . I didn't know how to get Helen to Howards End. That part is all contrived. There are too many letters. And again, it is all right once she is there. But ends always give me trouble.

INTERVIEWERS: Why is that?

FORSTER: It is partly what I was talking about a moment ago. Characters run away with you, and so won't fit on to what is coming.

INTERVIEWERS: Another question of detail. What was the exact function of the long description of the Hindu festival in *A Passage to India?*

FORSTER: It was architecturally necessary. I needed a lump, or a Hindu temple if you like—a mountain standing up. It is well placed; and it gathers up some strings. But there ought to be more after it. The lump sticks out a little too much.

INTERVIEWERS: To leave technical questions for a moment, have you ever described any type of situation of which you have had no personal knowledge?

FORSTER: The home-life of Leonard and Jacky in *Howards End* is one case. I knew nothing about that. I believe I brought it off.

INTERVIEWERS: How far removed in time do you have to be from an experience in order to describe it?

This form doesn't require the interviewer to be a writer; it only requires that the interviewer own a tape recorder. Such an interviewer may well have asked good questions, but he's provided no writer's consciousness to guide us along, helping us see connections, highlighting the interviewee's most important character traits. Although you're practicing a new research technique in this chapter (interviewing), you'll bring to the character sketch you finally write all the writing skills you've shown in your earlier work— selecting and organizing your material, interesting your reader in the subject, showing that you understand the implications of what you've written.

Your first step is to choose the person you'd like to interview. Start thinking of possibilites now, and tell someone—soon—who it is you plan to interview so that you will begin to believe that you will actually do it. Your interview will work best (believe it or not) if you don't know the interviewee at all, or if at all, only by sight. Also, you should interview a person at least 40 years old—old enough to have developed a perspective about what life means to her, or to him. I recommend that you interview someone who has chosen a path you don't plan to follow—a roofer, a bus driver, a mother of seven, a fire fighter, someone who has grown up in another country. I highly recommend going to a nursing home to find your interviewee. Most people in nursing homes are happy to talk; they have a wealth of experience, they have plenty of time, and they will have more free time a week later when you need to check a few things or ask a few more questions. You might bring along a small present to thank the interviewee with after the interview.

Whether you interview a person in a nursing home, though, or a busy working person, you'll be surprised how often people respond enthusiastically to the idea of talking, if only for a short time, about themselves. If the first person you ask doesn't want to talk or doesn't want to take the time, just thank her anyway and try someone else. You're not a reporter whose story will be incomplete until he has talked to a key witness. You're just a writer looking for *an* interview, and any interviewee will do. If your first try results in a refusal, your second one is not likely to.

In class, before you actually face your interviewee, you can practice several techniques that will make the process of interviewing and writing easier and more effective.

Exercise 14-2

Prepare questions.

Bring to class ten sample questions that you might bring to an interview. When class begins, pass your list to a neighbor and take a list from a neighbor. Choose the three questions of those ten that you think will elicit the most interesting answers. Pass the list along again, and take a different list. See if you'd choose the same three questions as the person who reviewed the list before you. Then, with your classmates, share the best questions and explain, in each case, *why* those questions were designed to bring out the best information. Take good notes, and feel free to use any of these questions in your own interview.

Exercise 14-3

Practice interviewing your teacher. (Instead of, or in addition to, interviewing the teacher, you and your classmates may want to interview each other.)

Use the expanded question list you now have to conduct a group interview of your teacher. Take notes on all questions asked, not just your own. Note how the teacher responds, just as any interviewee will respond. Some questions she will refuse to answer, some she will answer matter-of-factly, some she will enjoy talking about. When you note an area that the teacher is interested in, abandon your question list and follow up the provocative area. (The teacher will probably comment on the way you are interviewing at the same time that she is answering your questions.)

When the interview is over, write up (either in class or at home) a character sketch of your teacher. If all the sketches are compared, you will see a variety of choices—for introductions, conclusions, quotations. The following are some instructive samples from a teacher interview:

1. *Opening sentences:* Do these start the reader off well?

   • Cristina Cheplick left her friends and family to come to America to live with her husband.

openers (handwritten)

- Many questions come to mind when you talk to someone who has emigrated from another country.
- "My parents wanted me to be a doctor, but I wanted to teach," said Cristina Cheplick.
- "Life is a series of hassles," C. Cheplick said about life in Romania.
- Cristina Cheplick began to learn English in 5th grade, and read her whole book in a week.
- In 5th grade, Cristina was introduced to the English language; consequently, at the age of 28, she is an English teacher.
- Cristina Ionescu was born in a hospital in the Romanian town [*sic*] of Transylvania, which is near her hometown of Cluj.
- Cristina Cheplick is a woman who has already experienced more than most people have.
- Cristina Cheplick has chosen the lifestyle of the U.S. instead of the one in Romania.

2. *Telling facts:* Are these good ones?

- When she talks to friends from Romania, they don't ask about the government here but about food: "Do you have to stand in line for cheese?"
- Cristina smiled when she showed off the Romanian valentines her friends sent.
- Even though her own country has its problems, she still looks back on it with fondness.
- She saw *The Sound of Music* ten times, and even knows the dialogue by heart.
- It was a zip for her to read an English novel, she was so taken by the language.
- She went to all the movies she could and learned everything that she could about English culture. She met a visiting American and married him.
- In Romania, she lived in a two-bedroom apartment with the rest of her family.

3. *Using quotations:* Are these well-chosen?

- "It's a land where people vote with their feet," said Mrs. Cheplick, quoting her husband, "everyone wants to leave."
- Eight years of English and college gave her a good background to come here: "Everyone is poor and has to stand in line."
- "My marriage enabled me to leave, but that's not why I married."
- The national paper is only five pages long, due to government censorship. "When my mother saw the *Washington Post,* she thought it was the news for the entire year."
- The question that seems most prominent is: "How are people in America different from the people in your country?" This was the question that Mrs. Cheplick was asked. She replied that the big difference is the demeanor of the people.
- She emphasized it (the happiness of teaching English in Amer-

ica) through her enthusiasm and detailed descriptions. "Romania," she says, "is a very poor country."

4. *Paragraphing:* Would these paragraphs make a substantial contribution to a paper?

- She took the bus to her teaching job every morning, and returned in the evening. On her return trip, she witnessed the long line of citizens already waiting in line for the morning bread, cheeses, and other needs. When she retired for the night, she would sit up in bed, and read the 5-page *Scinteia* published by the gov't.
- C. Cheplick is an English teacher at the University of Maryland. She used to live in Romania until her marriage. She hopes to be an American citizen soon. She dresses in sweaters and slacks and ruffly blouses. The main difference she sees is the carefree attitude of Americans. America is a completely different world. Cristina smiled when she showed off her Romanian valentines.
- Her college education was free, with an agreement to work for the government. She took eight years of it in grade school and four in college. What a life!

5. *Choosing a focus:* Note how many choices you have.

- *Being practical:*
  Mrs. Cheplick picked her occupation in Romania, knowing that teachers and doctors made the same amount of money.
- *The linguist:*
  All of her life, she has had a love for different languages. Many a time, she would go to the movies to try and pick up some of the languages. Many times in class, she would read ahead, just for the fun of it.
- *The happy teacher:*
  An English teacher from Romania? Sounds like a contradiction in terms, but C. Cheplick, Freshman English teacher at the University of Maryland, is very happy in America teaching English. She emphasized it through her enthusiasm and detailed descriptions.
- *Seeking a new life:*
  She was refused entrance to the party government. She left her family and friends to try to make a new life with her husband in a strange new country. She knew she would never have a successful career in Romania.
- *Appreciating the new life:*
  Cristina left Romania to come to teach in America. She has much more freedom and enjoys the freedom of expression. Also, she does not have the everyday worry of where the next meal is coming from.
- *Hard times:*
  Mrs. Cheplick recalls the time when she was on a bus in Romania, and "the driver shut the doors on a person." People are rude and discourteous.

• *Hard worker:*
C. Cheplick began to learn English in the 5th grade and read the whole book in a week. She was always ahead of her class and studied for two years solid to get into college to study English.

Exercise 14-4

Remind yourself that you will be drawing inferences from the facts you discover about your interviewee.

List in your notebook ten facts from your childhood. When you've finished, perhaps the facts of one of the students—or of your teacher—can be written on the blackboard. Next, with your classmates, try to draw inferences from the facts on the board. Here's an example:

> Fact: I have eight brothers and sisters.
> Inference 1: "I bet you're Catholic."
> Inference 2: "I'd infer that you baby-sat a lot."
> Inference 3: "You learned to get along with people."
> Inference 4: "You're a fighter."

Discuss the validity of these inferences; then trade your own fact list for the list of another student, and draw inferences about that person based on the facts.

Finally, if each student presents a few of his or her facts and inferences aloud, the class can check for nonfacts and faulty inferences (and ask questions which would turn up more facts to substantiate the inferences that at this point seem most likely).

Exercise 14-5

Use videotapes to learn interviewing techniques.

Like the papers you'll write for this class, segments from *PM Magazine, 20/20,* and *60 Minutes* are successful because they are written to inform and entertain audiences—several of these ten- to twenty-minute segments try to reveal the predominant character trait of a person, making that person come alive for the viewer.

1. View a videotape which features a particular individual (the person does *not* have to be famous). If possible, get a copy of the script.

2. As you watch, keep in mind the following questions:
   • How does the introduction try to gain your interest?
   • What is the scriptwriter's focus?
   • How does the writer move from one revealing fact to the next (make transitions)?
   • *How* and *where* do quotations fit into the script?
   • Why is the ending provocative (if it is)?

The writing process is very much the same for a television script and for an article. Writing for presentation on paper must, however, be more descriptive than writing for a television script, because a camera can capture for the viewer what a reader—unless told—never sees. Note, in the tape you've chosen, how the camera shots (description) aid in emphasizing points made by the narrator.

If you've done some of these exercises, you should be well prepared to start now on your interview. Take your master list of questions and meet your interviewee at a scheduled time and place. Bring a small tape recorder if you wish and if your interviewee doesn't mind. A tape recorder will give you much (perhaps too much) raw material to work with and prune. But don't feel that you need a tape recorder. You'll be well prepared, and you'll save yourself hours of tape-listening time later, if you just bring two or three pencils and plenty of paper. Since you won't want to write down everything, your pencil will serve as a natural instrument of selection. Inevitably, both you and the interviewee will be nervous for the first few minutes, but soon you'll be talking freely. The questions you'll ask will depend on you and your interviewee and on the quality of the question-list selection you did in class, but there are some general guidelines you can follow:

1. Be sure to ask not only *what* the person has done but also *why* she has done it. You can be sure that the reader reading your sketch will consistently be asking, "Why?" Anticipate the question.

2. When you come upon any area that your interviewee is clearly interested in, ask more questions about that area. It may well be a key to the person's character.

3. Don't be afraid to stop and write something down to keep it from being lost. Your interviewee won't feel ignored. He'll be glad that you're being careful.

4. When you run out of good questions, leave, even if you think you'll need more information later. You can plan on being back in touch, at least by telephone. You haven't had your last chance at research yet.

5. As soon as you're on your own, fill out your abbreviated notes so that you can understand them. Two hours after the interview, your notes will be puzzling; two days later, they'll look like hieroglyphics.

When writing time comes, remember that, as with any other assignment, you are both a researcher and a writer; in this assignment, specifically, you are both an interviewer and a writer. Now that you have the raw material for a paper, it's your job to pull that material into shape: to *select* (don't fill your pages with everything you heard); to decide on a focus, an introduction, and a conclusion; to find a scheme of organization; to introduce your quotations skillfully and balance your emphases on quotations and commentary; to make sure you've provided enough breadth and depth of information; to omit irrelevant biographical details; to check for inaccuracies. As your draft begins to take shape, you'll find that you can't do all these tasks yourself, that your interviewee is still necessary. If you return to the interviewee, you can, in ten to fifteen minutes, ask the questions that you now know are important, though you didn't see their importance when you were only a first-time interviewer.

As you rework the final draft, there are some larger questions well worth asking. Have you found something that your readers wouldn't expect? Have you challenged your readers' assumptions? Have you told us something about human nature? If you have, we can now see a little better behind our human masks.

15

♦

Suggested Assignments

One thing which could be done would be to make all the papers the students have to write interesting. Make the subject something students would be interested in writing about.

student

I always thought a description was very short.

student

The proposal paper brought a lot of emotion out of me. It enabled me to convince not only the reader but myself of what I wanted to propose.

student

This chapter sets out several possible writing assignments that allow you to practice the many writing skills you have been developing in this class. These assignments should not be confused with the exercises in earlier chapters. Those exercises enable you to practice a skill or two (or even several); but these assignments place you as nearly as possible into a professional writing situation—that is, they demand that you collect and present information that will be helpful to your readers (teacher and classmates) or that will move them to action. Each assignment below begins by sending you out to research raw material. The assignment directs you to the raw material; then you have the freedom to select, to organize, and to interpret it. (The paper length called for in each case should be a clue to how much detail is expected.) Each assignment should stretch you, should ask you to do more than you initially think possible. Each will show you a new source of information so that you don't have to keep relying on yourself (a source too seldom replenished). Every time you write, then, you should be learning something new, acquiring a new perspective, a new understanding. Every paper you write should, in turn, serve to increase your readers' experience, and perhaps also their understanding.

#1 DESCRIPTION OF A CURIOUS PLACE

Method of Research: Observation and Note-taking

Most Pertinent Chapter: 2

Selected Details Due:

Clean Draft Due for Workshop:

Paper Due:

In this first assignment, your task is to bring a place alive on paper. Don't just describe the place for yourself. Think of your readers—your teacher and your classmates—as you write, and try to make them curious enough to want to see the place themselves. Show, in your description of the place, that you understand its social significance. Are the people who use the place rich, poor, or in between? What kinds of clothes do they wear? What does this place show about the way people treat others? Choose a place that people frequent, and include some characterization of those people in your description.

Past students have written about laundromats and auction houses, farmers' markets and decaying neighborhoods, museums and hospital emergency rooms, restaurants and department stores, junkyards and city centers, courtrooms and locker rooms. No matter how well you think you know the place _you_ choose, _visit_ it before the date your selected details are due, and plan to stay awhile (at least an hour). During this visit you'll do your research. Consider yourself a sound camera, and record the atmosphere and character of the place. If you have trouble noticing details, look for details that are contrary to your values or expectations, or think about similar places you know and look for the details that are different. If you are describing a fast-food restaurant, for example, and its rest rooms are labeled "gunslingers" and "señoritas," you have your first telling fact.

Bring your list of details to class on the date assigned, and collect opinions on them from your classmates: are they "telling" or "unrevealing"? After that class, select your best details, write a draft of your paper, and read the paper through to see if there are places where you need more information. Then visit your place at least once more. You'll be much more receptive during the second visit, because you'll have a better idea about the direction that your paper is likely to take.

Your paper must be at least three typewritten pages. It will include a variety of details, but it should convey some distinctive character (e.g., nearly everything about Beltway Plaza is cheap). Use as many telling details as you can. Use your introduction to make your readers take notice. Provide historical and material background if you can.

When you're finished writing, before the final typing, have a friend or two read your paper for you. Ask them which parts they like best. See if you've been able to make them laugh at something, or if there is anything they don't understand. Ask them if there are any parts that seem boring or too obvious. And ask them if they can identify the distinctive character you intended to convey—if they can't, you'll want to go back to your draft for a while before you do your final typing.

At the end of your paper, list three facts that you collected but that you decided, in the end, not to use in the paper.

SAMPLES

This sample, as well as other samples included in this chapter, is not a perfect paper (no paper is ever "perfect"), but it should give you some idea of what you are aiming for. Remember that in Chapter 11 there are weaker papers that correspond to each of the assignments in this chapter. You may find it helpful to examine those papers too.

BENSON ANIMAL HOSPITAL
Rani Garrison

Too broad — this is not clear

1 The sweltering mid-day summer sun dominates the day's activities: people hurrying to and from their lunch breaks, children recklessly racing down the sidewalks on their bicycles and skateboards towards the neighborhood's video arcade, construction workers drowning out the usual business-day street noises with the constant piercing and throttling sounds of jackhammers as they tear up the road. Yet, in the midst of this daily chaos, a secluded world is confined within the walls of Benson Animal Hospital. The building has been situated in the heart of Bethesda, Maryland for almost three decades. From the street, it is a plain, one-story corner building, the brick recently painted a mustard-yellow. Usually, there is hardly as much as a single cigarette butt on the surrounding sidewalk.

secluded? clear

2 Upon entering the hospital early in the morning, after the floors have been freshly mopped, one cannot help but notice the potency of ammonia lingering in the air. This is the only time of day that the floors actually shine. Tile floors are used instead of carpeting for easier cleaning and less animal odor. Another advantage of having tile floors is that once an animal sees a doctor and decides to make a quick exit, the hard, smooth floor and a firm grip on the leash keeps them running in place. By early afternoon miniature tumbleweeds of hair begin to drift around on the floor, and eventually settle in the corner.

3 After a client and patient are checked-in at the front desk and their record is pulled from the file cabinets, they wait, seated on long cushioned benches.

4 Above and behind the benches are glass windows, eight feet tall. These windows occupy most of the area provided for two walls. Two sets of bent-up venetian blinds hang in front of the windows. The only portion of the blinds that isn't damaged is the part that is out of reach. The clients often lean against the windows, sandwiching the blinds between the glass and their backs. Most of the damage is caused by the patients; usually excited puppies romp around the benches and crash into the blinds.

5 One of the two remaining walls is paneled with thick boards of oak. In that wall is a split-level door, like those in horse stables, which leads to the two doctors' offices. Dr. Benson's name plaque hangs on the wall by the door. Below it are bare spots where the name plaques of previous colleagues hung. Many new doctors and interns practice with Dr. Benson, then move

on to their own business a short time thereafter. On the other side of the door is a glassless window with shutters, as a service window in a fast food restaurant might look. The shutters can be closed when necessary. They are frequently closed when other clients are either excessively curious or equally disturbed by the sight of animals in emergency situations.

6 On the other side of the doctors' offices is the "backroom." Due to the absence of air conditioning and the lack of proper ventilation, walking into the room is like walking into a steamroom except that it has a rather unpleasant stench of heated feces.

7 The room is filled with cages lining all four walls, stacked three and four cages high. The "E. E. box" (excremental exercise box), otherwise simply known as "the box," takes up most of the area in the middle of the room. Looking into the box, you can usually see one or two dogs curiously sniffing the urine-soaked newspapers. In one corner of the room, between two walls of cages, is a stack of donated newspapers which are constantly in use. Another corner has three steps leading up to the rear exit. Next to the rear door are stacked cases of various prescription dog food, sometimes stacked six to seven feet high. At the bottom of the steps is a trashcan used to hide euthanized animals, each one placed in a trash bag, until they can be properly disposed of. In a third corner is a bathtub for bathing cats and dogs. Sticky jugs of flea shampoo are placed at random on the floor around the tub.

8 Behind the tub is a concealed lavatory. The door to this 4 ft. by 5 ft. room rests on its lower hinges. Inside the lavatory, a dusty toilet with a cracked seat and no lid is camouflaged by more cases of prescription dog food, as well as cat food. A window fan, in the same tiny room, slowly rotating in a breeze of muggy summer air, is temporarily placed in the window above the toilet. Outside that window is an alley where neighboring restaurants dispose of their refuse in huge dumpsters. Clouds of swarming flies and other pests feed on this collection of rotting scraps.

9 Leaving through the rear door into the alley, the noise and confusion revives the reality of the business-day hustle and bustle.

READY, SET, GO
Jan Weinstein

1 When I walked toward the girls' bathroom on the third floor of Denton Hall as the clock struck midnight, the experience began. The resemblance to Wall Street at five o'clock was amazing. The sudden rampage of girls with buckets full of equipment took your breath away. Your feet were in much danger too if you weren't careful.

2 The door never closed because of the constant in and out goers. It opened to an excellent overview of the misty, toothpaste smelling bathroom. Every sink, shower, stall, and mirror was occupied. The six showerers, ten toothbrushers, four pimple pickers, five bathroom goers and the

various eleven waiting for their places had to be on the ball. It was a great game of "Ready, Set, Go." As soon as one turned off the water, flushed the toilet, or walked away from the mirror, the next had to be ready. The pushing and shoving was enough to make anyone seasick. Once "the ready" and "the set" was taken care of, "the go" was up next. More than twenty separate games were all taking place at the same time. I could see the girls in "the go" stage so clearly. All of them were moving like darts.

3 As I walked through the entry way I got my first of many pushes. It was hard to tell which girl was responsible. By the time I turned around, she had already mixed in with the other clones. All were dressed in overly large t-shirts with their printed cotton underwear showing from the bottom. Their hair was tightly pulled back with mismatched barrettes. This way the white pimple medicine could smother their faces without the disturbance of loose hairstrands. The various shades of pink and red covered their toenails. If their fingernails did not match, it was only from nervous biting. No one would ever have Flowering Plum on her toes and Red As Romance on her fingers!

4 I noticed the floor first. The shampooy puddles all over could make anyone change their mind about cleanliness. Never have I seen such dirty soapy mush. I had to accept it. I was wading up to my ankles in it.

5 I started to look around a bit. I did this until I focused my attention on the girl standing next to me. The name on the back of her navy blue nightshirt was Jilly. She seemed to be from New York City. She was about 5′11″ and her physical condition was comparable to Dusty Roads. I figured she wasn't very interested that my wings were just clipped from my mommy in Miami, Florida.

6 She was extremely anxious. She clutched her black and blue towel in her left fist and her baby shampoo, soap, and razor in the right. Unfortunately, I was waiting for the shower too. My blood pressure was rising and my hands were starting to sweat beyond my control.

7 I was waiting in line for shower number two and Jilly was waiting for shower number three. We were both next. A few minutes passed and then shower number two turned off. Jilly gave me a look as the previous shower-er wiped, wrapped, and walked. Jilly had her eye on that vacant shower. She looked ready to fight for her chance at my stall. Well, I had to give it a five second consideration. I then came to my conclusion. Going to sleep dirty wasn't all that bad.

8 Changing my mind about the shower, I joined the other forty barefoot feet moving quickly in the dirty puddles. I waited to use the sink, stood in line for the toilet, and used my tippytoes for a peek in the mirror. The pink tile was getting cold. I had exhausted myself with waiting and worry.

9 I was ready to go to sleep. The crowd in the bathroom made me claustrophobic, the steam made me dizzy, the smell upset my stomach, the girls made me neurotic, and enough was enough.

[10] As I used my newly learned experience and pushed my way through the girls, I caught a look at Jilly. She had just stepped out of the shower. I stared at her wet, lanky body. Maybe I should have fought for my turn. She looked just as wimpy as she looked wet. Next time I'd know better. Beware! It's every girl for herself in this innocently pink-tiled obstacle course.

#2 AUDIENCE ANALYSIS OF TWO NEWSPAPERS

Method of Research: Finding Significant Facts and Drawing Inferences from Them

Most Pertinent Chapters: 2, 3

Fact-Inference Pairs Due:

Clean Draft Due for Workshop:

Paper Due:

An ethnographer studies what the people are like in a given area. The first ethnographers studied societies like those of the Tibetans and the Eskimos because they thought these peoples were exotic. But recent ethnographers have decided that history teachers or presidential counselors or Chicagoans can be just as exotic. In this assignment, your task is to act as an ethnographer and, using only two newspapers as evidence, draw some contrasting conclusions about the audiences those newspapers are published for. In other words, you'll be trying to determine how two newspapers view the readers in their respective communities.

To begin, find two newspapers that are likely to appeal to quite different audiences of readers. If you can find local newspapers from different parts of the country, say the *Seattle* (Washington) *Times* and the *Rutland* (Vermont) *Herald,* or the *Fort Worth* (Texas) *Star-Telegram* and the *Kenosha* (Wisconsin) *News,* that would be wonderful. If you can't get papers from distant communities, though, consider some papers that are available in most cities: *The New York Times, The Village Voice, The National Enquirer, The Christian Science Monitor,* a local religious newspaper, or a propagandistic newspaper of any kind. Also, most libraries carry papers from around the country (or around the world), and you could do your research using two of those.

Begin your research by looking through your papers and jotting down facts about the newspapers that reveal something about their intended audiences. Use as evidence the types of stories included, the way stories are written, the placement of stories within the paper, the types and number of advertisements, the wording of headlines, the opinions expressed and implied, and anything else that strikes you as you read. Then, next to each fact you've noted, write out an inference you think you can draw about the audience. Here's what your notes might look like:

Facts	Inferences
There are several ads in *The Village Voice* for plastic surgery, transparent braces, electrolysis, clinics for baldness, dermatology, and weight reduction.	Readers are very concerned about their appearance.
Produce advertised in a September *Seattle Post-Intelligencer* is very cheap: 23 pounds of apples, $4.98; squash, 9 cents per pound.	The Seattle area must have a good climate for growing fruits and vegetables.
A first-page article in the *Rutland Her-*	Emphasis suggests that the paper ex-

ald about oil drilling along George's Bank (off Cape Cod) concludes with two paragraphs about the plight of the fisherman.

pects its readers to side with the fishermen.

As with any other research, look for evidence that is contrary to your values or expectations, and you'll find evidence much more easily. Be bold in the inferences you draw, but remember that one fact is not enough to justify a bold inference, so look back to see whether there are any more facts that will help substantiate that inference.

At some point in your research, it will help if you bring your fact-inference pairs to class and discuss them with your classmates. Have your classmates evaluate your research by telling you whether they find your facts surprising rather than routine and whether they find your inferences thoughtful and not obvious. With that advice, continue to collect fact-inference pairs until you have thirty to forty; then decide on a thesis statement (a summary of your best inferences) about the newspapers' contrasting audiences that you feel you can substantiate using the examples you've noted. Once you have decided on a thesis, write a three- to four-page paper using as much evidence as you think is necessary to convince your reader that your thesis is accurate and reasonable, that you have a legitimate, thoughtful assessment of the differences between the two audiences. If your emphasis changes as you write your paper, be sure to make adjustments in your thesis that reflect the change.

SAMPLES

INFERENCES TO SHOW THE DIFFRENCES
Joseph Greenawalt

¹ The Seattle Post-Intelligencer and the Baltimore Sun are two very different types of newspapers. They differ greatly in their focus on international and national events, sports and leisure events, and editorial preferences. These differences not only indicate the publisher's point of view on various issues, but also the type of reader that each paper is attempting to reach.

² Firstly, the two papers have their respective headlines focusing on two very different subjects. The Seattle Post-Intelligencer reserves a good portion of its front page for its headline story dealing with the renaming of a Seattle airport in honor of the late Senator Henry Jackson. The headline reads, "SEA-TAC RENAMED FOR JACKSON." Since Jackson is primarily known in the Washington state area, and because the news is only of local interest, it is evident that the publisher believes that significant local news takes precedence over national or international news in the minds of the readers of the Intelligencer.

³ In contrast, the Baltimore Sun's headline, as well as the entire first page, deals solely on national and international events. Two articles deal with presidential news, including the headline, which reads, "REAGAN

DROPS PLANNED VISIT TO PHILIPPINES." Although an entire section, entitled "Maryland," is later devoted to state and local news, local news is nonetheless subordinate, in the publisher's view and unlike the Intelligencer, to the readers of the Sun. Also, because Baltimore is a port city, the publisher recognizes the fact that international events may have great bearing on Baltimore based import/export companies.

4 In the business area, the Intelligencer and the Sun show some sharp differences. The Intelligencer shares its business section with a sports section, spending roughly five pages on business matters. However, the articles deal mainly with general subjects such as Internal Revenue information, Federal Reserve Board rulings, and Dow Industrial and other stock averages. There are only two marginal articles discussing local Seattle business. However, the Sun deals with a greater number of specific local business matters. Its main headline is of a local issue, and reads, "TIRE PLANT GETS SOBER ASSESSMENT," while the headline of the Intelligencer deals with national I.R.S. news. It seems that while readers of the Sun are more interested in national politics, they are also more interested in local business news.

5 The Intelligencer and the Sun differ also on their treatment of sports. The Intelligencer and the Sun both have significant sports sections. However, the Intelligencer deals more with football and golf, only reserving one article for its baseball team, The Seattle Mariners. This is because the Mariners were not a very successful team this season. In contrast, the Sun not only has three articles in its sports section discussing Baltimore's baseball team, the Orioles, but also includes a separate eleven page section on their upcoming playoffs against the Chicago White Sox. With the addition of this extra section, the publisher is evidently capitalizing on the increased popularity of the Orioles. He's hoping that more people will buy the Sun to read about the success of their Orioles.

6 In the editorial page, the character of a newspaper and its readers can be readily and dramatically observed. The Intelligencer and the Sun seem to agree on basic political issues. In the Intelligencer, there are five articles criticizing the Soviet way of life. It is evident that this paper is to a degree anti-Soviet—but this does not mean that the paper is conservative or pro Reagan. Quite the contrary, for on the same pages, there are two cartoons criticizing Reagan administration policies. One cartoon shows how the Pentagon is using the Korean Airlines incident to acquire more armaments. In fact, one editorial expands on this criticism and attacks Reagan himself for using his speech condemning the Russians as a pretext for pushing his MX missile plan. The second cartoon criticizes the militarist supported violent response to the KAL incident by the American public. The paper has taken the position that moderate responses to the Soviets are appropriate, and that to build up the nuclear arsenal as a response is impulsive and wrong. Also, to support this, one editorial says America can not retaliate to the Soviets because of the threat of nuclear weapons, and only when this

threat disappears can America handle Soviet aggression. It seems, therefore, that the paper is an advocate of the nuclear freeze, giving the paper a decidedly liberal character.

[7] The Sun also demonstrates, through its opinion/commentary page, a liberal or Democratic oriented character. Firstly, a lengthy piece in praise of Democrat Walter Mondale appears. The article congratulates Mondale for his recent victory in Maine's straw poll and goes on to tell of his direct and forthright campaigning methods. Evidently, the paper supports Mondale and his Democratic ideals and hopes that he will defeat the Republican candidate for the presidency in 1984. Also two letters to the editor express dislike for Reagan policies, showing a similar Democratic position of the paper's readers. It is interesting to note that no pro Reagan letters or editorials appear, reaffirming the liberal character of the Sun and its readers.

[8] The content of a newspaper and its focus shows much about its particular readers. Even though the Seattle Post-Intelligencer and the Baltimore Sun share a similar liberal character and audience, they differ greatly in their approaches to presenting the news. The Intelligencer seems to be a locally oriented paper, with its readers preferring major local news to international or national news. On the other hand, the Baltimore Sun seems to present a broader view of the news to a business oriented subscriber who needs to keep abreast of major national and international news developments.

READERS OF THE SEATTLE POST-INTELLIGENCER AND THE NEW YORK TIMES
Jeffrey Gagliardi

[1] The New York Times and The Seattle Post-Intelligencer are two very dissimilar papers. There are a substantial number of differences between the papers which reflect the differences of subscribers, and therefore, the purposes of the papers. The major contrasts deal with the lifestyles and economies of Seattle and New York.

[2] The New York Times is a business oriented newspaper with a wide subscription area. The business section is fifty-two pages long and is packed with national stock exchange and investment data, ads for office supplies, computer systems, and even more ads for managerial and high tech jobs from around the nation. The major section of the newspaper is mainly national and international news. As is characteristic of all newspapers, the Times has car ads in its classifieds section. A large number of the car ads, though, are from dealerships, which are generally expensive, and have the option to lease. Leasing is the standard way a business acquires company cars. Although the paper, and New York, seem to center around Wall Street and the business world, New York's ports and shipping industry are also important to its economy. Two articles attested to this.

[3] The Times seems to have a very wealthy backing. On most of the pages

in the main section, over three-fourths of each page is advertisements. A majority of the ads are from the most expensive stores in the nation. Some ads are for products that only upper-middle-class or very rich people can afford, such as expensive jewelry, fashion wear, and luxury cars.

⁴ In the area of the Arts, New York is an important place. Not only does New York harbor thousands of musical and acting performances, it is also a major testing ground for the success of movies. In the Art and Leisure section of the Times, there are countless advertisements and articles on stage and musical performances. Movie ads are the most prominent, though, sometimes running full, or even double pages.

⁵ Although New York is a place of great opportunity and entertainment, it is also a highly pressured environment for its inhabitants. In the Times's travel section, there are a large number of ads for expensive overseas vacations. This helps support my view that there are many very wealthy people in New York, but it is the remaining ads which reflect the true nature of New York life. I am referring to the abundance of inexpensive weekend trips that are advertised as being restful and only ninety minutes outside of New York. These ads are meant to lure in average workers, as opposed to the ads for the well-to-do. The number of these ads points to the fact that New Yorkers like to get away from New York as often as possible.

⁶ Politically speaking, it is obvious that New York and The New York Times are mainstream Democratic. Not only did all the articles concerning the presidential campaigns favor Democrats, they supported and promoted Walter Mondale, who is presently in the lead in the race for the Democratic party nomination.

⁷ The purpose of the Intelligencer is drastically different from that of The New York Times. Whereas the Times is a nationally subscribed-to paper with a primary interest in the business world, the Intelligencer is localized for the Seattle area.

⁸ It seems that the Seattle area has a high percentage of blue-collar workers. There are a large number of articles, both national and local, concerning Seattle's major industries. The articles deal with the timber industry, agriculture, the shipping industry, the effect of international grain embargoes on farmers and shippers, and the recent drop in Washington state's unemployment from sixth to thirteenth in the nation. Shipping is probably Seattle's most important industry. There are a large number of articles on shipping and fishing, the name of the baseball team is the Mariners, and the name of the football team is the Seahawks.

⁹ The Intelligencer's business section is only four pages long. The employment and real estate ads are small too. With this in mind, it seems that the Seattle area has a limited job market and low economic opportunities. The Intelligencer is clearly meant to be a daily paper for the average person. With such informal titles of articles as "Fewer Couples Are Getting Unhitched," "Campaign Kitties Are Empty," and a front page feature entitled "Today's Chuckle," this is most likely true. There are also a page and a half of

games, eleven full pages of supermarket sales, several cooking recipes, and five advice columns.

10 The people of Seattle seem to hold more traditional American values. One title to an advice column read: "Fix supper early and relax with your husband," which represents a traditional view of the role of the female sex. The Intelligencer also has a religious advice column by the evangelist Billy Graham.

11 After reading these papers I find myself wondering whether I would rather live in Seattle or New York, based on the information I have gotten from the two papers. Honestly speaking, I would like to live in both Seattle and New York; both have qualities which I like. For economic reasons I would like to live in New York. Deep down, though, I have a desire to live in America's past, with some of its old customs and values. Seattle's farms and simpler lifestyle appeal to me more than the hustle and bustle of New York life. Seattle leaves me with the impression that it is a remnant of the Old West.

Day - essay,
p. 255

#3 AUDIENCE ANALYSIS OF A MAGAZINE

Method of Research: Finding Significant Facts and Drawing Inferences from Them

Most Pertinent Chapters: 2, 3

Clean Draft Due for Workshop: *Thurs. Feb. 19*

Paper Due: *Thurs. Feb. 26*

GOAL

To uncover and explain some of the magazine's assumptions about its audience and about the milieu, or the world, in which that audience lived.

YOUR READERS

Those of us who are curious about what our parents were like, or curious about the readers of some of the unusual magazines we see in the stores.

SUGGESTIONS

1960 —

1. Look at, read, and inspect your magazine carefully (any magazine published before 1945 or a current magazine addressed to people quite unlike yourself). Look at five or six consecutive issues or at one issue *very* thoroughly. Notice everything about the magazine—the kinds of articles, the names of articles, the advertising, the photos, the letters to the editor, the layout. Notice the kinds of articles, ads, and photographs that are *not* there too. Go into your investigation without a sense of what your thesis will be—with an open mind—*not* with a preformed idea about what you'll discover.

2. After you feel comfortable with the magazine, make a list of details about the magazine that strike you as interesting, unusual, or surprising.

3. About halfway through your note-taking, look at the notes and see if you can find some patterns or trends. What assumptions does the magazine make about its readers and their world? What do we learn about the people who bought this magazine? about their values? their interests? their habits? their likes and dislikes? their education? economic level? social class? moral concerns? age? sex? political views? family life? Now you can start to form a tentative thesis.

4. Finish collecting your details, remembering that the details you observe in the magazine are your evidence for your discussion.

5. Your final essay will contain both details and inferences. An inference is a conclusion that you've arrived at after studying the details. Not all your notes, of course, will make it into your final draft. But the details you include should be representative enough to let the reader see how you arrived at your conclusion.

6. To aid the reader and yourself, present your evidence—the details that support your conclusion—in systematic groupings, classes, or catego-

ries. Don't present information in the same random order in which you found it.

7. Be yourself when you write—straight, if you like; humorous if you like. Remember that you are a real person, and you are writing for a real audience. Read your paper aloud to make sure that it sounds recognizably human.

8. Catch us (your readers) with an introduction that will make us want to read on.

SAMPLES

REAL MEN READ SOLDIER OF FORTUNE
Unknown Student Author

[1] Are you interested in buying or selling guns, collecting military or war memorabilia, or learning survival tactics? Would you enjoy reading stories of combat and guerrilla operations from those who participate? Have you ever wondered what it would be like to be a mercenary, a professional soldier for hire? Or, would you like perhaps an hour or so of comic relief? If so, then this is definitely the magazine for you!

[2] Soldier of Fortune is a magazine devoted to the art of killing. It is a weapons catalogue, an instruction manual, and a "journal of professional adventures" all rolled into one. Published monthly and distributed worldwide, it is a super-macho, ultra-right wing conservative refuge where women, children and liberals are not allowed. Yet, it does not cater to the seeker of cheap thrills; the "messy" side of battle is nowhere to be seen. Although written in a surprisingly high-quality, if biased format, its coldly technical, matter-of-fact style is as chilling as the subject matter itself.

[3] Nearly all of the magazine's articles and features concern men and their lethal toys (affectionately referred to as "she," use of the female gender almost always refers to weapons, not women), or the occasional profile for such "enemies of free democracy" as Jane Fonda or Henry Winston. Monthly features include spotlights on particular small-arms weaponry and accessories; a section variously titled "I Was There," or "It Happened To Me," a grab-bag of first-hand accounts of mercenaries and ordinary soldiers in combat situations; and "Bulletin Board," a collection of current interest items. In one issue, the "Bulletin Board" focused on a variety of subjects such as El Salvador and Nicaragua, British mercenaries jailed in Angola, the annual DOD publication "Soviet Military Power," counterpropaganda activities of Radio Free Kabul, the magazine's sponsorship of Vietnamese refugees, and the postwar Falklands situation. There is also a letters column titled "Flak," in which readers respond to articles in previous issues. Notably, all the letters are written by men, and most indicate more than a passing familiarity with weaponry or military operations.

⁴ Articles in the magazine include: a series of combat stories, such as "Inside Free Angola," about anti-Soviet guerrilla fighters; "Intrigue in Africa," an account of Special Forces activities in Liberia; and a "frontline" report on strife in Central America. The magazine also lays heavy emphasis on Soviet and rebel warfare in Afghanistan, mercenary activities in third-world nations, and, for some reason, American Marines in combat in Vietnam, largely ignoring the contributions of the other military branches of service. Perhaps the editors are ex-Marines.

⁵ The photography is mostly of a dramatically glorified style; soldiers and weapons are pictured in much the same way as are new cars in full-color layouts. One gets the feeling that the photographers coach their subjects into displaying stoic expressions in emotional situations. Men are shown crouching behind their weapons with an air of intense concentration, slogging through muddy rivers or over dry wasteland in attitudes of seemingly joyful anticipation, or cradling their weapons in muscular arms while grinning at the camera as if to say, "this is child's play!" Few civilians are photographed; when they are, it is usually as part of a sympathetic article on a third-world nation.

⁶ The vast majority of advertisements concern the latest in foreign and domestic small-arms weaponry, accessories, assorted military clothing and insignia. Most are available through mail order and include such oddities as WWII German and Japanese memorabilia, Vietcong and NVA military issue items, and everything from grenades to exotic knives to airdart blowguns, steel ships, and ultra-sophisticated submachine and anti-tank weapons. Fireworks and plastic explosives are also on order; one ad goes so far as to offer instructions for making napalm! A striking fact is that only small, portable weaponry is advertised; also, ads commonly found in male-oriented magazines such as TV's, stereo equipment, cars, liquor, etc., are nowhere to be seen.

⁷ A good number of the advertisements are so totally outlandish, in a sick sort of way, that they are unwittingly funny. Some of the crazier ads include offers of folding kayaks, copies of CIA ID cards, mercenary newsletters, a manual outlining "dirty divorce tactics," tatooing supplies, a "Boy's Marine Academy" summer camp (specializing in boot-camp drills and physical training), and, especially, a cryptic appeal titled simply "A Warrior's Religion! Odin and Thor Live!"

⁸ For the aspiring professional assassin or covert activities specialist, there are mail-order ads for telephone bugs and anti-bugging devices, cigarette-lighter microphones, electronic surveillance equipment and "how-to" codebooks, frequency lists, etc. Of interest to the survivalist-cum-paranoid are bullet-proof houses, body armor, trained attack dogs, "safe" land in Canada and Alaska, survival caves, and nuclear shelters, complete with food and fuel supplies. One ad, for home security systems, is headlined "Catch the Scumbags!"

9 A great number of books, films and catalogues are available, offering everything from state and international law codes to video cassette recordings of combat, Marine boot camp, the Soviet Army, and the Third Reich. There are numerous ads for instruction in the martial arts, bounty hunting, etc. There's even a "complete vacation package" at a "fun-filled resort," offering hot-air ballooning, mountain climbing, simulated combat games, and survival training, in addition to tennis, swimming, horseback riding, and so forth. Not your typical get-away hot spot!

10 Lastly, the "open for hire" ads alone provide enough food for thought to fill an essay on criminal psychology. Some of these ads are quite specific about experience and skills offered (bounty hunting, courier service, bodyguards, electronic warfare specialists, even a "doctor trained in general anesthesia"). Some list post office boxes, some give full addresses, some merely list a phone number. They come from all over America, Italy, Canada, even the Dominican Republic. Those that are signed are apparently all-male, usually using macho-type professional or nick-names, such as Buck, Thorn, Mad Dog, Spotter, Stringer, Joe, and Troy. Others apparently are "agencies," like "Omega" or "MacDonald Associates," which sound more like real-estate firms than mercenary or assassination organizations.

11 Overall, Soldier of Fortune is frightening, pathetic, and/or comical, depending on the attitude of the reader. If the subject matter, including the freakiest of advertisements, were not treated with such utter seriousness, or if it did not contain so much solid reporting on military and paramilitary activities, it might be less threatening. In any case, it is sobering enough to consider that a magazine such as this evidently has the resources to provide such in-depth, technical information on modern weaponry and behind-the-scenes political intrigue; but especially, that it is available to anyone, anywhere in the world with three dollars to spend.

EVERYWOMAN'S MAGAZINE
Michael Parry

1 The time is November 1944, and a world war is raging on the other side of the Atlantic. An issue of Everywoman's Magazine gives us a good look back in time into the households of Americans and lets us see what the values and interests of women were four decades ago. By carefully examining the magazine, we can get a good picture of the needs and desires of the audience of the magazine—women—as well as an overview of the country during that era.

2 A quick glance through this magazine will tell that it is geared toward women, and more specifically, housewives. With only forty pages and twenty-three ads, it is quite easy to come to this inference. The table of contents lists articles such as "Children Can Make Housework Easier," "Mama Goes Shopping," "Thanksgiving Specialties," "Low-Cost Luncheons

for the Family," "Diary of a Housewife," and "For a Becoming Winter Wardrobe." There are numerous pictures and drawings of women, children, food, and new fashions, while there are only three pictures of men—all drawings and all in fictional stories.

3 The interests of women are presented as the typical housewife's interests: cooking, keeping a neat house, caring for children, and keeping up with the latest fashions. Seventeen recipes are included within three cooking articles as well as a turkey-stuffing article. Housework is assumed to be enjoyed and maybe even the highlight of a housewife's day. A quote like "Things get so dirty that it is a positive joy to clean them" does not seem out of place in this magazine. There are four articles about caring for and entertaining children, as well as three different photo essays on fashion covering six pages.

4 By closer reading it is possible to find some further clues about the magazine's audience. Three fiction short stories are placed at the front of the magazine. The articles are well-written and appear to be aimed toward a well-educated group of people. Although they are all about household situations, they are entertaining. Surprising for this period of time, women appear to be interested in working, probably because of conditions imposed by the war. An article entitled "Careers for Women" describes how to discover the things you really enjoy doing and how to market yourself for a job. I think women were becoming bored, with their husbands off at war, and were tired of being idle. In addition, many factories were in need of extra help during this period to produce war goods.

5 Money appears to be of concern to all, and most articles are interested in the best-looking but most cost-efficient way of doing things. Articles which mention this include cooking, fashion, and child care.

6 It is surprising to note that although this is a women's magazine and two-thirds of the articles were written by women, three-fourths of the magazine's management is conducted by men. Only the editor of the magazine is female, while the president, managing editor, art director, and general manager are male. This could mean that women may not have had enough experience to run a magazine and that most women held jobs of less prominence.

7 One large group that seems to have been completely excluded from this magazine is minorities. All (no exception) pictures, drawings, ads, and articles show white people, no minorities. As this is before the movements of the 1960s, there probably was a lot of prejudice surviving in America, and it could also be possible that most minorities had been denied an education, were thus illiterate, and could not obtain some of the better-paying jobs and luxuries that most middle-class families enjoyed.

8 If one puts this magazine in the proper time frame, it is almost surprising to realize that America was helping to fight a world war. In reading this magazine, it is hard to tell. There are only three ads which (not-so-clearly) state that there is a war going on. The most obvious is an ad to buy war

bonds, but it is buried on the second to last page. It shows two feet literally stamping out Nazism and Japanese Imperialism, and it states that war bonds will "give you that luxurious feeling of freedom that goes with a well-lined pocketbook." I'd say that was blowing it a little out of proportion.

9 The second and third war-related ads are to promote saving paper. The reason given in the second ad for this is that paper and paper products were needed to ship items to Europe. Although in the second ad they mention the words war, invasion, and ammunition, one would never conclude a world war was being fought. The third simply states, "Paper is still essential—save it." The playing down of the war could mean that people were getting tired of hearing all the news of the war, since it had been going on for a few years, and were just interested in "bringing the boys back home." The first two of these ads are the only direct references to a war in the entire magazine.

10 In conclusion, this issue of Everywoman's Magazine can be seen as directed toward middle-aged housewives interested in cooking, housecleaning, caring for children, and keeping up with the fashions. The world war presents a situation where women are looking for jobs while their husbands are away, are money-conscious, and are not too worried about keeping up with the latest war news. Finally, these women are well-educated, generally interested in reading articles about other households, and slightly prejudiced.

#4 STUDY OF A HISTORICAL ISSUE

Method of Research: Finding Facts and Journalistic Views of Those Facts from Library Sources

Most Pertinent Chapters: 2, 3, 4, 5, 6, 7, 13

Probable Topics Due:

Possible Sources Due:

Clean Draft Due for Workshop:

Paper Due:

GOAL

To look at journalistic reporting of some person or event at least 18 years old, and to study either (1) the event and its place in history or (2) the way journalists interpreted the material they reported.

THE PROCESS

1. Locate, in your library's periodicals room, the microfilm version of *The New York Times* from the day that you were born (e.g., June 5, 1967). If you have never worked with the microfilm, ask a librarian or a student library worker for assistance. Read through the entire paper (using one of the microfilm scanners), and choose one article which especially interests you. If you can't find an article that intrigues you from the day you were born, look at papers from days near the day you were born. You may choose your article from any section of the paper except the sports pages, but I recommend that you choose from the first section.

2. Once you've chosen an article, think up a topic for a paper you could write for the class that connects, closely or loosely, with your article. You might, for example, contrast some stories which indicate racial attitudes then and now; you might show how union and management stubbornness led to a long strike that neither side anticipated; you may be led to try to figure out why a certain event happened; you may show how several magazines or newspapers treated the same issue very differently. Readers of this kind of paper don't want you to tell them something that they could find out just as easily by looking in an encyclopedia. Your readers are curious about how people and events were viewed by the journalists of their own time.

3. On _____(date), bring to class a sheet of paper with the following information handwritten on it:

   - Your date of birth
   - A summary of the article you have chosen to work with
   - A topic, connected with that article, that you think you'd like to write about
   - The kind of reader you imagine being interested
   - Why you think such a reader would benefit from your paper

The class that day will compare potential topics, and suggestions will be made about where you and your classmates can find more information on the topics you've chosen. You'll learn a great deal by comparing your plans with those of your classmates. When you leave, you should feel confident that you have a topic that is not too broad so that you can research it thoroughly and still meet the deadline for the assignment.

4. Your next step is to check the library's indexes (your first stop should be *The New York Times Index,* for newspaper articles, and the *Readers' Guide to Periodical Literature,* for magazine articles) for sources of further information on your topic. Note down the sources you find in these indexes, and bring a list of ten possible sources of information to class on _____. You probably won't use all these sources in your final paper, and you may well use some others that you come across as you work.

5. Find these articles, then, and begin taking notes on items that will serve the purpose of your paper. You'll undoubtedly be noting facts (which of course must be acknowledged), as well as inferences made by the journalists you're reading (which also must be acknowledged). The quality of your paper will depend in part on your selecting these items carefully. But it will depend much more on the quality of the inferences (judgments, or conclusions) *you* draw about the facts and about the journalists' opinions. Your introduction, your conclusion, and the comments you make on each paragraph of material should show that you understand your material and that you, as a writer, are thinking and in control.

6. Before you begin writing, and as you sort through your notes, it may help to decide on an organizational pattern (cause-effect, comparison-contrast, narration, problem-solution) which best accommodates your evidence. Also, much of the information you've collected will have to be omitted. How will you decide what to include and what to omit?

7. Finally, you'll write your paper (again, at least three typewritten pages) and bring it to class for your classmates to read on _____. With their suggestions, you'll have _____ more days to rethink and revise your paper. Your typed paper is due on _____.

SAMPLES

CIVIL RIGHTS IN 1965 AS SEEN THROUGH THE NEW YORK TIMES
Jeffrey Gagliardi

[1] In 1965, race and racial equality were very controversial issues. The civil rights movement was gaining momentum, and blacks were gaining equality in practice as well as theory. The national government and the legal system were working substantially to erase discrimination. Opposed to the government and courts' attempts to bring racial equality, although not always directly or wholly opposed, were several important sections of the population, namely, the church, the police, some local and state governments, and a large portion of the people themselves.

² The national government and the court system were the main proponents in the establishment which promoted equal rights. The Civil Rights Act of 1964 eliminated more discrimination in its first year than all of the federal laws, court rulings, and executive orders of the previous decades. It barred discrimination in public places and in federally assisted programs. One of its immediate effects was to persuade more school systems to commit themselves to desegregation than since the Supreme Court desegregation ruling of 1954. One of the main differences was that now, the laws were being enforced, often through force.[1]

³ The black population was no longer sitting by impassively as they were being treated as inferiors. In Philadelphia, the city protested outside of Girard College. According to the founder's will, the institution was created for white, male orphans only. After trying for over eight years to change Girard College through the courts, the blacks took to the streets to protest. Led by three white ministers, the protestors stood vigil for close to two months. Despite the fact that the demonstration was peaceful, the police formed a massive barricade around the compound and arrested some protestors.[2]

⁴ Other civil rights protestors were not as lucky. Many were jailed en masse just for the simple fact of protesting, with no legal reason. In Mississippi, the state fair grounds were used to house "Civil Rights prisoners." The blacks claimed that the conditions at the compound were poor and that they were often beaten by the police. The mail hall, as told by the blacks, contained an imaginary line down the center to separate the blacks from the whites. If either the whites or the blacks crossed the line they were beaten back by police with nightsticks. Although they openly discriminated against the blacks, the police denied it, sometimes with ridiculous explanations. The police denied that the housing and boarding facilities were bad, and even that they abused the prisoners. When confronted with the fact that several prisoners had wounds on their heads, the police responded with the theory that they might have bumped their heads in the truck that brought them in. Furthermore, the police claimed that the blacks' accusations were propaganda for the civil rights movement. They even went so far as to claim that the blacks were abusing them; they claimed that the prisoners "cussed them out."[3]

⁵ One would expect that an institution, such as the church, that preached equality and love would back the civil rights movement. This was not so in Alabama. A Selma, Alabama, priest was removed from his post for helping the negroes of Selma launch a voter registration drive. The priest was accused of "exciting the negro population" and, among other things, planning to bring in five hundred negroes from outlying areas to destroy the town. The priest's view was very different. He maintained that he had cleared all of his actions with his superiors beforehand, and that he had never disobeyed them. The priest also said that he had been given implied threats from city and police officials that it would be in his "best interest" to

cease his activities. He was threatened with arrest, and was asked by his superiors to take a "vacation."[4]

[6] Teaching in the public school system also promoted racial discrimination. This was true not only with respect to segregation and the quality of the education, but with what was taught in the classroom and how it was taught. According to an article in The New York Times, a white teacher punished a black student by painting his face yellow. The teacher, however, claimed that other children wanted their faces painted too, but she only painted one because there was not enough time to do the others. Infuriated parents protested and demanded her dismissal. The principal of the school transferred her for the remaining three days of the school year, but maintained that the teacher did nothing wrong, even when faced with the testimony of a parent who was in the room at the time. The principal told the press that he only transferred the teacher because the parents made a big fuss.[5]

[7] In another incident, a teacher was dismissed for teaching her class about the civil rights movement and the principles of equality. The principal of the school, who dismissed the teacher, claimed that it would "hurt the pupils' self image."[6]

[8] The starkest example of the general population's attitudes toward the blacks was an article concerning a rape. On November 11, 1965, the first white man in modern Mississippi history was convicted of raping a negro. The sheer weight of the fact that the police and the courts had not, up until this point, convicted rapists because of the victims' color is appalling. The article called the court's decision "an unusual action."[7] To call a rightful conviction unusual because of race implies that the general population and the newspaper were racist. The boy's remarks during the trial were even more interesting. In his defense, he claimed that the girl had wanted to have an affair. He further claimed that the girl said she liked to have affairs with "white boys." In response to the fact that he left her in the woods, he maintained that he had thought he heard noises, and that he was afraid to be seen with her. All this was said despite the fact that overwhelming evidence pointed to the fact that he was guilty, as if his act of rape was justifiable or excusable because of her race—and that society would accept his answers.

[9] After reading this information, it is easy to create a general view of society's attitudes towards race in 1965. Society was split, though. The government and some of the people advocated equal rights, while a majority of the population either looked on it with distaste or openly opposed it. The overall view of the day, including the church, some elements of government, and the public school system, was that negroes were second-class citizens. The fact that the newspapers of the time printed articles informing the public of the crimes against blacks and, at the same time, wrote them in a discriminatory tone, shows that even the media was divided and confused on the race issue.

ENDNOTES

[1] All information from <u>The New York Times</u>: June 27, 1965, Nov. 13, 1965.
[2] <u>New York Times</u>, June 26, 1965.
[3] <u>New York Times</u>, June 26, 1965.
[4] <u>New York Times</u>, June 26, 1965.
[5] <u>New York Times</u>, June 27, 1965.
[6] <u>New York Times</u>, June 27, 1965.
[7] <u>New York Times</u>, Nov. 12, 1965.

<u>GOLEM</u>: AMERICAN REACTIONS TO ATOMIC POWER DEVELOPMENT
Craig Stoltz

[1] The first warning about the power of the atom was buried in Section III of the 7 June 1931 <u>New York Times</u>:

> ". . . What if the atom whose energy man has released should turn into a 'Golem,' which would destroy man? What if the explosion of the energy in one atom would automatically have the same effect on the other atoms surrounding it? On the sun . . . temperatures of 40,000,000 degrees are found. What if our tiny friends here on earth are capable of raising our temperatures to a similar degree of warmth? I doubt if anyone would welcome the change—unless it be a comparatively few Eskimos.
>
> . . . I hope in every experiment the scientists make they will endeavor first to make provision for every conceivable possibility. They will have to be particularly circumspect in this matter.
>
> For all we know in the 2,000,000 years . . . man has existed on earth there might have been other experiments which just got out of the hands of scientists in some prehistoric laboratory and resulted in the complete destruction of everything on earth."

And thus Philip Lieb of New York City became the first publicly to warn mankind about the destructive potential of atomic power. As speculative and sarcastic as Lieb's letter is, his fears that the atom is a <u>golem</u>, a Frankenstein-like monster, seem genuine, and have proven to be prophetic.

[2] Scientists had been speculating about and experimenting with atomic structures since the early 1920's; Lieb wrote his letter in response to a <u>Times</u> article reporting a group of English scientists' speculations that laboratory atom-splitting was a near possibility. Most of Lieb's contemporaries reacted to this progress with great interest and advocacy rather than with sarcasm and fear. Two weeks after Lieb's letter appeared, a <u>Times</u> editorialist recommended America's "pushing forward into this new frontier," for fear that the English and Germans might "outstrip us in this important technological race" (<u>NYT</u>, 20 June 1931).

[3] Approximately one year later, Lord Rutherford, a prominent British physicist, chipped particles from an atom and measured the energy released in the process. The media responded with speculations about atom-splitting as an energy source, and any Lieb-like fears about atomic research were overshadowed by anticipation of an atomic-charged "period of prosperity such as has never yet been seen" (NYT, 1 November 1933).

[4] As the 30's progressed, so did atomic research; atom-chipping, by which relatively little energy was released, gave way to splitting the atomic nucleus, by which tremendous amounts of energy were released. In 1939, German physicist Otto Hahn split an atom's nucleus in a Berlin laboratory, and in so doing released a 40,000-volt electrical charge. And perhaps not surprisingly, the Lieb interpretation of atom-as-golem gained support. Writers and scientists alike began to fear these high-energy releases, and to question whether these experiments could be controlled adequately. Lord Eddington, an English physicist involved in early atomic research, surprised some of his colleagues when he announced he would "prefer not to be too near the laboratory" when atom-splitting occurred. Both popular and scientific periodicals featured articles comparing the potential benefits and harm of atomic power. "Don't Worry, It Can't Happen: Explosions from Nuclear Fission Cannot Wreck the Universe," assured J. Harrington in a May, 1940 polemic appearing in Scientific American; A. G. Ingalls, a year earlier, had weighed the advantages and disadvantages of fission in "Incomparable Threat or Awful Promise?" which appeared in the July '39 issue of the same magazine.

[5] After the atom was split, most scientists working with the atom concurred with Lord Rutherford, who predicted that "atom-smashing of an energy source" was "years, even decades away." Typically, the pragmatic American public responded to this news with a predictable loss of interest. The mysteries of the atom were less fascinating to Americans than were practical energy sources and promises of economic benefits. Interest dwindled. Throughout the 30's, the Times had carried at least fifty articles, editorials, and features dealing with atomic research annually; as the 40's began, however, fewer and fewer articles appeared. By 1943, only four articles about atomic research appeared in the Times; in 1944, only one appeared.

[6] Ironically, these same years were the most important and prolific—but most secret—in atomic research to date. The U.S. Government was quietly sponsoring one of the largest and most expensive research projects in history, the Manhattan Project. This huge operation utilized four research and manufacturing centers and employed nearly 100,000 workers, only a handful of whom knew they were working to develop the first atomic bomb.

[7] When the result of the Manhattan Project's laborings exploded on Hiroshima in August of 1945, however, Americans' interest in the atom mushroomed. Immediately after the blast, many Americans felt a huge shrug of patriotic pride—we had given the Japanese what they deserved,

and we had used superior American technology to do so. President Truman's speech delivered eighteen hours after the bombing reflects this attitude: "What has been done is the greatest achievement of organized science in history. . . . We thank God that it has come to us, instead of to our enemies; and we pray that He may guide us to use it in His ways, and for His purposes" (Time, 13 August 1945). Truman's speech indicates pride in and justification of the atomic bomb's use, and most Americans shared these sentiments: a November 1945 Gallop poll indicates that 85% of Americans approved of the use of the bomb against Japan (Time, 3 December 1945).

8 As the fallout settled over the Pacific Ocean and the survivors and remains of Hiroshima, however, some Americans' opinions settled in a different pattern. Groups of Christians, leftists, humanists, and many others responded, as Christian scholar B. G. Gallagher said in a speech a year after the bombing, with "fear—massive, awesome, terrible apprehension" combined with "abhorrence and revulsion." Many Americans were outraged. "The U.S. has become the new master of brutality, infamy, atrocity. . . . No peacetime applications of this Frankenstein monster can ever erase the crime we have committed. We have paved the way for the obliteration of the globe" (Walter G. Taylor, NYT, 27 August 1945).

9 So it seemed to some. Despite early warnings about the devastating potential of the atom, the U.S. has forged ahead, developed the bomb, and in so doing not only killed tens of thousands of civilians, destroyed an entire city, and had done untellable damage to surviving and unborn Japanese; they had also created a weapon they feared to use but dared not ignore, one they felt they must control but had no idea how or how much to control it, and one whose lasting effects on the world and on history they could only speculate.

10 "There has been much talk about how to get the new monster into an unbreakable cage," wrote a Time editorialist in "Godless Götterdämmerung" on 15 December 1945, "but few admissions that the real monster is the human race."

11 For all his naiveté and shoddy writing, Philip Lieb had made a profound point fourteen years before others realized its truth. Atomic energy was a golem. But fourteen years later, while the fallout settled and the politicians barked, it could be seen as well that it was indeed a race of golem which had begot this golem.

#5 CHARACTER SKETCH

Method of Research: Interview

Most Pertinent Chapters: 2, 3, 4, 5, 6, 14

Clean Draft Due for Workshop: *Thurs. April 23*

Paper Due: *Final Paper = Thurs. April 30*

harmless - innocent

In a crowd we all look alike. But even the most innocuous looking among us has had some adventures, endured some hardship, and tried to make a sensible plan for his or her life. The purpose of an interview is to ask perceptive enough questions to find the details that make a person distinctive. You've done research by observing a place, by studying newspapers or magazines, and by working in the library. This time you'll do your research—gather your facts—in an interview with someone you don't know. Again, you need to concentrate and gather the facts that will speak for themselves and convey an impression. In the paper you will write, you will offer us not a random series of questions and answers, but a thoughtful portrait of the person you interview. You may be asked to read your paper to the class so that your classmates can get to know the person you have chosen. The hardest part of this assignment is getting your nerve up to ask someone to be interviewed. But it won't be nearly as difficult as you think; people like to talk about themselves.

insight into human nature

not like a newspaper

picking a topic

The person you interview must be (1) someone over 40 years old, or (2) someone whose occupation is one you don't know much about, or (3) someone whose background is very different from yours. Don't bother to interview a person your age, or a member of your family, or a neighbor whom you know well. You won't learn much from such an interview. One of my students interviewed a housewife who rode a motorcycle as a hobby. Another interviewed a derelict in Annapolis and got him to talk about how much time he would spend in Purgatory. Another student—from Korea—sat at a bus stop until he found someone—an immigrant from Turkey who had, coincidentally, fought in the Korean War—willing to be interviewed. He rode the bus home with the man and finished the interview at his home. And you can always find someone to talk to at a nursing home. Decide, as soon as possible, whom you'd like to interview so that you'll have plenty of time to organize your notes and write your paper.

Before you go to the interview, prepare a list of questions. Once you've asked a few of those questions, though, and you find yourself comfortable with the person you're interviewing, you should find yourself asking spontaneous questions and forgetting those on your list. Take careful notes, for the person's own words will usually be more effective than your own. Before you leave, ask permission to call the person back in case you need more information. Also ask whether the person would like a copy of the interview. Typing up your notes *immediately* after the interview will help you remember everything you want to.

Remember these key elements when you organize your material for your first draft:

1. Your first obligation is to the person you interview—don't change the meaning of what is said.

2. Your second obligation is to the reader; choose quotations and information your readers are likely to be curious about.

attaining quotes

3. Use the person's own words in your writing; they will be more telling than your own.

4. Don't try to unify too soon. Try to see the variety in the person you interview.

5. In your introduction, let your readers know why this person is worth reading about.

6. Don't relinquish control in your paper to your interviewee or to your notes. You are the writer. You organize and paragraph the paper, and you do it for your readers' convenience.

SAMPLES

A WATER PERSON: AN INTERVIEW WITH JOHN HOFFMAN
Diana Lambird

1 "Come on in, we're having an orgy," he said as he waved four more girls onto the elevator. By the time the elevator came down seven floors and reached the lobby, John Hoffman had everyone laughing. A handsome stalky man, the only sign of this thirty-five years are his laugh lines that are there whether he smiles or not. A deep tan and a couple scars on his hands are the only visible casualties of having the life that most people only dream of—sailing around the Virgin Islands and the Chesapeake Bay year round. "I fell into the job. If you had told me a couple of years ago, I would be sailing the islands for a living—I would have winked at you and said, 'sure.'"

2 Anyone can hire John. All you have to do is give him a call and he'll answer the phone, "Hey, this is John. What can I do for you today?" Just let him know what you want, and he'll try and get it done for a "reasonable price." He'll take you sailing on a fifty-five foot sailboat "anywhere, where the sun is shining and the wind is blowing." In fact, he's leaving for St. Croix with a couple of "lady doctors" and plans on staying down in the islands until the eastern sailing begins again. He admits that business is getting harder to find, but he's not worried: "I used to be booked up all through the winter by now. But not this year. Things must be getting tougher for people." But it doesn't seem to be getting tough for John. He dresses as if he stepped out of one of the pages of G.Q., drives a bright red 280Z T-top, and lives in an old house in downtown Annapolis.

3 The house is always occupied by his live-in maid and three Chesapeake Bay retrievers. "I don't find much time to live here, but I call it home." The house is filled with wood antiques and furniture he made himself. His favorite room is his bedroom, which is filled with unicorn artifacts. "The unicorns were all given to me by my friends—the ones that know me well." His close friends call him Uni because, he explains with a wink and a hug, "we're both fabulous animals." But the truth of the matter is his soon to be ex-wife pegged him with the nickname. During one of their frequent parties,

"she told a good friend of mine that she saw me as frequently as she saw a unicorn—and that I was as horny as one when I finally did appear. Anyway, the name stuck."

4 He took this present job because his marriage was over and it gave him the freedom he needed. "Pepper and I went through a lot together. But we finally had to let the relationship go. We didn't love each other anymore. That's one person I failed. I tried, but sometimes, I don't know." Silence. "I guess I can't change that I failed someone." They met while in college at the University of Michigan. They lived together for four years when "she just suggested that maybe we should get married. Hell, we were together for so long I figured, why not. So we did."

5 During this time John and friends from college started the Brooks Construction Co. With this, he made his fortune: "My partners and I were quite good at what we did; we were all good businessmen." But as the business flourished, the friendship of the partners dwindled. "To make a long story short, one of my partners—he was also one of my best friends—embezzled money from the rest of us. Another close friend and business partner committed suicide as a result of many financial and marital problems. I sold my shares and got out," which explains his wealth now.

6 He has always been accustomed to wealth. His parents are "well-off" and live in Houston, Texas. "I hate it there though. Can't really explain why because I love my parents, they're cool people. The other people there aren't like these people [people who sail]." "Water people" is what John calls people who like the water. "Water people are the greatest. They're open. Just ask anything of them and its done for you. I love 'em all." People are John's business, and he wouldn't go into another business unless he could work with them. "People are what make the world. I've seen some pretty ignorant ones, but they still are the only thing worth while in this world."

7 "Sailing," he said, "is when people are themselves. People let down their defenses under two conditions: when they're scared or when they're laughing. I like to do both. I like to make them laugh, and well, sometimes sailing can scare 'em a little." He doesn't plan on keeping the job forever, though. He has plans to start and run a chartering business in Annapolis and to settle down again, but people are definitely in his future, "whether they're water people or not."

YOU ARE ONLY AS OLD AS YOU FEEL
Robin Shaw-Maglione

1 Hal Saylor sits straight in his wheel chair, smoking his pipe. Swirls of apple-scented smoke surround him. Although unshaven, "I think I might just grow a beard," his clothes are of a recent style and his crystal blue eyes are clear and bright behind "bottleglass" spectacles. "Ah, you are here. That is good. I detest waiting for people—don't like to waste time."

2 We settled down in a cozy corner of the nursing home lobby near the

piano. A frail white-haired woman was softly playing chopsticks. "Used to play quite a bit," he said, nodding at the woman. "When I was young, my mother used to make me take lessons from every music teacher in town. Whenever she'd hear of a better teacher, I'd have to change teachers again. Once I had this teacher, Mrs. Maddox I believe her name was, who'd slam the piano cover down on my fingers if I made too many mistakes. Broke a finger once that way. Didn't want her as a teacher after that, but being as she was the best in town, I had to keep taking my lessons with her. After my finger 'n all, she started using a hat pin!"

3 Hal pursued his music and received his degree from the Cincinnati Conservatory of Music. He spent one of his summers during college working on the "Chris Green," a riverboat on the Ohio River. "I started out in the boiler room shoveling coal. One day the Captain happened by and we got to talking. He found out that I could play the piano and promoted me up to the lounge where I played for the passengers. Some promotion, eh?"

4 He looked down at his hands. His right hand moved and lifted his left hand into a more comfortable position. "You know," he spoke softly, "I spent eighteen years getting these fingers to play the major chords and now look at them. Useless. You might just say that I'm a one handed piano player."

5 Hal had a major stroke thirteen years ago this January. Recently his grandson, who is eight, asked him if he had ever walked. "I told him yes, but I don't think he believed me."

6 "Still and all, though, in and out of this chair, I've done a lot in life. Course, I haven't done it all yet, but I still have a few miles left in me. And if I don't get it all done—I'll just have to come back and do it."

7 After his music degree, Hal earned another degree in engineering. "There were too many starving musicians." Already an accomplished ham radio operator, having received his first license at thirteen (the youngest ever in the state), he entered the police force to head a radio communications team. "We were just a bunch of gun totin' radio operators." From there, Hal entered the FBI. "We used to call it the Farm Boys Institute because so many of the boys were from Iowa and Indiana." He joined the FBI to be close to the war effort. "I was too young for WWI and too old for WWII." He became an agent and traveled to every state in the union and every country in South America and Europe. "Once I traveled to a town just south of London to deliver a message to Churchill. The message was engraved on the lenses of my glasses. You couldn't see it with the naked eye, you needed a microscope to decode it." "Another time, using a device called an extortion package, we were attempting to capture a high-level banker involved in a blackmail racket. It (the E. P.) was thrown from a car window disguised as the money drop. It was equipped with a small tracking device that we could pick up by radio in the car. A faster beep meant that someone was close to it. It started to beep faster, so we went back to nab the guy. When we got there, there was this dog using it for a fire-plug."

8 When the war was over, Hal left the FBI for a job with less traveling. He went to work for CBS as a sound engineer. "The first thing CBS did was send me to Europe!" He worked with many celebrities including Lloyd Bridges, Peter Graves, and Guy Lombardo. "During one of the New Year's Eve shows Lombardo did, he wanted the violins to be highlighted at one particular point. He said he would signal me at the appropriate time. When I wanted to know why he didn't just mark it on the sheet music, he laughed. Lombardo couldn't believe that an engineer could read music!"

9 The time was nearly up. He had promised to talk to one of his radio friends. He has a complete ham radio set-up in his room at the nursing home. His friends at CBS installed the antenna on the roof for him. He's working on upgrading his ham license so that his equipment can reach out farther. "My world extends far beyond this nursing home. Where this wheel chair can't get me, the radio does."

10 We said goodbye, and I watched him wheel away to his room. On my way out, I passed his room and there he was, talking to someone in West Virginia and practicing speeding up his morse code. Go for it, Hal. As you yourself once said, "There isn't anything a body can't do, if you set your mind to it."

conclusion

#6 FILM EVALUATION

Method of Research: Studying a Film's Use of Subject, Language, Music, Shot Sequence, and Camera Angle to Determine Whether or Not the Sum Is Effective

Most Pertinent Chapters: 2, 3, 4, 5, 6, 9, 12

Clean Draft Due for Workshop:

Paper Due:

PRELIMINARY EXERCISE

Fill in the blanks in the following sentence:

_____ is a terrible _____.

Having filled in the blanks, specify three criteria by which you judge a "good," or at least a "not-so-bad," whatever-your-second-blank-filler was. Compare your statements, and your criteria, with those of the rest of the class. Which criteria are well thought through and based on common sense?

When you write an evaluation, keep in mind that your judgment must be based on criteria. Your statement that "Almond Joy is a good candy bar" is only a reflection of personal taste until you specify that (1) chocolate, (2) nuts, and (3) a nourishing base—like coconut—are the essential criteria for a good candy bar. Now your evaluation is publicly useful and can be discussed.

If you have completed this exercise carefully, you should be prepared to see the form your film evaluation will take:

1. _____ is a good (or bad) persuasive film.

2. What criteria must be met for a film to be persuasive?

   - Effective *ethos*
   - Effective *logos*
   - Effective *pathos*
   - Any others?

3. How well does this film meet these criteria? (The answer is likely to be at least slightly mixed—some aspects of the film will be effective, others not so effective.)

SUGGESTIONS FOR THE PLANNING STAGE

1. Films make their points using a wide variety of techniques unavailable to books, newspapers, or magazines. They use words, to be sure, but also music and a great number of pictures (shots) that vary in content, time exposed, camera angle and distance, and juxtaposition with other shots. So, in order to pick up on the visual strategies and others beyond the obvious ones, view the film at least twice—if possible, three or more times. At the first viewing, try not to be too critical. Just ask yourself, after viewing, whether you were persuaded to accept the filmmaker's point of view. If not, why not? If so, why so? Or if the audience did not include you, did the filmmaker persuade his or her audience? Your answer here will establish the basis, or thesis, of your evaluation (effective or ineffective?).

2. Use your second and subsequent viewings to make notes about *types of strategies* the filmmaker employs to convince you. Look for the following:

- *logos:* What verifiable facts does the filmmaker present? What assumptions does the filmmaker make? Does the filmmaker use an organizational structure that helps persuade, or fails to?

- *ethos:* What strategies does the filmmaker use to convince us of his integrity, that his argument is ethically sound and that he has our best social and moral interests in mind? Consider, for instance, the choice of a narrator, the choice of words in the narration, the biased or unbiased selection of material, and the choice of any other authorities who appear in the film.

- *pathos:* What strategies have been used to evoke a subjective response by appealing to our feelings rather than to our logic? Keep an eye out especially for visual and sound effects here.

3. It is not necessary to be an expert on film in order to do this assignment. But try to observe and analyze some of the basic cinematic techniques used: for instance, dramatic editing (juxtaposition of scenes, movement from one scene to the next), the use of unusual camera angles, dramatic lighting, pacing, the use of music in different scenes. *These will not be obvious from your first viewing.*

As you write, think of your readers as being skeptical of your point of view (it will help you to respond to that skepticism if, sometime while you're planning the paper, you write a paragraph or two explaining the reasons your readers might have for being skeptical). In your introduction, give us the facts about the film, and state your point of view clearly. After that you can organize the paper any way you wish. However, keep your thesis (effective or ineffective) in mind as you write. And be specific (citing dialogue, or describing shots) in supporting all your points.

SAMPLES

CONSIDERING THE HUMAN SIDE
Karen Teramura

1 Future Shock is a fast-moving film giving its viewers a variety of information and visual stimulation to emphasize the increasing rate of change the Scientific-Industrial-Revolution has brought about in today's world. The film makes no attempt to judge the controversial information it uses to demonstrate evidence of future shock but instead relies on the emotional and analytical abilities of the viewer to incorporate these facts—stimulating him into thinking about the consequences of "too much change in too short a time."

2 The introduction begins at a rapid pace combining and contrasting hectic city life to pristine woodland scenes. The viewer is tricked into believing that the woods provide a place of retreat from today's maddening pace of life until pseudo-human images emerge from the woods making a

mockery of its tranquility. Along with a variety of flashing and whirling clips of short duration, camera techniques which use angles that over-emphasize importance of objects and graphic images that denote conflict help to keep the viewer in awe.

3 The introduction's fast pace is halted by the enormous presence of Orson Welles. His soothing voice with its methodical tone compels the viewer to absorb his narrations of overwhelming change, setting the mood of the film. Repetition becomes an important element in the film, insuring its message is received by the viewer. Phrases like "endless decisions," "choice and overchoice," "the disposability of products and people," and "man's craving for warmth and closeness especially today when relation-ships are more temporary" make the viewer consider the effects of rapid change. Is our society ready for change? Can we absorb change and still control our lives? How does all this change relate to "me"?

4 The past is contrasted with the future. Traditional sources of rela-tionships which provide man with basic needs of warmth and security may no longer be relevant in a society which continually moves. Has newly found freedom and independence given way to a lost sense of belonging and long term commitments? Does the disposability of things and friendships affect our ability to cope? What is happening to our institutions of marriage, church and family?

5 These are all important questions the film raises which should be answered by everyone. Their answers give us a clue as to how we might cope in stressful situations, and allow us to understand that there is no one way to solve problems created by rapid change. The film begins to introduce this concept by giving examples of the different ways people have learned to cope with their loneliness, e.g., group marriages and homosexuality. It also warns us of the dangers of not being able to cope through its scenes of memory-process drugs and electric shock addiction. If people are unable to cope will they turn to self destruction?

6 In order to emphasize the rapid pace of novelty and innovation in the scientific community, the film attempts to show and question remarkable studies somewhat controversial at the time but already outdated. Remark-ably though, the bits and pieces of outdated research only reinforce the statements made about rapid change. It's still incredible to think that we're living in an age of test-tube babies. The genetic coding of DNA was a dynamic breakthrough in the '60s bringing about hopeful pursuits in cor-recting genetic defects. If these facts do not impress the viewer, then he is teased into considering somewhat preposterous events like baby shopping or the film's portrayal of city residents as nothing more than boobs only capable of unsophisticated reactions to skin color fads. It's hard to believe that anyone can become so superficial, but ironically these scenes make way for deep-rooted questions. Has or can scientific discoveries eliminate the joy of surprise in our lives? What happens when we begin to tamper with forces of natural selection before we fully comprehend the conse-quences?

⁷ Whether we care to admit it or not, future shock is relevant in today's world and will affect each of us in some point of our lives. Many of us have been protected from it through strong family ties. But once we become independent, taking on responsibilities for ourselves and our own families, we begin to opt for the decisions of success which finds us moving to wherever we can find it.

⁸ As a means of self-protection, more women are becoming financially independent. Couples put off having children until it becomes convenient. Both are wise decisions, but as the film points out in its marriage counseling scene, unless strong communication ties are maintained, unfulfilled expectations, restless clouds of instability, along with feelings of independence booster separations. Have we as individuals become too independent, too selfish to maintain life-long ties? How does this instability affect our children's ability to cope?

⁹ Time becomes the relevant issue in the film. Does time express change, or has change dominated time by being compressed more and more into each measurable unit? From the simplistic view of a child to the more complex attitude of the old, the film leaves the viewer with a scene that depicts how short life really is. The subtle message of being born, living, and dying passes before the viewer's eyes. Only he can challenge himself and make a difference in his life. Whether the film initiates his thoughts through emotion or logic, it stimulates them successfully.

¹⁰ It is impossible for any one person to fully comprehend all the knowledge being developed from our present Scientific-Industrial-Revolution. Too much knowledge without enough wisdom to understand its effects on the human spirit can be as devastating as its effects on the environment. Will we allow ourselves to be victimized by change? I hope not.

BRACE YOURSELF . . . FOR A SHOCK:
A LOOK AT THE FILM FUTURE SHOCK
Jeff Green

¹ We are being overthrown. Our civilization is crumbling. Our entire way of life is being shaken by the foundations. Even our way of thinking is being tragically bent toward destruction. The ironic thing is that this is all being caused by what we have always considered our greatest friend, yet has indeed proved to be our overthrower—technology.

² This is the warning presented to us in the film version of Alvin Toffler's Future Shock. The movie shows how America is quickly going into "future shock," a state caused by "the premature arrival of the future." The movie presents this ominous prophecy with great clarity, and it can be easily understood why people shook with fear after seeing this movie when it first came out in 1974. There are three main aspects which made this film so believable: the style in which the film presented each idea, the technological advances and modern trends used as examples of "the future getting out of

control," and the strategies used by the producer to strike a nerve in the viewer.

³ The movie begins immediately with an interesting film technique designed to capture the viewer's complete attention. It starts out with a pleasant scene of a couple walking alone in the woods. Suddenly a scene of sheer violence in a city street flashes on the screen, followed by the serene woods again with the silhouetted couple coming ever-so-slightly closer. The scenes rapidly switch back and forth between the peaceful woods and the terror-filled city until suddenly the couple is upon the viewer, and much to the viewer's horror too, for this couple, which seemed like a pair of peaceful lovers, is in fact a pair of grotesque-looking robots. Add to this the monotone voice of a narrator, and you leave the viewer in a state of utter confusion, which is just where the producer wants him.

⁴ The narrator of the film is none other than Orson Welles, and with his rough, monotone voice he makes the ominous thought of society's downfall seem very believable somehow. Throughout the movie, Welles wears a dark, heavy overcoat which seems to show a lack of permanence, as though he's ready to leave at any time. This supports one of the major points made in the movie concerning the lack of permanence in today's society.

⁵ Another interesting point about the film's style is the camera usage. Throughout the movie, the camera is constantly moving and pivoting and changing its focus. This gives the viewer a slight feeling of insecurity which the producer immediately thrives on by presenting his ideas as soon as this feeling appears. The best example of this is when the camera takes the viewer through two stores, first a supermarket and then a bookstore. The camera switches from item to item, aisle to aisle, floor to ceiling, doing complete 360° turns in order to show how far we have come in terms of choice. But the choice is so great it overwhelms us, leaving us staggering in indecision.

⁶ The second main aspect which makes the film seem frightfully believable is the technological advances and modern trends cited. The first and foremost trend cited is that of moving. More than ever before, Americans are packing up their belongings and moving. The movie shows how this is destroying our concept of the family and community. It explains how to kids today "home is just a place to leave." It also explains how the telephone directory is rewritten daily, showing further that "where we live means less and less."

⁷ The film also focuses on modern medical advances. These include artificial limbs, artificial kidneys, and heart bypass surgery. It singles out the case of Carl Schaefer, who, after suffering a stroke, was given eight hours to live, but who was saved through a heart bypass operation. This in turn prompts the idea that the body is slowly becoming replaceable and, in a way, "disposable."

⁸ The film also discusses the case of Verlin Cobb, a prematurely wrinkled lady who decided to get a face-lift, suggesting that "even faces are tempo-

rary." Finally, Dr. C. Epstein discusses the feasibility of reproducing human embryos within a test tube. This shows that "even motherhood is becoming obsolete," and if we don't gain control of technology soon, we will find ourselves "baby shopping in babytoriums or genetic supermarkets."

9 But medical advances are not the only new changes discussed in the film; also noted are changes in basic, traditional institutions, including religion and marriage. The film discusses the cases of group marriages, commune living, and homosexual marriages, which for many are truly shattering to the foundations of these institutions. These new changes, according to the film, are the setting for "a quiet revolution," which in turn is "part of a bigger revolution." This big revolution can be seen forming through such new developments as the battle for homosexuals' equal rights, constant strikes against traditional methods, ideas, and values in various occupations, and the battle for women's equal rights.

10 The producer combines the mind-controlling film style with the awe-inspiring data and then mixes in the final touch, an appeal to the viewer's raw emotions, making the movie undeniably effective. This appeal is first seen when Welles is discussing everything's lack of permanence. A little girl walks into a toy store carrying a beaten-up doll and trades it in for a different one. As she leaves, we see the shopkeeper dump the old doll into a garbage can while Welles narrates, "Even old friends don't last forever."

11 Another appeal to the viewer's emotions is a scene showing people of the future getting up in the morning. When the male wakes up, he takes a quick energy pill and then plugs himself into a socket for some instant happy stimulation. He then plugs his wife in and gives her a good morning kiss. The thought of this horrifies the viewer.

12 The final and most effective appeal to the viewer's emotions comes in the final scene. It not only does the best job of reaching the viewer but actually puts a cap on the film and sends the viewer away ready to act against this terrible plague called "future shock." It shows a baby lying alone on a vast beach with the narrator saying, "Our children—will we save them from future shock? The choices we make will determine the outlook of their world. There is still time . . ."

#7 PROPOSAL

Method of Research: Studying an Audience and the Facts of the Case

Most Pertinent Chapters: 2, 3, 4, 5, 6, 9

Clean Draft Due for Workshop:

Paper Due:

PRELIMINARY EXERCISE

Write down in your notebook a brief description of a problem—in your family, in this school, in your community, in society—that bothers you.

Now think of a worse problem, a problem that affects more people, and write a brief description of it.

One of these two problems will probably be the subject of the proposal paper you'll be writing. Before you do any research, can you think of a method of attacking your problem? What's the cause of the problem? Have any solutions to the problem already been tried?

Finally, pair up with one of your classmates, and explain your proposal. After you've explained it, give your partner enough time to write out three possible problems with, or objections to, your proposal. Consider these objections as you write your paper.

OVERVIEW

Injustice rears its head daily in our experience, even when we belong to a society that tries to be just. There is always room, therefore, for proposals to improve matters. In writing a proposal you will be using writing not only to get people to listen to you as you explain something, or to agree with you about the value of some part of our culture, but to get them to do something about a problem that you think should be remedied. Think up a way to solve the problem that bothers you most. It may take a while to work out the details, but be patient and keep thinking. Keep in mind practical details like cost. And try to figure out how the solution will help everybody—not only you, the employee, for example, but also the boss and the whole company.

Write your solution in a letter to the people who would have the authority to make the change you are recommending. See whether you can make them happy that they received your letter.

SUGGESTIONS

In your letter, you will need evidence to show why there is a problem and how your solution is the best one available. Use your detective instinct to do your research: consider books, newspapers, journals, company papers, phone calls, interviews, observation. Use, in short, whatever material you need to make your case.

Remember to anticipate the objections your reader or readers will have. What will your readers not like about your plan? And how will you answer their objections? Assume that your readers are skeptical, but that they are not hostile and will at least begin to read your paper with an open mind and a sense of goodwill. Your problem is to wedge yourself into that slight opening and expand it as far as you can.

Remember, too, the importance of your own *ethos*. Not only do you have to know what you are talking about, you also have to be generous and understanding of your readers' position. You want to do everything you can to persuade them to say "Yes" to your proposed change.

Structure your essay so that it progresses smoothly, with each point building on the preceding one. You'll probably want to include the following elements:

1. Opening words that win attention and goodwill by introducing the problem in a tone expressing optimism about solving it.

2. A history of the case, including possible causes of the problem.

3. An acknowledgement of your readers' probable point of view.

4. A concession to parts of that view and a refutation of other parts.

5. A direct statement of your proposal, along with evidence that it is the best alternative and a detailed explanation of the good effects likely to be produced. It often helps to acknowledge constraints that would affect *any* solution to this problem.

6. A final, heightened appeal for support. (You don't want your reader to sleep easily that night until your plan has, in some form, been accepted.)

SAMPLES

PROTECT THE PROTECTORS
Unknown Student Author

[1] One of the biggest concerns of American citizens is crime on the streets and, in particular, violent crimes where victims are stabbed or shot. Every day there are stories in newspapers and on television about someone who has been injured or killed during the commission of a crime. Some of the victims are innocent bystanders who happen to be nearby and are struck by a stray bullet. There is also a special class of victims of these crimes who are usually not directly involved in the original act and they are not mere bystanders. These victims are police officers who, because of their oath and duty, must pursue and attempt to apprehend violent people. Police officers are expected to get involved in dangerous situations and to relieve citizens of the threat of violence. It is because of this danger that a police officer faces that I address the Montgomery County Council.

[2] In recent years there has been an increase in the number of law enforcement officers killed or injured in the line of duty. Between 1960 and 1967, there was an average of 51 officers killed each year in the United States. Since 1970 there have been at least 100 deaths reported every year, and some of those years the figure was 125 or more. Most of the officers were killed with handguns. A few were murdered with knives, rifles, or shotguns. Four police officers have been killed in Montgomery County since 1972. Some of these deaths could have been prevented if the officers had been equipped with an inexpensive protective vest.

³ Protective devices for the chest are not new and unknown pieces of equipment for the police community. Bullet-proof vests have been used for years by police departments in special situations where there was an obvious chance of being shot. This equipment was always expensive, big, heavy, and cumbersome and could not be worn all the time. In the past few years a more compact, lightweight, and inexpensive vest has been developed and is now available for purchase. This newer vest can be worn at all times concealed under outer clothing and provides constant protection against stabbing or shooting. My proposal to the Montgomery County Council is that money should be immediately appropriated, under emergency legislation, to purchase one of the new bullet-proof vests for every officer on the county police department.

⁴ Several brands of chest protectors are on the market, but an average description can be given to describe them. Newer models weigh approximately two and a half pounds. They cover an area of about twelve inches by sixteen inches on the chest and back. Construction is of various lightweight synthetic materials that are sewn together in layers and hang from shoulder straps over the chest and back. Elastic straps on the side of the body pull the front and back together but are not restraining and allow freedom of movement. Tests have been conducted by the manufacturers and by the Law Enforcement Assistance Administration of the Department of Justice. These tests have shown that the vests will stop almost all handgun bullets including the powerful .44 caliber magnum. Repeated forceful thrusts with knives have failed to penetrate the protectors. Only a relatively small number of thin sharp-pointed objects and bullets were able to go through the material. Overall, the modern bullet-proof vest has shown in tests that it provides good protection from knives, handguns, and other low velocity weapons such as small rifles and shotguns. Statistics show that most murdered police officers die from wounds in the chest or back inflicted by these kinds of weapons.

⁵ The cost of buying a bullet-proof vest for every officer is low, especially when compared to the benefit derived. The average price is approximately $100.00 per vest when purchased by an individual officer, but a discount could probably be obtained if a large order was placed with one of the manufacturers. At the price of $100.00 per unit, every officer on the police department could be equipped with a vest for about $75,000.00. The murder of the lowest paid officer in the department would cost the county at least a quarter of a million dollars in death benefits. If just one life was saved by a bullet-proof vest, it would also save far more money than the initial cost to the taxpayer.

⁶ One possible drawback has been suggested if every officer were to be given a protective vest. Some people feel that the officer would have a false sense of security and would take chances that he or she would not take without the vest. Even if this is true, I suggest there is no way to measure the possibility or predict that it will happen with a particular police officer.

Valuable life-protecting equipment should not be withheld from a person merely because it will make the person feel secure. Also, because some officers may not wear the vest, it is felt, by some people, that the equipment should be bought by the individual. I agree that some police officers may refuse to wear the vest because, at times, there is a slight discomfort from excessive heat, but the major reason is that many officers cannot afford the purchase. The Montgomery County government has the money to buy bullet-proof vests that could eventually save far more than the initial investment.

[7] Bullet-proof vests are efficient and inexpensive protection for police officers. They are light enough to be worn at all times and do not hinder normal movement. Cost is low to supply every officer with a vest and a cash outlay now could possibly prevent a far more costly loss in the future. Extensive testing has shown that bullet-proof vests will provide protection against the wounds that usually cause the death of a police officer.

[8] Now is the time to take a bold step to provide protection for the police officers of this community and to show that someone cares about the welfare of the men and women who try to shield others from aggression. The duty of a police officer is to provide protection and to assume the danger that a citizen might have to face. This duty cannot be ignored, but there should also be the duty of the citizens of a community to furnish basic protective equipment to the police. These men and women who serve are just mortal humans who can bleed to death, and this fact is being proven with greater and greater frequency. Right now, without hesitation, let's do something that will help shield our police.

TO: DR. J. P. STEWART, PRINCIPAL OF BUCHANAN ACADEMY

[1] She is the one at the end of the welfare line, holding in her arms a dirt-smudged one-year-old. She rolls her eyes as she realizes the baby is wet, and she blows a puff of smoke into his round, dirty face. He cries; she hits him. Fifteen years old, this mother would probably rather be outside throwing a frisbee, or roasting corn on a beach with a bunch of friends, but she is just one of the one million teenage girls who became pregnant in 1978 and could be one of the ten girls who became pregnant while attending Buchanan Academy in the last five years. Unable to return to school, and painfully aware of the difficulties of getting a good job without a diploma, she depends on the small check she receives each week to pay the rent, buy diapers, and provide food for the two of them. She didn't plan on getting pregnant, and there is a good chance, had she known how, she would have prevented it. But her parents never told her about contraception, and the school she attended offered no classes on the subject.

[2] Her school did have a sex education class on puberty, pregnancy, heredity, and V.D., but prohibited discussion of contraception, abortion, homosexuality, and masturbation. Like most of the schools in the county,

the course taught the students about gonorrhea, syphilis, and chancroid, they warned them of venereal warts, dreaded lesions, and blindness, but they never told them how to prevent them. After endless diagrams, films, and lectures, all the students really knew about sex was how to "identify the parts." Speaking with Laura Jackson, Director of Health and Physical Education at Buchanan Academy, I learned of the students' lack of information. "These teenagers do not know the first thing about contraception. They think an I.U.D. is something like an IOU, that all jellies are made by Welches, and that a prophylactic shield is a piece of armor used in the holy wars by the ancient men of Prophylon." She went on to tell me of one pregnant sixteen year-old who came for counseling. After asking the girl if she had taken "precautions," the wide-eyed girl assured her, "Of course, we were afraid someone would find out, so Joe shut all the windows and I locked all the doors. We were real careful. . . ." Although amusing, this student's "misconceptions" should be corrected, and because this duty is sometimes neglected by forgetful or embarrassed parents, I propose that you, Dr. Stewart, add this type of sex education to the curriculum at Buchanan Academy.

3 A four-week mandatory course could easily become part of the health education class which is already required for graduation. Those teaching the course will decide on a standard course description and syllabus including the four major units:

    A. Understanding the sexual functions of the human body.
    B. Pregnancy prevention and alternatives.
    C. Venereal disease and its prevention.
    D. Making responsible decisions.

The first unit should include a brief explanation of the anatomy of sex and pregnancy, followed by the second unit which could include contraception and abortion. The third unit would solely be devoted to V.D. and its prevention. Diminishing the emphasis on the anatomy of sex, the teacher could bring contraceptive devices into the classroom for the students to see, and would answer questions on abortion, masturbation, and homosexuality. The fourth unit should attempt to correlate the first three units with the student's need to be able to make a responsible decision. It is in this fourth and final unit that the teachers should try to make the student understand that owning a body and having the ability to function sexually do not give the student free license to use these assets indiscriminately.

4 Because some embarrassed students have difficulty asking questions they think they should already know the answer to, a shoe box could be set by the door and students could place, as they exited, their written questions into a slot, ensuring the students' anonymity, preventing wide eyes, dropped jaws, and embarrassed giggles, and allowing the teacher time between classes to answer the questions adequately.

5 Lest the mention of practical sex education conjure up in the minds of

fretful parents images of Fourteenth Street, <u>Hustler</u> magazine, and Farmer's Daughters jokes, a Friday night parent-teacher assembly could be arranged to tell the parents exactly what their children will be taught. During this meeting, the parents could ask questions and offer any suggestions they felt would improve the course.

6 The present Health Education Directors at Buchanan Academy could teach the class as part of the health class, avoiding hiring new teachers and the burden of extra hours and rescheduling. The cost of the course would vary, depending on the cost of audio-visual media, samples, and teacher's text, but could initially be held to a small sum, a minimal amount if we are to consider the $10,000.00 bill the state must foot for the delivery, postnatal care, and welfare of a single jobless mother. The class will try to give all the students a sense of responsibility and make them aware of the decisions that they must make as adults. But even if the program were to reach just one person and help keep her from becoming pregnant, the program would have justified itself monetarily, as well as reaping the unmeasurable rewards of saving a student from the trauma of an unwanted pregnancy. But for this program to work, the course must be mandatory. There may be some students who are adamantly opposed to listening to "things they already know," but even if they answer to the name Masters or Johnson, there are always more questions to be asked. It is often the ones who swear to having read <u>The Joy</u> ten times who ask the fewest questions, yet know the least about preventing V.D. and conception. Working this course into the already mandatory sophomore health class solves the problem of insuring 100% enrollment.

7 Parents attempting to shield their "innocent" children from this subject may, for religious or personal reasons, question the course's necessity and ethical value. Addressing the question of necessity, Northern Urban Area studies show that the mean age for the boy's first sexual intercourse is twelve years old and that by the age of sixteen, one in five girls has had sex. Each year there are one million pregnancies, and 300,000 abortions. These figures are not being lowered, and the problem of teenage pregnancy and V.D. are not diminishing. We, as parents, administrators, and concerned citizens, cannot erase the millions, but we can do something to help the small percentage coming from our school. Neglecting to inform these teenagers about sex is obviously no guarantee that they will not have intercourse, yet informing the students increases the chance that they will think twice before they do have sex, and if they decide they want to, they will know enough to make an intelligent decision.

8 To satisfy those who for religious reasons will not want their children learning about contraception and abortion, the teacher could make it clear that the alternatives to pregnancy may not be desirable for all, but simply that these alternatives exist. It is similar to the class on evolution presently taught in your school. The teacher does not in any way imply evolution to be

the preferred view: in fact, the teacher is a creationist, but the students are taught that other views exist whether they choose them as their own or not.

⁹ I realize that the subjects of contraception and abortion have been traditionally taboo, and there may be difficulty in getting the school board to even discuss the matter, much less appropriate money, but I feel that this subject has been too long ignored by the people who have the power to make a change. If Buchanan Academy were to initiate this type of program and if it were successful, not only would the school gain recognition and added respect, but it might set a precedent for other schools in the county.

¹⁰ The proposed course could save a young couple from being forced into marriage, eliminate the pain of a parent who might otherwise have been devastated, and prevent the heartbreak of a child who might have grown up unwanted and unloved. As a parent and a school administrator, don't you think that it is worth it?

Respectfully yours,

Tracey E. Landis
Class of 1979

#8 PERSUADING A CLASSMATE
TO CONSIDER AN ISSUE FURTHER (Taylor, 507–10)

Method of Research: Studying the Classmate's Opinion, Then Finding Information and Further Opinions in the Library and Elsewhere

Most Pertinent Chapters: 2, 3, 4, 5, 6, 7, 9 – *Ch. 13 – Research*

Clean Draft Due for Workshop: *Mon.* *Review –*

Paper Due: *Dec. 8.* *Enclmates –*
to March 12

Your assignment this time is to use writing to its fullest potential—that is, to change someone's mind, even if only slightly.

Stop for a moment.

Fill out, in as much detail as possible, a copy of the opinion sheet following this assignment. When you've finished, hand your opinion sheet to another student, and you'll receive one in turn (try not to trade papers with the same student).

In your paper, you will show your partner that the issue is more complicated than he or she thinks.

Stop again.

In order to better understand your reader's views, take fifteen to twenty minutes to question her or him about those views. Then allow yourself to be questioned by the writer who will be writing for you. Before you leave, exchange phone numbers so you can ask follow-up questions.

This paper will allow you to show almost all the skills that we've practiced in this course—using facts to back up an opinion, using library resources, conducting interviews (if you wish), writing effective introductions and conclusions. In addition, this paper will force you to become clearly aware of your reader, another crucial writing skill.

You may structure your paper any way that suits your material, but you may find your research proceeding more clearly if you keep in mind the following format:

Introduction of the problem –
Concession to your reader's point of view –
Advancement of your own argument –
Conclusion –

As you write, you may want to consider any of the following common methods of persuasion:

1. Use of facts, statistics, and examples found through research
2. Use of examples from your personal experience
3. Definition of terms in a way in which your reader does not usually define them
4. Discussion of possible causes or effects
5. Appeal to authority (combined with evidence that the authority deserves to be listened to)
6. Description of a similar situation and its results

My guess is that as you do your research, you'll consult about ten sources (remember that you'll be researching both sides of the question), and your final paper will acknowledge at least three.

OPINION SHEET

NAME: _____ AGE: _____ SEX: _____

SUBJECT: _____

I am _____ strongly opposed.
_____ moderately opposed.
_____ moderately supportive.
_____ strongly supportive.

I consider myself to be _____ very well informed on the subject.
_____ moderately informed on the subject.
_____ not very informed on the subject.

Sources of information on the subject have been (check as many as necessary):

_____ father   _____ mother
_____ other family member   _____ friend(s)
_____ religious authority   _____ club or social organization
     name: _____   name: _____
_____ book(s)   _____ movie(s)
     name: _____   name: _____
_____ newspaper or magazine article(s)   _____ television program(s)
     name: _____   name: _____
     name: _____   name: _____

There _____ have _____ have not been one or more personal experiences which have influenced my opinion on the subject—specifically: _____
_____
_____
_____
_____

On the back of this sheet are my reasons for holding this opinion, both emotional and intellectual, major and trivial.

I respond _____ more emotionally than logically to this subject.
_____ more logically than emotionally to this subject.
_____ both emotionally and logically to this subject.

I _____ enjoy talking about this subject.
_____ dislike talking about this subject.
_____ am indifferent to talking about this subject.

I _____ do _____ do not believe my opinion can be changed.

SAMPLES

FOOTBALL IS NOT ALL BAD
Edward Berry

[1] Football on both the college and professional levels is a big money sport. Schools are paid between $300,000 and $800,000 for having a good season and playing in a bowl game (Washington Post, Nov. 13, 1983). On the professional level, athletes are paid hundreds of thousands of dollars to play only sixteen games on some fall Sunday afternoons (Sport Magazine, July 28, 1982). So naturally, some people do not like football because of some of the things the athletes do to "get the money." Also, because of the money, athletes (just as other pro & college athletes) are placed on a special pedestal and sometimes get special favors or treatment. But even with all its problems, football will not go away, and most of the time it serves as good entertainment.

[2] First, as in all sports, football has its problems. The game suffers from some of the violent actions of the players. This almost strictly applies to the pro game. Some players seem to go out of their way to hurt their opponents. On Thanksgiving Day 1982, in a game between the Detroit Lions and the New York Giants, Giants punt returner Leon Bright was not given the customary and required two yards to field the punt, and he was hit by the Lions' Leonard Thompson, who tried to hit him as hard as he could. The result? Bright suffered a sprained neck and back (Washington Post, Nov. 26,1982). The injury could have been avoided if Thompson had not been so intent on hurting Bright. In another event, in a game between the Chicago Bears and the Philadelphia Eagles, defensive tackle Mike Hartenstein hit Eagle quarterback Ron Jaworski with a forearm across the head. Jaworski was knocked out of the game and had a mild concussion (Washington Post, Sept. 21, 1981). That also could have been avoided, for all Hartenstein had to do was tackle Jaworski, not punish him.

[3] The media do not help either. The media portray athletes as invincible figures. Yet when one of the athletes does something wrong, they make it seem as if it is a major event in history. When Mercury Morris, a former Miami Dolphin running back, was caught selling and using cocaine, the media had full coverage of his trial and what he did when he went to prison (NFL Today, Nov. 13, 1983). If it was you or me, very few, if any, would care. There would be no media coverage and hardly any press clippings.

[4] Then there are the fans. They want to see plenty of hard hits for the average $12.50 ticket (Redskin ticket office, Nov. 21, 1983). They boo if the action of the game is slow and get upset when a player complains about the rough action of the game. Most of the players, meanwhile, seem to retire from the game with injuries that will ache them for the rest of their lives. They inflict pain all of their lives and pay for it when they retire. Former Dallas Cowboy receiver Buddy Dial has a ruptured disc in his back from a

football injury suffered in 1967 (Redskin Report, Oct. 8, 1983). Former Bear great and Hall of Fame linebacker Dick Butkus walks with a permanent limp from floating cartilage in his knee suffered in 1969 (interview with Dick Butkus, "The Linebacker," Nov. 7, 1983).

5 On the other hand, we must realize that this is the way that these men, along with other men, make their living. No one forced these men to put on a set of pads and a helmet and bang each other on Sunday afternoons; it was by their own free will. Butkus said, "I loved the game and it was my only way from the slums of Chicago. I wanted to play each Sunday, pain or not!" (Butkus, "The Linebacker"). They get paid enormous amounts of money to play football, and they are expected to play. The game is their job, and they perform it the best way they know how, even if it means inflicting some pain to the opponent.

6 The media's job is to report the news, which includes pro football. They are expected to know why Mercury Morris used cocaine, why he sold it, whom he sold it to, and what he is doing while he is in jail. The public asks those questions, and the media are expected to answer them. Besides, what would the public rather hear about, Morris's drug problem or the average junkie's drug problem? Football is a dominant sport in American society, and we must live with it because most of the public likes it, wants to hear about it, and cannot get enough of it.

7 The fans pay money to see the game, and they have the right and choice to voice how they want to see the game played. When we go to the movies, if the movie is not any good, we get upset and mad with the movie because we feel that we have wasted money on the movie. Football fans feel that way when they do not see enough action for their money. Fans like long runs by Eric Dickerson and pinpoint passes to Charlie Brown. But even if they want to see more hard hits, it is their choice.

8 Football is a good sport, but it has its problems. The public demands some things in football that are wrong, and they should be corrected. One of the things should be if a player commits a flagrant foul, he should be thrown out of the game and fined $5,000. Maybe if the league hits the players where it hurts, some of the violence will disappear. But do not expect these things to happen. If the league was to make the game any more passive, the public would wonder whether they are watching a touch football game or NFL football. They already have the fans upset with the rule stating if the quarterback is in a defensive man's grasp, then it is a sack. The quarterback is a player too, so why can't he get hit? Pro football now and in the near future will have a domineering effect on society.

ABORTION: DON'T REJECT IT OUTRIGHT
Stephanie Gunkel

1 Abortion is a very sensitive and controversial subject. Many people believe that having an abortion is the same as committing murder. How-

ever, I believe there are a few serious circumstances where an abortion would be the best answer.

2 Susan Beach, an eighteen-year-old freshman in college, is strongly opposed to abortion because of her religion. She is Roman Catholic, and like all persons of her religion, Susan was taught that abortions are wrong. Catholics believe that the fetus is a human life from the time it is conceived, and to have an abortion would be the same as murdering someone. She feels that there are no exceptions for having an abortion.

3 Although I do not strongly believe in abortion, I do feel that there are four main circumstances when a woman or couple should consider an abortion. Three of my reasons for favoring abortion are medical, pertaining to either the health of the mother or child, and the fourth is socioeconomic.

4 When a child is conceived through a rape or incest, an abortion is often requested by the mother. I strongly believe that most women, no matter what their religion, would also want an abortion if either of these incidents actually happened to them.

5 If the mother chose to have the child anyway, it would be considered illegitimate. Bearing an illegitimate child could cause serious emotional problems for both the mother and the child. Psychiatrist Charles Hayman states that "engaging in sexual intercourse through rape or incest can be a traumatic experience for any woman" (Abortion Controversy, by Betty Sarvis and Hyman Rodman, p. 80). Most psychiatrists feel that if a woman were to conceive a baby because of a rape or incest, it would not be to her advantage to have the baby. Most women would prefer to forget that traumatic events such as these ever took place, and if they have the baby, it will be a constant reminder.

6 A more serious circumstance is when the mother's health, in many cases her life, is in danger. I feel that under some of these circumstances, an abortion is a smart alternative.

7 The mother's heart is one of the most important organs involved in any pregnancy. In the 1940s, heart disease was the leading cause of maternal death (Abortion Controversy, p. 92). Between 1946 and 1950 over one half of the abortions performed in the United States were performed because the mother had a form of cardiac disease, and as a result, the abortions saved the women's lives. Now, over thirty years later, because of medical advances in anesthesia and surgical procedures, the threat to life because of heart disease has decreased, and many abortions can be avoided. Nevertheless, the mother's health should always be taken into consideration first.

8 Two other organs which are very important during a pregnancy are the kidneys and lungs. Therefore, if a pregnant woman had a serious kidney disorder or tuberculosis, her doctor would most likely recommend an abortion.

9 In many instances, when a woman has cancer, especially cancer of the breast or cervix, and then becomes pregnant, the cancer cells usually spread more rapidly than normal (Abortion Controversy, p. 72). This

makes the pregnancy extremely complicated, and an abortion is almost essential.

[10] When a woman has a disease such as epilepsy, multiple sclerosis, or rheumatoid arthritis, carrying a child usually makes her health conditions worse, and the effects are unpredictable. In these cases, to avoid further complications and health hazards, it would be in the mother's best interest to have an abortion.

[11] The decision to have an abortion under any circumstances is an extremely difficult one, and should never be taken lightly. When her own health must be taken into consideration, she must then decide whether or not she wants to risk her own life to have the baby. Under medical conditions such as these, talking to a physician or psychiatrist can be very comforting.

[12] The third reason that I feel it is acceptable to have an abortion is a very sensitive issue. When a couple has a child that is mentally retarded or physically deformed, it very often causes financial strain on the parents and great emotional strain on both the parents and the child. Although it is unfortunate, because our society is so critical, the deformed child can also experience some distressing social problems.

[13] In the 1970s, the amniocentesis test was invented to diagnose malformations in the unborn fetus (Abortion Controversy, p. 83). It then becomes the parents' choice whether or not to terminate the pregnancy through an abortion.

[14] There are three main causes that can explain why a baby could be born deformed. The first and most serious cause of deformity is from overexposure to radiation. When a pregnancy has not yet been diagnosed and a woman undergoes extensive x-rays, in most instances the radiation will cause drastic fetal malformation. These malformations can be anything from missing toes and fingers to nonexistent arms (Abortion Controversy, p. 74). Rubella, which is a virus, and syphilis, a form of V.D., can both cause fetal deformities. Over the past twenty years, doctors have discovered that if the mother receives a rubella vaccine or undergoes extensive physical and psychological therapy, if she is a syphilis carrier, then some of the more serious abnormalities will not be apparent in the newborn. However, there is not an absolute cure to avoid either of these diseases yet, so some of the minor malformations may still occur.

[15] The main point in these three cases is whether or not the parents are going to be able to accept and care for the deformed child, just as they would a physically normal child. Raising a deformed child can be an enormous emotional burden, and I think the parents should be one hundred percent sure that they will take on any obstacles that may occur in the future, no matter how difficult they might be. Many women and men are not emotionally strong enough to raise a disabled child. In the long run, a woman may experience fewer psychological problems from having an abortion than from having a deformed child.

¹⁶ The last reason that I feel it is acceptable to have an abortion is for socioeconomic purposes. This is the first circumstance to be presented where the parents should consider how the child will feel, instead of themselves.

¹⁷ A large majority of our society believes that all children have a right to live whether they would be rich or poor. However, I feel that a child also has the right to a life where he or she will be as happy as possible. Since poverty is a very large but unfortunate problem in the world today, is there a need to bring another human being into the world who will grow up as unhappy as the rest of the poverty-stricken people in the world? When parents are not financially stable enough to provide their children with decent clothes and nutritious food, which are both essential, then abortion could be a good alternative.

¹⁸ Abortion is a subject that will be debated for many years in the future. There are many strong arguments, both pro and con. Our society should try to keep in mind that although many abortions are performed to avoid unwanted pregnancies, just as many are performed out of love, to avoid traumatic complications that may occur if the pregnancy is carried to full term.

#9 MY WRITING PROCESS AND WAYS TO IMPROVE IT

Method of Research: Recollection of Chronological Sequence of Events While Writing

Most Pertinent Chapters: 2, 3, 10, 11

Clean Draft Due for Workshop:

Paper Due:

What was the last piece of writing (in or out of class, formal or informal) you did that you were proud of? Or if you can't think of a piece you were proud of, what was the last piece that you hated writing? Once you decide, describe the steps—physical and emotional—that you went through as you wrote. Think of the writing process in its broadest terms: you first start work when you hear you have to write. Your writing process isn't finished until you turn your work in to the person who asked that it be written.

This paper will be a good test of your powers of observation, which you have been trying to improve all semester. You'll probably remember the most details if you try to recapture them in chronological order. Remember that thinking and wasting time are as much a part of writing as is setting pen to paper. Also, don't pretend that writing is an emotionless activity: recall—and express—the feelings you had along the way.

If you would like to give your paper a persuasive edge, you could conclude your paper by evaluating the effectiveness of the stages you went through, perhaps suggesting how you may change your method of writing in the future. Your paper would then answer both of these questions:

- What are the steps of the writing process?

- What is an *effective* writing process?

What you write will help your teacher give even better advice to the students who follow you.

SAMPLES

SGWPP: SELECT, GATHER, WRITE, POLISH, AND PRODUCE
Michi Weant

1 Sitting down and writing an essay was not a very pleasant process for me. I struggled along, perfecting each paragraph as I wrote it. With such a method, I invariably became entangled in one place, with nowhere to go but away from my topic. My writings became forced and brittle, even after the troublemaker was tossed into the trash. Doubtfully, I decided to try the method at the other extreme: writing and writing, with no stopping for punctuation, grammar, or coherence. Well, it worked.

2 My first paper of the year was a good testing ground for this new method. The paper required me to demonstrate the effect of possessions on their owners. After I looked over the information I'd collected on various

people and their material obsessions, I chose the option that was most interesting and held a ready supply of facts. I brainstormed happily, using a set of index cards to record bits of information, anecdotes, and conversation. I arranged the cards in a fashion that provided a smooth flow of ideas and returned to my thesis statement. Once arriving at a point of general organization, I felt confident enough to begin the writing.

3 I chose a small, empty room in my dorm's basement for the writing and typing of my paper. The room is officially a study room but is rarely used. It would be quiet and nondistracting, because except for a desk, two chairs, a sofa, and a carpet, it was barren. I settled in behind the desk and closed my eyes. For ten minutes I assured myself that I was very interested in my topic. I mentally loosened the grit and debris from old ideas that clogged my creative arteries. Gripping my pen firmly, I opened my eyes and began to write.

4 Once started, it was surprisingly easy to write constantly, using the index cards as guidelines. There were the usual rough spots, but rather than let them deter me, I blundered through. Even though I rambled away from my subject a few times, I stayed closer to the topic than usual. I tied things up without problem and wrote a quiet and efficient ending. Sitting back, I smiled. As I shuffled through the papers, I was surprised to find that the draft wasn't as messy as I'd expected. When I read through it lightly, I saw that it had potential to flow well. Of course, there were various technical problems to take care of and polishing to do. Although I was anxious to rewrite it, I forced myself to wait until the next day, when it would be fresher to me.

5 I wrote my second draft, making alterations and deletions and smoothing over the rough spots. Reasonably satisfied, I called in an old classmate whose intellect and advice I respected. We worked through the material, scribbling, adding, and arguing. I typed the third draft, with revisions, as we went along. We took an hour break to satisfy our ravenous appetites, and when refreshed, we reread the work aloud. It showed much improvement, but not enough. Again, I decided to leave the paper alone so it would be new to me the next day.

6 Feeling good about this new method, I enjoyed sitting at my typewriter the next morning. I cleaned, typed, and proofread my essay. With a nod of approval from a classmate in my dorm, I trotted off to have it xeroxed and take it to class. Once in the classroom, it was dissected and examined, with written critiques as a bonus. Classmates who read my essay enjoyed it, but each commented on the weak introduction. I sighed, knowing they were right. It was not effective in stating my thesis. I immediately began toying with the introduction, cutting and rewriting. Finally, I was happy with it, and it got a good reception from my "editors."

7 An hour later, my beautiful essay lay upstairs in my room, a polished and shining work that did what I wanted of it; it met the assignment's requirements comfortably, not in a cramped or an affected manner. I had

successfully selected a topic, gathered ideas, written drafts, polished, and produced a good paper. I was happy. And more importantly, I had begun to enjoy writing papers.

WRITING—THE DUE PROCESS
Michael Schulman

1 Writing is an individualized process. No two writers do, or should be asked to do, the same things in writing or preparing to write. By the same token, no one writing process could be said to be more effective than any other, just different. Even the most haphazard or unlikely method of writing must undoubtedly have contributed some work of value to the artistic or journalistic domains. This paper will outline my approach to writing. It will not, however, attempt to assess the effectiveness of my process or compare it to other methods for the purpose of evaluating the quality of any method. Individualism renders any such attempts extraneous. My process can be divided into three basic blocks: thought, articulated thought, and the writing stage.

2 The pure thought stage of my writing process is probably the most time-consuming part. Given an open, basic theme for an essay, I must first think of a specific topic. Usually I do not sit down with the express purpose of thinking of a topic. My rumination is done on the fly while I am doing other things: daydreaming in class, driving around downtown, doing my homework, eating, or even listening to my stereo. I am far too lazy to devote dedicated effort to something as ethereal as thought. Eventually, after much halfhearted deliberation, a simply splendid topic will sail gracefully into my notice. That topic is knocked around for a while, and if it is reasonable, I will go with it. My instincts are important in this stage of the process; I try not to let my mind do too much of the thinking, for only doubts spring out of my excessive thought. With a topic now firmly in mind, the real work starts. I roll the idea around in my head again, this time thinking of unusual ways to attack it, what I want to say about it, and what tone I may want to affect. The essay now begins to take shape in my head, and it is time to put that shape on paper.

3 This is what I call the "articulated thought" part of my writing process. While still thinking about and defining my topic, I write an elaborate, beefy outline crammed with specific facts that will go in the paper. This step involves much pacing and meditation in order to squeeze thoughts out of my head to let them drip onto the paper. This stage overlaps, and sometimes merges with, the first stage of pure thought. By the end of the articulated thought step, my essay has a fixed shape and thesis, and the only work left to be done is the actual writing of the paper.

4 Writing the first draft of the paper basically consists of filling in the outline. It is a fast first draft, much of the effort already made in the first two stages. After the first draft is written, it is revised on the same paper.

Being lazy, I never write a second draft but merely alter my pencil-written rough draft on the same pages. Major changes are rare, most being variations of word choice and sentence structure to increase clarity. Once the revision is complete, the typing begins. Because I am an agonizingly slow and poor typist, there is a good deal of time to revise while typing, which I do profusively. My remedial habit of reading aloud while typing allows me to hear strange, confounding syntax that otherwise escaped my fatigued eyes. The only thing left to do after typing is proofread, which, because of my consummate lack of typing skill, is always quite a chore.

5 My approach to writing is obviously a lazy, minimum manual labor approach, but it works for me. If I think too long about something, it begins to look wrong, and doubts creep into my mind. That a system for writing works for the writer is all that one should ask. Effectiveness is gauged only by the results gained by the user of the method, and the fact that other writers use different processes should not demean what works for a certain writer.

#10   LITERARY INTERPRETATION

Method of Research: Careful Reading, Underlining, and Note-Taking

Most Pertinent Chapters: 2, 3, 4, 5, 6, 7, 12

ASSIGNMENT

1. Read a work of fiction, either on your own or with the rest of the class.

2. Take reading notes as you read, giving special attention to the ways in which parts of the book are connected to each other and (ultimately) to the purpose of the book as a whole.

3. Write an essay in class on _____ (date).

SUBJECT OF THE ESSAY

Show how one of the sections, perhaps a chapter, in your book fits into the overall scheme of the book. Assume that your reader doesn't believe that it fits well. Bring in at least two other sections for purposes of comparison, contrast, illustration, or elaboration of your point.

BRING WITH YOU TO CLASS

• More than one pen or pencil.

• Your book.

• A dictionary (if you wish).

• An outline of what you plan to write. (The key to success with in-class writing when you are given the question in advance is *preparation*. Carefully plan your paragraph outline, and choose possible supporting quotations.)

ABOUT YOUR ESSAY

Make your writing show that you've mastered this course's priorities:

observation	organization	clear connections
selection of details	telling quotations	tightening
thoughtful writing	introduction	conclusion
purpose	paragraphing	

WHEN YOU THINK YOU'RE FINISHED

Look over your whole essay and cross out (and replace, if necessary) any BS.

SAMPLES

DOCTOR PARCIVAL
Marina Gopenko (a native of Russia)
(written in class)

1 I have never lived in a small town, but in my mind the small town is always associated with places where all people are very close to each other mainly because they see each other almost every day, know how other people live, and know what problems they have. In other words, people in a small town are like one big family. But after I read Winesburg, Ohio by Sherwood Anderson, I changed my mind.

2 "Many people must live and die alone, even in Winesburg," said Alice Hindman, one of the heroes of Winesburg, Ohio. Unfortunately, she is right. Winesburg looks like a place where all people have the same big problem—difficulty in communicating with each other. Different people try to change that differently, but most of them, like Dr. Parcival, choose a wrong way.

3 From my point of view, Dr. Parcival is one of the most typical persons who represent Winesburg. He, like many other citizens in Winesburg, is very lonely. Since he was a little boy, he has never had enough attention. His mother always loved her older son more, and for a little boy it was very painful, especially because it was unjust. He worked very hard as a newspaper reporter for just $6 per week, and all his money he gave to his mother, while his older brother spent all the money he earned on himself.

4 The lack of attention from his parent, influenced all his life. To be understood and loved became his main wish. Probably, it was the reason why he came to live in Winesburg. He thought that it would be easier to become noticeable in a small town. He came to Winesburg from Chicago and when he arrived was drunk and got into a fight with a baggageman. As a result he was escorted to the village lockup, and when he was released, he announced himself as a doctor. His story seems very strange, and intended to get his listeners' attention, but the citizens of Winesburg don't pay any attention to him.

5 Misfortune didn't stop Dr. Parcival, and he decided to try another way. He made friends with George Willard, who is in the center of people's attention in Winesburg. Dr. Parcival wants to influence Winesburg's citizens by influencing George: "I have a desire to make you admire me. That's why I talk," said Dr. P.

6 For that reason, to admire himself, he tells George a story that he was a murderer and thief in Chicago. He is like Seth Richmond, who loves Helen White, but instead of just simply explaining his feelings, he begins to tell her about his plans to leave instead of just keep talking, and so on. Instead of using simple words and explanations, people in Winesburg make life much more difficult and unclear.

⁷ So, Dr. Parcival decided to be famous at any price. It becomes a point of his life, and because he doesn't see any simple way, he decided to be popular as a writer. "To write the book, Dr. P. declared, was the object of his coming to Winesburg to live." But his book is not clear and realistic in its ideas. He began to live according to his book idea that "Everyone in the world is Christ and they are all crucified" and completely lost the relationship with real life principles and ideas. He started to live in a world of his ideas like Kate Swift, who can tell a story about people who lived a hundred years ago or about her best friends, but cannot get along with people whom she lives with. Or he is like Enoch Robinson, who "with quick imagination began to invent his listeners to whom he explained the things he had been unable to explain to living people." So, loneliness and problems in communication is the main characteristic of Winesburg's people.

⁸ To be famous becomes Dr. Parcival's sickness: "You <u>must</u> pay attention to me. If something happens, perhaps you will be able to write a book," he said to George Willard.

⁹ Dr. Parcival went so far with his idea to become a center of everybody's attention that he returned a request to go to a child who died in an accident. The way to become famous doesn't make any difference for him. "Now everyone will get excited. And I will be hanged to a lamp-post on Main Street," said the Dr. proudly. He wants to fill George with the same ideas, but G. doesn't believe in that kind of popularity. By that Sherwood Anderson gives us an optimistic feeling about the future of Winesburg. The new generation, which is represented by George, must be better. And with the author we hope that the new generation won't have so much trouble trying to be in touch with each other.

ALICE HINDMAN AND THE SPECIAL PROBLEMS OF WOMEN
Woienshet Kebede (a native of Ethiopia)
(written in class)

¹ "Adventure," in <u>Winesburg, Ohio</u>, is the story of Alice Hindman. The story, like almost all the other stories, is about the problems of communication. In addition to the communication problem which all people in <u>Winesburg, Ohio</u> face, Alice also faces a problem due to her sex (female).

² Alice, when she was sixteen years old, met Ned Currie. She wanted to marry him. But Ned only wanted to care for her. His idea of only caring for her changed just before he left Winesburg to look for another job. After that they said things they would not have said otherwise. Anderson puts it this way: "It did not seem to them that anything that could happen in the future could blot out the wonder and beauty of the thing that happened." Ned left the next day. For a while, since he was lonely, Ned wrote to Alice. But once he made friends in the city, he forgot about her.

³ Alice, though, did not forget Ned. She felt lonely, but she thought to

herself that she should stay without friends. She did not try to make friends. Anderson says about this as follows: "For all her willingness to support herself she could not have understood the growing modern idea of a woman's owning herself and giving and taking for her own ends in life." She believed she had to be devoted to her husband and not to anybody else. Her loneliness, despite her attempt to put up with it, did not go away. Because of this she began to be attached to inanimate objects. Finally she tried to give in a little bit and walked along with Will Hurley. In the darkness she tried to touch his coat. But, she still did not change her mind about Ned. In fact she did not want the clerk to walk with her anymore.

4 Alice in some way is like Elizabeth Willard. Elizabeth married Tom because society pushed her to do so. For example, "Other girls of her age in Winesburg were marrying men she had always known, grocery clerks or young farmers. In the evening they walked in the Main street with their husbands and when she passed they smiled happily." Alice, like Elizabeth, was not able to make another friend, because there was always the notion that she was Ned's girl. Again here society made life difficult for the young woman.

5 In some other ways Alice is not like Elizabeth nor like Kate Swift. Elizabeth, for example, had tried to do things that society does not allow her to do. "Once she startled the town by putting on men's clothes and riding a bicycle down Main Street." Elizabeth does this which is not expected of a female. Kate Swift also tried, despite what the society expected. For example, "The people of the town thought of her as a confirmed old maid because she spoke sharply and went her own way."

6 Alice, when compared to the men, is like Wing Biddlebaum, who is lonely and walks on his veranda hoping George Willard will come. Alice was also hoping Ned would come. She is also like Enoch, who later on did not want any people except his paintings. He was married once. He also had friends. But he could not get his message through to them. He preferred to be with his paintings. Alice did the same thing too. She began to like her furniture rather than humans.

7 When compared with all the above characters, Helen stands out as knowing better than them all. Helen, in the story of "Sophistication," distinguishes between her interest and that of society. Her mother, for example, wanted her to marry her college instructor. But she did not do what her mother wanted her to do. She also did not leave with George. In the story of "Departure," George left Winesburg in search of a better place. But Helen's staying behind indicates her being independent. She did not have to be devoted to a man like Alice did.

16

◆

What Next?

No, I didn't like the textbook. To me, all English books rank right down there with The Scarlet Letter.

student

I don't think this course requires a book. This course only requires pencil and paper.

student

I never liked to write much and I still don't like to unless it is necessary. But I think I now have more power to write.

student

This was a tough course to take while on academic probation. It involved a lot of time. It is slightly more enjoyable to write, but it still is a pain at times.

student

I'd still rather work with numbers but I do think I learned how to write better.

student

A blank piece of paper isn't as frightening to me any more.

student

I feel more comfortable about writing, but I still have a lot of room for improvement. I wish I could take this class again so that I could keep improving my writing skills.

student

Few are taught to any purpose who do not become their own teachers.

Sir Joshua Reynolds

Exercise 16-1

You are now finishing a course which was designed to help you become a more correct, more effective, and more confident writer. You certainly have not solved all your writing problems—nobody ever does. But you have made some progress. Take a few minutes to take stock, now, of your current writing ability.

What kind of writer would you call yourself now? In what areas have you made the most improvement this semester? What problems do you still have as a writer? *Why* do you think you still have those problems? Can you think of methods you can use to help solve your remaining problems?

In this book, I've tried to address writers who are skeptical of their own writing ability, and skeptical about whether writing can help them in their careers and in their lives. I hope now that you are less skeptical, that you've tasted the pleasure of teaching yourself and of profiting from the advice of your teacher and your classmates. I hope now that you'll take your writing education into your own hands and try to find the books that can help you learn more fully what the resources of our language are. I recommend highly:

1. A college dictionary (at least 50,000 words). When you don't know a word, the only way to make it part of your vocabulary is to write it down and look it up in the dictionary right away. This process may get easier when we get computer dictionary programs that will print up a definition as quickly as we can punch in the word. But no one looks up every unfamiliar word, no matter how much teachers have advised us to do so; very few of us do it as much as we say we do. Try doing it during your summers. Or for a week at a time during the school year. Surprisingly quickly, your determination will pay off in increased word and thinking power.

2. William Strunk and E. B. White's *The Elements of Style,* 3rd edition (New York: Macmillan, 1981). An inexpensive, brief review of all the basics of writing, including differences I haven't even mentioned in this book, like those between *lie* and *lay, accept* and *except, flammable* and *inflammable.* This book is deservedly the most widely consulted book about writing.

3. H. W. Fowler's *A Dictionary of Modern English Usage,* 2nd edition (New York: Oxford University Press, 1965), whose 700 pages cover thoroughly and delightfully almost every nuance of the English language. Once you decide that writing is a craft you want to excel in, you'll certainly want a copy of this book.

4. Robert Pirsig, *Zen and the Art of Motorcycle Maintenance* (New York: Bantam, 1975). Even if you're not interested in Zen (I'm not), and even if you're a hopeless motorcycle mechanic (I am), this book is an excellent introduction to the kinds of practical and critical think-

ing that are so important for writers. Besides, it's a good story of a motorcycle trip.

5. Reginald Bragonier, Jr., and David Fisher, *What's What: A Visual Glossary of the Physical World* (New York: Hammond, 1981). This picture book identifies the component parts of everything from chain saws (guidebar, guidebar nose, spark-arresting muffler) to front doors (center stile, butte stile, lock stile) to flagpoles (finial, truck, staff) to electric guitars (bridge, frets, pickguard) to fire hydrants (bonnet, hose nozzle cap, cap chain). Just browsing through this reference book will help you think more clearly and develop a better eye for detail.

Having taken this course, you should now realize that writing helps us remember; it helps us make sense of our experience; it helps us work out our passions and frustrations; it gives us the power to make a mark, for better or worse, on the world around us. You know that learning to write is—far more than we might expect—learning to understand other people. You know that writing, not just for you but for everyone, is work, but that the satisfaction of a finished paper—well-observed, well-organized, and well-written—can make all that work worthwhile.

You have practiced many individual skills in this course, from observing to inference drawing to paragraphing to organizing to punctuating. Successful writing won't result from keeping those skills in the front of your mind all the time. The limitations of remaining fully conscious of your technique are illustrated in a story I heard last year about Walter Hagen, a golfer who won many of the top tournaments in the 1920s and 1930s, including four or five PGA championships in a row. Hagen was a notorious carouser, and in one of those PGAs, he showed up for the final round hung over, unshaven, and red-eyed. His opponent—it was match play—was one of those sweet-swinging, cold-blooded types, and just before they teed off, Hagen said to him, "You know, you've got the most beautiful swing I've ever seen. That little pause at the top of your backswing really works. How do you do it?" By the time the poor kid had figured out what Hagen had done to him, Hagen had won—five holes up with four holes to play. Skills are more useful after they've become intuitive than they are when we remain fully conscious of them.

I hope this course has strengthened your observation, your thoughtfulness, your organization, your sense of audience, your sense of self, and your ability to bring all of these to bear on your writing. The course has been designed to help you strengthen all these skills both consciously and intuitively—we hope fast enough for you to do well in this course. But even if you haven't done as well as you would have liked in this course, your intuitions have made some progress, and if you continue to nurture and strengthen them, they will eventually serve you well.

◆
Works Cited

Adams, James L. *Conceptual Blockbusting*. 2nd ed. New York: Norton, 1979.

Adelstein, Michael. "Writing Is Work." In *The Practical Craft*. Ed. W. K. Sparrow and D. H. Cunningham. Boston: Houghton Mifflin, 1978, 116–25.

Aristotle. *The Rhetoric of Aristotle*. Ed. Lane Cooper. New York: Appleton, Century, Crofts, 1932.

Ashe, Arthur. "First Sign of Decline, Color Discovered." *The Washington Post,* 17 Mar. 1979, 4.1.

Bernstein, Carl. "Graduation Speech from the Bottom of the Class." *The Kenosha News,* 7 June 1979, 5.

Berthoff, Ann. *Forming, Thinking, Writing*. Rochelle Park, N.J.: Hayden, 1978.

Bibliographic Index. Ed. Laurel Cooley. New York: Wilson, 1982.

Bolles, Richard Nelson. *The Three Boxes of Life*. Berkeley, Calif.: Ten Speed P, 1978.

Britton, James. "The Composing Processes and the Functions of Writing." In *Research on Composing*. Ed. Charles R. Cooper and Lee Odell. Urbana, Ill.: National Council of Teachers of English, 1978, 13–28.

Cowley, Malcolm, ed. *Writers at Work*. Vol. 1. New York: Viking, 1959.

Crosby, Harry. "Titles, A Treatise On." *College Composition and Communication,* Dec. 1976, 387–91.

Descharnes, Robert, and Jean-Francois Chabrun. *Auguste Rodin*. Secaucus, N.J.: Chartwell Books, 1967.

Dickens, Charles. *A Tale of Two Cities*. Harmondsworth, England: Penguin, 1970.

Dowst, Kenneth. *Basic Writing*. Pittsburgh, Penn.: The U of Pittsburgh, 1977.

Faigley, Lester, and Thomas P. Miller. "What We Learn from Writing on the Job." *College English,* Oct. 1982, 557–69.

Flower, Linda, and John R. Hayes. "Problem-Solving Strategies and the Writing Process." *College English,* Dec. 1977, 449–61.

Galbraith, John Kenneth. "Writing, Typing, and Economics." *Atlantic,* Mar. 1982, 102–05.

Garrison, Roger. *How a Writer Works.* New York: Harper & Row, 1981.

Gebhardt, Richard. "Imagination and Discipline in the Writing Class." *English Journal,* Dec. 1977, 26–32.

Gebhardt, Richard. "The Writing Process." *Freshman English News,* Spring 1980, 19–22.

Geduld, Harry M., ed. *Filmmakers on Filmmaking.* Bloomington: Indiana U P, 1967.

Graves, Robert and Alan Hodge. *The Reader over Your Shoulder.* New York: Random House, 1978.

Hall, Carla. "The Radical Voice of Moderation." *The Washington Post,* 14 Mar. 1983, 2.1.

Harris, Art. "The Wild Bunch, Heros Once More." *The Washington Post,* 4 Nov. 1983, 4.1–4.2.

Hayakawa, S. I. *Language in Thought and Action.* 2nd ed. New York: Harcourt, Brace, and World, 1963.

Howarth, William, ed. *The John McPhee Reader.* New York: Farrar, Straus, and Giroux, 1976.

Hyams, Edward. *The Changing Face of Britain.* St. Albans, England: Paladin, 1977.

Kennedy, George. *The Art of Persuasion in Greece.* Princeton, N.J.: Princeton U P, 1963.

King, Leonard. Class handout. The Maret School, Washington, D.C.

Kolb, Harold. *A Writer's Guide.* New York: Harcourt Brace Jovanovich, 1980.

LeSueur, Meridel. "I Was Marching." In *Women Working: An Anthology of Stories and Poems.* Ed. Nancy Hoffman and Florence Howe. Old Westbury, N.Y.: The Feminist Press, 1979, 228–40.

Linton, Calvin. *Effective Revenue Writing.* Washington, D.C.: U. S. Government Printing Office, 1962.

Los Angeles Times, 12 Nov. 1983, 2.2.

Macrorie, Ken. *Telling Writing.* 2nd ed. Rochelle Park, N.J.: Hayden, 1976.

May, Rollo. *The Courage to Create.* New York: Norton, 1975.

McPhee, John. *Basin and Range.* New York: Farrar, Straus, and Giroux, 1981.

McPhee, John. *The Curve of Binding Energy.* New York: Farrar, Straus, and Giroux, 1974.

McPhee, John. *The Pine Barrens.* New York: Farrar, Straus, and Giroux, 1967.

Mitchell, Henry. "The Waugh to End All Waughs." *The Washington Post,* 18 Jan. 1982, 3.1.

Mill, John Stuart. *On Liberty.* Indianapolis: Appleton Century Crofts, 1947.

More, Thomas. *A Dialogue of Comfort against Tribulation.* Ed. Louis Martz and Frank Manley. Vol. 12 of *The Complete Works of St. Thomas More.* Ed. Richard Sylvester. New Haven: Yale U P, 1963.

Murray, Donald. "Internal Revision: A Process of Discovery." In *Research on Composing.* Ed. Charles R. Cooper and Lee Odell. Urbana, Ill.: National Council of Teachers of English, 1978, 85–103.

Murray, Donald. "Write before Writing." *College Composition and Communication,* Dec. 1978, 375–81.

New York Times Index, July–August–September 1916. New York: Bowker, 1965.

Newsweek, 6 May 1968.

Pianko, Sharon. "Reflection: A Critical Component of the Composing Process." *College Composition and Communication,* Oct. 1979, 275–78.

Pirsig, Robert. *Zen and the Art of Motorcycle Maintenance.* New York: Morrow, 1974.

Plato. "Cratylus." In *The Dialogues of Plato.* Oxford, England: Oxford U P, 1892.

Public Affairs Information Service Bulletin. Ed. Lawrence J. Woods. New York: Public Affairs Information Service, 1982.

Raymond, James and Ronald Goldfarb. *Clear Understandings.* New York: Random House, 1982.

Readers' Guide to Periodical Literature, March 1957–February 1959. Ed. Sarita Robinson. New York: Wilson, 1959.

Reed, Fred. "Lean, Healthy and Forty-Five." *The Washington Post,* 29 Sept. 1979, 4.1.

Rogers, Carl. "Communication: Its Blocking and Its Facilitation." In *Rhetoric: Discovery and Change.* Ed. Richard E. Young, Alton L. Becker, and Kenneth L. Pike. New York: Harcourt, Brace and World, 1970, 284–89.

Ross, Nancy. "Guide Offers Hints to Bring Markets to Inner Cities." *The Washington Post: Business,* 7 Dec. 1981, 5.

Safire, William. "The Fumblerules of Grammar." *The New York Times Magazine,* 4 Nov. 1979, 16.

Shelley, Mary. *Frankenstein.* New York: Pyramid, 1957.

Smith, George Rose. "A Primer of Opinion Writing for Four New Judges." *The University of Arkansas Law Review,* 1967.

Sterne, Lawrence. *Tristram Shandy.* Ed. Howard Anderson. New York: Norton, 1980.

Stoltz, Craig. "Doing Archaeology." Unpublished manuscript, 1983.

Taylor, Pat Ellis. "Teaching Creativity in Argumentation." *College English,* Dec. 1977, 507–10.

Worsley, Peter. *Inside China.* Harmondsworth, England: Penguin, 1975.

Zinsser, William. *On Writing Well.* 2nd ed. New York: Harper & Row, 1980.

♦

Acknowledgments

For permission to use the selections reprinted in this book, the author is grateful to the following publishers and copyright holders:

Sherwood Anderson, "Hands," from *Winesburg, Ohio*. © 1919 by B. W. Huebsch; © renewed 1947 by Eleanor Copenhauer Anderson. Reprinted with the permission of Viking Penguin, Inc.

Arthur Ashe, "First Sign of Decline, Color Discovered," © 1979. Reprinted with the permission of The Washington Post Company.

Russell Baker, "No No Smoking," May 2, 1976. © 1976. Reprinted with the permission of The New York Times Company.

Russell Baker, "Why Being Serious is Hard," April 30, 1978. © 1978. Reprinted with the permission of The New York Times Company.

Michael Berheide, "Brief Guide to Revision." Reprinted with the permission of the author.

Edward Berry, Jeffrey Gagliardi, Rani Garrison, Marina Gopenko, Jeff Green, Joseph Greenawalt, Stephanie Gunkel, Woienshet Kebede, Diana Lambird, Tracey Landis, Michael Parry, Robin Shaw-Maglione, Michael Schulman, Karen Teramura, Michi Weant, Jan Weinstein. Papers reprinted with the permission of these authors.

Richard Nelson Bolles, *The Three Boxes of Life*, © 1978. Selection reprinted with the permission of Ten Speed Press.

Robert Farrar Capon, *The Supper of the Lamb*, © 1967, 1969. Selection reprinted with the permission of Doubleday & Company, Inc.

Carol Coston, fundraising letter for *Network*, August 1981. Reprinted with the permission of the author.

Harry Crosby, "Titles, A Treatise On," *College Composition and Communication*, December 1976. © 1976. Selection reprinted with the permission of the author.

Harry Geduld, *Filmmakers on Filmmaking*, © 1967. Selection reprinted with the permission of Indiana University Press.

Ellen Goodman, "When Grateful Begins to Grate." © 1979. Reprinted with the permission of the Boston Globe Newspaper Company and the Washington Post Writers Group.

Ruth Hammond, "But I Never Said I Could Take a Picture . . .," *Waseca's Daily Journal*, February 24, 1976. © 1976. Reprinted with the permission of the author.

S. I. Hayakawa, *Language in Thought and Action*, 2nd edition. © 1963. Selection reprinted with the permission of Harcourt Brace Jovanovich, Inc.

William Howarth, *The John McPhee Reader.* © 1976. Selection reprinted with the permission of Farrar, Straus & Giroux, Inc.

Martin Luther King, Jr. "I Have a Dream." © 1963 by Martin Luther King, Jr. Reprinted with the permission of Joan Daves.

Harold Kolb, *A Writer's Guide.* © 1980. Selection reprinted with the permission of Harcourt Brace Jovanovich, Inc.

Ken Macrorie, *Telling Writing*, 2nd edition. © 1980. Selection reprinted by permission of Hayden Book Company.

John McPhee, *The Pine Barrens.* © 1967. Selection reprinted with the permission of Farrar, Straus & Giroux, Inc.

John McPhee, "The Search for Marvin Gardens." © 1975. Reprinted with the permission of Farrar, Straus & Giroux, Inc.

E. Ethelbert Miller, "Airport: A Takeoff on a Poem." © 1980. Reprinted with the permission of the author.

George Orwell, *The Road to Wigan Pier.* © 1936. Selection reprinted with the permission of Harcourt Brace Jovanovich, Inc.

Fred Reed, "Lean Healthy, and 45," *The Washington Post*, September 29, 1979. © 1979. Reprinted with the permission of the author.

Jewell Rhodes, "When Your Sense of Humor is Your Best Traveling Companion," *MS*, March 1983. © 1983. Reprinted with the permission of the author.

Nancy Ross, "Guide Offers Hints to Bring Markets to Inner Cities," *The Washington Post,* December 7, 1981. © 1981. Reprinted with the permission of The Washington Post Company.

Craig Stoltz, "Doing Archaeology." Selection reprinted with the permission of the author.

Pat Ellis Taylor, "Teaching Creativity in Argumentation," *College English*, December 1977. © 1977. Selections reprinted with the permission of the author.

Lewis Thomas, "Notes on Punctuation." © 1979 by Lewis Thomas. Reprinted with the permission of Viking Penguin, Inc.

Lewis Thomas, "On Societies as Organisms." © 1971 by the Massachusetts Medical Society. Originally published in *The New England Journal of Medicine*. Reprinted with the permission of Viking Penguin, Inc.

Richard Wright, *Native Son.* © 1940 by Richard Wright; © renewed 1968 by Ellen Wright. Selection reprinted with the permission of Harper & Row, Publishers, Inc.

◆
INDEX

INDEX